MAKING TOUGH DECISIONS

Paul C. Nutt

MAKING TOUGH DECISIONS

Tactics for Improving Managerial Decision Making

Jossey-Bass Publishers

San Francisco • London • 1989

MAKING TOUGH DECISIONS
Tactics for Improving Managerial Decision Making
by Paul C. Nutt

Copyright © 1989 by: Jossey-Bass Inc., Publishers
350 Sansome Street
San Francisco, California 94104
&
Jossey-Bass Limited
28 Banner Street
London EC1Y 8QE

Library of Congress Cataloging-in-Publication Data

Nutt, Paul C.
  Making tough decisions.

  (A joint publication in the Jossey-Bass management
series, the Jossey-Bass public administration series, and
the Jossey-Bass nonprofit sector series)
  Bibliography: p.
  Includes index.
  1. Decision-making. I. Title. II. Series:
Jossey-Bass management series. III. Series: Jossey-Bass
public administration series.
HD30.23.N88 1989   658.4′03   88-46079
ISBN 1-55542-138-5 (alk. paper)

Manufactured in the United States of America

Credits are on page 611.

JACKET DESIGN BY WILLI BAUM

FIRST EDITION

Code 8911

A joint publication in
THE JOSSEY-BASS MANAGEMENT SERIES

THE JOSSEY-BASS
PUBLIC ADMINISTRATION SERIES

and

THE JOSSEY-BASS
NONPROFIT SECTOR SERIES

Contents

Contents

For Charles and Isabell Nutt

Preface

Decision making is one of the most important recurring responsibilities facing managers in organizations. Choices are called for on a regular basis with important consequences. To make a decision, the manager must choose among ways to deal with problems confronting an organization. The choice among these alternatives often makes irrevocable commitments. Once a decision is made, resources have been committed that are seldom recoverable should something go awry. A manager's decisions also have considerable impact on the performance of the organization. Both the prospect of sunk (unrecoverable) costs and the need to improve organizational performance suggest decision making as a topic meriting the attention of managers.

Surprisingly, managers are often unaware of how they go about making decisions. The steps taken during decision making are frequently habitual and seldom subjected to careful scrutiny, making it difficult to improve decision practice. The purpose of this book is to offer a critical review of decision making and suggest remedies that are responsive to these criticisms. Bad decisions are explored to isolate what can be done to improve them. Four related themes are addressed: decision makers' limitations, remedies in the form of steps to take that mitigate these limitations, matches between decision processes and types of decisions, and techniques that can be used to support the decision-making process. To meet these aims, the book is eclectic—summarizing, integrating, and extending several literatures, including human information processing, cognitive psychology, the behavior and management of groups, learning, social psychology, organization theory, decision theory, decision analysis, utility theory, subjective estimation, sensitivity analysis, and systems theory.

This orientation requires considerable reformulation of material that was developed from a micro human information processing standpoint, extending and generalizing these findings to managerial concerns. Also, the analytical and structuring procedures discussed in the book were extended from narrow applications, for which they were devised, to the more strategic concerns of managers. These extensions are not without risk. In some cases, the generalizations to strategic decisions are untested and may be untestable. The prescriptions that result are offered in the hope that positive steps can be taken to move decision making from an art to more of a science, or at least to balance art and science so that intuition and analysis both have an appropriate role in the decision process.

A particular kind of decision made in and for organizations is called a "tough decision." To one degree or another, uncertainty, ambiguity, and conflict are always present in tough decisions. Ambiguity shrouds the events provoking action in a tough decision, making it difficult to determine what the decision is about. Tough decisions also have considerable potential for conflict. Key people often have something to lose or to gain and may take action to pursue their interests. To make a tough decision, steps must be taken to sweep away this ambiguity, cater to powerful individuals, or both. Finally, uncertainty is always present in tough decisions, making it difficult to determine the magnitude of important factors, such as projected use of a service or levels of sales for a product.

To help managers cope with tough decisions, a paradox must be confronted: Good decision practices cannot ensure good outcomes. Outcomes are ruled, to one degree or another, by chance. For instance, a product can be well designed and carefully marketed but still not sell, owing to changes in economic conditions that could not have been anticipated. To make good decisions, managers explore foreseeable future conditions and use sound procedures to acquire and process information to inform their choices.

Barriers to improving decision making also stem from

clashes of interest, which can produce divisiveness and conflict. Managers feel considerable pressure to deal with conflict and often resort to rules of thumb that simplify and speed their information handling. Inferences are made by applying person-centered notions of what counts. These steps can result in assumptions that are unrealistic and mislead the manager. The groping and panic-stricken behavior that result often lead to failure. Decision makers caught in such a trap find it impossible to systematically seek out and consider information that reveals what the decision is about, let alone mingle chance information about future conditions with objective information to carefully compare alternative courses of action. This book offers managers and students of management a way to deal with these dilemmas.

Audience

Making Tough Decisions is written for the responsible agent who has the power to commit resources, usually after consulting with some type of decision body. Such a decision maker must present that group with a well-reasoned assessment, to defend his or her choices or involve them in the decision. A delineation of how this responsibility is shared (for example, whether groups must be consulted or merely informed) identifies the responsible parties to a decision.

Both managers and students of management can benefit from the book. Managers face many distractions that soak up their time, and wading through yet another book may be low on a list of priorities. However, if the subject of improving decision making captures your interest, read further. The material offers valuable lessons from bad decisions, as well as helpful hints designed to prevent avoidable pitfalls. New ways to think about decision making that help cope with tough decisions will emerge from a careful reading of this book. Decision making is discussed from the vantage point of real managers in real organizations. The examples contained in this book should resonate with people who have experience in facing tough decisions.

The book is appropriate for a number of courses in

business, public management, health care administration, engineering, and other academic areas in which management is
taught. The book will appeal to students because of the diversity
of sectors covered, its offering of useful career comparisons, and
its step-by-step procedures. The material has already been offered, in a slightly different form and with good results, to
students who are interested in a variety of settings and who have
considerable differences in terms of experience. Some of the
material may provoke spirited discussion, which is desirable.
The more questions asked, the more one can learn.

The treatment of decision making as a process is original
and should provoke the interest of decision scholars. Many
questions about decision making remain, and any treatment of it
can be controversial. Debate is welcomed — indeed, sought.
There are many views of decision making that depart from the
ideas offered here. The challenge of new ideas creates movement
toward new and better ways of doing things. This is the goal of
scholarship, at least as it should be.

Overview of Contents

The book is made up of twenty chapters, a glossary of
terms, and three appendixes. It is organized into five parts. In
Part One, the nature of tough decisions is described. Case histories of decisions made using poor decision-making practices,
which had bad outcomes, are presented to point out avenues for
improvement. Good decision-making practices, in these cases,
would have revealed some if not all of the pitfalls that were
encountered. This linkage of good practice to the cases provides
specific illustrations of the recommended decision procedures.
The present level of knowledge about decision making cannot
ensure good outcomes but can offer steps to avoid pitfalls that
can cause a decision process to fail.

In Part Two, the origins of poor decision-making practice
are explored. Chapters Four and Five show how rules of thumb
that managers often use create bias and errors. Chapter Four
explores how bias can creep into the reading of information that
describes what a decision is about, setting in motion a direction

of inquiry that can be way off target. Chapter Five shows how rules of thumb applied to information processing create misleading conclusions and closed loops, in which learning about poor practice cannot occur. Chapters Six and Seven demonstrate the cognitive origins of habitual forms of decision behavior, which differ from the shortcuts described in Chapters Four and Five. Habitual behavior stems from the deep-seated preferences of decision makers, which coax them to act in particular ways. When these preferences are particularly rigid, they produce stilted understanding that severely limits the decision maker's opportunity for "knowing." Preferred ways of making decisions (in self and others) are introduced, and the strengths and weaknesses of these preferences are discussed. Emphasis is placed on making a diagnosis that offers insight into the behavior of self and others. Together, these chapters identify the nature of the shortcomings that can be observed as people make decisions. This discussion sets the stage for chapters that offer ways to overcome habitual behavior and ill-advised shortcuts.

Part Three lays out three decision processes developed to deal with the limitations described in Part Two. These decision processes are described in Chapter Eight, walking the reader through steps useful in making tough decisions. In Chapter Nine, these three decision processes are matched to types of decisions that a manager is apt to encounter in practice, creating a contingency framework. Matching process to decision types brings out the benefits of each process. By tailoring the processes to specific kinds of uses, the costs of decision making are minimized, while the benefits that each process can offer are realized. Following these prescriptions cannot ensure success but can mitigate our susceptibility to bias and habitual behavior, which often leads to poor decisions. These suggestions have had considerable impact on the performance of organizations through improved decision making.

Part Four elaborates process steps. Chapter Ten describes tactics useful in forming, coalescing, and controlling decision groups, drawing on the rich research traditions in social psychology. Chapter Eleven addresses the paradox of problems. There is no test that can ensure that the "correct" problem has been found, but steps can be taken to avoid being misled by symptomatic signals. Techniques that aid in the search for core problems are presented. Chapter Twelve introduces the notion of multiple perspectives, providing practical ways to ensure that several views of a decision will be considered as the process unfolds. Analytical techniques that overcome a decision maker's difficulties in making inferences are introduced in Chapter Thirteen. Simple examples are provided to illustrate various decision rules, show how alternatives can be valued, and demonstrate the process of "what if" questioning about key assumptions (such as future conditions that are ruled by chance events). Chapter Fourteen provides insights into the factors that inhibit learning and ways to improve decision practices through reflecting on outcomes to detect missed opportunities.

Part Five presents techniques that can be used to support a decision process. Chapter Fifteen summarizes several "group processes" that can be used to manage a decision group, as well as rules to select among these group processes for specific types of decisions. Chapter Sixteen addresses setting objectives, determining criteria, and generating alternatives, as well as the ethical considerations that each activity can pose. Chapter Seventeen provides techniques to make the subjective estimates needed in the analytical procedures presented in Chapters Thirteen, Eighteen, and Nineteen. Key analytical concepts are presented in Chapters Eighteen, Nineteen, and Twenty. Chapter Eighteen describes the decision tree technique, which merges the influence of a cascaded set of future conditions that influence the value of alternatives. In Chapter Nineteen, multicriteria decisions are considered, offering both short-fuse and analytical tactics that can deal with the complications posed when several criteria are required to compare alternatives. Chapter Twenty shows how decisions can be analyzed to determine the implicit values of decision makers. The results of the analysis promote insight into these values and, in this way, into learning about how values influence a decision process.

Several forms of "what if" questioning, called *sensitivity analysis*, are presented in these chapters. Risk is assessed by a demonstration of how assumptions about a future condition can alter the choice among alternatives. This approach is also used to estimate unknown payoffs, such as the amount one should pay for various forms of insurance. Sensitivity analysis is also used to show how much criteria weights must change to shift the decision from one alternative to another. These notions are then extended, to show how several future conditions can be considered at the same time to explore risk.

Using the Book

The material in *Making Tough Decisions* can be used in several ways. A basic understanding of decision making can be gleaned from reading Parts One and Three (Chapters One, Two, Three, Eight, and Nine). Emphasis on overcoming the problems in decision making is supplied by Part Two. In addition to Parts One, Two, and Three, Chapters Eighteen, Nineteen, and Twenty in Part Five could be included, to provide an analytical emphasis. A basic, conceptual understanding of decision making can be derived from Parts One, Three, and Four.

One final note: Citations contained in this book are not intended to be exhaustive. Representative references and classical works that set in motion major research efforts are used in place of the most recent elaborations or extensions, as is the practice of many contemporary authors.

Columbus, Ohio   Paul C. Nutt
March 1989

Acknowledgments

I am indebted to many people whose ideas sparked my interest in decision making and supported the long process of developing this book. The book is built upon several foundations. They include the problem-formulation ideas of Ian Mitroff; the analytical techniques developed by Howard Raiffa; the human information processing research of Amos Tversky, Daniel Kahneman, and Ward Edwards; the work of C. West Churchman and Ian Mitroff, who extended Carl Jung's notions of cognitive style to management; the synthesis of several decades of research in social psychology by Bud Collins and Harold Guetzkow; the learning concepts developed by Chris Argyris; Hal Linstone's multiple perspectives; the notions of decisional conflict developed by Irving Janis; and, finally, the work of David Gustafson and George Huber, who found practical ways to apply utility theory to decision making.

The cases appearing in Chapter Twelve were developed by Jodi Holman DeVillier, Bernard Presutti, Michael Slusher, Beth Scheiderer Traini, and William Woolverton. The case in Chapter Nineteen was provided by Gregory Beham. All are former students who have gone on to become decision makers. Ralph Goldston showed me how NFL scouts use player ratings. The kiva ideas were developed in conjunction with Robert Backoff. Bob also provided many thoughtful suggestions that strengthened both the cognitive-style material and my thinking, in many other areas too numerous to mention. Suzanne Nutt and Alis Temerin provided many ideas that improved the organization and presentation of the material. Sara Toomey and Helen Dean typed and edited the manuscript. Both are conscientious and dedicated co-workers, who maintained a frantic work schedule under trying circumstances, often at considerable personal inconvenience.

Special thanks are due Nancy, Suzi, and Charles. The book was written during a very trying period in our lives. A supportive family, always there when needed, made the long process of thinking and writing much easier, under difficult circumstances.

This book is dedicated to my parents, Charles and Isabell Nutt, who pointed me in the right direction and provided values that guided me.

P.C.N.

The Author

Paul C. Nutt is a professor of management at the Ohio State University, with faculty appointments in the Colleges of Business, Medicine, and Engineering. Nutt holds a B.S. degree (1962) and an M.S. degree (1963) in industrial and operations engineering from the University of Michigan and a Ph.D. degree (1974) in industrial and systems engineering from the University of Wisconsin, Madison, and is also a registered professional engineer.

His research and consultation have emphasized strategic decision making, from both a descriptive and a prescriptive viewpoint. Before his appointment to the faculty at the Ohio State University, he worked as an engineer for the Voice of Music, Eli-Lilly, TRW, and Eastman Kodak and was a self-employed consultant. His work experience includes developing and operating private nonprofit consortia for state government supported by federal contracts.

He has served as a consultant to many organizations, including the National Science Foundation, the National Center for Health Services Research, several agencies in the U.S. Department of Health and Human Services, several state governments, and many private organizations.

He is active in several national and international professional societies and is a sought-after speaker who has written over seventy-five articles for academic and professional journals. His previous books include *Evaluation Concepts and Methods* (1980) and *Planning Methods* (1984). Another book to be published by Jossey-Bass, coauthored by Robert W. Backoff, deals with organizational regeneration and change.

MAKING TOUGH DECISIONS

 Part One

Tough Decisions

Part One shows how tough decisions can become bad decisions and outlines steps that can be followed to prevent a debacle. In Chapter One, the notion of a tough decision is discussed, showing how ambiguity, uncertainty, and conflict are always present. Chapter Two presents five decision cases that demonstrate how tough decisions can become bad decisions when conflict, ambiguity, and uncertainty are not confronted. Chapter Three uses the cases to illustrate steps that can be followed to improve the prospect of heading off a debacle. These steps are the cornerstone on which the decisions procedures recommended in the book are built.

1

How Uncertainty, Ambiguity, and Conflict Produce Tough Decisions

Janis and Mann (1977, p. 17) illustrate the dilemmas inherent in tough decisions by quoting Warren G. Harding as he ruminated about a policy question: "I can't make a damn thing out of this tax problem. I listen to one side and they seem right. I talk to the other side and they seem just as right, and there I am where I started. I know somewhere there is a book to read that would give me the truth, but hell, I couldn't read the book. I know somewhere there is an economist who knows the truth, but I don't know where to find him and haven't the sense to know him and trust him when I did find him. God, what a job."

Although President Harding would not have wanted to hear it, the situation is even worse than he believed. No book, expert, or test can be used to find the "truth" in decision making. Bad outcomes can occur no matter what steps are taken. The best that a decision maker can do is follow steps that increase the prospects of understanding foreseeable risks and prepare for possible bad outcomes. This chapter describes the nature of tough decisions and what can be done about them, introducing the steps recommended for making tough decisions and explaining why each step is essential.

Tough Decisions

Tough decisions have uncertainty, ambiguity, and conflict. These features of tough decisions are often interrelated, with one leading to another. Ambiguity frequently produces conflict, and conflict produces several types of ambiguity. Uncertainty, which arises in all tough decisions, can lead to both ambiguity and conflict. Harding's frustration with his tax decision stemmed, in part, from uncertainty surrounding the consequences of a tax, ambiguity about whom to consult, and the prospect of conflict no matter what choice he made. Both the tax and the no-tax courses of action were apt to produce opposition. The scope and intensity of this opposition was ambiguous: Harding saw no way to identify and consult with all the interest groups that could take a position on the tax decision. Some of the important players who would voice opposition were known, but every experienced decision maker realizes that others are apt to emerge, making the extent of the conflict ambiguous. Conflict between some of the tax–no-tax proponents should have been apparent from Harding's discussions with people representing both sides of the issue, but the reasons behind this conflict were not understood, making the decision seem ambiguous. Steps to head off the arguments of interest groups were frustrated by this ambiguity. Lying behind the conflict and ambiguity was Harding's inability to predict what the impact of the tax would be and what the future would be like without a tax.

Uncertainty. Uncertainty will always be present in tough decisions, making it a key feature. For instance, in Harding's tax decision there was uncertainty about future conditions, such as inflation and economic growth, that could render the tax ineffective or even counterproductive. Uncertainty arises when decision makers believe that they cannot make accurate predictions because they lack critical information or cannot sort the information they have into relevant and irrelevant categories (Downey, Hellriegel, and Slocum, 1975). To make predictions, information is needed that characterizes future conditions, the effect that these future conditions will have, and how various responses can improve matters (Milliken, 1987).

Future conditions become uncertain when the behavior of suppliers, competitors, government, customers, voters, and the like is beyond the control of the decision maker. For example, economic trends may suggest that people's buying power has been improving and may influence product sales. Similarly, events, such as deregulation and import taxes, may influence people's consumption behavior. Together, a cascaded set of future conditions made up of strikes, new technology, consumer preferences, price wars, inflation, and other factors make product sales or service use volatile and thus uncertain. The uncertainty grows as the number of factors that are deemed to be important increases.

Uncertainty also stems from the way in which future conditions influence a decision. For example, economic conditions may appear to be worsening, but this trend may not lower the sales of a specific product in a specific firm. It is also difficult to predict the consequences, degree, and timing of well-known trends. The numbers in high-consumption cohorts, such as the eighteen-to-twenty-five age group, are easy to specify, but the cohorts' consumption behavior is not. Preferences, such as the popularity of Vietnam movies with the eighteen-to-twenty-five age group, may shift unexpectedly for unknown reasons.

Response uncertainty stems from difficulties in valuing alternative courses of action. The careful valuation of alternatives is inhibited by uncertainty about how future conditions will influence an alternative, making it more or less favorable, and the relative importance of the means used to compare alternatives, called *criteria.* For example, a new product line can be very profitable (the criterion) if sales reach certain levels. Sales, however, are the result of many factors that interrelate in complex ways, making their effects difficult to predict. Also, some products produce more growth but less profit, suggesting that uncertainties about the relative weight of these criteria must be confronted to make a decision.

To cope with uncertainty, decision makers make subjective estimates about the nature of the environment that indicate what they believe sales, utilization, and similar factors will be. When these assumptions are off target, poor decisions are likely.

Many decision makers have little tolerance for uncertainty and sweep it away by making simplistic assumptions. As a result, chance events, such as the likelihood of favorable and unfavorable levels of sales, are treated as though they were certain. In reality, decision makers may have very little under-standing of future events, such as economic conditions that could devastate their expectations about sales, and little under-standing of how changes in these conditions influence the rate of sales. To identify a preferred course of action, the decision maker makes an assumption about sales that is seldom, if ever, tested. People who do recognize the need to acquire informa-tion depicting events beyond their control have difficulty in making estimates that describe chance events, such as a sales level. People make notoriously poor estimates of chance events and seldom use techniques that can improve the precision of such estimates. Chapters Two and Three elaborate on the ori-gins of this behavior, and Chapter Seventeen offers ways to make the needed estimates.

A related problem stems from extreme postures toward risk that lead managers to make unrealistic estimates of chance events. A balanced view of uncertainty is desired because such a view produces a more realistic assessment of alternatives. Often decision makers are unaware of their tendency to treat chance events in extreme ways, as if they are nearly certain to occur or as if they will never occur. To create such an awareness, decision makers, or members of a decision-making body, can use the questionnaire in Appendix A to measure their risk-taking pref-erences. Decision makers or group members are asked to fill out and self-score the form. The risk norms, also found in Appendix A, help the decision maker or group member see his or her preferences in light of the range of values for others with the same role. Individuals who have preferences that are very differ-ent from those in similar roles are cautioned about being overly risk averse or risk tolerant. This exercise is carried out just prior to making subjective estimates of uncertain future events.

Ambiguity. Ambiguity arises when key elements in a deci-sion cannot be characterized. Ambiguity occurs when impor-tant factors are either unclear or unknown, as contrasted with uncertainty, in which important factors are clear but making a prediction using a factor is not. Many decisions are both ambig-uous and uncertain. Decisions are ambiguous when future con-ditions, the links between future conditions and courses of action, criteria to compare the courses of action, and problems provoking the need to act are, to one degree or another, unknown. For example, ambiguity in the Harding tax decision arose because of the magnitude of possible disagreements among interest groups, future conditions as yet unforeseen, problems in gathering information that captured the relative merit of the tax–no-tax alternatives, and failure to explore the core problems provoking the need for a tax. Most of this ambiguity was never recognized, let alone confronted.

Decisions that are novel, complex, or contradictory often create ambiguity (Budner, 1962). Novel decisions are beyond the decision maker's experience. There are no familiar analogies to use as templates to extract clues that suggest core problems, future conditions, courses of action, and criteria. Complex decisions have many problems, future conditions, alternative responses, and means to compare these responses to consider, making it difficult to sort out the important from the rest. Contradictory decisions have at least two competing interpretations of core problems, future conditions, alternatives, or criteria. Adopting any one of these interpretations calls for commitments that preclude consideration of the others.

Decision makers facing ambiguous decisions respond in a variety of ways, depending on their tolerance for ambiguity. Decision makers with low tolerance for ambiguity engage in submission or denial, which can lead to disastrous results. With submission to ambiguity, no attempts are made by decision makers to clarify problems, future conditions, or options. Denial leads them to make silly assumptions that render the decision amenable to the tactics used in past decisions or to suit their desires or hopes. For example, Harding could have recalled the last time he had to deal with a tax increase and treat the decision as analogous or have selected the no-tax option because of a campaign pledge.

Ambiguity can be repressed or avoided but doing so often creates anxiety and discomfort and leads to reconstructive or destructive behavior. Reconstructive behavior recasts the decision in ways that are apt to ignore core problems, fail to recognize crucial future conditions, miss useful responses, and overlook ways to compare responses. Harding, for instance, could have equated income and excise taxes in terms of who pays and who benefits, factors that produce a noticeable budget surplus, and how the two might combine to produce a potentially explosive situation that his administration would not have wanted to face. When decisions seem too complex to sort out, decision makers may adopt destructive behavior, such as muddling through (Lindblom, 1965), doing what others are doing (Cyert and March, 1963), or ignoring the decision by treating it as unimportant. Muddling through caters to the powerful, and tradition enshrines the past. Both tactics avoid immediate problems but may create even bigger problems in the future. Harding catered to interest groups in the tax decision, as past administrations had done, which created more severe problems down the road. Ignoring the decision treats the problems provoking it as insignificant, potentially letting them fester, only to arise in more severe forms in the future. As with uncertainty, many decision makers have little tolerance for ambiguity, which can lead them into traps created by reconstructive and avoidance behavior and thus to poor decisions. Chapters Two and Three elaborate on the origins of this behavior. Subsequent chapters offer a variety of techniques to help decision makers overcome real and perceived ambiguity by providing ways to search for and identify core problems, future conditions, and options.

Managers' attitudes toward ambiguity range from tolerant to intolerant. Managers who are unwilling to tolerate ambiguity create special problems. Such individuals are apt to push for rapid decision making, even when time pressure is modest. In tough decisions, premature closure can be deadly. To deal with this tendency, the key parties to a decision, such as members of a decision group, can fill out and self-score a form, found in Appendix B, that measures their tolerance for ambiguity. The norms, also shown in Appendix B, help decision makers come to terms with their views about ambiguity. This step helps those who have a hard time with ambiguity become more accepting by seeing that many executives do not share their views. It also helps to manage the personal views of decision participants that force premature closure on a decision process that must grope for answers amid conflicting signals and information inherent in tough decisions.

Conflict. Conflict can stem from ambiguity, or it can result from the disagreements among key parties with stakes in the decision, people called *stakeholders* (Freeman, 1983). Conflict often arises when decision makers experience frustration in dealing with stakeholders or in coping with the ambiguity and uncertainty surrounding a decision, or both. Core problems may be vague and future conditions obscure or take on several meanings and values, for some interest groups and not others. As a result, each interest group may see the decision as addressing different problems, which may be more or less amenable to systematic assessment.

Conflict is typically expressed in terms of disagreements among stakeholders about acceptable levels of risk, future conditions that arise and may influence outcomes, core problems that provoke the need to act, courses of action to deal with these problems, and criteria to assess the alternatives. Tough decisions can produce serious and irreversible consequences for an organization and the individual or group responsible for making the choice. The threat of serious consequences produces psychological stress. Stressed decision makers often find it impossible to conduct systematic searches and careful analyses, the very action that describes what a decision is about and ways to respond.

Stress often gives tough decisions a strong emotional coloring. The deliberation that precedes a choice among courses of action (called *alternatives*) involves many sticky and value-laden issues that lead to "hot cognitive" processes (Janis and Mann, 1977). Threats and perceived threats produce a level of arousal that can lead to irrational choices. This arousal is often expressed as a tension that calls for an alternative to be simultaneously adopted and rejected. Such tension can be observed in the hesitation and vacillation of a decision maker. For example, Harding hesitated in his tax decision because he could not satisfy everyone and he could not understand why people were so worked up. During the Cuban Missile Crisis, members of the President's Advisory Committee reported sleepless nights, believing that all actions open to them would provoke the Soviet Union's leadership into irrational acts (Sorenson, 1966).

Stress creates a paradox. There is a strong need to take action, to relieve the stress, and a fear that any action will produce undesirable consequences. Studies of stress find that avoidance feelings reach a peak when a decision is made, not when actual danger is the greatest. Experienced parachutists, for instance, experience the greatest stress the moment they decide to participate in a jump (Epstein and Fenz, 1965). Stress declines by the time they actually make the jump.

Arousal or anxiety, when it becomes intense, seriously disrupts decision makers' capacity to be vigilant and systematic in their information processing. Janis and Mann (1977) identify five conditions that can produce conflict in tough decisions: different or conflicting aims, forces calling for traditional and innovative alternatives, undesirable features in all available alternatives, time limitations, and resolution that seems difficult or impossible. Each of these conditions can stem from ambiguity or uncertainty or both.

Aims or objectives provoke conflict when stakeholders view different needs, problems, or issues as priorities. Arousal stems in part from the prospect that a choice will produce winners and losers. Stakeholders who believe that they can become losers have incentives to thwart the decision maker's objectives and impose their own.

Stakeholders may emerge to support alternatives based on traditional practices, as well as alternatives calling for change and innovation. Clashes can be based on fear, stemming from the unknown or from vested interests that may be threatened. Conflict can result when commitments to tradition are confronted by arguments for innovation and change. These competing values can lead to a clash between power centers who believe in preservation and those dedicated to change, or the clash may be symptomatic of interests that are threatened by change or adhering to tradition (Quinn, 1988). In either case, the confrontation frequently produces conflict. As a result, the decision maker will perceive both the traditional and the innovative alternatives as having negative features. Following a fruitless search for alternatives that can offer a compromise, a pattern of behavior called *defensive avoidance* emerges. Warning signals are distorted, and the decision maker engages in wishful rationalization (Janis and Mann, 1977). Decision makers can no longer process information systematically, and they blindly grope for an alternative that can end the conflict.

During this period of groping, time horizons shrink. This foreshortening can be real or perceived. Real losses of time stem from the need to repeat process steps, such as setting objectives or identifying alternatives. Perceived time pressure is produced by repeated failures to find an acceptable choice. According to Janis and Mann (1977), these conditions produce "hypervigilance." When time is (or is thought to be) short and there is no way to escape making a choice, decision makers can act irrationally. Analytical techniques that extend and augment the decision maker's information-handling capacity, allowing vigilant information processing, seem unrealistic. The decision maker resorts to simplistic ways of thinking, which will be described more fully in Chapters Four and Five. In this situation, a decision maker is likely to feel panic. Hypervigilance produces a frantic search that is likely to overlook alternatives and fail to adequately assess available alternatives. This behavior leads decision makers to contrive a solution that provides immediate relief but often leads to postdecisional regret.

Moderate levels of conflict, in contrast, can be useful, increasing interest and productive behavior, such as seeking information, discussing a decision with others, and thinking systematically. This behavior permits decision makers to use tactics that augment and extend information handling, as long as they feel there is adequate time and resources to apply these tactics. These steps are seldom taken when conflict is high or missing (Ebert and Mitchell, 1975). High conflict leads to hypervigilance. If conflict goes unrecognized, decision makers tend to see the decision as unimportant, not meriting the effort called for in a careful search or systematic analysis.

How Tough Decisions Are Made

Most tough decisions are made by using criteria of tradition and imitation (Mintzberg, Raisinghani, and Theoret, 1976).

As choices are made, decision makers are guided by their past practices or the practices of other organizations thought to be effective (Nutt, 1984b). Innovative alternatives are overlooked and logic traps are never confronted, let alone managed. As a result, decision makers often treat tough decisions as though they were easy. The problems provoking action are accepted as given, because decision makers fear that an exploration will create conflict. They make decisions by choosing among alternatives that are much alike. Staying with past or accepted practices helps decision makers deal with the conflict and confusion that often remain submerged, out of sight.

Analytical decision procedures are seldom applied to tough decisions, because decision makers fear unmanaged valuation information (Suchman, 1967). Information that can strip away ambiguity can also mobilize centers of power whose interests are threatened, provoking conflict. Pouring oil on these troubled waters draws decision makers away from an objective assessment of problems and ways to cope with them. Restoring order and ensuring peace often supplant all other activities.

Key Points

1. Tough decisions stem from conflict, ambiguity, and uncertainty that arise as managers grapple with the problems provoking the need to act and consider ways to respond.
2. Decision makers who concentrate solely on managing conflict must make assumptions that sweep away ambiguity and uncertainty, treating tough decisions as if they were easy.

2

Tough Decisions
That Become Debacles:
Five Case Examples

Five cases are presented in this chapter to describe the uncertainty, ambiguity, and conflict inherent in tough decisions. These cases are also used in Chapter Three to illustrate basic steps that are recommended to deal with uncertainty, ambiguity, and conflict. Bad decisions were selected because they point out the need for each of the steps recommended in this book and show how those steps could have been applied to real decision situations.

Bad Decisions

Bad decisions, like most things viewed from the vantage point of hindsight, often appear in overly sharp relief. It is difficult to believe that the cues and signs of failure, which seem so clear after the fact, were originally overlooked. However, decision makers do not have the luxury of waiting to see how things work out before they make commitments. With these cautions in mind, calling a decision bad runs considerable risk of being unnecessarily critical, even unjust. As a result, cases that go beyond bad decisions to what can be termed debacles were sought. *Debacle* is an emotive word that is intended to convey the notion of a decision gone very wrong.

To call a decision a debacle, at least one of two types of

outcome must have occurred: abandonment and mistakes (Hall, 1980). Abandoned decisions are marked by actions that were substantially modified, reversed, or ultimately withdrawn after considerable effort and money had been expended. Mistakes represent decisions that were made in the face of substantial criticism by informed people and provoked, and continue to provoke, considerable controversy. Abandoned decisions can be illustrated by the English Channel tunnel and its proposed high-speed rail system to link England and France and by Ford's Edsel. The Bay of Pigs fiasco and governmental regulation of hospital capacity to control costs by using a "utilities model" are examples of decision mistakes. On the basis of these definitions, a decision debacle results when choices are widely regarded as unwise, are overturned, or are never implemented, after a considerable expenditure of resources.

The Cases

The following cases provide illustrations that seek to capture both the diversity and the complexity of decisions that occur in public, private, and third-sector (private nonprofit) organizations. The threads of these cases will be gathered to identify what seem to be the root causes of failure and to offer steps that deal with the problems, described more fully in the next chapter.

President Carter's Iranian Rescue Mission. The overthrow of the Shah of Iran produced a backlash of intense anti-American feeling in Iran. For reasons still not clear, the titular leaders of Iran authorized the taking of American diplomats as hostages, violating a previously ironclad principle of diplomatic immunity for embassy personnel stationed in a foreign country, a principle officially adhered to by every country on the globe. For over a year, Americans were subjected to nightly hostage updates on national television. The American Broadcasting Corporation (ABC) used the situation to launch a late-night news program. ABC appeared to use the ruse of giving the American people daily updates on the hostage situation to test the waters for its new venture. The program was a smashing

success, vaulting its anchor, Ted Koppel, into national promi-
nence and justifying the gimmick of newsmen who do not move
their heads while talking.

Whatever ABC's motivations may have been, the nightly
spectacle on the evening news of lunatics menacing Americans
supposedly protected by diplomatic immunity galvanized the
country. No administration could withstand the nightly implicit
accusation by ABC that not enough was being done to obtain
the release of the hostages. The unrelenting criticism was unprecedented. Not even during the most intense periods of the
Vietnam conflict was there a single coherent call in the media
for a particular action. Enormous pressure was brought to bear
to free the hostages, no matter what the cost.

Responding to this pressure, President Carter authorized
a rescue mission. Helicopters were flown from an aircraft carrier
to a remote spot in the Iranian desert. The plan called for the
helicopters to assemble in the desert, fly to the Iranian capital of
Tehran (some thousand miles away), land in the center of the
populous and crowded city, take the hostages (by force, if need
be), and return the way they came. A sandstorm intervened
before the second leg of the flight, which was to carry the
rescuers to Tehran, could begin. One helicopter's engines,
fouled by sand from the storm, malfunctioned on takeoff. With
its pilot blinded by the storm, the helicopter collided with a
transport plane that was to carry out the hostages, killing eight
of the would-be rescuers. Calls to the aircraft carrier revealed
that there were no functional backup helicopters. In the ensuing
chaos, the rescue was aborted and the surviving members of the
rescue team returned to the carrier.

In the aftermath of the rescue attempt, ABC had even
more to broadcast, now showing Iranian tapes of the burned
planes and dead servicemen. Images of Iranian leaders, pur-
portedly holy men, poking at dead U.S. servicemen with sticks
were dutifully broadcast, further increasing the loathing of U.S.
citizens for the leadership of Iran.

The decision to rescue was vehemently criticized. Critics
claimed that, even with good weather, such a rescue was sure to
fail because of impossible logistics. The distance to the Iranian

capital, finding nearly a hundred people who might have been dispersed, and ferrying them out of a crowded city made the rescue attempt seem foolhardy at best. According to some critics, the helicopter accident was grimly fortuitous, because it averted a nearly certain larger loss of life had the rescuers reached Tehran. The sorry state of the helicopters' level of readiness, which was revealed in subsequent news stories, made the rescue attempt seem even more ill-advised.

The Iranian rescue decision was riddled with conflict caused by ambiguity and uncertainty (as summarized in Table 2.1). Speculation about the leadership of Iran was futile because information was either lacking or contradictory. Beliefs about who was in control and who could act as a spokesman resulted in heated disagreement, producing considerable ambiguity and uncertainty. All conceivable responses seemed to have undesirable consequences for U.S. foreign policy and little chance of freeing the hostages.

The seeming threat to the hostages — and, not incidentally, to the Carter administration — led to a classic case of hypervigilance, which made a systematic consideration of options impossible. The paradox of a strong need to take action and fear that no feasible action could produce a desirable outcome created considerable stress. The ability to systematically develop and consider responses was disrupted as administration officials jumped from one scrap of information to another, hoping something helpful would turn up, amid increasing pressure from the media to act. A frantic search was mounted to find a way out of the dilemma. As the administration blindly sought a way to respond, it was easy to latch on to the rescue mission and ignore other options. The rescue attempt provided an escape that offered immediate relief but created considerable postdecisional chagrin.

RCA's Video Disk. RCA introduced the video disk in 1980, long after Sony and other Japanese manufacturers had established a beachhead for the video cassette recorder. The Sony Betamax and its imitators offered recording and playback features, whereas the video disk had only a playback capacity. The video cassette recorder, or VCR, provided a "time shifting"

Table 2.1. The Features of Tough Decisions in the Cases.

Features of Tough Decisions	Carter's Rescue Mission	RCA's Video Disk	BART System	Sydney's Opera House	ITT's Paper Plant
Conflict	Intense, producing hyper-vigilance	Hidden from public view	Avoided, producing post-decisional regret	Displaced, surfacing later to cause problems	Repressed, to make superior appear to be right
Ambiguity	Avoided, leading to anxiety	Repressed, leading to treating the decision as typical	Repressed, leading to muddling through	Ignored, leading to muddling through	Dismissed, leading to anxiety that a poor decision was being made
Uncertainty	Ignored, to deal with pressure to act	Unwittingly made favorable estimates	Deliberately made favorable estimates	Politicians took considerable risks that went unrecognized	Unwittingly made favorable estimates; discovered but never corrected

feature that freed the viewer from network scheduling. RCA justified the video disk player by noting its high-quality picture and freedom from pending litigation by producers, who were contending that VCRs were violating copyright laws by allowing uncontrolled taping of TV programs. Control of taping by imposition of a surcharge on every tape was being proposed. Such legislation, if approved, would probably slow the demand for VCRs and open the market for a substitute product, such as the disk. RCA treated the impending legislation as a certainty and projected sales of 500,000 units in the first year, with competitors selling an additional 250,000 units (Landro, 1983).

Three years later, the legislation had failed to gather any support in Congress and RCA had yet to sell 500,000 disk players, making it clear that sales expectations were much too optimistic. Sales one-third of those forecast were obtained only after RCA offered deep price discounts on both its player and disks, introduced stereo and remote-control features, and invested $20 million to create an inventory of disk recordings and programs. The company's losses were nearly $300 million at this point, and customer surveys suggested that 85 percent of the buying public were not interested in video disks.

Disregarding these signals, RCA introduced a new video disk player with new features and signed marketing contracts with major distributors. In 1984, less than a year after the new product was introduced, the *Wall Street Journal* reported that RCA had taken a $175 million write-off and abandoned the video disk market. The decision to exit the market was made following a period of increased sales in commercial markets, suggesting that buyers were beginning to recognize some of the disk's desirable features (storage capacity, image and sound quality, instant access, and its library of programs).

"Sunshine laws," which allow observers to watch public decisions unfold, as in the case of the Carter rescue mission, do not apply to business firms. As a result, reports of the deliberations of firms appear comparatively free of conflict. The absence of conflict is often attributed to a firm's authority structure when, in fact, conflict between and among levels is hidden from public view or submerged as smoldering resentment. However, the account of RCA's decision makes the treatment of ambiguity and uncertainty quite clear. RCA's failure to treat the video disk as a tough decision led to failure not once but twice (Table 2.1).

RCA repressed ambiguity by reconstructing the decision as typical of its product development choices when it actually depended on a new factor: the prospect of governmental action. The firm dispelled uncertainty by treating governmental legislation that would restrict the use of VCRs as a certainty, making VCRs less attractive and opening a market for video disks. Calculations of profits were misleading because RCA first overstated the size of the market, reflecting assumptions about the expected legislation, and then understated it, failing to detect the eventual potential of the video disk's commercial market. The decision to enter the market was not recognized as a tough decision, which led to two poor decisions: to enter the market and then to leave it.

Bay Area Rapid Transit. The Bay Area Rapid Transit System, better known as BART, represents a decision whose time is yet to come. In many ways, BART is an examplar of urban transit: air-conditioned cars with carpet, easy ticketing, quiet operation, clean and attractive stations, and a span of 71 miles in the San Francisco Bay Area (Hall, 1980). Nevertheless, BART has many critics who are both well informed and vocal. They contend that BART failed to come anywhere near the expectations set for it in 1959, when the decision was made to create an urban transit system.

The need for urban transit was defined in terms of a growing population and increasing use of the automobile. The resulting projected congestion posed a threat to the employment, commerce, and culture of the Bay Area. BART was proposed as a way to offset these trends. The routes selected to link the cities of San Francisco and Oakland followed from these needs. The cost, projected to be between $590 and $720 million, was to be met by bonds, with an annual subsidy to offset projected shortfalls in operating revenues. Neither the means to collect the subsidy nor its acceptability to Bay Area residents was considered in the decision process.

Both the system's cost and its operating subsidy quickly

became controversial. Construction costs ballooned to $1.3 billion, nearly double the original forecast and $400 million above legislative authorizations. The 123-mile route was trimmed to 75 miles in an attempt to keep the cost below $1 billion. During construction, the use of new technology created delays and forced design modifications that cut the maximum operating speed from eighty to seventy miles per hour and reduced the average speed to forty miles per hour. Unanticipated problems in constructing a tunnel across the bay, in the control system and lightweight car designs, and in dealing with and coordinating the work of subcontractors ultimately hiked the cost to $1.6 billion for 71 miles of coverage.

By its second year of operation, BART had realized only a fraction of its forecasted use. As a result, the effect of BART on Bay Area traffic was so small it could not be measured. Traffic congestion continued to grow from pre-BART levels, and BART's operating losses created a deficit of $40 million. To offset these losses, a half-cent sales tax increase was passed in emergency session of the state legislature. After the dust settled, taxpayers were providing two dollars of subsidy for every dollar of BART revenue. The BART system that was designed to serve white-collar, suburban workers was largely paid for by people who had no access to or need for the system.

Capital costs proved to be 150 percent of forecast and operating costs were 475 percent of forecast. The costs of operating BART were twice as high as a bus system and 50 percent more expensive than using an automobile. Even with the subsidies that cut user costs by two-thirds, fewer than half of the projected riders used the system.

The belief that a clear and efficient urban transit system would change commuters' preferences, enticing them to abandon their cars for BART, was unfounded. There was (and is) no evidence that urban transit will be used in place of a personal car or that people will flock to live near transit stations, giving up their long-standing preferences for low-density, detached housing. Nevertheless, cities such as Washington, D.C., continue to build rapid transit systems, citing these very justifications.

The cost estimates for BART were overly optimistic, perhaps even naive. Assumptions of no technical snags and modest to nonexistent inflation were seemingly challengeable and may have been patently ridiculous. The political bodies that supported BART seemed to believe in public relations hype, such as "the question is not if we can afford BART but if we can afford not to have BART" (Hall, 1980, p. 112), rather than hard facts about its costs and its prospects of reducing urban congestion.

Proponents of the BART decision avoided conflict by ignoring critics and, when forced to defend the system, using dubious analysis to make unrealistic assumptions which were carefully buried in masses of detail (Table 2.1). Ambiguity in the BART decision was repressed, leading to a decision that was made by muddling through, dealing with each new crisis as it arose. Favorable assumptions about the number of BART riders and the costs of construction and operation were made so that projections of fares, subsidies, and capital outlays would make the system seem attractive. Proponents ignored uncertainty by dismissing the prospects of low ridership, inflation, and construction problems. Again, a tough decision was treated as if it were an easy decision. As critics became vocal, pointing out the errors and mistakes, considerable postdecisional regret ensued, embarrassing both the city of San Francisco and the state of California.

Sydney's Opera House. The opera house in Sydney, Australia, according to most who have seen it, is an architectural tour de force. It has become the symbol of modern Australia's commitment to the arts. Gracing one of the world's most beautiful harbors, the opera house dominates natural beauty in a way that must be seen to be appreciated. The night view of the harbor from inside the building is particularly stunning. Perhaps no visually superior building has been created in the twentieth century.

So why was it a mistake? First, the decision process that produced it is unmatched in terms of delays and cost overruns (Hall, 1980, p. 138). The opera house projected in 1963 to cost $A7 million was finished in 1973 at a cost of $A102 million. Its internal design was changed repeatedly to avoid further cost overruns and delays until it was too small to meet the needs of its intended users. The building was designed to house operas as well as symphony concerts, choral works, ballets, and meetings in a large hall and to accommodate drama, intimate operas, chamber music, and recitals in a smaller hall. The project was conceived in the late 1940s as a grand gesture by Labour prime minister John Cahill. In other words, a purely elitist undertaking was proposed for a society that has no use for elites, and it was funded by lotteries designed to raise money from people who would have no use for the building other than to look at it or show it to tourists.

Of 233 design entries, a jury selected the proposal of Jorn Utzon. Utzon proposed a set of huge concrete shells placed side by side to create the image of sails, like those of the sailboats that continuously grace Sydney's harbor. The design was indeed wonderful, but Utzon had no idea how to construct the building to serve its intended purpose. After years of trying to get firm plans to build the opera house, officials discharged Utzon and hired new architects. Costs continued to mount amid critics' claims that attempts were being made to design a perfect build-ing, regardless of its cost. To deal with the complaints, the plans to accommodate user requirements were drastically cut back, adversely influencing hall size, reverberation time, rehearsal room provisions, and many other features crucially important to the performing arts. These changes would ultimately render the building unsuitable to stage a major opera. When the opera house opened in 1973, the cost-saving mentality had even elimi-nated parking facilities.

Operating the building proved to be labor-intensive, also hiking costs. The projected price of a ticket became unthinkable when linked to rental charges proposed to balance the budget. Still more subsidies, now on a continuing basis, were needed from lotteries to keep the opera house in operation. The Aus-tralians' lust for gambling was used to satisfy a minority's interest in culture. The political risks in such an action should be obvious.

Hall (1980) sums up the controversy as who pays, who benefits, and who decides. The gamblers paid, but society may also pay because the lotteries have become so popular that they have been institutionalized, with all the attendant potential for abuse. Art lovers have benefited, along with all who have seen the building. But the cultural climate of Sydney, it can be argued, has benefited less than it should have because the cost of the building and its operation bled away funds that could have been used to support and enhance the arts. The politicians decided. They either took foolhardy risks or showed great courage and vision, depending on your point of view, to promote an elitist idea in a country committed to populism.

Conflict was displaced in the opera house decision through subordination of how the opera house would be used to "making a statement" about modern Australia with a building (Table 2.1). It was implicitly assumed that nice buildings are also nice places for all types of theatrical performances. Conflict did not emerge until the details of the design, which took shape years after the project was conceived, made the building unsuitable for many of its intended users. Ambiguity was ignored in the failure to recognize how the building's design would influence its cost. Cost estimates and operating expenses were seemingly biased to keep them optimistic, particularly during the period in which the commitment to build was made. Like the BART decision, this decision was made by muddling through, dealing with problems and crises as they arose, failing to recognize it as a tough decision.

ITT's Paper Pulp Plant. In the late 1970s, International Telephone and Telegraph (ITT) built a plant in the Province of Quebec to produce high-grade paper pulp (Loomis, 1979). The opportunity to acquire logging rights in Quebec for an area nearly the size of the state of Tennessee made the decision to build the plant seem low risk. Although revenue estimates were modest, the value of the timber rights seemed substantial. The Province of Quebec offered these rights at a large discount in the hope of increasing employment. The shrinking of harvestable timber stands implied a shrinkage of the supply of high-grade paper pulp to ITT decision makers. The continued growth and demand for this product seemed a reasonable assumption. Decisions to close high-grade paper pulp plants in Canada and

Scandinavia were noted and used to justify the prospect of strong markets in both North America and Europe.

The chief executive officer (CEO) of ITT first became aware of plans for the pulp plant at the close of a board meeting. The size of the timber stand attracted his attention. Participants left the meeting thinking that the project had been approved. Studies and negotiations followed in which estimates of the plant's potential were made. Doubts about market and financing were uncovered by divisional executives but were not offered to the CEO, in the belief that he had approved the project and would not want to hear negative information at this point. In 1971 the decision was announced. The plant was to be one of three that ITT would build to process timber obtained from the logging rights negotiated with Quebec.

Problems plagued plant operation from the outset. The market was soft; long-term sales contracts were impossible because of a glut of high-grade pulp on the market. Firms that exited this market signaled a problem, not an opportunity. Labor difficulties arose. The plant was located in a foreign country with a history of militant unions and fierce nationalistic pride. ITT mismanaged Canadian workers by failing to understand these instincts. ITT's political acts in Chile during the period further riled the workers by giving the impression that management could not be trusted. The plant was completed six months late and $60 million over budget, in part because ITT had problems dealing with the complex pollution-control devices required by Canadian law. Because of the harsh climate and short growing season, the timber stands were made up of low-yield, slow-growing trees.

The operation costs for the plant were driven up by labor disputes made worse by language incompatibility between the French-speaking union members and English-speaking managers. Logging costs increased because of a shortage of loggers to meet production schedules. Logs had to be obtained from other areas, adding transportation expenditures to the mounting costs. Production problems stemmed from ice embedded in the bark of trees, which reduced the quality of the pulp. Because the plant was designed with a production-line approach, problems in one area (for example, ice removal) shut down large segments of the production process. Only 13 percent of the plant's capacity was achieved after the first year of operation. After five years, the plant managed to average just 75,000 tons of the projected annual volume of 375,000 tons, all of it low-grade pulp. Expensive advertising designed to dramatize the value of ITT's pulp for use in products such as rayon proved futile. The plant was closed in 1979 with a pretax loss of $200 million.

The hidden conflict that often occurs in firms emerges to a degree in the ITT paper plant decision (Table 2.1). The CEO of ITT made an off-the-cuff remark at a board meeting that was interpreted as approval of the project. Subsequent doubts were not expressed. As the old story goes, the messenger bearing bad news is often executed. In such a situation, both supervisor and subordinate can come to view each other as incompetent, which also leads to conflict. Ambiguity in the decision was dismissed on the assumption that the timber could be processed to produce high-quality pulp and to fill a market void. When key line managers saw the folly of their earlier assumptions, they became anxious but saw no way to express their concerns. Uncertainty was dismissed on the assumption that a strong prospect for sales was signaled by the market exit of European firms when the reverse was true. No one attempted to explore the uncertainty in the paper pulp market or to make cost estimates with both favorable and unfavorable assumptions about factors that influence cost. Again, the key characteristics of a tough decision appear to have been ignored.

Key Point

Tough decisions can become bad decisions when ambiguity, uncertainty, and conflict are ignored, treated superficially, or assumed away during decision making.

3

Preventing Debacles by Improving Decision Making

This chapter shows how tough decisions can become bad decisions. Some of the key factors that cause bad decisions are discussed in terms of the cases presented in the last chapter, to provide concrete illustrations. The cases are then used to illustrate steps that can be taken to improve decision-making practice.

What Causes Bad Decisions?

Bad decisions occur when a decision process is managed poorly and when important process steps are skipped or treated superficially. Key problems that arise in carrying out a decision process include addressing the wrong problem, using autocratic behavior that discourages participation, being distracted by conspicuous alternatives, overreacting to time pressure and stress, relying too much on intuition and judgment, using dogmatic decision practices, failing to understand the values driving stakeholders' behavior, difficulties in making subjective estimates, failing to use analysis, problems in communicating the results of analysis, ignoring ethical considerations, and failing to learn from mistakes.

1. *Addressing the wrong problem*

    The most troublesome dilemma facing decision makers is teasing core problems or concerns from the signals calling for action. The problem to be addressed provides a window that focuses all subsequent activity, calling for considerable care in its selection (Kolb, 1983). Core problems are often taken for granted, and premature commitments to action are made without any clear notion of what is provoking the need to act. Solutions can displace problems, symptomatic signals can be considered, and urgency can be misinterpreted.

Solutions often seduce decision makers (Cohen, March, and Olsen, 1976). Having an "answer" eliminates a major source of ambiguity in tough decisions. For example, in the BART case, decision makers became enamored with using the latest technology to create a model subway system, forgetting that they would be held accountable for reducing urban congestion. Another danger is to focus on a problem that is symptomatic of deeper concerns and that would have emerged with deeper probing. Kolb (1983) finds that all decision situations contain a range of problems and opportunities. Some are obvious and some are not. The appearance of urgency can divert attention away from more important but less pressing concerns. Artificial time pressure is often created in decisions, as in the ITT case.

2. *Failing to use participation*

Decision makers who do not use participation often have an incomplete understanding of the decision and what it is about. The participation of stakeholders who have a diversity of perspectives provides numerous ways to view a decision. These different perspectives or vantage points can reveal insights into both opportunities and dangers inherent in a decision. The autocratic behavior of decision makers at RCA and ITT limited what could have been known about the video disk and pulp plant decisions. For instance, in the ITT case, had the CEO consulted with any one of several vice-presidents, he might have uncovered their reservations and averted a bad decision.

Participation can be helpful in eliciting a broader and deeper understanding of problems provoking the need to act, ways to respond, future conditions that influence action possibilities, and means of comparison or criteria. Moreover, by reconciling the perceptions of stakeholders, decision makers enhance the prospect of "buy in," leading to greater decision acceptance. Decision makers exhibit varying degrees of willingness to use participation (Vroom, 1973). Managers often fail to see situations in which acceptance is required and therefore need cues that identify decisions that would benefit from using participation. Ways to elicit participation and cues to identify situations calling for its use are described in Chapters Ten and Fifteen.

3. *Being distracted by conspicuous options*

Conspicuous options, pushed by people with vested interests, are often adopted. For instance, in the BART case, decision makers assumed that technology would be the solution to urban congestion. A conspicuous alternative limits the motivation to search for ideas, which leads to low rates of innovation. Solutions often appear to be changing problems. The availability of timber rights in the ITT case, the desire to create a landmark in the opera house case, and an assumed market niche in the RCA case created decision processes that searched for ways to justify the conspicuous options. The distraction of a conspicuous means often leads decision makers to ignore ends.

The makers of public policy seem to have learned little about the dangers of becoming prematurely committed to a single option or idea. The policymakers responsible for the U.S. decision to enter the Korean War (Snyder and Paige, 1958) considered several options, but each option had armed intervention as its theme. Decision makers in the Cuban Missile Crisis (Allison, 1971) considered only two functionally unique options: armed intervention and blockade. In both cases, policymakers were under the impression that a large number of options had been canvassed before a decision was made. Seen in this light, the Iranian rescue decision seems a continuation of a preference to take only a restrictive look at policy and an unwillingness to depart from traditional notions of policy actions.

4. *Overreacting to time pressure and stress*

      Stress and time pressure contributed to the Iranian rescue debacle. Oftentimes, decision makers seem to be overwhelmed by complexity, stemming from ambiguity and uncertainty, and unable to take action to deal with these factors, which limit their understanding. When stress and complexity combine, decision makers seldom approach decisions systematically. The result is hyper-vigilant information processing in which decision makers frantically grope for a way to respond. Finding ways to manage stress-induced conflict is essential if decision making is to improve.

      Decision makers frequently behave as though all decisions must be made under the pressure of time. Often this is realistic. The Iranian hostage decision is one example. Time pressure, however, can be created unintentionally, which creates serious limitations in applying systematic decision procedures. RCA and ITT had no real pressure to act as quickly as they did. Decision makers in the BART decision acted over a period of several years. Nevertheless, decision makers in all three cases felt considerable pressure to act, even though such pressure had no bearing on the actual needs of the decision. This is typical. Unintentional time pressure is often created when decisions move through many organizational levels (Ritti and Funkhouser, 1986). Unintended signals are read into managerial pronouncements, such as "exercise on this," that invariably result in the creation of artificial deadlines. Astute observers of organizational behavior note that most decisions can wait until Tuesday, many until a year from Tuesday. Nevertheless, many decisions become "short fuse," calling for knee-jerk responses like those of frogs. Unlike frogs, people have their brains uncoupled from their eyes, which allows them to reflect before acting. When artificial deadlines are imposed, opportunities to understand what a decision is about begin to vanish. Relaxing artificial deadlines has many benefits.

5. *Overusing intuition and judgment*

Decision makers frequently prefer to rely on their intuition and judgment rather than on analysis and systematic, step-by-step procedures. Such a preference can lead to serious distortions of reality, which can produce decision debacles such as those discussed in this chapter. Selective perception, information loss, memory limitations, computational limits, rules of thumb, failure to appreciate randomness, inconsistency, and learning biases make intuition suspect. Recall limits and memory lapses are common problems facing all decision makers. Unless memory is augmented, decision makers use rules of thumb that lead to the carrying out of a simpleminded information search. Such a search produces very few alternatives, judged by such conspicuous criteria as cost, without any appreciation of contextual factors that will influence the merit of an alternative. The biases associated with using intuition inappropriately are discussed in Chapters Four and Five. Remedies can be found in recognizing the kinds of judgmental bias that can occur and dealing with these biases by using decision procedures (found in the next chapter) that are designed to cope with them. Decision makers who recognize these biases, and the limitations they produce, use their intuition more effectively and make better decisions.

6. *Using dogmatic decision practices*

Decision makers often evolve preferred ways to make decisions. For example, they may prefer to use reasoning and analysis, gauge people's sentiments, rely on personal values or draw on personal storehouses of facts, uncover possibilities, and many other approaches. When one of these approaches is used and the rest are ignored, decision makers can become dogmatic, as discussed in Chapters Six and Seven. Decision makers who recognize their own preferred way of making decisions and see how it differs from that preferred by others develop an appreciation of the diversity of useful tactics and of how to resolve conflicts. Also, appreciating the variety of perspectives that can and should be applied to decision making deepens understanding and thereby reduces decision-making risks.

7. *Failing to deal with values*

Values and beliefs also create serious problems, because decision makers are frequently ill-equipped to deal with them. Decisions are often assumed to be value free, and huge sums are spent on analyses that ignore values, even as stakeholders maneuver to support their vested interests. In both the BART and Sydney opera house decisions, values played an important role in provoking conflict that remained submerged for years. Instead of ignoring values, decision makers need to find a way to identify, compare, and appreciate how values differ, a key step in making tough decisions. Chapters Eleven, Nineteen, and Twenty offer techniques to uncover and explore value differences in a framework that promotes accommodation and compromise.

8. *Problems in making subjective estimates*

Overly optimistic estimates of crucial factors are often made to make a particular course of action seem desirable. Estimates of costs in the opera house and BART cases were kept unreasonably low, perhaps to keep the favored options in each case viable. Optimistic estimates of demand and other factors made the video disk and paper plant seem desirable. Methods are needed to collect both qualitative and quantitative information so that each can play a role in decision making.

Techniques are offered in Chapter Twenty to collect subjective estimates of factors that are ruled by chance events. These subjective estimates can be treated as assumptions, allowing the inherently stochastic elements of many key factors, such as use and demand, to be considered and sensitivity analysis to be conducted by using these factors. The "what if" questioning that results allows decision makers to explore assumptions about key factors to see how the merit of an alternative varies with optimistic and pessimistic forecasts.

9. *Failing to use analysis*

Careful analysis is more apt to be used to justify the purchase of a typewriter than to make far more significant decisions, such as leadership changes (Mintzberg, Raisinghani, and Theoret, 1976). Ambiguity, uncertainty, and conflict make analytical procedures appear to be overly academic: detached from reality and incapable of rendering the complexity surrounding tough decisions understandable. Used in the absence of steps that explore possibilities and carefully establish the premises under which analysis is to be undertaken, these fears about analysis *are* justified. Analysis without framing is meaningless or, even worse, misleading, as pointed out by the cost estimates for BART and the opera house and the profit projections for the video disk and the paper plant. Properly used, analysis helps to strip away ambiguity and uncertainty; in doing so, it offers a way to cope with conflict. The steps needed to frame a decision with direct analysis are laid out in Parts Three and Four of this book.

10. *Problems in communicating analytical results*

Decision makers often lack skills in the analytical aspects of decision making, which creates fear in their hearts when they attempt to communicate analytical results. Analysts who produce such results often become "witch doctors." They acquire considerable power in organizations because decision makers must defer to them to describe the results of analysis. Cutting through the veil that obscures analysis should reveal its limitations and how it is done and offer a way to describe the results. Communication prospects are enhanced when the shroud is lifted from analytical procedures that can be profitably used in decision making.

Decision makers faced with the need to use analytical procedures are often intimidated by the appearance of complexity and fail to appreciate their value. What is quite understandable often appears complex before a careful exploration. Decision makers with the patience to work through any systematic treatment of decision making will be rewarded with deepened insights and sharpened skills. Managers who acquire these skills and insights are no longer dependent on organizational witch doctors.

11. *Ignoring ethics*

Concerns about ethics arise because tough decisions are seldom ethically neutral. The choice among alternatives in the BART system ignored who pays for the system and who benefits from using it, which posed serious ethical questions to BART critics. Ethical concerns crop up in sole-source contracting and various kinds of conflicts of interest, and in more subtle ways through distortions to protect perceptions of an employer's interests (Catron, 1983). Subtle ethical concerns arise during testimony to Congress or to upper management, in which financial needs are distorted. This type of deception is tolerated, even applauded, when directed toward outsiders, such as competitors, suppliers, oversight bodies, and subordinates. Carried to an extreme, such actions can prompt whistle blowing and acute embarrassment to the organization.

To pose ethical considerations, the "billboard" tactic is suggested by Catron (1983), which asks decision makers to reflect on how the organization would be seen if the steps used to make the decision were described on the front page of the evening paper. Would BART decision makers have acted as they did if faced with an exposé showing that two-thirds of the price of a ticket for white middle-class riders was paid for by taxes on nonriding, low-income minorities?

12. *Learning*

Learning about missed opportunities and causes of failure seldom occurs, leading decision makers down the same blind alleys over and over again. The realities of organizational life make it more difficult to own up to failures. Information about decision results seldom sepa-

rates good decisions with bad outcomes from bad decisions with good outcomes, posing still another type of
threat. As a result, bad outcomes are revealed in carefully
measured doses, if at all. ITT top management was not
apprised of the pulp plant problems until they were un-
manageable. BART decision makers busied themselves
with defenses to single out targets for blame and made
service-area changes to keep the ballooning cost from
becoming conspicuous.

To avoid potentially embarrassing questions, bad
news is offset with good news. The coverup is two-tiered:
the distorted good news, and the act to create misleading
information. The games of deception become "undiscussable," because to reveal them would also reveal the
lose-lose position created for the organization. Put in this
situation, people will treat key aspects of a decision from
which others need to learn as undiscussable (Argyris, Putnam, and Smith, 1985). Incentives that allow decisions to
be discussed must be used to break down the blamefinding mentality of postdecision review.

Improving Decision Making

To improve decision making, steps must be taken to identify core problems, pose ways to respond to these problems, and
foster vigilant information processing as these responses are
assessed, by linking them to future conditions and criteria that
influence their merits. Both a systematic search and a careful
appraisal of the products of the search are essential. As the cases
point out, decision makers face many distractions that divert
their attention and lead them to adopt approaches to simplify
and speed up the decision process. Furthermore, dealing with
these distractions seems to have kept decision makers from
exploring factors that provoke conflict, ambiguity, and uncertainty; yet such factors must be grappled with if managers are to
make good decisions. The steps that make up the process to
make decisions have been designed to help managers deal with
these concerns.

To introduce analytical information, one must subject it to careful control: There can be no surprises. The manner in which a decision is made is as important as the analysis of courses of action. To allow a thoughtful exploration of alternatives in a tough decision, important centers of power must be carefully managed. The decision maker must consider and attend to the needs of these centers as they emerge. A coalition is built that represents these power centers, managed by group procedures and informed by analysis.

A summary of key stages and steps in the process follows. The value of each stage and step is illustrated in the cases. Full process details appear in Chapter Eight, and techniques that support each process step are detailed in subsequent chapters of the book.

The Decision Process

The stages and key steps recommended to carry out a decision-making process are summarized in Figure 3.1. The process stages of "exploring possibilities," "assessing options," "testing assumptions," and "learning about missed opportunities" are recommended. These stages reflect the dilemmas encountered by decision makers as they attempt to cope with the conflict, ambiguity, and uncertainty embedded in tough decisions, as observed in more than twenty years of practice and research into practice (Nutt, 1984b, 1986d).

The *exploring* stage is used to uncover and then test problems believed to be provoking action and to seek ways to respond. The insights that stem from the problems stakeholders believe to be important are used to provide several competing ways to view the decision, reducing the chance of dealing with the wrong problem. Core problems are sought. These core concerns offer ways to identify aims or objectives and potentially useful courses of action.

The *assessing* stage is used to value the merits of alternative courses of action that seem to be useful responses to the core problem identified in stage one. To carry out an assessment, decision makers must seek criteria to compare the alternatives

Figure 3.1. The Decision-Making Process.

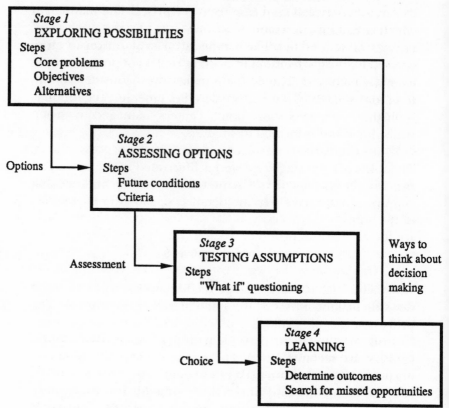

that reflect their aims (objectives). Using these criteria, decision makers can identify future conditions that influence the benefits assigned to a course of action. The linkage of future conditions and criteria is used to value each of the alternatives. For example, sales are linked to profits by the number of units that can be sold under favorable and unfavorable economic conditions.

In the *experimenting* stage, decision makers examine the values attached to each option or alternative by relaxing key assumptions, such as predicted sales or utilization levels, to expose the degree of risk in courses of action they are considering. Finally, in the *learning* stage, the outcome of the decision and missed opportunities is sought.

These stages and steps identify in general terms how decision makers can deal effectively with tough decisions. The chapters that follow expand on these stages and show how each step can be carried out. The botched decisions in the cases will be used to illustrate the value of these stages and steps and the insights that can be gleaned from using them. The activity these steps and stages call for is illustrated by means of the cases in Table 3.1.

Exploring Possibilities

In the first stage of the process, core problems are used to identify the objectives to be addressed and courses of action that offer a way for the decision maker to respond. Necessary steps are identifying the problem, setting the aim or objective, and generating responses as alternative courses of action.

Core Problems. Failing to uncover submerged problems and issues often proves to be the fatal flaw in bad decisions. Note that core problems were seldom sought, let alone confronted, in the cases.

Problems that are provoking the need to act often create a paradox. It is essential to seek core problems, but there is no way to know how much time and effort to devote to problem identification. For example, if you are house hunting and continually think that the next house will be just what you want, the search will go on indefinitely. More effort devoted to search will reveal useful information, but it is hard to know when to stop. However, ignoring the dilemma reduces the ambiguity but also increases the risk of a poor decision. Consider the Iranian hostage rescue decision. Why were the hostages taken? Was it a wanton act, typical of postrevolutionary chaos, or did it have deeper significance, such as a symbolic gesture to retaliate for decades of American interference in the internal affairs of Iran? The objectives and remedies depend on which of these core problems one assumes.

Consider the ITT and RCA cases. What problem provoked the ITT paper plant and the RCA video disk decisions? Increasing profit was implicitly assumed, but many U.S. firms go

Table 3.1. Improving Tough Decisions.

Exploring Possibilities	Carter's Rescue Mission	RCA's Video Disk	BART System	Sydney's Opera House	ITT's Paper Plant
1. Core problems	Why hostages were taken	Perceived corporate opportunities	Projected urban congestion	Need for a statement about modern Australia and need for an arts center	Perceived corporate opportunities
2. Aims	To obtain hostages' release before 1980 election	To increase profit	To relieve congestion	To respond to needs	To increase profit
3. Responses	Use force	Video disk player	High-speed transportation	233 proposals	Buy timber rights and build paper pulp plants
Assessing Options					
4. Criteria	Early and safe release	Profit	Cost	Budgets	Profit
5. Future conditions	Stability of Iranian government Who is in charge	Prospect of restrictive VCR regulation Consumer and commercial demand	Level of ridership Effect of inflation on construction costs	Potential for gambling to raise funds	Timber accessibility and quantity Market for pulp
Testing Assumptions					
6. Asking "what if" questions	Logistics in reaching Tehran and finding hostages	Demand without restrictive legislation Commercial applications	Ridership and assumptions linked to subsidies Inflation rates on construction costs	Optimistic and pessimistic cost estimates and operating budgets	Timber regeneration speed Demand by pulp types Labor costs
Learning					
7. Outcomes	Hostages released after 1980 election	$175 million loss	71 miles of track and cost of $3/trip to operate	Cost fifteen times estimate and took sixteen years to complete	$200 million loss
8. Searching for missed opportunities	Core problems never confronted Diplomatic initiatives and help from other countries ignored	Critical conditions influencing profit never tested	Cost estimates unrealistic Buses far less costly and more effective	Core problems never confronted Cost estimates unrealistic	Critical factors influencing profit never tested

through periods in which growth, stability, and human resource development are preferred to profits. A different decision might have been made had corporate aims been explored before each company became committed to an action that presumed a problem.

The problems leading to action in the Sydney opera house were bifurcated. According to Prime Minister Cahill, the core problem was the need to create a landmark that would make a statement about modern Australia. The core problem for the arts community was not having a place to showcase their emergence as world-class performers. The need for a performing arts hall, campaigned for unsuccessfully since 1947 by the arts community, was interpreted by Cahill as an opportunity to create a cultural landmark. The contradictory actions implied by these core problems were not confronted. The politicians essentially ignored the arts community. As a result, function was subordinated to form as the decision was made.

The BART decision appeared to use a problem to justify an idea. Protagonists used the projections of urban congestion to argue for a high-speed urban transit system instead of using the congestion projections as a stimulus to search for economical ways to reduce congestion. Again, a solution seems to be looking for a problem (Cohen, March, and Olsen, 1976).

Objectives. The aims of decision makers, reflecting the interests they are pledged to represent, are identified by using objectives. To set objectives, decision makers use core problems, selected to be confronted or overcome, as a means to indicate the outcome they desire.

The implicit objective in the rescue decision called for hostage release at the earliest possible time, meaning before the election of 1980. The objective implicitly pursued by the Carter administration seems infeasible. The Iranian captors had no motivation to act quickly and considerable incentive to drag out the process to embarrass a sitting U.S. president as long as possible. The press made it impossible to identify and explore realistic concerns about the motives and goals of the captors. What little was known was swept aside because the situation was made explosive by unrelenting media pressure.

The Sydney opera house decision was made without a stated objective. Australian decision makers (the prime minister and his cabinet) slid into a decision without ever clarifying their intent. Each party to the decision made assumptions to suit its own interests: creating a landmark and creating a cultural center. Conflicts between functional and aesthetic concerns were never recognized, let alone resolved.

The BART decision substituted a means, creating a high-speed urban transit system, for the objective of reducing urban congestion. Creating the system displaced concerns about congestion to the point that estimates of impacts on congestion had no influence on the BART decision. The objective the decision makers claimed to have addressed, relieving urban congestion, seemed to have no impact on their actions. Had urban congestion been taken seriously, other options, such as buses, would have surfaced. Substituting means for ends seems also to have occurred in the ITT pulp plant and RCA video disk decisions. The act of creating a plant and a product became the objective guiding the actions of decision makers, not some expectation of outcome. In each case, however, audits eventually showed how far the decision had wandered from the aims implied or hoped for, causing intense embarrassment to those involved.

Alternatives. Nearly every discussion of decision making calls for the decision maker to identify several alternative courses of action before committing to one (for example, Dewey, 1910; Simon, 1947; Thompson, 1967). However, most studies of decision-making practice reveal that only one alternative receives serious consideration as decisions are made (for example, Mintzberg, Raisinghani, and Theoret, 1976; Nutt, 1984b). This behavior leads to missed opportunities, ignoring innovation, and decision processes particularly susceptible to conventional wisdom and the pet ideas of people with an ax to grind.

Both ITT and RCA committed to an idea and made no effort to reflect on their objectives and see if other options might better serve their interests. Carefully exploring these interests helps decision makers see the need to identify a variety of ways to deal with them. Without this focus on aims, disastrous options can become innocuous or even intriguing. Timber rights seduced ITT and impending legislation misled RCA, making their ideas seem viable. The Iranian air rescue decision seems particularly bad because diplomatic alternatives had not been fully explored, because of instability in Iran at the time, and would cease to be a viable option for some time if a rescue mission failed. The BART decision makers made no effort to explore alternative transportation ideas, such as fast-lane buses, and seemed to be caught up in producing a technological marvel.

Assessing Options

The assessment of options calls for an analytical procedure that determines the merits of alternatives by using several criteria and considering several future conditions that could occur (Von Neuman and Morgenstern, 1947). The information needs are given by objective measures of performance, which require the use of criteria, and subjective estimates of future conditions, such as interest rates. Both objective and subjective information have a role in the assessment of options before a choice or commitment can be made.

Criteria. Poor choices are more likely when objectives are ignored, sequestered, or ambiguous because there is no clear basis to infer criteria to compare alternatives. For example, profit is often assumed to be the dominant criterion used by firms when, in fact, other interests often motivate their actions (Dill, 1965). As Perrow (1979) points out, the objectives pursued by the managers of firms often depart from corporate aims and rhetoric. Profit is the official credo, but decision makers act as though they are driven by market share, technological leadership, and the needs of people in various divisions. If these criteria had been applied to the RCA video disk and the ITT pulp paper plant decisions, they would have revealed that the video disk and pulp plant were inadvisable from several vantage points. A focus on objectives makes it easier to find criteria that provide useful proxies for the aims of decision makers. Deriving criteria from objectives focuses attention on aims and helps ensure that the criteria used to value alternatives embrace aims that management wants to endorse.

The BART urban transit system and the Iranian rescue decisions seem plagued by unclear criteria. The BART analysts focused on using technology when the potential for reduction of urban congestion seemed to have been the dominant concern. The Iranian rescue decision seems to have applied no criteria at all, being made for visceral and not rational reasons. In both cases, criteria teased from objectives would have revealed problems with current options and the need to explore other alternatives before the decision makers became wedded to the choices they made.

Future Conditions. Future conditions identify factors that influence estimates of payoff. Demand, use, interest rates, and the like require subjective estimates because they are inherently stochastic, subject to chance variation that can render the best forecast completely off target. To deal with the inherent variability in these factors, decision makers are urged to make both optimistic and pessimistic estimates of what may happen.

Informed decision makers use good decision practices and hope for good outcomes. Outcomes will always be ruled, to one degree or another, by chance. Inevitably, both desirable and undesirable outcomes will stem from good decisions. The best prospect of realizing a good outcome, however, is associated with following procedures that allow responsible individuals or groups to confront the question of how they prefer to deal with risk (Matheson and Howard, 1972; Kenney and Raiffa, 1976).

The manner in which information about these values is sought is a crucial step in the decision process. A key consideration is representing uncertainty that is inherent in tough decisions. Uncertainty is captured in two ways. The first encodes estimates of the likelihood of events, such as oil embargoes leading to price hikes that move through the economy. The second elicits values to assess the importance of various criteria used to compare alternatives, such as profit and quality.

The decisions in the cases were influenced by many future conditions that were known or knowable. Estimates about the occurrence of important conditions were so poorly made that they almost seem to have been deliberately biased to justify a particular alternative. The BART system made very conservative estimates for rates of inflation in a long-term, multiyear project, in which inflation was clearly an important factor governing costs. Even though the inflation that actually occurred was very high, it was not unprecedented in this century. Moreover, the rates the decision makers assumed were low by any recent experience of similar projects known at the time. To make their projects sound feasible, decision makers in the Sydney opera house and the BART cases may have deliberately made low estimates of costs. Had costs been couched in both pessimistic and optimistic terms, the need for contingency plans to help justify and rationalize possible cost overruns would have been revealed. RCA's video disk and ITT's pulp plant decisions were based on overly optimistic estimates of demand. Considering future conditions from a pessimistic as well as an optimistic viewpoint would have revealed the prospect of huge losses and would have sent out waves of caution that might have headed off both of these debacles.

Other estimates that should have been made from an optimistic and a pessimistic point of view include the prospect of ridership in the BART decision, costs for the ITT pulp plant stemming from union unrest and tree-harvesting problems, the likelihood of lax guards and easy entry into and exit from Tehran in the hostage decision, public acceptance of state lotteries to raise funds for the opera house, and the prospects of legislation restricting the use or increasing the cost of videotape in the video disk decision. Each case contains numerous events and factors that, when explored, reveal upside and downside risks. None of these factors were viewed from this perspective in any of the case decisions.

Testing Assumptions

The likelihood of chance events is inherently uncertain and cannot be known with precision. As a result, estimates of uncertain quantities should be treated as assumptions that can be relaxed to explore the implications of trade-offs. Differences

among parties to a decision often lie in their values, which dictate the assumptions about risk that they make and how they
weigh decision criteria. Subjecting these assumptions to analysis helps decision makers find out which assumption seems more
defensible. The analysis helps decision makers illuminate and
resolve differences in assumptions by showing how (or whether)
a decision changes with changes in key assumptions. These
procedures are logical and normative, suggesting how individuals can make decisions that best attain their objectives and
help manage the uncertainty inherent in all tough decisions.

The uncertainty in future conditions is managed by a
tactic called *sensitivity analysis*. For instance, in the RCA video
disk decision, demand estimates could have been used to project profits and losses under assumptions of restrictive and
nonrestrictive legislation. This type of analysis could have been
used in both the initial decision and the subsequent decision to
invest even more in a technological updating of the video disk
system. The BART decision was particularly sensitive to cost and
the resultant subsidies called for under various assumptions
about the level of ridership. The Sydney opera house decision
could have explored the potential for revenue generation under
various assumptions about the propensity of Australians to
gamble. The feasibility of fund-raising in this case was fortuitous
but could have been foreseen, heading off problems in dealing
with members of the Australian Parliament and the press who
opposed the decision and were constant critics as the opera
house was being built. The costs for ITT's pulp plant could have
been explored by means of sensitivity analysis to ask "what if"
questions about the plant's advisability under various assumptions about labor costs, log availability, plant downtime, and the
like. In each case, experimenting would have revealed conditions under which the decision was unwise, allowing decision
makers to reflect on the advisability of a decision under a range
of optimistic and pessimistic assumptions.

Decision criteria can also be subjected to sensitivity analysis to see how values influence a decision. For instance, the 233
proposals for the Sydney opera house could have been assessed
by changing the weights attached to functional and aesthetic

criteria to see if the proposals were sensitive to changes in the weights. This type of analysis has two purposes. First, proposals that satisfied both the functional and aesthetic criteria would have defused criticism from both users and the aesthetically minded. Second, decision makers could determine how much of a shift in their values (how they weighted the criteria) was needed to tip the decision from one proposal to another. Often disputes between parties, such as among the members of the jury that selected the design proposal, can be managed by demonstrating how much a member supporting a functional proposal must give up in the name of aesthetics. Note that the jury in the decision behaved as though functional criteria were unimportant in the selection of the Utzon proposal. This led to serious problems for users. A more balanced approach to aesthetic and functional concerns would have averted many of the subsequent user problems and attendant cost overruns.

The BART decision made totally unrealistic assumptions about the ridership behavior of Bay Area residents. No evidence was solicited to determine the nature of incentives that would be needed to coax people not to drive to work. This assumption was never tested but became the cornerstone on which the decision to change traffic patterns was built. This assumption is still being made to justify multimillion-dollar expenditures for urban transit projects that are unable to deal with traffic problems they were designed to alleviate.

Learning

The last stage of the decision process calls for determining outcomes and reflecting on what occurred to identify missed opportunities. After a choice has been made, its desirability often becomes known or knowable. Using this information, decision makers consider whether they could have foreseen a bad outcome to reduce the prospect of repeating preventable mistakes.

Outcomes. The video disk resulted in a $175 million loss for RCA, and the pulp plant caused a $200 million loss for ITT. These losses were carefully documented for tax purposes. However, many decisions are made with little or no careful accounting. Outright fear of possible consequences creates little motivation to reflect on what happened.

In some situations, decision outcomes are hard to specify or interpret. For example, the hostages were released after the 1980 election, but it is difficult to know what motivated their captors to act at this time and what role the aborted rescue mission played in hastening or delaying the release. Assessing causes in such situations is tricky business. The BART system provides commuter service in the San Francisco Bay Area for 71 of 123 miles that were planned. The cost of these 71 miles was $1.3 billion, more than twice the estimate, and ridership is so low that public subsidies are needed to cover two-thirds of BART's operating costs. The opera house has become a major tourist attraction in Sydney, but it has not served the performing arts well and requires huge public subsidies to keep ticket prices affordable. The structure cost fifteen times what was estimated and took sixteen years to build, and yet it is universally recognized as just what Cahill intended: a landmark symbolizing modern Australia. Did it succeed or fail?

Reflecting on Outcomes. The failure to reflect on what went wrong can lead to more bad decisions and the associated recriminations. Legislators and politicians still have to learn from the BART system's failure. Similar systems have been installed in Washington, D.C., and elsewhere, and they have experienced the same problems of low use, resulting in huge subsidies and no relief of inner-city traffic and other problems that are, at this point, foreseeable. The opera house case offers guidance for problems that arise when architects design buildings. The "form versus function" debate has arisen countless times. Decision makers seem remarkably naive in their dealings with architects and raise this same issue over and over again (Nutt, 1984c).

Key Points

1. Tough decisions can produce bad outcomes no matter what precautions decision makers take, because key factors that influence the outcome are often governed by chance events.

Bad decisions occur when foreseeable events are not recognized and managed. Informed decision makers adopt good decision practices and take realistic steps to appraise outcomes, seeking ways to improve their decision-making capacity.

2. The decision process presented in this chapter is designed to overcome the problems encountered by managers in coping with tough decisions. The recommended order of activity is as follows:

   a. Explore possibilities by uncovering core problems, setting objectives, and identifying ways to respond.

   b. Assess options by using criteria derived from objectives linked to the likelihood of future conditions and the values of key stakeholders.

   c. Experiment by relaxing key assumptions to assess risk.

   d. Search for missed opportunities by reflecting on outcomes.

 Part Two

What Inhibits
and Misleads
Decision Makers

Part Two describes behavioral factors that often inhibit and mislead decision makers. These factors stem from two sources: the rules of thumb or heuristics used to overcome limitations in handling information and cognitive makeup. Chapters Four and Five describe the information-handling limitations that hamper decision makers and show how decision makers cope with these limitations. Chapter Four discusses how information is acquired that muddles decision making by creating traps that can lead to poor decisions. Chapter Five identifies errors that arise in information processing, expressing judgments, and attempting to learn. Together, Chapters Four and Five describe the behavior of decision makers who have become hypervigilant in their attempts to acquire diagnostic information as they cope with the ambiguity, uncertainty, and conflict in tough decisions.

Behavior is also influenced by deep-seated preferences governed by the cognitive makeup of decision makers. These preferences, which influence how a decision maker prefers to act, are discussed in Chapters Six and Seven. Chapter Six uses Jungian notions of psychological type to describe the cognitive makeup of managers, defining styles of making choices and taking action. The unique features of each style are delineated. The chapter points out the potential for conflicts between styles, how each style deals with tough decisions, and the lost opportunity for insight that stems from relying on a single style.

Chapter Seven combines choice and action preferences into "decision styles" (Nutt, 1986b). A self-scoring form is provided in Appendix C so that the reader can determine his or her dominant style, auxiliary styles, and styles that are seldom used, called *shadow styles*. Comparison of the styles in Chapter Seven enhances decision makers' awareness of their own behavior and points out the merits of other ways of making decisions, which are often overlooked. The goal of Chapters Six and Seven is to sharpen the reader's self-awareness and point out new ways to carry out decision making. Appreciation of these tactics is essential if one is to develop this balanced perspective.

4

Errors in Sizing Up
the Situation

The chapters in Part Two characterize the behavior of decision makers who do not use analytic techniques and memory-
extending aids. Figure 4.1 summarizes this behavior, showing
how many decisions are made. As illustrated in this figure, the
literatures on information processing and cognitive style provide related and yet distinct ways to understand decision-making
behavior. Information processing captures behavior at the
micro level, demonstrating fallacies in how people acquire and
process information. These fallacies stem from rules of thumb
applied to sweep away conflict, ambiguity, and uncertainty
through simplifications and shortcuts that are applied to information handling during decision making. Cognitive style de-
cribes behavior at a more macro level, characterizing how unconscious preferences dictate the conduct of decision making in
which managers create premises to arrive at a decision. Understanding the behavior of decision makers poses issues that must
be addressed to improve decision-making problems, pointing
out pitfalls and traps that can mislead a decision maker and
result in poor decisions. The decision processes and techniques
that support these processes, which are discussed in Parts
Three, Four, and Five of the book, were selected to help decision
makers avoid these traps and pitfalls by dealing with the conflict,
ambiguity, and uncertainty inherent in tough decisions.

The Window

There is a hotel just below the great barrier reef in Gold
Coast Australia that provides a striking view of the Pacific Ocean

Figure 4.1. How Many Decisions Are Made.

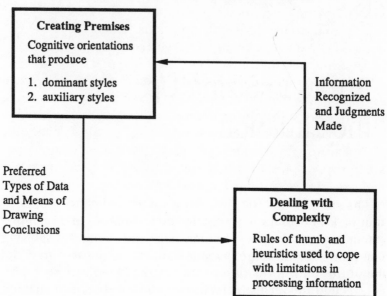

breakers. At sunrise the pounding surf mingles with the dawn's light to create a memorable view. The view is so striking one tends to be riveted to the spot, disinclined to move. However, moving to the right reveals Miami-like highrises to the north, protruding through the mist with the rising sun backlighting the buildings. Moving to the left reveals pristine, seemingly untouched beaches, stretching away to the south as far as one can see. A slight change of position reveals dramatically different views. Changes in the way one views a decision produce a similar shift in perspective. From one angle, the decision maker sees one set of perspectives and, from another angle, another set of perspectives. Tough decisions require this type of multiple viewing to window or frame a decision (Nutt and Backoff, 1987).

A key source of bias is context, which captures the background information needed to understand what the decision is about. To avoid bias, the context must be appreciated through the acquisition of relevant information. A fundamental kind of bias stems from finding a misleading context. Decisions made with a misleading context have little chance from the outset, no matter what other steps are taken.

Contextually derived assumptions, which specify what a decision is about, can be way off target. For example, a decision process initiated to deal with the work load grievances filed by telephone operators focused on the operators' work schedule to find a schedule that was acceptable. The context was assumed to be work load. When the grievances reappeared, a closer examination revealed that they were caused by an autocratic supervisor. The work load context provided a window that looked over a landscape that had few, if any, clues about the supervisor's being the source of the grievances. Such a decision is doomed to failure even before the decision process has begun. To avoid failure, the language describing context must be varied to open up the decision to new views. For instance, a company can view complaining customers as annoyances or as valued informants about the firm's products or services. Automobile manufacturers in the United States can measure their market share against one another or against Japanese and European manufacturers as well. Regional markets frame decisions differently than global markets, which recognize the inroads of Japanese and European manufacturers.

This chapter and the next describe sources of bias in decision making that can produce poor decisions. Bias is strongly related to context. A misleading context can create a frame that illuminates an environment with cues that will mislead subsequent activity. The search for an insightful context is *the* most important step in avoiding bad decisions. When decision makers use a particular context or frame, the "environment" yields cues grudgingly. Bias can also arise in how decision makers view a given context, acquire and process information, and learn about successes and failures. Biases concerning the way decision makers acquire information are discussed in this chapter, and processing and learning biases are described in the next.

Tough decisions require careful framing, looking at the decision from several perspectives before any commitments are made. Rules are needed to help a decision maker decide which

perspective to adopt. Tactics to deal with contextuating or framing a decision are provided in Parts Four and Five of this book.
Ways to organize a decision to deal with the biases inherent in
processing information for decision making are also required.
Tactics to overcome these obstacles are provided in Parts Three
and Four. Together, these tactics offer a way through the maze
that deals with many of the obstacles a decision maker is likely to
confront in making tough choices.

Intuition and Its Use in Decision Making

Knowing, without the conscious use of reasoning or logic,
is called *intuition.* In decision making, intuition is applied to
identify and interpret information and to make judgments
using this information. Instant apprehension leads one to acquire information and make judgments that are often insightful.
Intuition is indispensable in the efficient conduct of routine
choices in our daily lives. Intuition serves a decision maker to
provide simplifications that cut through the bewildering mass of
details that can obscure instead of reveal and to draw inferences.
Decision makers can also use their intuition productively when
they apply it to creative tasks. Applied to tough decisions,
however, intuition can be misleading. Tough decisions require
systematic information acquisition and careful processing. Intuition can be misleading because incorrect or insufficient connections are often made. When confronted with tough decisions, decision makers must learn to mistrust their intuition.
The purpose of this chapter and Chapter Five is to explore the
conditions under which intuition can lead to bad decisions.

To draw conclusions, decision makers use rules of thumb
based on their experience in dealing with prior decisions: both
personal and work-related. To simplify a decision, to make it
understandable, decision makers classify and label objects and
events according to categories. These categories can be appropriate, helping to clarify an impending choice, or misleading,
providing a poor representation of the decision. A poor representation can lead to bad decisions, choices that are hard to
sustain and defend given the facts available when the decision

was made. This chapter and the next explore conditions under which people's information-handling limitations lead to bad decisions. A process of judgment is described to identify how decision makers use rules of thumb to deal with these limitations. This discussion identifies flaws in the approaches often used to acquire information and make judgments based on this information and shows why decision makers persist in using approaches that are prone to failure. Muddled information processors often stumble when they use shortcuts that lead to bad decisions. For example, people often make a snap decision to join the Christmas club at a local bank when a savings account provides the same service *and* pays competitive interest. A modest search would have revealed the superior alternative.

How Judgments Are Made

Figure 4.2 provides a way to visualize how people render judgments. The components in this model of judgment are widely recognized by psychologists and management scientists who study decision making. This illustration presents an amalgamation of ideas drawn from Hogarth (1980), Nisbett and Ross (1980), and Hammond, McClelland, and Mumpower (1980).

The model has several key components: the decision maker, the nature of the decision and its requirements, and the environment in which a decision maker renders a judgment. The results of the actions that are taken affect the decision maker who has made a judgment, creating an opportunity to learn, and may also alter the environment.

Consider a person faced with a choice of accepting a cash settlement for replacing a car badly damaged in an accident or getting it repaired. The environment contains information about the marketplace that suggests what constitutes a fair cash settlement, the risks of repairing the vehicle, such as hidden damage that limits the car's useful life, and the insurance company's willingness to cater to the car owner's desires. Faced with these options, a decision maker (the car owner) applies what are called *schemas* that capture beliefs about the environment and ways to deal with these beliefs. The car owner may suspect that

Figure 4.2. Model of Judgment.

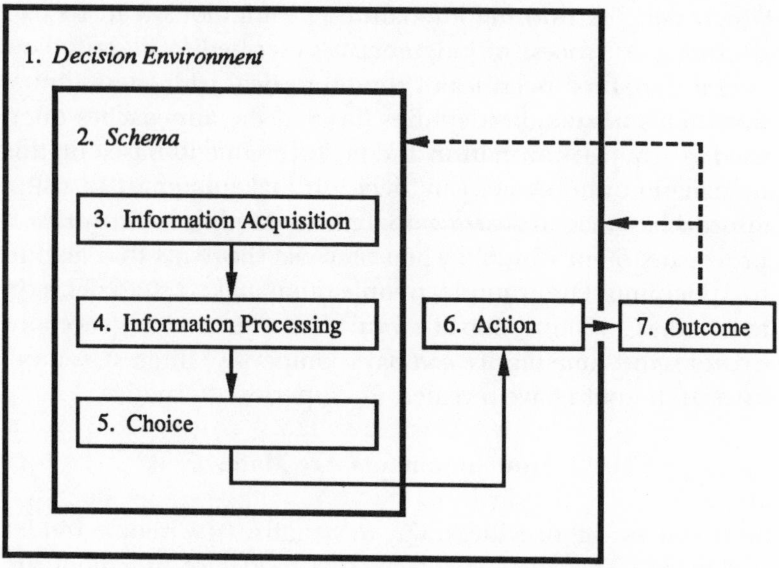

the insurance company has hidden reasons for wanting to "total out" a car that seems fixable. For instance, if a repair estimate is 60 percent of the value of the car, the car owner may believe that the insurance company can make money on the transaction, which minimizes its total cost. Such a belief dictates subsequent action, ignoring the possibility of hidden damage that can hike the cost of repair to the point that it exceeds the car's replacement value. Hidden damage is a very real problem. Insurance companies know from experience when the costs of hidden damage are liable to exceed the car's replacement value and use cues to decide when to declare the automobile a total loss. If the owner has the car repaired and hidden damage emerges during repair, the insurance company may refuse to underwrite the expenses, reinforcing the view that the insurance company had no intention of making a fair settlement. Under such conditions, the car owner's belief becomes a self-fulfilling prophesy.

Behavioral Decision Making

The car repair decision can be used to illustrate key components in a model of judgment. The notion of an "environment" is used to capture factors that influence a decision. The environment is composed of collapsed levels of systems, such as an insurance company's reserves, insurance industry practices forged by valued beliefs of opinion leaders, and general economic conditions. Psychologists who have studied decision making ignore these levels and treat the stimuli they produce as a single set of influences. In reality, the stimuli emerge from a cascaded set of considerations that influence and are influenced by decisions. For simplicity, such influences as levels given by company, industry, and general economic concerns will be ignored to concentrate on how decision makers elicit pertinent information from the environment, made up of these levels, that surrounds a decision.

The decision environment contains salient information about core problems that are provoking the decision. First cues are drawn from the decision environment, shown as the outermost box in Figure 4.2. Beliefs about the environment (box 2) shape and direct steps that are taken to deal with the environment. These beliefs can cause a decision maker to focus on the wrong set of issues or to represent the issues incorrectly. In the previous example, the car owner framed the decision as "coping with a devious insurance company" instead of identifying the best available option in meeting his or her transportation needs. This representation creates a schema. The decision maker's memory provides past experiences of self and others in which insurance companies have appeared to act in devious ways, providing a way to represent the impending decision. Schema captures the "what" and the "how" in the representation used by the decision maker. In the car repair decision, the "what" is coping with a "devious" insurance company and the "how" is stonewalling to get what the car owner believes to be a fair settlement.

The act of judgment engages steps of information acquisition (box 3) and information processing (box 4) to produce a choice (box 5). The car owner produces information from memory (beliefs concerning insurance settlements) and the environment (the market value of the car and settlements that seem fair and should be offered) and processes this information to determine whether to accept a cash settlement or to reject it and

barter to get the car repaired. In making a choice, the car owner
uses a schema to extract and interpret information drawn from
the environment (box 6). In box 7, the car owner learns the
outcome: the true cost and true condition of the car. Should
problems arise and the insurance company refuse to underwrite the additional cost of repair, the belief that insurance companies are devious and hard to deal with would be reinforced.

Comparison of Normative and Behavioral Models

The decision-making steps captured in Figure 4.1 are
behavioral, describing steps decision makers take when facing
tough decisions. These steps differ markedly from the recommended steps called for in Chapter Three. The motivation to
speed decision making entices decision makers to substitute
schemas that simplify information acquisition and processing
for exploring possibilities, assessing options, and testing assumptions. The activities in box 2 of Figure 4.2 replace the steps
called for in the first three stages of the recommended decision
process. The stage devoted to learning corresponds to the action and outcome feedback loops in Figure 4.2. This feedback,
however, is informal and often incomplete or missing without
formal attempts to secure and reflect on information that clarifies the decision's outcome.

The Origins of Bias

The car repair example illustrates how various kinds of
bias can creep into making decisions. First, information that is
acquired from both memory and the environment can be incomplete, misleading, and wrong. Information becomes salient
when past experiences were pleasurable or hassles, making
some of these experiences more vivid, and thus more memorable, than others. Second, information can be processed by using
approaches that produce erroneous inferences. Third, the way a
choice is expressed can cause bias. Finally, informal feedback
that links a choice with decision steps can lead to erroneous

deductions about what leads to success and failure in decision making.

Factors that hamper decision making stem from information processing carried out to understand and deal with issues and problems provoking action to form judgments that take shape as decisions. Human information-processing behavior can be characterized by selective recognition, sequential read in, rules of thumb applied to simplify inference making, memory limitations, and imposing patterns as templates to characterize the choice to be made. Bias stems from how information is acquired and processed, possible actions imagined, and learning about success and failure. People's limitations in information handling are offset by experience gleaned from observing the world about them. This experience suggests how information should be anticipated, acquired, and interpreted. The way patterns are imposed to give meaning to information must be understood to see how decision makers make choices. Biases stem from errors that arise in acquiring information, processing information, expressing preferences, and learning about successes and failures. These biases are described in the remaining sections of this chapter and in Chapter Five.

Errors in Acquiring Information

Decision makers are partial to information that becomes conspicuous (Cyert and March, 1963). Bias can occur when decision makers extract information that appears salient from their memory of seemingly related decisions and from the decision situation. Errors stem from misunderstanding frequency effects and being misled by vividness.

The Availability Heuristic Applied to Information Acquisition

Available information can produce significant biases. For example, a manager can be duped by mediocre but politically astute subordinates who remind the manager of their modest success just before salary decisions are made. Salespeople make a similar error when they recommend a product that they were most recently trained to sell instead of searching for a product that best meets a particular customer's needs. Decision makers are often drawn to the most readily available evidence when they can and should seek diagnostic evidence. When framing is based on available information, a decision process can be misled. For example, in the salary and product decisions, context was determined by incomplete information. A search for additional information would have revealed a more complete definition of what constitutes success for the salary decision and a more appropriate array of product choices for customers for the product decision. Available information can become even more misleading when an assumed context has no relevant cues about what is at issue, as in the telephone operator grievance example mentioned previously.

Decision makers who respond to readily available information use a rule of thumb that Tversky and Kahneman (1973) call the "availability heuristic." Decision makers use the availability heuristic to make judgments about the frequency and likelihood of future events that simplify the decision task and speed information acquisition. Misuse of the availability heuristic can lead decision makers away from information they need in order to understand what a decision is about. The availability heuristic is applied spontaneously and to a large extent indiscriminately, without well-defined rules of procedure, by decision makers who apply it and attempt to justify its use even after it is shown to be prone to error (Maier, 1931).

Bias in frequency estimation falls into three categories: initial sampling, storage, and recall.

Initial Sampling Bias. Decision makers often rely on personal experiences and treat these experiences as though they represent a random sample of events. For example, if your first trip to Las Vegas results in a gambling loss, you are more apt to agree with the old adage that there are two kinds of people who leave Las Vegas, losers and liars. The unemployed are more apt to meet others who are unemployed, making the frequency of unemployment seem greater than it is (Nisbett and Ross, 1980). This stems from the everyday activities of job hunting, getting unemployment compensation, and seeking out people to provide commiseration. These contacts tend to magnify the extent of unemployment in the mind of the unemployed.

People draw data from the environment to substantiate initial impressions. For example, Las Vegas losers are drawn to newspaper articles that describe how much people have lost in playing state lotteries. The unemployed are more apt to read about and recall news stories that promulgate homilies (for example, when energy is short, jobs disappear). They pay special attention to the length of an unemployment line because they have to stand in it. The line may have been about the same length during their period of employment, but this information is not salient at this time and thus not recalled. In both instances, long lines may be due to chronic understaffing in the unemployment agency and have little relationship to unemployment rates. The unemployed are not likely to realize this bias, nor are they likely to collect information that gives them a more accurate picture of employment problems.

Like Las Vegas losers and the unemployed, decision makers focus their powers of observation when a problem or crisis occurs. The context to judge urgency and the like is often missing, making preliminary estimates of performance seem worse than they may be when correctly normed. Your feet do not hurt unless you stand in the line. Similarly, decision makers focus their attention on events that have special meaning to them.

Storage Bias. Bias in the storage of information also creates errors. People are more apt to notice and remember things that take on special significance. For instance, ask someone to recall trivial events that happened the day John Kennedy was assassinated. A graduate of your college or university testifying at the Watergate hearings during the Nixon administration, or at the Contra aid hearings during the Reagan administration, makes this person's testimony more memorable than testimony by someone with whom you have no identification. We are drawn to the successes and failures of individuals with whom we have some sense of kinship. You are likely to read a letter to the editor of *Time* magazine from someone living in your hometown, even if you have never met the individual. Decision makers are drawn to, and thus acquire and remember, information that they notice because of a sense of identity, apparent kinship, prior association, and the like. Other features (very big or small, very attractive or ugly) can also make information salient (Nisbett and Ross, 1980). Unless these factors are relevant to a decision, biased information will be stored that produces errors when used.

Recall Bias. Recall is dependent on patterns. The more distinct the pattern, the better one's recall. For example, chess players have good recall of the location of chess pieces when the pieces have positions on the board that can occur during a chess game (Tversky and Kahneman, 1971). When the pieces are located randomly on the board, both nonplayers and chess masters have poor recall, as demonstrated by their inability to reconstruct the chessboard. However, chess masters have much better recall of piece location from actual games than does the nonplayer, suggesting that experience with patterns helps in recall. Past decisions that apply to a current choice offer a template that one can use to capture information. Patterns that do not apply, such as random chess piece placement, create confusion.

Recall bias is influenced by information patterning. As described in the chess example, some patterns ease and others obscure recall. For instance, my personal filing system has evolved and has a special logic to me but would create nothing but confusion for you. Information consistent with this type of evolved pattern is more apt to be remembered and recalled without error or distortion.

Selective Perception

Perceptions of relevant information are not complete but selective. The problems of selectivity become even more pervasive when information is obtained over a period of time instead of all at once. Studies of perception find that people are exposed to many times more information than they can process. For instance, an individual can read less than 2 percent of what is present visually (Simon and Newell, 1971). Being continually assaulted with information forces selectivity. People apply rules that result in their "seeing" only what they are willing to see. As a result, decision makers selectively recognize diagnostic information. The selectivity stems from their experience, anticipation or expectations, and prior notions of causality and results in disregarding or discounting conflicting evidence.

Experience Bias. Experience can be the "great teacher," but it tends to focus us on what we already understand. Decision makers are likely to identify and act on problems that are consistent with their experience. Marketing managers tend to view decisions in market terms, accountants in financial terms, and so on (Dearborn and Simon, 1958). For example, marketing managers tend to see problems as the need to stimulate sales and measure performance in terms of market share. Financial managers treat the same situation as a cash flow problem and measure performance in profitability terms. Other examples include engineers who see problems in technological terms and call for the updating of productive capacity. Professionals tend to view a decision from the special vantage point of their own interests. The interests of others tend to be dismissed or discounted, leading each professional to identify a different type of information: market share, cash flow, and innovations.

Anticipation Bias. Decision makers may anticipate what information they will observe when faced with certain types of decisions and then, by looking for this information, create a self-fulfilling prophecy. For example, new medical students at a student orientation program tend to recognize information that confirms their decision to attend medical school and their choice of a university. A hospital administrator who opposed a merger is apt to search for information that emphasizes post-merger problems, such as loss of autonomy and decline of service to the community, in conducting a postmortem of the merger.

Causality Bias. Decision makers also seek information that is consistent with their notions about causality. For example, interviewers tend to search for information to confirm first impressions. Information that refutes the initial position is downplayed or disregarded. To downplay information that refutes an individual's initial views of a candidate, the individual relegates the disconfirming information to a special-case category. For instance, when a favored candidate for the position of superintendent of schools was found to have been fired from a prior position, the firing was dismissed as a local "personality conflict." Terming the conflict "local" provides a rationale to disregard the information. In forming an impression of the candidate, a decision maker will not give much weight to information that does not fit the expected profile.

Vividness in Weighting the Importance of Information

Decision makers, like people everywhere, are impressed by *vivid* information (Walster, 1966). Smart advertisers play on vividness. For example, television ads for Volvos begin by showing beautifully restored MGs, Thunderbirds, and Corvettes to capture attention.

As George Bernard Shaw pointed out, the death of a single person is a tragedy, the death of millions a mere statistic. No amount of skill can make such statistics as the death of 6 million Jews during World War II as compelling an image as that drawn in *The Diary of Anne Frank*. Experiences that have powerful impact evoke images that influence how people see themselves and others. Nisbett and Ross (1980) point out how well-reasoned arguments are swept away by vivid information. Rational discussion of slavery, war, and migrant workers had little impact, compared to the compelling imagery of *Uncle Tom's Cabin*, *All Quiet on the Western Front*, and *The Grapes of Wrath*. In each case, the vivid presentation of plight and consequence influenced how people thought about these issues. The polemics of Stowe, Remarque, and Steinbeck created a public outcry that, in each case, led to societal change.

Vivid information is more likely to be recognized and remembered than pallid information. To be seen as vivid, information must be emotionally appealing, concrete, image-provoking, and personal (Nisbett and Ross, 1980). Each factor contributes to the way in which decision makers weigh information.

Emotional Appeal. Decisions that do not have the sweeping consequences of war or peace can still provoke considerable emotional involvement. For example, information affecting people we know has vividness. Our attention is riveted to newscasters describing the accidental death of a friend. The same kind of information can pass nearly unnoticed when the accident involves someone we do not know. People are able to recall specific details surrounding the friend's death, such as the time or location of the accident, condition of the road, whether seat belts were worn, and whether the driver of the other car, who caused the accident, was intoxicated. Subsequent recall influences people's views of highway safety, vehicle safety standards, drunken driving, and the like. The prospect of recall is accentuated as the consequences of the event become more severe, such as when a drunk driver causes property damage as compared to permanent injury. The emotional interest of an event is influenced by the degree to which the event influences desires, hopes and wishes, needs, motives, and values (Nisbett and Ross, 1980).

Concreteness. Detail and specificity help to create vivid information. Indicating who was involved, what actions were taken, and the situational context in which something occurred makes information concrete. Concrete examples evoke images that are more apt to be remembered (Nisbett and Ross, 1980). For example, a newscast describing the firing of a CEO can state: "The president of XYZ Corporation will leave his post next month to teach at the local university." This announcement has less impact than one that notes, "Joe Doe, president of XYZ Corporation, was relieved of his duties amid a controversy over the impending merger of XYZ with its chief competitor, and he will teach part-time while looking for permanent employment." The latter version is more vivid even if the listener has never met Joe Doe and has no knowledge of his stewardship of the XYZ company. People who are contemplating resisting or attempting to overturn a company policy are more apt to reconsider after hearing about Joe Doe's firing than they would be after a story about a company president leaving his job to teach.

People have difficulty learning about negative instances and finding missing information, because concreteness is lacking. For instance, managers who are swept away as a salesperson describes the virtues of a new computer system seldom inquire about breakdowns or the adaptability of software. Positive and available information is more vivid and more apt to be used.

Proximity. Vividness is influenced by a person's proximity or closeness to an event in terms of location, time, and familiar surroundings (Nisbett and Ross, 1980). An event that one personally observed an hour ago is more vivid than last week's occurrence observed by someone else in another city. The effects of proximity have considerable influence on action. Eyewitnesses of crimes call for stiffer sentences than do people who merely hear about crimes. Smart defense lawyers use this type of information in jury selection. Emotional impact can heighten or dampen the effects of proximity. If your friend or relative were victimized in a particularly brutal manner, the vividness of the incident would be greater for you than observing a crime directed against someone you have never met. Both incidents have proximity, but the friend's plight is more vivid because of its emotional impact.

Firsthand information has more weight than indirect information. For instance, to enhance the credibility of information, managers often note, "I was there." Those who oppose a decision are told, "Go and see for yourself." There is a pervasive belief that personally observed information should be given more weight than any other kind of information. This belief can lead managers to impose a degree of skepticism that is unwarranted, refusing to believe computer printouts, statistical analyses, or even printed accounts in journals until they have personally witnessed the event or situation of interest. This type of behavior makes the managers' store of information provincial and truncated. New information or insights will tend not to surface when decision making relies on firsthand information.

Data Presentation

Decisions are also influenced by how information becomes available. Ordering, mode of presentation, the mix of qualitative and quantitative, displays, context, and negative or disconfirming information can have biasing effects that limit one's objectivity and result in errors (Dickson, Senn, and Chervany, 1977).

Order Effects. Information in a decision process is acquired sequentially. The ordering may lead to an emphasis on initial or recent information, depending on attention-focusing events. For example, sales managers often extrapolate sales on the basis of their most recent experience, especially if the experience suggests a dramatic increase or steep decline in sales. Anchoring effects can also occur. Early information suggesting poor performance in a situation that has high emotional impact, such as high cost following the installation of a very expensive inventory control system, can persist even when subsequent information suggests acceptable levels of performance. The perceived "performance failure" may be due to learning effects, as people acquire the skill needed to operate the system, or to fluctuations in business activity that temporarily stress the system. Nevertheless, these initial expressions can create an aura of failure in much the same way that initial impressions of people often persist in the face of disconfirming information.

The order in which information is acquired produces what are called *primacy* or *recency effects.* Information acquired early in the decision process often has a disproportional impact on a final choice. The homily "first impressions are important" conveys the pervasiveness of this effect. Recency effects, in which the last information obtained has an undue influence on a decision, are also observed, although this effect has less influence than primacy effects. Both types of effect point to a large "excluded middle" of information that is lost or discounted in decision making, creating bias in acquisition.

Primacy effects occur because decision makers tend to approach a decision with a theory or explanation. They collect initial information to confirm what the decision is about and fit subsequent information to this view. In experimental situations (Asch, 1946), an interviewer may alter his or her impression of an inteviewee when initial information is positive (individual seems intelligent and industrious) or negative (the same individual is depicted as impulsive or stubborn). This initial view persists even when persuasive disconfirming information is presented. The rejection of disconfirming information can be understood in terms of an early formed theory or explanation that sweeps away unnerving uncertainty and gives the decision maker something to go on. Once formed, these impressions are difficult to set aside. Initial information also seems more salient in the absence of ways to describe a decision. As more information accumulates, each new discovery loses this apparent salience.

Premature commitment and failure to revise are reinforced by experience. Decision makers often see things as static or unchanging and expect these tendencies to persist (Heider, 1958). This commitment to a provincial theory, an early notion of causality, or first solution that appears to resolve conflict is consistent with the emerging view of decision making by managers. Decision makers find uncertainty intolerable. They experience relief when they obtain information that allows them to begin to deal with a decision (Nutt, 1984b). This information is hard to discard, even when its value becomes dubious in subsequent discoveries.

Displays. Information displays can help or hinder a decision maker. Information overload can be reduced by displays. But when a data display *seems* logical and complete, important omissions are less apt to be noted. For instance, consulting the price and performance information for VCRs published by *Consumer Reports* magazine often dictates information that the consumer will seek in store visits. Using the *Consumer Reports* format to collect information reduces the effect of such factors as the persuasiveness of a salesperson dramatizing various features that favor a particular product. However, the consumer may overlook new developments, such as digital effects, because the *Consumer Reports* format ignores these features.

A display may create an information overload when it swamps a decision maker with information. For example, if an article in *Consumer Reports* describing the cost and performance of VCRs offered too much detail, the potential buyer would be unable to discern important features. Novice staff people often flood the sensory apparatus of decision makers in this way, making it difficult for them to pick out the features of a decision that are important to the organization. Management information systems (MIS) frequently create this type of problem. Management information systems are being abandoned by organizations for two reasons: the inability of the MIS to provide information pertinent to decision making, and the burdening of decision makers with voluminous information having no apparent use (Nutt, 1986c). Redundancy in a display can cause a decision maker to be led to a single, possibly incorrect, conclusion.

Key Points

1. A model of judgment can be used to identify sources of bias in acquiring and using information as people grapple with tough decisions.
2. Decision makers recognize information selectively and give information that is readily available too much weight.
3. Errors in recognizing and weighting information stem from:
   a. Difficulty in accurately estimating the frequency of events.
   b. Giving events with which one has a kinship too much weight.
   c. Emphasizing information consistent with past experiences.
   d. Being drawn to vivid information and discounting the value of pallid information.
   e. Order effects, in which information that is initially recognized has more weight than information recognized later.
4. A misleading context will frame a decision so that diagnostic information is overlooked.
5. Relying exclusively on available information can create a misleading context.

ꙸ 5

Faulty Reasoning

Rules of thumb used to simplify and speed the processing of information in drawing conclusions also stem from people's information-handling limitations. These limitations entice decision makers to use analogies, imagining how a current decision is similar to a past choice. The analogy is used to derive ways to process information, make inferences, imagine possible actions, and learn. Rules of thumb that muddle information acquisition and interpretation in decision making are discussed in this chapter.

Information-Processing Errors

Decision makers use a variety of approaches to process information. The approaches are made up of the mental operations or steps that decision makers use to draw conclusions from information that they have collected. Bias can occur when the required information processing is hampered by the shortcuts decision makers use to simplify the decision and lower the level of mental effort. For example, applicant selection in which various candidates are considered for a job opening is often carried out by visualizing the characteristics of previously successful jobholders and selecting the applicant who seems to have the same characteristics. No attempt is made to isolate characteristics that were key to the previous jobholder's success. When asked how they carry out decisions, such as applicant selection, decision makers often imply that they used a more rigorous approach. Decision makers contend that they have made a comprehensive inventory of desirable characteristics and look for them in job candidates.

A similar kind of logic was used by Woody Hayes, who recruited black ministers' sons for Ohio State's football team for more than twenty years. Woody believed that individuals in this group would have better values, which would lead to more coachable players who would contribute to his team and get something from college — which to Woody meant graduating. This elaborate selection rule was never validated, but it was suggested for others to emulate, and many did.

As these examples suggest, decision makers are not passive collectors of data who carefully record what becomes available as they make a decision. They make interpretations on a continuous basis as data become available by resolving ambiguities, making educated guesses about events that resist direct observation, and forming causal explanations about what they observe. To go beyond available information, decision makers apply "knowledge structures" (Nisbett and Ross, 1980). Knowledge structures take shape as broad generalizations, preconceptions, and anecdotes about decision making that contain a decision maker's views about how to make a decision. They offer the decision maker a repertoire of rules that lead to rapid and coherent as well as incorrect interpretations.

Understanding is based on the decision maker's experience, which provides an elaborate and abundant storehouse of knowledge about relationships among objects, people, and events. Some of this knowledge takes the shape of beliefs that form theories about these relationships. For example, experienced hands in organizations believe that a conservative decision rule called *minimax*, in which options are selected that minimize the magnitude of possible losses, is used by everyone but the top management of an organization. (Minimax and other decision rules are discussed in Chapter Thirteen.) Managers also have "schematic" structures that pose relationships in certain ways, making certain conclusions more likely than others. For example, some leaders use stories or parables, believing that the punchline creates a subtle nudge to act in a certain way.

Both the availability and representativeness heuristics (Tversky and Kahneman, 1974) are key approaches decision makers use to simplify and speed up information processing.

The availability heuristic, used to acquire information, relies on *apparent* linkages that offer an explanation. The representativeness heuristic applies an examplar and treats the decision as if it matched this prior decision. Each heuristic offers rules of thumb that can produce biased information processing, leading to judgmental errors. Certain rules may be more readily accessible than others because of a decision maker's experience. Other rules of thumb are applied because they seem to fit the decision situation.

The Availability Heuristic Used for Interpretation

Availability can influence which of many plausible relationships between events is recognized as causal. Dispositional factors describing people, such as traits and attitudes, can be used to explain actions that a manager believes were dictated by situational considerations. For instance, assume that a manager gives an employee with a serious health problem time off with pay. This action can be seen by observers as stemming from the manager's considerate nature, when the manager actually based the decision on the compelling needs of the employee. From the manager's perspective, the plight of the employee was causal; from the point of view of an observer, a consideration trait was causal. The manager's causal interpretation is based on the employee's needs (the figure) relative to the magnitude of those needs (the ground or frame). Observers see the manager as the figure, and they ground or frame the observed behavior in a different context on the basis of their view of the manager's traits and attitudes.

Experiments reveal that focusing attention on one of several plausible causes results in the adoption of the highlighted causal interpretation. Highlighting can occur when subordinates are singled out by a manager as prime movers or as disruptive forces. Attention can be focused in subtle ways, such as seating arrangements, or by omission, in which one member of a group of supposed equals is always overlooked for temporary leadership assignments when the boss is away.

Outcomes seen in retrospect are more apt to be viewed as

preordained because of availability effects. Causal agents have greater after-the-fact availability when a predicted event occurs than when it does not. For example, a psychiatrist's explanation of a patient's suicide is often based on the patient's prior history. This explanation creates a causal scenario that seems more important than other explanatory factors, such as unknown events surrounding the suicide. Decision makers respond to the presence of causal scenarios and to the ease with which they can be identified and constructed. Decision makers assume that explanations have more salience when they are easy to create. The ease of creation conveys a special significance to the scenarios' implied causality.

Indiscriminate use of the availability heuristic in forming causal explanations can lead decision makers to make serious judgment errors. This occurs when decision makers are unaware that disconfirming evidence is difficult to come by. For instance, decisions about who gets a scholarship seem to have been made correctly when the recipients do well. The performance of individuals not receiving a scholarship tends to be ignored because these individuals are not available as potential disconfirming examples. Errors can also occur when memorable associations are unrelated to a decision that must be made. Decision makers who shift salient experiences from one decision to another without accounting for contextual differences are apt to process nondiagnostic or misleading information. For example, respondents to surveys are influenced by their personal situation, such as being unemployed or recently divorced, which is apt to color their attitudes and views. It is difficult for the respondents to shift contexts as they respond to questions about foreign policy and personal achievement.

The Representativeness Heuristic Used for Interpretation

To make decisions, an examplar is often used as a template from which premises about relationships are drawn. Decision makers identify the relationships from assumptions about generating processes, categories, and antecedents (Nisbett and Ross, 1980). If the analogy has a good fit for the decision, the assumptions provide clues about important relationships that strip away layers of ambiguity. If the fit of exemplar to decision is poor, the relationship can be misleading, creating a false sense of security that limits the search for cues, making it more difficult to draw an accurate inference.

Process Inferences. Decision makers often judge the likelihood of an event by drawing inferences about the process that produced it. The bias that can result is illustrated by the well-known "gambler's fallacy." After a long series of odd outcomes from dice rolls in a craps game, some people believe that an even outcome is "due" even though each event (roll of the dice) is independent of all other rolls. The likelihood of an odd or even outcome remains 50/50, no matter what runs were observed in a previous set of outcomes. This type of logic is often used when a fan says that the Celtics are "due" for a win after losing a game or two in the NBA finals or that a company is apt to win a government contract after losing out on several previous contracts. In these cases, the process is assumed to be dependent on prior outcomes, when it is only somewhat dependent or completely independent of these events. When the decision maker does not understand a generative process, errors can result from this type of extension.

Categories. The categories that decision makers use to classify events can be off target. A five-alarm fire has different meanings to fire fighters from different cities. The fire fighters who hear this phrase create an image of the people and property at risk and the number and types of crews needed to cope with this type of fire on the basis of their prior experience. Because fire fighters have very little job mobility from one city to another as the result of local union rules concerning seniority, these people develop very localized images of fires and their severity.

Stereotyping also creates categories that may be misfits. Consider, for example, a couple in which one spouse likes to garden, shop for clothes, and look at new homes to get decorating ideas. Many people would guess that this spouse is the wife. There seems to be a better fit between the activities cited and the wife because of the way women are stereotyped. Stereotyping occurs because decision makers apply a form of base rate information, which keeps decision makers from searching for a more relevant category. More women than men are thought to fit the gardening, clotheshorse, and house redecorating stereotypes, so this base rate is used to make a judgment, even though the categories are clearly insufficient to make the male-female choice. Decision makers are often victimized in this way by the apparent representativeness of categories.

Questions can be posed in two ways. In the first, one asks how likely it is that a woman was described by these categories. In the second, one asks the likelihood that someone resembling this profile would be a woman. The second question elicits an odds estimation, whereas the first forces an all-or-nothing judgment. The odds estimate is more apt to provide an accurate causal inference than the all-or-nothing judgment. Errors are more frequent when decision makers use categories instead of likelihoods to make judgments.

Antecedents. To account for the consequences of a decision, such as the after-tax losses from a sell-off of a merger partner, decision makers are motivated to search through a list of available antecedents to find a plausible explanation. Anything that logically preceded the decision and seems to point to the merger failure could be entertained. This matching of causes and consequences can be misleading when undue emphasis is placed on causes that are similar to observed consequences. If the merger sell-off was prompted by low profits, a search for antecedents is likely to turn up telltale signs of high cost or poor revenue prospects. However, a merger sell-off prompted by needs for capital is apt to prompt a search for unrecognized indicators of capital requirements, which were available prior to the merger.

After firing someone for lack of motivation, managers are more likely to find signals of a poorly motivated individual at the time of hire than other factors that might have produced low motivation, such as the absence of work challenges or limited opportunity for advancement. Similarly, the causes of disgruntled managers who resign can be explained in terms of predispositions, such as "they were hard to please" or "they had unrealistic expectations." If these same managers hide their true feelings and cite the attractions of a new position as reasons for leaving, causes are sought in terms of salary differentials and other aspects of the new job that make it attractive.

Antecedents and consequences need not be similar and may often be unrelated. The causes of poor motivation are likely to be multiple and complex, calling for an assessment of the work and its prospects for growth as well as what subordinates view as menial and challenging and the proportion of menial to challenging activities in jobs with high turnover.

There is more to causal assessment than a simple extrapolation of the features found in consequences to identify causes. Bias that leads to errors can result when antecedents, derived in this manner, are used to explain outcomes. Managers delude themselves into believing that the problems of turnover are related to job selection instead of the nature of the job. This delusion can result in their institutionalizing costly and unneeded devices, such as psychological testing to select applicants. In this example, the costs of testing could be better directed toward job redesign to try to resolve the turnover problem.

As Nisbett and Ross (1980) point out, Anwar Sadat's diplomatic initiatives toward Israel, which resulted in the Camp David accords and a lowering of tensions between Egypt and Israel, can be viewed as an economic necessity or a heroic vision. Future initiatives by the United States are shaped according to which antecedent is adopted as an explanation of the Sadat initiative. The wrong assumption can offend the current leadership of Egypt and produce foreign policy that is doomed to failure.

Knowledge Structures

Experience provides an abundant supply of general knowledge that suggests how people, objects, and events are related. Decision makers acquire knowledge about these relationships and store themes to create theories. Theories formed from beliefs and schemas are used to suggest the nature of relationships (Minsky, 1975; Nisbett and Ross, 1980).

Theories. Knowledge is captured through propositions that characterize what one believes to be true about people, object, and event relationships. Examples include the following: managers with insecurities have strong needs for control, introverts make poor leaders, and staff people, not managers, are hired to introduce new ideas into an organization. These theories are applied to explain what happens, for instance, when an organization attempts product innovations. The belief that innovation rests with staff conjures up a process in which staff propose and the manager disposes. The notion that managers can and should be responsible for introducing ideas would never arise under a staff-centered innovation set of beliefs.

A theory can range from a broad generalization about human behavior and its determinants to narrow conceptions about an individual. Decision makers rely on many such theories, derived from their experience and from their reflections about the culture of their organization. They use these theories to assimilate impressions and beliefs that guide what data are sought and encoded. For example, some managers have a tendency to explain the decisions or preferences of stakeholders in terms of dispositions, ignoring situational factors that offer more likely explanations of a choice. The preferences of stakeholders are thought to stem from enduring attitudes instead of incentives in the situation to which the stakeholders respond when making a decision. This view gives rise to the notion that a decision maker's acts are guided by plans and goals in which benefits are maximized and costs minimized. These propositions form tacit global theories that are used to explain what a decision maker observes and to predict what will happen. Examples of global theories include the Protestant ethic, personal responsibility and free will, virtue is its own reward, money motivates, and many others. Each creates dispositional theories that can be trotted out each time an individual attempts an explanation of action. Studies of decision making reveal that action is seldom guided by or even consistent with a particular set of dispositions. Decisions are more apt to be explained by intentions that are produced by incentives in the decision situation at the moment of choice. Opportunities create attractions, and risks create repulsions. By relying on dispositional explanations as theories to predict what is likely to develop, people frequently make judgmental errors.

The extension of dispositional theories to human behavior is particularly prone to error. To explain behavior as a predisposition ignores the situation-specific factors that form powerful incentives for people to act in certain ways. If managers who become entrepreneurs are assumed to be predisposed toward change, innovation becomes an act of faith and not one of many logical responses that an organization can adopt. If such a view is held by many of our current industry leaders, it may help explain our lack of competitiveness in world markets.

Schemas. Another source of inferred causality is created by a succession of scenes that are formed into a coherent structure, or schema (Bartlett, 1932). Two types of schema are used. The first is based on events and the second on scripts.

An *event schema,* the most basic type of schema, creates relationships between significant events. An example can be found in a manager's attributions that identify factors thought to be causing the performance downturn of an organization (Ford, 1985). A choice can be made between internal causes, such as low quality or poor training, and external causes, such as interest rates and shifts in consumer preferences. Because internal attributions of causes imply the possibility of wrongful action and managerial responsibility for that action, managers more frequently cite attributions of external causes. External attributions often produce a learned helplessness response and not the more proactive response that is needed to produce an organizational turnaround. Event schemas are often multiple, complex, and abstract. Managers often employ event schemas in very complex ways, discounting the search for causality in certain situations and inhibiting it altogether in others.

Script schemas are derived from sequences that occur repeatedly over a long period of time (Nisbett and Ross, 1980). For instance, a decision can be remembered as having various steps, like scenes in a play, that began with recognition and then identified alternatives, evaluated them, and implemented a preferred choice. Each scene (that is, recognition, identification of alternatives, evaluation of alternatives, and implementation of a choice) summarizes a set of basic actions that were taken. Previous decisions had various sequences of scenes, which resulted in good or bad outcomes, personal recriminations or congratulations, insights, or confusion. Certain sequences get reinforced, others abandoned.

Central to a script are participants, much like the players in a game. The typical behavior of a class of participants mediates the script. These individuals become stereotyped or, more appropriately, person-prototyped, in terms of occupational roles (nurse Mary), personal experience (Billy-Bob, the redneck school director, or Mr. Pretentious, the departmental chairman), culture (the organization man or "save the whales" liberal), fictional characters (a Horatio Alger or a Captain Ahab), and from the jargon of psychiatry (neurotic or paranoid). When person-prototypes are evoked, such as claiming that a manager is paranoid, they often exert considerable influence on judgments. Once evoked, the prototype creates expectations of individual behavior that are set by the predictions of what, for example, a "save the whales" liberal would do if faced with the situation at hand.

Unlike stereotypes, which have taken on a pejorative connotation, personas or person-prototypes are intended to convey a variety of postures, both useful and destructive. Person-prototypes are often embellished by metaphors drawn from various sources. "That CEO has an ego just smaller than the orbit of Venus" and "When you talk to him, hold on to your wallet" are examples. Credibility can be enhanced or cut down by using personas in this manner.

Provoking Knowledge Structures. Decisions are almost always approached as representatives of a class or category, not as one of a kind or unique. Theories and schemas, along with personas, play an important role in classifying a decision prior to making a choice. Theories and schemas are used if they are available and seem representative. Managers make a match between the situation at hand and relationships that seem pertinent by drawing on available relationships, found in stored theories and schemas, that appear to correspond to the decision they are confronting. The composite of these uncovered relationships creates a "knowledge structure" (Nisbett and Ross, 1980). Knowledge structures provide a way to deal with decisions that are believed to fall into particular categories. Such tactics are essential in managing the time and effort required in making choices, but they can be misleading.

The selection of a knowledge structure can be wrong, leading to misapplication, or it may be used too often, when less rapid but better tactics are available to identify important relationships. For instance, misapplication has led to poor political judgments. President Johnson evoked the Munich Conference to call for aggressive military policy in Vietnam (Nisbett and Ross, 1980). President Reagan applied a macho image of militarism to call for action plans that ultimately led to illegal aid to Central American rebel groups. This type of script is often dogmatic and unresponsive to legitimate queries, keeping a decision maker from thinking through a decision with pertinent and situationally accurate information.

Person-prototypes can also mislead. President Truman trusted Stalin because he reminded him of a ruthless and corrupt figure, Tom Pendergast, who aided Truman in the early stages of his political career. Because Pendergast had been trustworthy in his relations with Truman, the president assumed that Stalin would be as well (May, 1973).

Misapplication of schema also occurs when a posited relationship lacks relevance to the situation at hand. For instance, following an interview in a graduate school admissions process for an MBA, a candidate may be called "another John Smith" to evoke the negative image of a student totally disinterested in course work, seeking only the MBA "union card." If John Smith is widely regarded as an "admissions mistake," this person-prototype may be shifted to the new candidate. Person-prototypes can also crop up in letters of recommendation. An MBA candidate could be described as competitive, with a decided "Eastern attitude," to conjure up images of an abrasive, tactless individual unfit for any managerial role. This relationship posits a link between "Eastern attitude" and abrasiveness that may be utterly without foundation for MBA candidates, or for people in general. If person-prototypes are used in place of available and more valid criteria, such as GPA and GRE or GMAT results (graduate school test scores), undergraduate university, relevant major, and experience, a bad decision is likely.

Inferential Adjustments

Both the application of inappropriate theories and schemas and the failure to revise and adjust them can lead to bad decisions. Attempts to revise a poorly selected theory or schema occur less often than one would expect, producing what is called the "anchor effect" (Tversky and Kahneman, 1974). Anchor effects can be illustrated by the tactics of antique auctioneers. The auctioneer always asks for a price well above what the antique is expected to bring. The bid price is quickly reduced, often by huge amounts, to attract bidding activity. Nevertheless, the initial price creates an anchor that tends to increase what bidders will pay for the item being auctioned, no matter what its true dollar value may be. Haggling with car dealers and the initial appraisals of real estate agents are also guided by this principle.

The same type of bias can occur when decision makers make estimates. If the starting point of an estimate is too low, an upward revision of the initial estimate will be overly conservative (Edwards, 1968). For example, consider two managers who make initial estimates of the likelihood of a high level of demand for a product at one in ten and one in two. The manager making the pessimistic one-in-ten estimate will resist increasing his or her estimate to a greater extent than will the manager making the more optimistic one-in-two estimate. The initial estimate becomes a "cognitive anchor." This anchoring has been found to persist in decision-making experiments even after the initial estimates that were given to a subject were shown to be arbitrary.

Experiments in information processing show that managers, after making their first pass at a problem, resist new information, other modes of drawing inferences about factors such as demand, and carefully reasoned challenges of their estimates. The managers give ground grudgingly, primed to challenge the relevance of new information, defend their inferences, and set aside the reasoned views of others. This anchoring effect seems to stem from the preferred schema or theories that the managers apply. The eagerness to use simple and immediately available rules of thumb has a disproportionate effect on the managers' views that resists revision. Once a rule of thumb has been used, managers find it hard to abandon it.

Memory

Limited memory capacity is a primary cause of the shortcuts used in decision making. These shortcuts are carried out by applying heuristics that help decision makers discover and learn.

Currently accepted theories of memory contend that a series of associations is used to reconstruct past events for contemplation (Pribaum, 1983). Memory is a continuous process of reconstruction, unlike computers, which access information in the same form as the information was entered. Errors can occur when decision makers reconstruct events from information fragments. For instance, arguments over graduate admissions can stem from graduate committee members' interpreting current admissions according to different expectations. For one faculty member, admission rates are down unless they exceed the *highest* number of applications in the past several years. For another faculty member, no action seems necessary until the number of applications falls below the lowest recent number of applications. Both faculty members look at the same information, but each recognizes only a fragment of the information that is available.

Vivid information that depicts causal relationships is more apt to be stored in memory. Such information is more likely to be recalled to make inferences when it is concrete and evokes powerful images. Memory is aided by redundancy, recruitment, rehearsal, and reflection (Hogarth, 1980).

Redundancy occurs when multiple sources of information are present. Managers confronted at various points in time by different stakeholders who demand action have salient information about the decision stored in separate pathways of memory, enhancing recall. If the information offered by each stakeholder is also vivid, the combined effect of vividness and redundancy makes the information comparatively easy to recall. Recruitment occurs when memory is used to call out information that agrees with what was just observed or confronted. Vivid information is more apt to draw out supporting information from memory that tends to confirm the inferences implied.

Rehearsal and reflection are more apt to occur for vivid, as compared to pallid, information. Vivid information captures our attention, remaining in our thoughts for longer periods of time. As this "time in thought" extends, our attitude toward the information becomes more fixed and inflexible. For instance, managers who ponder the advisability of a particular choice for extended periods of time make more extreme judgments about the merits of their choice than do managers who give the decision less consideration. This extended time in thought leads to rehearsal. Interesting or vivid information is played out from several vantage points merely because it is attention-getting, not because it is relevant. Extended playing of information leads to more elaborate encoding in memory, which improves recall. Vivid information forces reflection. Managers are seduced by information that remains in their memory, using homilies such as "If it were not important, it would not keep coming back to my thoughts." Managers appear to tacitly assume that what occupies their thoughts must be important and give additional weight to it.

The Inferential Effects of Vivid Information

Managers who weigh information according to its vividness are apt to give less weight to more diagnostic information. Data aggregations or summaries, statistical analyses, and probability statements may be set aside because they are particularly pallid and also lack concreteness and emotional attachments.

Table 5.1. Comparison of Mythic and Evaluative Information.

Mythic Information	Evaluative Information
Partial, personal, interested	Impartial, impersonal, disinterested
Anecdotal, stressing cultural motifs and images	Generalizable, stressing logic or experimental inquiry
Stirs emotions in a drama	Suppresses emotions by avoiding the dramatic
Bias accepted	Bias eliminated
Repetitive and redundant	Coherent and sequential
Implicit and intuitive	Explicit and precise
Takes moral stands	Amoral

Source: Adapted from Mitroff, Mason, and Nelson, 1974.

People are prone to read the anecdotes set out in boxes of news magazines such as *Time* in lieu of the accompanying article. Indeed, these anecdotes are offered because they have high reader appeal and are more apt to be read.

The vivid case history, with its anecdotal inferences, has more effect than an analysis. This effect is so extreme that "myth-information systems" have been recommended to transfer pallid analyses into the more vivid anecdote that captures an inference drawn from analysis (Mitroff, Mason, and Nelson, 1974). Table 5.1 compares some attributes of pallid information drawn from analysis with vivid information made up to describe the results of an analysis (Nutt, 1980b).

Vivid information can also distort inferences. Demonstration programs that illustrate the effects of technological advances to strategic managers have higher adoption rates than persuasion that relies on tables, charts, and statistics (Nutt, 1987b). Demonstrations also have the power to mislead when the evidence for adoption is dubious or lacking. The high-pressure sales tactics of many vacuum cleaner and encyclopedia salespersons provide illustrations. More than two decades after the surgeon general's report linking smoking with lung cancer, many people, including physicians, continue to smoke. One exception is physicians whose specialties put them in contact with people who have lung cancer. For example, radiologists have a very low rate of smoking (Nisbett and Ross, 1980). In the same way, seasoned members of the press who follow the campaigns of presidential candidates systematically reject negative evidence from polls known to be highly accurate. Members of the press assigned to McGovern, Mondale, and Dukakis were continually exposed to enthusiastic crowds made up of those candidates' supporters. The reporters gave these vivid examples of popularity greater weight than objective evidence in the polls, causing the reporters to make wildly inaccurate estimates of the popular vote. Gary Hart reentered the 1988 presidential campaign after receiving a thousand letters, 90 percent of which were supportive. Hart, like the press corps, was misled by vividness, this time of letters from supporters that gave no indication of the general depth of his support after disclosures about his philandering life-style.

Inferences based on vivid information persist after managers have been exposed to diagnostic information, show they have learned the more diagnostic information, and understand and appreciate the inference that can be drawn by using the diagnostic information. When given vivid information, decision makers set aside pallid information. This behavior occurs even when the inference that can be drawn with the vivid information seems dubious to intelligent and informed observers. Managers may ignore accurate analysis and data summaries and use in their place anecdotes, the views of trusted colleagues, and personal experiences.

Personal recommendations have more influence than aggregated data and analysis. Managers prefer to discuss the meaning of information drawn from a management information system before using it for decision-making purposes (Nutt, 1986c). Bias can occur during decision-making discussions, with individuals or in groups, when they exclude, by design or ignorance, important information.

Defending Reasoning

When managers draw inferences from vivid information and favored theories or schemas that contradict what others contend or claim, the managers mount elaborate defenses. They use several tactics to protect their inferences, including homilies such as "You can prove everything with statistics" or "Seeing is believing." Managers also offer ritualistic anecdotes, called "man who" statistics (Nisbett and Ross, 1980), to contradict those who disagree with their inferences. For example, a smoker's response to the surgeon general's report often takes the form of "I know a man who smoked four packs of cigarettes a day and lived to be a hundred." The argument is presented as a single case that contradicts the other party. Managers define their strategy by noting the "man who" carried out a similar strategy with superior results. "Man who" justifications can also be second party, such as peers or respected individuals who have taken a similar or supporting position. To counter such tactics, the homilies can be reversed: "Just because it's vivid doesn't mean it's important." "Don't use your 'man who' reasoning on me" (Nisbett and Ross, 1980).

Making Inferences

To make a choice calls for a decision maker to acquire diagnostic information, deal with illusory associations, construct causal schemas, and make predictions. Intuitive rules of thumb are used in each case to speed and simplify information processing. Incorrectly applied, these rules of thumb make it difficult to draw inferences about the associations buried in the pieces of information that have been acquired (Kahneman and Tversky, 1973; Slovic, 1975).

Describing Data. A manager must be able to code data, characterize data aggregates, and generalize from what he or she observes in order to draw inferences. Coding, characterizing, and generalizing can be biased, thereby creating misleading inferences.

Data coding is influenced by the preconceptions of theory and schema discussed previously (Hogarth, 1980). Bias can occur when these preconceptions prevent managers from encoding diagnostic information and entice them to consider nondiagnostic information. The manager who likes an informant is more apt to consider the information he or she offers, regardless of whether or not the informant is diagnostic. Similarly, stereotypes regarding an informant, such as females as notoriously emotional and apt to overreact to problem situations, influence what is coded. Treating a single case as indicative of a class or failing to see a series of diagnostic cases as exemplars also biases coding. For example, physicians can make incorrect diagnoses when they classify and fit into diagnostic categories a few stray symptoms offered by their patients.

Theories and schemas provide cues that suggest categories in which to code seemingly relevant data for classification purposes. Once a theory has been formed or selected, information that fails to fit is given less weight and is less apt to be coded, no matter what its relevance. Misplaced confidence in a theory or schema, highly available theories or schemas, and a failure to deal with ambiguity can all lead to poor inferences. For example, assume that an interview procedure used to select job applicants is thought to be effective. A manager with this view is led to believe that the interview procedure is the best way to judge a candidate's job fitness. Information acquired through the interview would be coded, and other information, such as work history and background, would be ignored. Inflexibility in acquiring information for job selection decisions can produce poor choices.

To classify data, managers must estimate frequencies, proportions, and averages (Bowman, 1963). Distortion in making such aggregations stems from salience, availability, and extremity. Salient data are weighted too heavily, as are available data and extreme values in data. In each case, eye-catching data swamp the more mundane, according to the vividness and availability arguments previously offered.

To make generalizations about data, one must characterize the members of a particular class of objects, events, or people. Decision makers arrive at conclusions about the merits of mergers, sell-offs, golden parachutes, executive incentive plans, and the like according to examples of each that they have encountered. Such observations can be misleading if a manager is exposed to just a few cases or a biased or parochial set of cases.

Managers often behave as though they have little apprecia-tion of the need for large samples (Estes, 1976). According to statistical principles, bias is far more likely with small than with large samples of cases. Even managers with statistical training often abandon the insights of this training, substituting the illusion of personal experiences to make policy. The speed with which the wife of the hospital CEO was handled in an emer-gency room is substituted for more accurate and available infor-mation about emergency room treatment efficiency. In courts of law, data presented to describe average wages in a labor dispute are set aside in favor of case histories, called precedents. The committee hearings of a legislature ask for testimony from affected parties, discounting analyses. Murder rates in states with and without the death penalty, as well as changes in murder rates following death penalty laws, are countered with the case histories of felons who claim that they were not deterred by a death penalty threat (Nisbett and Ross, 1980). In these examples, the representativeness heuristic allows one to make strong in-ferences on the basis of very weak data.

Bias also stems from observing unusual or typical cases. To control for the errors that can result, managers must be able to eliminate or make allowances for the atypical case or ensure that an unbiased set of cases has been observed. The best way to obtain a descriptive set of cases is to sample randomly, but the need for this procedure is widely misunderstood. For instance, Tversky and Kahneman (1971) describe a politician who sets aside the results of a poll because it selected participants "com-pletely at random."

Sampling ignorance can also stem from context-specific experience. The CEO of a suburban hospital will have a view of debt collection problems and bad debt costs that is markedly different from that of a CEO in an inner-city hospital. Exporting the views between these contexts without careful adjustment can lead managers to set misleading norms in their decision making.

Illusory Associations. Establishing relationships demands considerable skill in coding, categorizing, and generalizing di-agnostic data. Bias stems from spurious or illusory associations decision makers believe they have discovered. An example of illusory correlations can be found in Rorschach tests (Nisbett and Ross, 1980). Many psychiatrists continue to use this instrument even though its sign-symptom associations have been found to contain invalid associations.

Erroneous relationships stem from associations decision makers believe should exist. Practicing clinicians, for example, do not encounter signs and symptoms independently. Separating one from the other without making an inappropriate association can be difficult. Further, these associations can form lasting impressions. Managers who see a dramatic turnaround following a job appraisal interview may relate the tactics used to the results observed, when in fact the employee's change had other origins. If so, the managers may form an illusory association that can persist over an extended period of time, leading the managers to advocate job appraisals for all low-performing employees.

Managers whose attention is focused by large increases or decreases in important indicators of performance are motivated to look for causes in the performance change. These attributions of causality can be illusory. For example, if an increase in the utilization of an outpatient clinic occurs during a marketing effort, the merit of marketing may be indelibly stamped in the mind of the hospital administrator even when the association of marketing and increased utilization is spurious.

Random or mistaken events associated with actions create "superstitions." For instance, sales volume jumps due to increases in business activity can be attributed to a marketing effort that was carried out prior to the period in which sales increased. A failure to consider the need to learn how to operate the new inventory ordering system as a reason for poor initial performance of the system can lead managers to resist using industrial engineers and inventory control procedures in the future. If these views are reinforced by subsequent events, such as the experience of trusted peers, the superstition grows and takes root. It is then repeatedly trotted out as an explanation for a class of phenomena that seems to fit these experiences.

The growth of superstitions stems from random reinforcement, which Skinner (1969) has shown to have the most
lasting effects on behavior. Training is quicker, with longer-
lasting effects, when desirable behaviors are reinforced by
means of a random schedule. For instance, Skinner used random scheduling to teach birds to peck a target by dropping a
food pellet when the desired behavior (pecking for food) was
observed. A random schedule was more effective in reinforcing
the desired behavior than any other schedule, including providing food each time the target was pecked. Random reinforcement was so strong that birds became compulsive, pecking the
target continuously until they were exhausted. Imagine what
would happen if a bird initially pecked the target while standing
on one leg. One-legged birds can be equated with managers
who, through superstitions, become committed to certain practices. Both may compulsively apply tactics that are ineffective.

Causal Schema. In cases that are theory- and schema-poor,
managers search for a causal model to explain what they have
observed (Golding and Roper, 1972). In forming the model,
managers must identify causal factors that help them explain,
for instance, the observed performance downturn of a department or person. The origin of such models is derived from
maxims, parables, and myths that make up a corporate culture.
They are used, in the same way that analogies to seemingly
related situations and anecdotes offered by important peers are
used, to find clues that identify desirable actions. When the
prescriptions drawn from such sources contradict, as in "Look
before you leap" and "He who hesitates is lost," each homily is
placed in a context in which it can apply. The moderator variable that is used may or may not be relevant. For instance, a
manager may conclude that extended contemplation of non-
strategic decisions is acceptable but that product and market
choices are not. This informal store of haphazard knowledge
can be off target and misleading.

The "motor oil is motor oil" commercial provides an
illustration. This pronouncement is made by an old man who is
driving a car that is belching a thick veil of blue smoke in a
Fourth of July parade. An observer early in the parade notes,

"Quite a parade this year," to which another responds: "It's the economy." By the end of the parade, the smoke has driven away most of the paraders. An observer notes, "Not much of a parade this year," to which another responds, "It's the economy."

Overconfidence in the use of such models stems from a failure to judge their predictive accuracy. Search is limited to finding a plausible model, leading to a cycle of use and reinforcement from use without tests that confirms value. In this way, smokers develop elaborate theories of tension release through smoking, failing to consider that smoking may heighten tension, continually creating the need to smoke, and ignore job and family sources of tension in their lives.

Making Predictions. Most decisions call for the decision maker to predict outcomes, such as how proposed products will do in a national marketplace. Decision makers process a variety of information to make this prediction, including market surveys, the views of their family, who sampled the product in trade trials, and their own track record of being overly optimistic or pessimistic when faced with similar decisions. Predictions of this type are both important and difficult for executives to make. Accuracy is influenced by the selection of relevant datums, using appropriate theories and schema, and the drawing of valid inferences. Precision is hampered by the cues derived from illusory relationships, vivid information, and a failure to consider the context in which a prediction is made (Meehl, 1954).

Managers, as well as people in general, are notoriously poor at prediction. Formulas make better predictions than the individual who provided the rationale that is included in the formula (Bowman, 1963). Even people who are skillful in making certain types of decisions, such as stockbrokers (Slovic, 1969) or physicians (Goldberg, 1970), are outperformed by models that aggregate information to make predictions. Other examples include admissions officers predicting the performance of college students and personnel managers choosing employees (Dawes and Corrigan, 1974). Special training and feedback on results have a small but insufficient effect, leaving the "model of man" better than the man in the business of predicting. Experts seem to know how to make predictions but are unable to apply this knowledge consistently as they process the information that is required to predict. When a manager lacks expertise and experience, the accuracy of his or her predictions becomes even more dismal.

Sources of Prediction Error. The poor predictive ability of people is attributed to their failure to use base rates, dilution, and misconstrual. Base rate data are drawn from prior likelihoods, proportions, and averages. Intuitive predictions tend to rely on target cases, or seemingly relevant anecdotes, and to ignore base rates. Managers become overly concerned with matching the case to the decision at hand instead of acquiring base rate information.

The dilution effect occurs when diagnostic information and nondiagnostic information are mixed. Decision makers have difficulty in separating the relevant from the nonrelevant, so the latter dilutes the impact of the former. For example, managers predicting performance of new employees are unable to separate their nonrelevant prior experience from the relevant; the managers have similar difficulties in identifying desired performance in relevant college courses and pertinent information in letters of recommendation.

Rationalizations used to explain the failure of a highly touted junior executive, gleaned like postgame rap sessions after a loss, account for the how but not the why of seemingly likely events. This type of prediction failure typically stems from an imperfect forecasting relationship. Forecasting the success of executives is a risky business in which some failure must be expected. If managers expect a perfect track record, they may revise the predictive approach when there is no need for a revision. The new approach is seldom as good as the old and embodies wasted effort.

Windfall predictions also result in misconstruals. When things turn out better than anticipated, rationalizations provide a way to avoid changes. Success, however, can be due to anomaly or chance. Continuing to rely on the best predictors ensures the best results. For example, to assess the prospects of reform in an employee, it is wise to note that the best predictor of future behavior is past behavior. However, the inherently stochastic nature of outcomes makes reform possible, no matter what steps are taken. The correct interpretation of such a prediction is that reform is possible but unlikely.

Errors in Expressing Judgments

The way decision makers express their choice can also create bias. Response mode is influenced by the question format, scale, wishful thinking, and illusions of control.

Format

The way in which respondents to a survey are asked to express their choice influences their response. The wording of questions can have a profound effect. Consider, for example, a question posed as a preference for treatment when "50 percent are expected to live" or "50 percent are expected to die." The aura, but not the fact, of an optimistic tone in the former ("50 percent survive") produces more optimistic estimates in respondents. In the management of hospitals, occupancy is a widely used indicator of organizational performance. Questions regarding federal policies resulting in "75 percent occupied" and "25 percent empty" create very different connotations in the mind of industry experts. The latter (25 percent empty) conveys a pejorative tone because the positive phrasing (75 percent occupied) is expected. Describing a project as having a 70 percent chance of success is more likely to result in an approval than depicting it as having a 30 percent chance of failure. Each of these examples shows that decision makers given identical information are apt to be swayed by its form. Generally, an implied positive expectation in a question can induce positive or risk-inclined responses, and negative expectations can induce negative or risk-averse responses. Conservatism also affects the way people respond to scales. Edwards (1968) finds that people crimp their responses at extreme ends of a scale, estimating high-likelihood events too low and low-likelihood events too high.

Response modes can entice people to emphasize different aspects of alternatives they are asked to judge. For example, open-ended fill-in-the-blank-type questions about salary, such as "When I work hard around here. . .," are apt to produce different kinds of response than scales that ask the respondent to link salary and effort. The scale mode produces an agree/disagree response but the open-ended question can elicit a variety of responses, including "No one will talk to me" (Nutt, 1982a).

Wishful Thinking

Wishful thinking has several kinds of undesirable effects. First, it can cause estimates of likelihoods to be higher than the facts warrant (Cyert, Dill, and March, 1958). People will act as if the likelihood of an outcome they desire is higher than a realistic appraisal would allow. For instance, what can be called the lotto mentality surfaces when the payoff of a state lottery reaches some new high, such as $20 million. People know the likelihood of winning is very close to zero, but they buy tickets anyway. Managers display a form of lotto mentality when they go after big government contracts that they have no chance of winning. Second, wishful thinking can produce responses that attempt to reduce conflict. Stress will increase the potential for bias because decision makers have more difficulty assimilating information and are less apt to carefully process information in a stressful state.

Illusions of Control

Decisions that require a forecast can produce illusions of control (Langer, 1975). The act of forecasting or predicting an inherently uncertain future event often creates a feeling of control over that event. The event remains uncertain, but the manager behaves as though the act of making a prediction makes the predicted outcome become more certain. For instance, costs associated with plans that pose new ways of operating are often treated by decision makers as known, clear, and certain when, in fact, they are uncertain and apt to vary substantially from estimates.

Failing to Learn from Experience

Managers learn from what they can observe. Feedback is essential for learning to occur. Decisions that fail to produce recognizable measures of success can make learning impossible. In some cases, feedback is not available; in others, it is ignored or misinterpreted. A decision that rules out options also tends to rule out learning about the discarded options. Unlike the line in the Frost poem, "the road not taken" could have been the better way. Without taking it, there is no way to know. All choices among plans or alternative ways of acting, such as giving students scholarships or selecting people for jobs, rule out learning about the rejected applicants. The performance of people rejected for jobs or scholarships is unknown and hidden from efforts to learn about the selection process.

The timing and delay of feedback can make it impossible to conduct prompt appraisals. When outcomes are finally observable, the decision process may not be recallable. The results of mergers and acquisitions, for instance, may not be fully understood for many years. With the passage of time, the process undertaken in unsuccessful mergers or acquisitions may be forgotten and repeated.

Managers learn from what they are able to observe. They will be reinforced by decisions that create rewards and stop what seems to produce failure and recrimination. Managers implicitly learn these relationships by linking successes and failures with factors that appear to have produced these outcomes.

Selection of Norms

To make a decision, managers often use standards of expected performance, called *norms*. For instance, to select an individual for a job, a manager may use a norm of at least ten years of experience. To understand the types of bias that can occur, consider managerial job selection that uses an examination, a practice that is common in civil service. Norms concerning job performance and the score on the exam are shown in Figure 5.1. Norm 1 (N1) represents a cutoff that is applied to

Figure 5.1. Norms and Outcome Feedback.

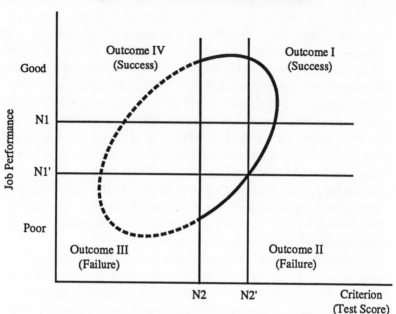

Source: Adapted from Hogarth, 1980.

separate good from poor job performance as determined by formal job appraisals and the like. Norm 2 (N2) captures the test score cutoff that was used in the selection process.

The prospect of being able to observe success and failure depends on patterns of job performance, the norms used for selection and those used to measure success, and the assumption of independence between the rules used and whether or not the manager has been successful (Hogarth, 1980).

Performance Biases. To understand performance biases, assume that the performance of managers selected for civil service management positions, such as office manager, are captured by the ellipse in Figure 5.1. The ellipse contains the range of performance outcomes for the successful applicants. If the norm is stringently applied, with no exceptions, the portion of the ellipse to the left of the cutoff is unknown, designated by the dotted line. Occasionally, mitigating factors, such as equal opportunity rulings, require the selection of individuals who fall far below the selection norm. In the discussion that follows, it is assumed that equal opportunity and related cases are few in number.

The norm applied to test scores influences the relative number of successes and failures. As the rule becomes more stringent, moving from N2 to N2', the relative number of successes to failures appears to increase, although the true success rates remain the same. A more stringent norm also reduces the number of outcomes (successes and failures) that can be observed.

Biases Due to Norms. The norm applied to measure job performance has similar effects. If expectations are lowered from N1 to N1' in Figure 5.1, as would be required in equal opportunity cases, the apparent predictive ability of the test increases because the relative number of successes appears to increase. The increase is illusory, as the true numbers of successes and failures have remained unchanged. The true rate of success, the proportion of all applicants that would be successful, is seldom if ever known. Assumptions about this rate influence performance expectations. The ratio of successes to failures is influenced by the cutoff standards that are set, which in turn influence what decision makers conclude about the predictive value of the test. Note that the decision maker's expectations shape this conclusion: High expectations result in lowered expectations regarding the test's predictive abilities.

The Postselection Bias. A bias in interpreting success can be produced when job selection makes available training and other types of special attention that improve the successful applicant's chance of doing well on the job. The new hire may be aided by the more experienced hands and shown the ropes, which include many tips on how to do well. In many decisions, it is difficult to separate the decision from the outcome. For example, a physician's decision to treat a patient calls for a judgment that treatment is needed, which is followed by therapy. A physician acting in this manner has no way to tell if a condition is self-limiting, introducing misleading cues about the merits of treatment. The physician has no knowledge of what will occur with-

Figure 5.2. Treatment Effects Biasing Feedback.

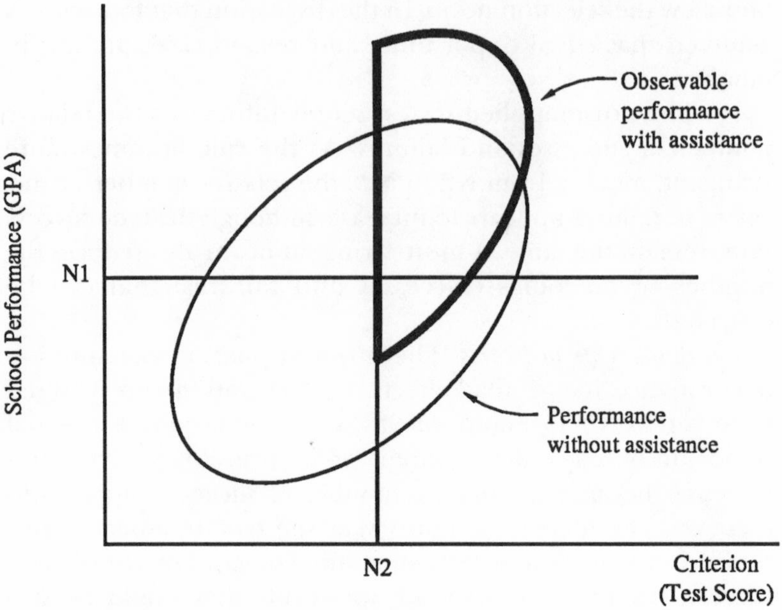

Source: Adapted from Hogarth, 1980.

out treatment. Overtreatment, such as excess surgery, may stem from physicians who fail to see the self-limiting nature of some ailments.

The selection of a recipient for an award, such as a scholarship, also produces this effect, as shown in Figure 5.2. Students receiving such an award are often able to associate with better students, have superior instructors, and get more help and the like in honors classes, thereby improving their skills. The heavily outlined part of the ellipse shows the effect of this performance elevation in terms of grade point average (GPA) and how it creates a favorable bias in feedback because the relative number of successes appears larger than it would be without the special attention.

Biases That Inhibit Learning

Time lags and the huge diversity in decision types erect barriers that make learning about one's choices complex and time-consuming. Learning depends on acquiring feedback about outcomes, taking time to reflect on the steps taken in making a decision, and records that link predictions with outcomes (Goldberg, 1968). Feedback that describes the consequences of a decision is essential if learning is to occur. Learning is greater when several similar decisions can be captured so types can be grouped and linked to outcomes. The unique or infrequent decision is far less apt to produce learning than are repetitious choices. Records are also essential. Methods of bolstering memory capacity are helpful to ensure that consequences are understood in context. If feedback includes both outcome and how the decision was made, such as the bases of a prediction, learning can be more effective. Barriers to learning stem from erroneous attributions, misplaced confidence, and hindsight bias.

Erroneous Attributions. "Chance" events are circumstances beyond the manager's control that result from a bundle of causes that are not fully understood. They seem to be random but actually represent the outcome of a combination of complex events that are not predictable when one makes a decision. Managers often find it difficult to determine whether outcomes, such as occupancy, are due to their actions (starting a public relations campaign) or the acts of a competitor, as in the remodeling of a competing local hospital, which temporarily decreases its capacity. When a manager's acts and chance events occur at the same time, the two can be hard to separate.

Managers make an erroneous causal attribution when they assign the wrong cause to an outcome. The same factors that produce the gambler's fallacy and illusory relationships, discussed in Chapter Four, come into play. A manager can fail to see that an extreme value for cost is likely to be followed by less extreme cost value because cost outcomes are stochastic and vary around some unknown average cost. When extreme costs are noted, managers often take action. If a cost reduction follows this action, managers must recognize that a decrease in cost might have occurred, even if no action had been taken.

Illusions of Control. An illusion of control occurs when managers make decisions that require skill and find it hard to untangle their skill from chance effects. Good outcomes are attributed to skill and bad ones to chance. Reacting in this way, managers can create an illusion of control over situations that, in fact, were out of control. The track records of managerial success can be made up of self-fulfilling attributions about the powers of managers' decision making that bear little resemblance to reality.

Hindsight Bias. After one experiences an outcome, a decision often seems to have been inevitable and easily related to cues available at the time of choice (Fischhoff, 1975). For instance, some claim that the space shuttle disaster of 1986, which killed seven astronauts, should have been foreseen because of the known risk of low-temperature launches. At Morton-Thiokol, the rocket booster contractor, engineers claimed that O rings in the booster do not seal properly at temperatures below 50°F, that their concerns were well documented in various reports, and that NASA decision makers were aware of these reports. The engineers further claimed that these concerns had been expressed during the countdown of a previous shuttle launch. NASA administrators ignored the engineers' claims, contending that nothing would ever be launched if they listened to all of the claims and advice of this type put forward during a launch countdown. The engineers countered by insisting that only a sudden increase in temperature during a previous launch averted an earlier disaster.

From the vantage point of hindsight, the shuttle disaster seems to have been preventable. A prior prediction was made and ignored. An earlier tragedy was averted only because of a chance event, a sudden increase in temperature at the Cape Canaveral launch site. NASA administrators were (and are) nearly all political appointees, with a terminal case of technological ignorance. They were unable to understand the engineers on the rare occasions when they tried. With this background in mind, blame for the shuttle disaster seems to rest squarely on the launch decision makers at NASA.

Before one buys into this explanation, however, the "creeping determinism" (Hogarth, 1980) that emerged during the inquiry following the shuttle disaster should be noted. *After one listens to all the testimony, aspects of it, which one can call* the O-ring story, become more salient than they were at the time of the launch decision. Creeping determinism makes what happened seem to flow from preceding events, causing stochastic events to appear deterministic.

Creeping determinism sweeps aside other, equally plausible explanations, such as bureaucratic smugness and ponderous decision processes (Mitroff, Mohrman, and Little, 1987). NASA's management has grown from 1,050 employees per launch in 1966 to an estimated 1,850 per launch budgeted for the shuttle program. Transactions that once took six weeks now take six months. However, panels investigating disasters must find scapegoats and fall guys. NASA's top managers were sacked and replaced with their predecessors, who are also political appointees with little technological sophistication. NASA's decision processes remain largely unchanged.

The results of experiments confirm the effects of creeping determinism. Decisions in which outcomes were known caused subjects to see these outcomes as inevitable and clearly related to available cues. The same decision described as having an unknown outcome produces less predictive certainty and far fewer as well as less intense cue associations.

The knowledge that a particular outcome has occurred seems to restrict memory. Instead of recalling the past in terms of the uncertainties present at the moment of choice, the decision maker comes up with a reconstruction to account for the outcome. The history of the decision is revised to make sense of what happened by creating a coherence in antecedents that are linked to the outcome. For example, the Japanese attack on Pearl Harbor seems predictable in retrospect, as does the economic chaos that stemmed from the Arab oil embargo in 1973 (Hogarth, 1980).

Distinguishing Hindsight and Foresight. Making forecasts or predictions of yet-to-be-realized events or conditions is laced with uncertainty. There are many paths, each capturing important contingencies, that cannot be understood with clarity at the time of a choice. Decisions concerning gas rationing in 1973, for example, required accurate estimates of the shortfalls of hundreds of petroleum products and the economic consequences of each. Moreover, totally unexpected events occurred. Consumers acted irrationally, as when they lined up at gas pumps with nearly full tanks of gas to "top off" their tanks, which created a chaotic and explosive situation across the country. Forecasts and predictions require imagination, flexibility, and a thoughtful response to unexpected events as they arise. Hindsight requires little imagination and allows one to impose a clear-cut structure made up of the *now* deterministic cues and consquences. These cues and consequences seem to be plausible diagnostic aids because they preceded a now realized outcome.

Hindsight Bias and Learning

The bias associated with hindsight reasoning poses important questions that influence how decision makers deal with success and failure, distort their recall of decisions, and learn from their decision foibles.

Dealing with Failure. Neville Chamberlain is recalled as the English prime minister who was duped by Hitler just before World War II (Hogarth, 1980). The wonderfully compelling BBC series depicting Winston Churchill out of power during the 1930s and reacting to Chamberlain and his "peace in our time" agreement, and to others who failed to see the Nazi menace, is riddled with hindsight bias.

Chamberlain-like incidents frequently occur in organizations. Claims are made that the CEO should have known about the intentions of competitors before launching a new product; such claims are accompanied by a rendition of a litany of signals that the CEO chose to ignore. Parole boards are vigorously criticized when a felon is released and commits a crime, as the critics ignore evidence of model behavior in confinement and the degree of risk in comparable cases on which the decision to parole was made. When a decision is made public and shown to be wrong, hindsighting invariably occurs. If one is to learn, the case must be disguised so that one can see whether the facts available at the time of choice seemed to warrant the decision that was made.

Memory Distortions. After the outcome of a decision is known, memory plays tricks on decision makers, distorting what happened and permitting rationalizations. Blame is quick when there seems to have been an avoidable error, as in the shuttle disaster. Some decisions produce good outcomes for serendipitous reasons. Decision makers become visionary leaders when their decisions turn out right and bumbling idiots when they do not. Limited memory capacity creates the need to consolidate events to permit recall. Forgetting attributions that proved to be incorrect is both expedient and essential. Many learned relationships are useful, such as the somewhat rote way in which most of us drive our cars, but other relationships create bogus linkages that persist over time and distort learning. Distortion in memory, caused by knowing how things turned out, is apt to create spurious associations that are difficult to unlearn.

Lack of Surprise. Experience, it is said, is the great teacher. The hindsight bias poses several questions about what is taught. Decision makers fail to treat outcomes with the amount of surprise they merit. This has two implications. First, the lack of surprise may suggest that there was little to learn. Decision outcomes are treated as though they were preordained. Second, causal explanations that are too easily constructed may fail when applied in future decisions. Consider a company CEO reflecting on the costs and benefits of product advertising. If the ads precede an increase in sales, a linkage between the ads and sales can be easily posited. Other, equally plausible explanations, such as a dedicated sales force and good training, can be discarded, leading to disillusioned salespeople and trainers. After-the-fact explanations cannot be put to any useful validity test, making them shaky, if not a wholly unusable means of learning. There is a tendency not to seek information that tests and possibly sets aside these explanations, so they can persist over extended periods of time.

Key Points

1. Steps taken to simplify and reduce effort in processing information to make decisions can produce errors. Such processing errors stem from the following:

a. The availability heuristic, in which one of many plausible relationships between events is seen as causal because it is conspicuous.

b. The representativeness heuristic, which uses a prior decision to guide the current choice. Errors can result when the decision used as an analogy is deceptively similar to the current choice.

c. Knowledge structures, based on experience, used to form beliefs about how people, objects, and events are related. These beliefs can be overgeneralizations, such as "money motivates," or based on a stilted experience that results in stereotyped responses.

d. Reluctance to adjust preliminary judgments or means of making judgments as more diagnostic information or better means are uncovered.

e. Vivid information that is more likely to be recalled, no matter what its relevance to a decision.

f. Illusory associations, which emerge because plausible observable causes are mistaken for true causes that were hidden. An illusory association can become a superstition when no tests of its predictive ability are applied.

g. People's limited ability to make predictions stemming from superstitions, vivid information, ill-chosen exemplars; failure to use base rates (for example, averages); dilution of diagnostic with nondiagnostic information; and misconstruals, in which a bad decision produced a good outcome because of chance events.

2. Errors in expressing judgments that stem from misleading formats used to acquire information, wishful thinking that makes desirable outcomes more likely, and illusions of control that occur when predictions make estimates seem preordained and not subject to chance.

3. Failure to learn from success and failure. Learning failures are due to the following:

a. The hidden value of discarded options.

b. The selection of norms that create a biased impression of the proportion of decisions that are successful.

c. Giving special attention to the selected option, which

enhances performance prospects, thus making decisions become self-fulfilling prophecies.

d. Difficulties in separating chance events from actions, which can lead to assigning the wrong cause to an outcome.

e. The hindsight bias of creeping determinism that makes an outcome, after it has been observed, seem likely or even inevitable.

6

Unconscious Preferences

This chapter and the next illustrate how Jungian notions of cognitive makeup create preferences for certain types of reasoning that lead managers to use particular types of decision procedures (Nutt, 1979b, 1986a). Chapter Six describes the variety of ways that managers prefer to make choices and take action, which are called choice and implementation styles. Chapter Seven explains how these traits are combined to create decision styles, points out conditions under which managers shift their style, and notes the least and most preferred decision-making tactics implied by each style. Using the self-administered questionnaire in Appendix C, readers can determine their own style and then read Chapters Six and Seven to find a description of their style and note its conflicts with other styles, identify their least and most preferred ways of making a decision, and consider the corrective action that is offered. Reflection on one's style provides a basis for self-appraisal and a means to recognize and appreciate how managers with a different style believe that decisions should be made. This appreciation helps managers see that no single approach to decision making can be used exclusively and lays the groundwork for matching decision types to the decision approaches presented in Part Three of the book.

Barriers to the Use of Multiple Perspectives in Decision Making

Decision aiding is a recurrent theme in the ideas offered to improve decision-making capacity, but the success of a deci-

Note: The author wishes to thank Robert W. Backoff for his many useful suggestions in the development of this chapter and the next.

sion aid depends on its compatibility with the way in which managers prefer to make decisions. The influence of a decision maker's "style" must be considered to realize the benefits of using multiple perspectives during decision making. Understanding the deep-seated preferences in one's decision style helps to explain why decision makers often fail to develop a repertoire of decision approaches and use them when pertinent. This raises two important questions. The first deals with self-awareness and the second with overcoming barriers to the use of certain types of decision tactics. The self-awareness dictum has its roots in both psychotherapy and Eastern religions. Self-motivated change, based on enlightenment, is thought to stem from self-awareness that leads to self-directed change. Once managers or budding managers become aware of the inner sources of their behavior and their unconscious needs, they may be able to liberate themselves from these influences when they make decisions. Even if this liberation is partial or incomplete, awareness provides managers with the motivation to seek a balanced perspective, complementing their strengths with the strengths of others who have very different worldviews. This type of team building is essential to the formation of groups and coalitions and the selection of support staff who embody the variety of perspectives needed to deal with tough decisions. Decision makers need both self-awareness and skills in recognizing why coalitions form naturally, without outside impetus.

Observing the Behavior of Decision Makers

The way in which managers carry out decision making becomes apparent in routine contacts and more formal gatherings, such as the meetings of directorates, that are considering various actions. Managers go about making decisions in very different ways, which can provoke controversy. The conduct of decision making becomes observable as managers offer justifications to support a decision and, if pressed, the means used to arrive at that decision. Conflict can occur when a justification is repeated until it becomes a cliché. For instance, some managers preface all observations by "At our shop, we. . ." Such a justification may goad some listeners to wonder, "Does this generalize?"

Others justify their claims by noting, "Logic dictates that. . ."
Such a position can provoke a retort that action based solely on
logic is apt to fail because the feelings of people committed to
venerated practices must be managed before change can occur.
"Life is change, so we must seek out and adopt new ideas" elicits
rejoinders about commitments to preserve the core values of an
organization. Laying out the steps to be followed in managing
the feelings of potential dissenters brings criticisms of a failure
to focus on ends.

Differences in preferred bases from which to draw a
conclusion can also cause conflict and dissension. Some managers rely on reasoning and analysis to draw conclusions. Others
resonate to operant principles. Still others emphasize people's
sentiments, personal values, testimony of the senses, personal
stores of facts, emergent possibilities, and inspiration.

These different approaches to decision making pose several questions. First, why do some managers seem to gravitate
toward particular approaches and use them repeatedly? Second, what makes this behavior habitual? Third, why are some
managers so predictable and others less so? Cognitive theory
offers some answers to these and related questions. According to
this theory, differences in the cognitive makeup of managers
color their preferences. This leads them to form different views
of how to make a decision (Churchman, 1971). People are more
apt to regard the approaches used by others as trite and
hackneyed when their own cognitive style differs from the styles
of others.

Carl Jung's theory of psychological types provides a widely
accepted theory of cognitive style (Jung, 1923). The Jungian
classification categories and Briggs's (Myers and Myers, 1980)
interpretation of their role in human activity are used in Chapters Six and Seven to identify styles of decision making. Style
comparisons point out distinctions in the ways managers
choose and act to implement their choices. These distinctions
also suggest when potential conflicts in interpersonal relations
are likely to occur and why organizational leaders advocate
certain types of action and use particular tactics to carry out
their vision. A deeper understanding of these style-based prefer-

ences, along with their strengths and weaknesses, suggests steps that a manager can take to build on the strengths and manage the weaknesses inherent in each style.

Choice Styles

Jungian theory suggests that choice styles can be defined by the preferences managers exhibit as they gather and analyze information to make decisions.

Gathering Information

Information can be gathered by sensing (S) or by intuition (N). Sensing data take shape as facts and details, breaking the stimulus into discrete elements. In *sensing*, a person gathers information with a coding device that searches for deviations from accepted standards. For instance, sales managers who search through reports, comparing this month's sales to those in the same month a year ago for individual salespeople, use this type of information. Such a tactic is used to ensure that significant details can be extracted from the copious information that a sales manager with this kind of preference would want to have.

Intuitive information attempts to capture a comprehensive picture or a gestalt of a decision situation. A perceptive approach to information gathering is applied. The decision maker attempts to find patterns, rather than apply a preconceived coding strategy. For instance, an auditor examines large quantities of data to construct a picture of financial performance for an organization. Similarly, open-ended survey questions provide intuitive information for a decision maker to ponder.

Each type of information has strengths and limitations. In sensing, the coding device used to acquire data may miss relevant details. For instance, cost-variance reports used to measure the performance of a department may not document the turnover of department heads, which has led to the poor performance identified in the report. On the other hand, intuitively acquired information may never coalesce into a coherent picture. Decision makers can become overloaded with information, making them unable to find relationships in the data that they can use to devise premises on which to base action. For instance, a content analysis that seeks patterns in open-ended survey questions may be complex, influenced by setting, mood, individual differences, and the like. However, the sought-after patterns can remain obscure even after extensive study.

Decision makers with these different preferences look for very different types of information. For instance, in arguing for an increase in support for medical research, a sensing individual would be prone to use data, for example, pointing out that farm support payments to tobacco growers are greater than the entire budget of the National Institutes of Health (NIH). Individuals who prefer intuitive types of information would want to highlight programs that could benefit from an increase in NIH funding. Although their aims may be similar, people with S and N preferences are likely to disagree about the best way to support these aims. The intuitive policymaker hears the "facts" and wonders what the point is. Is the irony of spending more money to produce disease than to deal with it likely to be appreciated? According to the intuitive, facts without context are often misconstrued. The sensate wants to have possibilities backed up with fact: how much these programs cost, their benefits, and so forth. Specifics and examples are thought to make an argument compelling.

Processing Information

An individual may use either thinking (T) or feeling (F) to process information in order to reach a decision. Thinking relies on logic and a step-by-step process. The decision is carefully structured so steps in processing data can be laid out in advance. Decision makers who use thinking modes of reasoning stress generalization and believe decisions should be amoral and impersonal. They believe analysis, not personal considerations, should dictate choices.

Feeling personalizes the decision. When a decision maker relies on feeling, the personal circumstances of all concerned, as well as the unique nature of the decision, form the basis for decision making. Decision makers who use feeling tend to be heuristic, jumping back and forth among solution ideas and testing each one. An incubation phase follows, which leads to a flash of insight: A new idea emerges and may provide a unique or innovative response.

Each mode of processing also has strengths and weaknesses. Thinking is efficient and reliable. Premises are set out and assumptions checked, permitting the rationales to be made explicit. Unfortunately, many ill-structured decisions, such as choices about strategy made by top management, are not manageable when one uses only logic (Mintzberg, Raisinghani, and Theoret, 1976). In other instances, a step-by-step analysis is abandoned, because it is perceived to be time-consuming and hard to comprehend (Nutt, 1984b). Feeling promotes acceptance and, on occasion, innovation. But personalizing a decision may smack of favoritism or moralizing, and it may cause a person to miss opportunities to select a superior course of action.

These two ways of processing data produce very different rationales. A manager using feeling may justify his or her actions by noting, "I care." Individuals with thinking preferences are apt to wonder, "About what?" Critics realize that feeling can be used to protect or create a power base or to select alternatives that benefit individuals they must cater to or want to impress instead of selecting the best alternative. The best alternative, however, can be difficult to identify when objectives are vague, which makes criteria to judge an alternative argumentative. The F-oriented manager is aware of the need to understand key value differences to frame the decision. This framing is often useful because in many important decisions the interests to be served must be understood before a decision can be made.

Preference Stability

According to the innate view of style, people are born with S or N and T or F preferences (Myers, 1976). These preferences dictate choices and actions during a person's early cognitive development and have been observed in the actions of children during play. Subsequent job, educational, and other experiences are thought to result from rather than to cause these preferences. Strongly held preferences suggest that style is deeply rooted in a person's psyche and does not evolve as one experiences new stimuli found in life, education, and jobs (McKenney and Keen, 1974). Job seekers look for occupations and work roles that are compatible with their cognitive orientations. As a result, people unconsciously seek organizations and jobs within those organizations that are compatible with their preferences. People choose undergraduate courses, continuing education programs, and other types of learning to build on their preferred skills, which in turn reinforces them.

The Styles Implied

Managers often prefer one information type and processing option (Churchman, 1971; Mason and Mitroff, 1973). As shown in Figure 6.1, these preferences lead to four styles of choice making: ST (sensation-thinking), NT (intuition-thinking), SF (sensation-feeling), and NF (intuition-feeling). These styles have provided a window to view the cognitive makeup of managers, which has proved to be insightful in illuminating the distinct ways in which choices are made.

Systematic Style. Managers using an ST or "systematic" style consciously structure their decisions by developing ways to look for cues in evaluating data. The tactics they use to search may vary from one systematic decision maker to another, but each stresses hard data and logical analysis, and each attempts to devise rules that will govern the decision process. Variations and adaptations occur as tactics are applied to new and different decision tasks.

Figure 6.1 summarizes the preferred types of information; preferred bases, or warrants to draw conclusions (Toulmin, 1979); and decision aids that are consistent with the preferences of each style. The preference for careful analysis with hard data suggests that systematics would prefer to use analytical decision aids such as mathematical models or statistical techniques. War-

Figure 6.1. Choice Styles.

	Preferred Mode of Gathering Information	
	Sensation (S)	Intuition (N)
Thinking (T)	*Systematic* (ST) **Information:** quantitative measures **Warrant:** statistical significance or axiomatic logic **Decision Aids:** cost-benefit analysis and evaluation research	*Speculative* (NT) **Information:** future possibilities **Warrant:** assumptional flux and stochastic parameters **Decision Aids:** decision trees with sensitivity analysis
Feeling (F)	*Judicial* (SF) **Information:** current situation or circumstances **Warrant:** acceptance and compromise by interested parties **Decision Aids:** decision groups	*Heuristic* (NF) **Information:** current possibilities **Warrant:** experience and judgment **Decision Aids:** mutual adjustment

Preferred Mode of Processing Information (row label for Thinking (T) / Feeling (F))

rants such as statistical significance and mathematical logic are used to validate the need for action.

Systematic decision makers prefer to compare options by using quantitative criteria and to base their decisions on the findings of the analysis. ST managers become uneasy with decisions that are not amenable to this type of treatment. Some type of cost-benefit or cost-effectiveness analysis is thought to be necessary to consistently make "good" decisions. Unwarranted theorizing and moralizing are believed to result when qualitative information or personalities clutter up a decision. Managers with these views see people with different styles as misusing quantitative information. These views are often expressed by the statement that most things are measured with a micrometer, marked with chalk, and cut with a meat ax. The systematic decision maker feels no compelling urge to consider context and frequently ignores the way shifts in the environment, such as changing oil prices, could influence the merits of alternatives.

Speculative Style. The "speculative" or NT decision maker tries to subject hypothetical possibilities to logical analysis. Like systematic decision makers, speculative individuals follow logical steps in the analysis, but they are more concerned about contextual factors, using analysis to devise and test several premises. Information that describes the influence of crucial contingencies, such as demand or use estimates, illustrates key premises that speculative decision makers often consider.

Decision aids congruent with this style are decision trees and sensitivity analysis, described in Part Five of the text. The NT regards future possibilities, expressed as data-assumption linkages, as key facts suggesting a warrant of assumptional flux. To isolate a preferred course of action, NTs relax assumptions about key factors to see if a pessimistic as compared to an optimistic view of these factors would call for different choices.

Speculative decision makers want to use a structure to organize their decisions and regard those without a structure as fuzzy thinkers. They are intrigued by unknown-unknowns and how they know they know. Speculatives are leery of decision makers who espouse the use of intuition derived from experience to make decisions, wondering whether good judgment comes from experience or experience comes from bad judgment. According to this view, once something happens, no matter how accidental, it tends to be regarded as a manifestation of a hidden reality.

Judicial Style. A "judicial" or SF decision maker prefers to rely on consensus to select a course of action. Such individuals disregard general issues to focus on human relations that appear to influence choice, using facts and details to describe these relationships. Decisions are treated as unique, and each is considered on its merits. Reality is what a key body, such as an organization's board of directors, can agree about. The judicial decision maker seeks quantitative information but processes the information by seeking an agreement about the information's meaning.

Advocating interaction to sort and reconcile evaluation data is consistent with the preferences of a judicial manager. People's perceptions of the current situation are facts to a judicial, and what people will accept is the key warrant used to endorse action. Action taking becomes feasible for an SF when negotiation has identified an acceptable course of action.

Judicial managers prefer to consider information from a variety of sources, using decision aids, such as group process (see Chapter Fifteen), to do so. Judicials try to avoid the "straitjacket" they believe is imposed by formal models. Only interpersonal contact can cater to judicial decision makers' preference for hard data and their need to understand the views of their peers when making choices. The "community of minds" sorts through the information that is uncovered to isolate a course of action. Cost-benefit and cost-effectiveness criteria are considered, but the importance of such information hinges on its presentation and its source. The result is a synthesis of cost-effectiveness and cost-benefit data based on the synergistic insights of the group, which is believed to produce good decisions.

Heuristic Style. Managers with a heuristic or NF style rely on unverbalized hunches or cues and prefer to defend their choice by its "fit" to their experiences. Social responsibility and quality of life often form the basis for a choice. Analytical approaches are viewed as unable to capture the complexity in most important decisions. The heuristic decision maker believes that values are a crucial aspect of most decisions and that choices cannot be made without considering the decision's value context.

To make a decision, the heuristic decision maker attempts to balance conflicting claims. Politics and bargaining, through mutual adjustment, are preferred approaches. Heuristics believe that important decisions can seldom be uncoupled from personal views and desires of powerful stakeholders who are influenced by the decision. Facts become the NF's perception of these views and desires, backed by a warrant that stresses the NF's judgment and experience (Figure 6.1). Reconciling the values and beliefs of key stakeholders is a precursor to action.

Heuristic decision makers see decision making as a practical exercise that must cater to the whims of key people and the culture of the organization they represent. A point between conflicting claims and counterclaims that balances opposing views is sought, and the political and moral consequences of each alternative course of action are stressed. Heuristic decision makers view analytical approaches as inappropriate because they ignore or fail to capture the political and moral concerns posed by alternatives. They resonate to George Bernard Shaw's observation that all the economists in the world laid end to end would not reach a conclusion. Group decisions are avoided because a group may force the decision maker to disclose information before the consequences of disclosure can be assessed. Decision groups are seen as producing "pooled ignorance," which in the mind of the heuristic decision maker seldom leads to wisdom.

Steps Preferred by Each Style

Managers with different styles have been found to make choices in very different ways. For example, loan officers in a bank were asked to describe how they believed loans should be made (Mitroff and Kilmann, 1975). Loan officers with a systematic style believed that loans should be based on a careful review of each applicant's assets and liabilities and that would-be borrowers should be granted loans when their level of indebtedness to income was below a certain value. Speculative loan officers wanted a short statement of the applicant's financial position and why the loan was needed. The decision rules tended to be contextual; indebtedness-income ratios would vary, depending on the loan's intended use. Judicial loan officers wanted to call the loan applicant's employer and others who could "vouch for" the applicant. They advocated a group session in which all loan officers would share information gleaned from their applicants, with the group selecting loans to be approved from this pool of applicants. Finally, the heuristic loan officers wanted to hold an open-ended interview with each applicant and, if they remained undecided after the interview, would prefer calling a trusted fellow loan officer to discuss the results of the interview. The applicant's personal situation was cited as a basis to grant a loan.

Planners who prepared an essay describing their view of an ideal planning process produced similar results (Nutt, 1979b). Planners with a systematic style called for a step-by-step planning process that isolated need, coupled need with financing, and outlined a procedure to identify ways to carry out programs within budget constraints. Speculative planners preferred a planning process that was guided by generic concepts such as a formal statement of goals and objectives. The goals were described as guiding a process that develops a general model, specifying macro components of the plan. Budget constraints were seldom mentioned. Judicial planners contended that people's needs should direct planning. Consumer surveys and small-group rap sessions were often cited as ways to judge needs. The heuristic planners evaluated people's needs by using their own notions of what make up critical values. The plan was often described as springing from the minds of skilled professionals as a consequence of their carefully considering people's needs.

Managers considering criteria to select a university hospital CEO have been found to follow a similar pattern. Search committees made up of systematics identified criteria such as knowledge of procedures and emerging trends in prospective reimbursement rules and regulation. Committees made up of speculatives sought CEO candidates with skills in market segmentation and promotion. Committees composed of judicials claimed that interpersonal skills were critical and sought candidates with a proved ability to deal with medical staffs and boards of trustees. Finally, committees made up of heuristics sought candidates who had experience dealing with external actors, such as insurance companies and other third-party payers, and preferred people with proved skills in coalition building and coalition management.

Approaches to risk management in highly regarded banks illustrate how style can be manifest at the organizational level (Nutt, 1989). The Wachovia Bank and Trust Company dealt with risk by using the same procedures it applied to making loans, procedures compatible with systematic rationales. Exposure was measured by credit standing according to a moving three-day average, which was monitored daily. The Philadelphia National Bank followed judicial rationales. A committee was chartered to identify risks and develop procedures to deal with them. The committee came up with nineteen risk factors, which were used to rate loans on a five-point scale, from minimal to critical risk. The committee reviewed this information to identify areas needing attention. The Northwest Bank of Minneapolis applied speculative rationales, devising a guide that specified procedures and steps to be used in risk assessment. This guide was to be used to identify areas needing attention in order to offer possible actions that might apply (remove customer; increase float time, interday balances, and so on). The Chase Manhattan Bank used heuristic tactics, supporting accountable individuals with the needed experience and judgment to identify questions and pose answers. Advisory councils made up of functional area specialists were created to provide expertise that the responsible manager could summon to answer questions. The council was intended to supplement but not replace the responsible manager's judgment.

Disposition Toward Action

Managers faced with identical decisions exhibit differences in their desire to act that have been related to their style. For example, studies of a multiphased merger acquisition task with feedback (Blaylock and Rees, 1984) and simulated capital expansion decisions (Henderson and Nutt, 1980) found that managers with a judicial style were inclined to act, managers with a systematic style were uncertain about acting, and the others fell in between. Systematic managers were found to be risk-averse and judicial managers quite risk-tolerant. Systematic managers' action aversion and judicial managers' desire to act were even stronger for top executives than for middle managers (Nutt, 1986a).

Action-Averse Styles. The insistence on using hard data and logic, preferred by decision makers with a systematic style, creates many pitfalls in dealing with people who have another style. Judicials can allege that systematics are naive because they ignore the human element. Speculatives can claim that systematics measure only what is convenient, ignoring the stochastic properties of factors such as demand that often dictate success. However, dealing with the heuristic poses the most serious problems for systematics. Heuristics, with their "relevant" anecdote, use vivid imagery to capture attention (Mitroff and Kilmann, 1978). As the systematic sees it, anecdotes often lack generalizable qualities but people buy into the action they imply because of their seeming relevance. As Bertrand Russell pointed out, action often depends on the emotional interest of the instance, not the number. The death of a single person is a tragedy, but millions of deaths a mere statistic. During the Vietnam War, executions in the streets and the image, on national television, of dead Vietnamese stacked like cordwood, aroused the conscience of the nation in ways that reports of the military's kill ratios could not.

In dealing with heuristics' arguments, the systematic often finds them shallow or used when the heuristics attempt to put aside logic so that their interests can be served. However, systematic managers are often trapped by their preferred tactics. Claims that a heuristic manager is biased must be supported by facts, which can be difficult if not impossible to secure; thus systematic managers often must put up with what they see as endless maneuvering by heuristic managers. Because systematics have difficulty in coping with the other styles, they prefer to deal with other STs.

Action-Oriented Styles. Judicial, speculative, and heuristic managers tend to be action oriented. Managers with these styles would prefer to deal with their opposite (the NF with the ST, and the SF with the NT, and vice versa) than with others who have the same style (Nutt, 1986a). Managers with SF, NT, and NF styles act as if they believe that managers with a style the same as their own are more likely to detect and shoot holes in their tactics than are those with opposing styles.

The heuristic finds the systematic easier to deal with than another heuristic. Setting aside logical arguments for the "pragmatic and feasible" is perceived to be easier than dealing with someone who understands heuristic (NF) tactics and hence may focus on the NF's motives and values. The heuristic can manipulate the systematic by playing on the motifs and symbols of the organization. The personal, moral, and interested posture of the NF is more likely to win converts than is the impersonal, amoral, and disinterested posture of the systematic (Mitroff, Mason, and Nelson, 1974). The heuristic confronting another heuristic must defend his or her interests, notions of morality, and selected beneficiaries to someone with potentially different views of what is moral and who should benefit. Arguing that personal interests are more important than abstract generalities is more apt to win more converts than is a dispute over who should benefit.

Speculative managers are more apt to act in a judicial than in a speculative environment; and judicial managers would rather act in a speculative than a judicial environment. Both types of managers would prefer to deal with their style opposites than with managers who have the same style they do. These findings suggest that judicial managers believe that they can sweep along speculative-oriented individuals with cooptation by using, for example, a decision group. Experience shows that judicial managers are more likely to detect and attempt to undermine an emerging group consensus if it conflicts with their views. The speculative in a group using NT logic to argue against an emerging group consensus is less apt to sway the group. Similarly, speculative managers seem to regard other speculatives as more of a threat than judicials. When put off by a decision, speculative managers seem better equipped to detect holes in decisions arrived at by NT logic, noting fallacies in subjective data and the warrants that lie behind sensitivity analysis, than do judicial managers. The apparent comprehensiveness of the NT argument may seem convincing to the judicial and hard to counter. In contrast, speculative managers can reveal key assumptions in NT arguments when they seek to undercut a decision.

Choice Styles and Decision Processes

The systematic and heuristic and the judicial and speculative choice styles are often treated as opposites because each of these pairs uses totally different information and processing tactics (Churchman, 1971).

Systematic decision makers excel at finding a model they can use to represent decision problems. The model specifies data that should be collected and provides a format to permit a logical, step-by-step analysis. Heuristic decision makers exhibit superior performance in dealing with poorly structured decision tasks, such as deciphering codes. Rather than employing a model, heuristic decision makers attempt several dissimilar attacks on a problem to see where each approach will lead. For example, several false starts, followed by incubation, led to a flash of insight that suggested how to break a code.

Heuristic decision making was used by operators of paper mills who were found to control the papermaking process by literally tasting the broth. An extensive investment in both time and resources was required before management scientists were able to devise a control process and install quantitative decision rules that worked as well as broth tasting. Erwing (1977) notes the skill of Estée Lauder in selecting a fragrance that has mass market appeal but points out that the internal operations of the firm during its growth and expansion were guided by systematic decision makers. This suggests that managers with a systematic style are adept at dealing with decisions that call for complex manipulations of information and that managers with a heuristic style are better at dealing with search decisions, in which information and ways to understand the information are ambiguous, as described in Chapter Nine.

Judicial decision makers are good at producing compromise and agreement. This skill is particularly important for decisions involving considerable information but little agreement about the meaning that can be extracted from this information. Information-rich decisions seem best handled by managers with a judicial style (Chapter Nine). However, judicials can become too caught up in producing agreement to deal with plausible contingencies. In contrast, decision makers with a speculative style are more adept at using information with stochastic properties. In situations involving considerable uncertainty, this skill is important in the development of contingency plans that deal with shifts in key factors that influence a choice among alternatives. The speculative decision maker is likely to be good at dealing with decisions in which information can be derived from analysis (Chapter Nine). However, speculatives can be indifferent to the need for compromise and lack the consideration skills needed to promote agreement.

The link between decision styles and decision procedure suggests that a procedure may not be used unless it is congruent with the decision maker's style. This can lead to poor decisions because each procedure has specific uses. For instance, vague and ill-structured decisions can be treated to rigorous analysis when such analysis is futile without careful framing to see what the decision is about. Analysis cannot capture or represent critical criteria that must be understood if one is to choose among alternatives in this type of decision. In contrast, tasks that involve clear-cut closed-system decisions may receive homeostatic tinkering when analysis can efficiently isolate a desirable course of action. Managers should avoid endless political maneuvering when an analytical assessment of contingencies can help to shed light on a superior course of action.

Effective decision makers should understand the rationales drawn from each of the choice styles. The value of choice styles described in this chapter lies in part with their definitions (Hall, Bowen, Lewicki, and Hall, 1982). The strengths and weaknesses of each choice style help managers consider various types of information and processing options. This helps managers appreciate the value of the three decision processes to be discussed in Chapter Eight. Matching decision processes with types of decision most apt to benefit from each process, which will be discussed in Chapter Nine, also follows from an appreciation of the choice styles.

Implementation Style

Jung's extroversion/introversion (E/I) and judgment/perception (J/P) preferences are an integral part of his theories about human action taking (Jung, 1970). These preferences deal with the type and focus of preferred action and offer several potentially important distinctions useful in articulating implementation styles (Nutt, 1986a).

The Action Frame

Preferences regarding action focus and action type will be used to identify implementation styles. An individual's predisposition for extroversion or introversion specifies an action focus, and the use of judgment or perception specifies a preferred type of action. A distinction is made between people who prefer to concentrate on their outer world and those who prefer their inner world. These people are called *externals* and *internals*, respectively. These terms are used because the preferences they describe are cognitive and not behavioral, which the introversion-extroversion terms imply. Individuals with an internal action focus (Jungian introverts) concentrate on concepts and ideas, whereas externals (Jungian extroverts) prefer to deal with people and things.

According to Jung, there are two ways to deal with the world: by judging and by perceiving. A judging individual wants to regulate and control, whereas a perceiving individual tries to understand and then adapt. Judges (J) are action-oriented, and perceivers (P) are more passive. For example, managers with a J orientation who are taking a new recruit "under their wing" feel a need to tell the newcomer "what's right." Managers with a P approach set up experiences so that new recruits can "find out for themselves." The J manager is unhappy with such an exercise because its results may be misleading or even wrong, and the P manager listening to the J wonders if a new recruit will be able to appreciate the distinctions. According to the P manager, personal awareness, even if somewhat wrong, produces growth and development. The J manager sees this outcome as leaving the new recruit with erroneous information that he or she feels compelled to correct.

Jungian theory suggests that "business cases" can be difficult for students to use when they have a strong action type preference because a business case forces them to take both P and J types of action. People with strong preferences will find one of these types of action difficult. Perceptive powers are stressed in preparing for class to tease out hidden meanings that the case writer has buried in the case, and students need judgmental orientations to sum up and propose an action. P-oriented students are apt to come to class with an understanding of these hidden meanings but find it difficult to make a recommendation at the end of class, particularly if class discussion has failed to uncover their insights. J students often find it difficult to search for hidden clues but are willing to sum up at the end of class, using information that surfaced during discussion. These tendencies can make the J student and not the P student seem insightful during class when the reverse may be true.

As with data and processing preferences, individuals have implementation preferences that lead them to focus on their inner or their outer world and to take a control or an adaptation attitude toward taking action. Combining preferences drawn from the action focus and action type identifies an individual's preferred implementation tactics.

Defining Implementation Styles

Figure 6.2 shows how the action focus and action type can be used to define styles of implementation. In the following discussion, these implementation styles are illustrated according to tactics, including warrants and data that form inferential licenses and implementation techniques, that seem consistent with the preferences of each style.

Managers with an IJ or "influencer" style prefer to collect information that describes and rationalizes the need for action. Influencers seek to regulate and control without contact with people. This suggests that influencers engage in

Figure 6.2. Implementation Styles.

	Preferred Type of Action	
	Judging (J)	Perceiving (P)
Internal (I)	*Influencers* (IJ) **Data:** ability to manuever **Warrant:** end justifies means **Techniques:** incentives and rewards, behavioral modification	*Tuners* (IP) **Data:** hidden meanings **Warrant:** mutual understanding **Techniques:** game scenario
External (E)	*Persuaders* (EJ) **Data:** merits of a case **Warrant:** understanding imperatives to act **Techniques:** persuasion and personal power	*Brokers* (EP) **Data:** organizational pressure points **Warrant:** evoke sanctioning mechanism **Techniques:** negotiation and bargaining, cooptation

(Dominant Focus When Taking Action)

implementation-related action by managing the situation to pave the way for adoption. Influencers' tactics are often subtly hidden and seen only through their effects. Once the influence process has been built, IJ managers attempt to use it artfully to enhance adoption prospects. When observed, influencer tactics can appear Machiavellian. To illustrate, consultants who encourage clients to begin on their own, knowing that they will fail because they lack basic skills and then will ask for help, use this approach. Kissinger's actions in two presidential administrations illustrate the application of similar tactics on the world stage.

Influencers use information that describes their room to maneuver. If the need for action is clear, influencers select the means thought most likely to achieve action, discounting other considerations, such as morality or prerogatives. The means selected provide a path of least resistance to achieve the desired

end. Implementation techniques consistent with this action-
taking style include unfreeze-refreeze approaches used by organizational design, or OD, specialists (for example, Lewin, 1958;
Schein, 1964), Skinnerian contingency reinforcement techniques that managers can use to shape subordinates' behavior
(Scott and Cummings, 1973), and incentive schemes
        Managers with an EJ or "persuader" style concentrate on
the tangible aspects of the situation in which action is contemplated, as shown in Figure 6.2. To justify an action, EJ managers
use persuasion tactics in which they make overt appeals to
reason or values. Using persuasion to call for action satisfies the
urge to regulate and control. Persuaders appear to be common
in organizations because these tactics require that claims be
made overtly. To call for action, persuaders present information
drawn from the merits of the case. Inferences based on either
logic or values can be used to develop the argument.
        Pure persuasion (Parsons, 1963) or information power
(French and Raven, 1959) are tactics that an EJ might adopt.
Persuaders are prone to cite facts by using illustrations, anecdotes, or demonstrations that offer insights in an attempt to
convince people or change their views. One must have a reputation for honest and candid dealings with people and a record
of accurate situational assessment if persuasion is to work
(Nutt, 1983).
        Managers with an EP style often become organizational
brokers, using their knowledge of organizational pressure
points to create situations that produce compromise by shaping
an idea until it is acceptable to key parties. Brokers see themselves as agents making contracts and view implementation as a
process of negotiation. To realize these aims, brokers often elect
coordinational roles in organizations, working various groups
until bridges that facilitate negotiation are built. Information
must be viewed as accurate and appropriate to the case being
considered before a broker will take action. Brokers use the
prospects for carrying out a successful bargaining process, one
designed to create an environment conducive to compromise,
to infer the desirability of taking action (Figure 6.2). For instance, a broker views distinctions between negotiational tactics

that work best with groups, as opposed to individuals, as high-quality management research. Brokers prefer to implement by using participation to promote cooptation, which leads to agreement (Delbecq and Van de Ven, 1971).

Managers with an IP or "tuner" style rely on adaptation and reflection. Data are collected to describe a situation so that adjustments can be made before action is attempted. The data are used to identify zones of compromise that can be offered to parties to a decision. Tuners promote harmony by finding areas of agreement, showing ways in which positions are similar in an attempt to make differences appear minor and insignificant. According to statements made by Anwar Sadat and Menachem Begin, President Carter's approach during the development of the Camp David accords involved IP tactics.

The game scenario is an implementation technique (Bardach, 1977) that seems ideally matched to the tuner's style. The metaphor of a game is used to identify players, stakes, rules of play, conditions for participation, and the like in order to visualize the ways in which people are likely to respond to an implementation attempt. Archetype games based on resource control, objective modification, and evasion of control offer a framework in the game scenario tactic to systematically elicit ways of foreclosing these options (Nutt, 1983).

Taking Action

Managers with different implementation styles may have very different attitudes toward taking action. Influencers seem inclined to act, tuners and brokers appear to be somewhat action-oriented, and persuaders see action as difficult, requiring considerable continuous effort. Managers with an influencer style seem quite action-oriented because situational alignment provides them with an ideal means to manage threats. Such an approach allows influencers to consider action under a variety of circumstances. A caution stems from the chance that influencer tactics will be exposed, making the IJ appear manipulative and thus not trustworthy. The tuner's willingness to adapt also creates action opportunities. This commitment to compro-

mise should help to overcome the objections and suggests leverage that the IP may learn to use to make changes. This tactic,
however, is ineffective when stakes are very high. The broker's
negotiational stance also seems somewhat action-oriented. However, the openness of this tactic suggests that it also may be
ineffective in situations with high conflict. Experience suggests
that information and demonstrations will not move people
wedded to a certain position because of personal or selfish
reasons. Persuasion has fewer tools for managing vested interests. As a result, persuaders may drift toward a conservative
action posture.

Style Conflicts

Various types of clashes can be envisioned when managers with different implementation styles encounter one another
as they attempt to carry out a decision. Table 6.1 summarizes the
ways that a manager with each implementation style would react
to managers with the other styles, assuming that one manager is
acting and the other is observing.

Managers with an influencer (IJ) style attempt to be subtle, hoping to shape behavior without being detected by others.
Success depends on arrangements that are accepted without
much discussion or analysis because these tactics are manipulative and the spectre of manipulation is often viewed negatively. Persuaders (EJs) who observe influencers find these tactics
devious and thus unacceptable because they are incompatible
with the candor used by persuaders. Influencers find persuaders naive because influencers believe that incentives, not
rational arguments, are needed to coerce people with special
interests. As a result, influencers may avoid persuaders so that
influencers do not have to play "their cards" until they are ready
to act. Persuaders' arguments can become a source of irritation
as they harp about the need for a change when the influencer is
seeking arrangements to make the change a reality.

Managers with an influencer style find the broker's action
orientation to be useful but incomplete. As the influencer sees
it, both the formal and informal organization must be activated,

Table 6.1. Perceptions of the Implementation Styles.

Acting Style	Reactions Provoked in:			
	Influencers (IJ)	Persuaders (EJ)	Brokers (EP)	Tuners (IP)
Influencer (IJ)	Lost opportunities to manage the situation	Devious	Violate rules of conduct	Take unnecessary risks
Persuader (EJ)	Naive	Critique quality of argument	Act without means	Insensitive to necessity of compromise
Broker (EP)	Limited by focus on means	Act without rationale	Exploit bargaining leverage	Unable to learn
Tuner (IP)	Limited by what others want	Prone to inaction	Reflect when means must be cultured	Values and feelings uncovered

whereas the broker (EP) concentrates on the formal organization. However, influencers like to have brokers working for them
because a broker gives the impression that an influencer has
been following formal organizational rules. Brokers see the
influencer's tactics, when they can observe them, as violating
the norms people expect in their interpersonal relationships.
The broker concedes that manipulation works but believes that
the repeated use of manipulation has long-term negative consequences for the organization.

Managers with a tuner style appear limited but useful to
managers with an influencer style. Focusing on people's wants
and learning about desired adaptations are treated as necessary
but not sufficient to ensure success. Combining EP and IP tactics
would provide influencers with an ideal data base from which to
act. Brokers think through formal means, and tuners identify
the informal: important compromises that must be considered.
This information can be essential for influencers in mapping a
path that avoids confrontations. When tuners discover influencers taking action, they seem prone to apply their reflective
powers and study the approach being used. The tuner sniffs out
the influencer's trail to reflect on what was done and its merits.
Because influencers hope to cover their tracks, these tactics can
alienate tuners from influencers. Influencers may see well-
positioned tuners as people who must be carefully managed so
that they are not in a position to tip off individuals whom
influencers hope to entice. In summary, influencers prefer to
work with brokers, attempt to carefully manage tuners, and
avoid persuaders.

Managers with persuader and broker styles often clash,
and these clashes can be quite open. Persuaders find that brokers deal with the mechanisms of change without clear-cut rationales. Brokers are perceived to be process-oriented, often
losing sight of the end to be achieved. The public view of the
legal profession and lawyers is an illustration. Brokers find
persuaders have reasons but lack a means to act. People do not
act, as the broker sees it, until they have been cued by organizational rules and swept along by cooptation.

Persuader-tuner relationships seem less contentious. Persuaders see tuners as prone to inaction, or at least not likely to take action in a timely manner. Tuners find persuaders' rationales lacking in sensitivity to what people think. To tuners, this seeming unwillingness to compromise makes persuaders appear to be failure-prone. Tuners reflect on these failings but seem unlikely to share their reflections, keeping persuader-tuner conflict lurking beneath the surface during exchanges between them. As a consequence, persuaders may find brokers hard to work with and seek out tuners. However, the need to vocalize their arguments in order to test them leads persuaders away from seeking tuners' advice, which they often need.

Brokers and tuners have empathy for each other's implementation style and usually form good working teams. However, brokers see a tuner's style as incomplete because of its focus on abstract issues when the key question (for a broker) concerns priming the mechanisms in an organization that are required to take action. The issue, as the broker sees it, revolves around key people and groups and their prerogatives. Tuners see brokers as practicing the "politics of the singular." Excessive pragmatism leads to treating everything as a special case. The politics of the singular inhibits learning because brokers' single episodes of success are not reflected on to gather insight. When tuners and brokers share their views, both gain important perspectives. As a result, brokers and tuners can have mutually supportive roles when a manager with either action style is open to the insights of a subordinate or a peer with the other style.

Brokers, persuaders, influencers, and tuners evaluate the implementation attempts of managers with their same styles in terms of warrant. For example, an influencer evaluates other influencers in terms of their abilities to recognize and capitalize on opportunities to manage a situation to promote implementation, using clever incentives to create the desired behavior. Similarly, a broker evaluates another broker on the bargaining leverage exploited, a persuader another persuader on the quality of an argument that is offered, and a tuner another tuner on the extent to which "true" feelings and values have been uncovered (Table 6.1). Cooperation, not conflict, seems likely because managers with the same implementation style use similar tactics to promote change. Communication focuses on which tactic to use, such as debating the type of incentives to offer.

Key Points

1. A manager's cognitive makeup creates preferences for particular types of reasoning. Such traits are expressed as styles of making choices and implementing a preferred course of action.
2. Four choice styles and four implementation styles that use very different approaches to making choices and taking action were defined. A balanced perspective, drawing on the insights to be gleaned from each style, produces superior decisions.
3. Managers who use their style blindly often create conflicts with others who have a different style. These conflicts can be productive if the decision makers learn to appreciate the unique insights people with different styles bring to a decision process. This appreciation leads to self-awareness and demonstrates the value of using multiple perspectives in decision making.
4. Matching decision approaches to types of decisions depends on appreciating the value of various types of reasoning that one can use to make judgments.

7

Different Styles of Decision Making

The previous chapter showed how a decision maker's cognitive makeup can identify his or her preferred way to make choices and implement those choices. This chapter illustrates how preferences for a particular type of information, the way to process this information, action focus, and action type together define "decision styles" (Nutt, 1986a). These decision styles are illustrated in terms of preferred ways to draw an inference, choice-making steps, and tactics congruent with each style to capture the way that managers with each given style prefer to make decisions. Examples are used to illustrate the unique approaches to decision making preferred by managers with each style.

In addition, the basis for a manager's shift in style will be developed. Managers who lack clear-cut preferences may substitute several subsidiary or auxiliary styles for their dominant style. Auxiliaries are also used when perceptively oriented managers have a strong internal focus. To act, these managers must adopt another style, which makes their behavior differ from their cognition. Shadow styles are defined to identify tactics that are seldom, if ever, evoked during decision making. Finally, the prospect of conflict or cooperation among individuals is predicted by using decision style. Effective groups and coalitions must deal with conflicts and incorporate the perspectives that people with diverse styles have to offer.

Constructing Decision Styles

Decision styles are defined by a manager's preferences for one of the action foci, data types, processing options, and action types, as shown in Table 7.1. These preferences specify a primary and a secondary choice process and an implementation tactic for each style.

The primary process is made up of a decision means (one of the rival appreciative instruments: thinking, feeling, facts, or possibilities), which is focused externally or internally. Managers who see situations in terms of people and things have an external action focus (E). The first act of an external thinking type (ET) is to subject a perceived need or opportunity to criticism or analysis. External feeling types (EFs) would decry or crusade for a perceived need or opportunity, external sensates (ESs) would try to put the need or opportunity to use, and external intuitives (ENs) would attempt to shape the need or opportunity.

Managers who see situations in terms of concepts and ideas implicit in a perceived need or opportunity have an internal focus (I). They attempt to identify the essence of the need or opportunity to create meaning for observed patterns. IT managers engaged in decision making try to reconcile various causal interpretations. IF managers attempt to understand the values of people affected by the decision, IS managers try to classify and compartmentalize decision-related data, and IN managers attempt to identify decision possibilities. Thus, the primary step taken in decision making is specified by an orientation toward T, F, S, or N, focused by E or I.

The secondary process and implementation tactics flow from the preferred action type: the use of judgment or perception. The secondary process uses the preferred action type (J or P) to bring out and focus the appreciative instrument missing in the primary process, as shown in Table 7.1. The secondary process also accounts, in part, for the behavior of internals, whose observable acts often fail to convey the process they use to reach a decision, and qualifies the actions of externals. The

Table 7.1. Constructing Decision Styles.

Dominant Consideration	Action Focus	Dominant Process	Secondary Process (Consideration Brought Out by Action Type)	Decision Style	Decision Style Code*	Implementation Style	Impl. Style Code
Thinking (T)	External (E)	Externally (ET) focused thinking	Data (S) with judgment (J)	Procedural	ESTJ	Persuasion	EJ
			Possibilities (N) with judgment (J)	Evaluative	ENTJ	Persuasion	EJ
	Internal (I)	Internally (IT) focused thinking	Data (S) with perception (P)	Ordered	ISTP	Tuning	IP
			Possibilities (N) with perception (P)	Intellectual	INTP	Tuning	IP
Feeling (F)	External (E)	Externally (EF) focused feeling	Data (S) with judgment (J)	Political	ESFJ	Persuasion	EJ
			Possibilities (N) with judgment (J)	Mediator	ENFJ	Persuasion	EJ
	Internal (I)	Internally (IF) focused feeling	Data (S) with perception (P)	Flexible	ISFP	Tuning	IP
			Possibilities (N) with perception (P)	Committed	INFP	Tuning	IP
Sensation (S)	External (E)	Externally (ES) focused sensing	Thinking (T) with perception (P)	Traditional	ESTP	Brokering	EP
			Feeling (F) with perception (P)	Relational	ESFP	Brokering	EP
	Internal (I)	Internally (IS) focused sensing	Thinking (T) with judgment (J)	Empirical	ISTJ	Influencing	IJ
			Feeling (F) with judgment (J)	Anecdotal	ISFJ	Influencing	IJ
Intuition (N)	External (E)	Externally (EN) focused intuition	Thinking (T) with perception (P)	Visionary	ENTP	Brokering	EP
			Feeling (F) with perception (P)	Proselytizing	ENFP	Brokering	EP
	Internal (I)	Internally (IN) focused intuition	Thinking (T) with judgment (J)	Iconoclastic	INTJ	Influencing	IJ
			Feeling (F) with judgment (J)	Cooperative	INFJ	Influencing	IJ

* The underlined code letter indicates dominant consideration in decision making.

warrants as well as some of the traits, considerations, and weaknesses of each decision style are summarized in Table 7.2.

Externally Focused Thinking Types

The external thinker analyzes, organizes, and regulates tangible manifestations (people and things) of strategy, plans, and the like to make decisions (Table 7.2). External thinkers are convinced by reasoning and use their secondary process to support thinking through their information preferences, S (actualities) or N (possibilities), giving rise to two styles: EST̲J and ENT̲J. The underscored letters denote the primary process. The external and judgmental preferences of ET managers lead to implementation by persuasion.

The Procedural Style. Managers with an EST̲J or procedural style base their decisions on facts that describe realities. Adherence to procedure in the establishment of fact is a key consideration. The proceduralist uses logic, within a framework of organizational SOPs and rules, to develop a complete factual documentation of prescreened options found to be realistic. These preferences make managers with a procedural style quite conservative, often preferring the status quo to change because full factual documentation is frequently time-consuming, costly, and a difficult standard to meet. Because the intangible, abstract, and wishful are hard to grasp, proceduralists often ignore what might be. For example, proceduralists choosing among MIS options follow established organizational rules as they carefully document the merits of feasible options. One of the MIS approaches has to be *clearly* superior before managers with a procedural style will argue for its adoption. To call for adoption, such managers use persuasion tactics to voice the compelling merits of the idea. They describe the merits in terms of the factual analysis they applied to reach the conclusion and how their assessment followed established organizational procedure.

The key weaknesses of managers with this style are their preference for established practice and the status quo and a failure to reflect on their logic structure to evolve it. Strengths stem from caution and adherence to rules in decision making.

Complete documentation and a clear-cut rationale prior to action make proceduralists' actions defensible and understandable to others.

The Evaluative Style. Managers with an ENTJ or evaluative style also use logic but employ a secondary process of intuition, which leads to a search for possibilities rather than factual descriptions. Such managers place emphasis on what might be rather than on what is when looking for possibilities, long-range implications, and consequences. For instance, strategic choices stress wishful new products and markets. Managers with an evaluative style attempt to tease out the consequences that flow from various market-product combinations. The merits of the case hinge on whether or not expectations for demand or utilization make a product feasible. Evaluative managers describe the viability of the preferred option in these terms, selling it by pointing out how its benefits can be realized under several feasible conditions. This kind of reasoning was used to sell an expansion plan for an airport to a city by using the size of subsidies offered by airline carriers and the length of the leases carriers were willing to sign and by pointing out that the length of the lease created a stable financial base under several population growth assumptions.

Evaluatives tend to be quick on the uptake, recognizing implications others overlook. The weaknesses of evaluatives stem from their preference for the company of other quick studies, denying them the counsel of people who have pertinent facts, and from their impatience with people who are slow to grasp or understand. Ignoring fact-based advice and running roughshod over people who are groping to understand can create problems for evaluative managers. They often fail to appreciate or give time to the arguments of others without forceful intervention.

Internally Focused Thinking Types

Internally focused thinking type (IT) managers look for principles that underlie a decision, using a curious, detached approach. This process of principle seeking goes on unabated

Table 7.2. Decision Style Characteristics.

Dominant Process	Warrant Applied	Decision Style and Code*	Secondary Process	Key Consideration	Key Traits	Weakness	Implementation Style
			Ways to Support Thinking				
Externally focused thinkers	Reasoning and analysis	Procedural (ESTJ)	1. Judgment by means of data	Factually described realities	Caution, rule adherence	Conservatism	Persuasion
		Evaluative (ENTJ)	2. Judgment by means of intuition	The consequences of possibilities	Quick study of implications	Ignoring of fact-based advice	Persuasion
Internally focused thinkers	Operant principles	Ordered (ISTP)	1. Perception by means of data	Data that give order and meaning	Realism	Economy of effort	Tuning
		Intellectual (INTP)	2. Perception by means of intuition	Unique and ingenious options	Development of all possible qualifications	Failure to deal with implementation problems	Tuning
			Ways to Focus Feeling				
Externally focused feelers	People's sentiments	Political (ESFJ)	1. Judgment by means of data	Tangible views of key people	Reconciliation of opposing views Human relations skills	Acting on wrong assumptions	Persuasion
		Mediator (ENFJ)	2. Judgment by means of intuition	Ways to harmonize		Preoccupation with approval	Persuasion
Internally focused feelers	Personal values	Flexible (ISFP)	1. Perception by means of data	People's values	Creation of flexible arrangements	Commitment to needs of the moment	Tuning
		Committed (INFP)	2. Perception by means of intuition	What's right	Development of personal views and beliefs	Slowness to act	Tuning

Ways to Support Data

Externally focused sensates	Testimony of the senses	Traditional (ES<u>T</u>P)	1. Perception by means of thinking	Practical action	Concentration on variations of what is known	Possibilities overlooked	Brokering
		Relational (ES<u>F</u>P)	2. Perception by means of feeling	Tact	Maintenance of good relations	Tough choices deferred	Brokering
Internally focused sensates	Personal store of facts	Empirical (IS<u>T</u>J)	1. Judgment by means of thinking	Facts that contain inferences	Use of experiment and observation	Wary of change	Influencing
		Anecdotal (IS<u>F</u>J)	2. Judgment by means of feeling	Personal experience	Recall of incidents and anecdotes	Finding an appropriate precedent	Influencing

Ways to Consider Possibilities

Externally focused intuitives	Emerging possibilities	Visionary (E<u>N</u>TP)	1. Perception by means of thinking	New ideas	Unpredictability, independence	Finding best ideas	Brokering
		Proselytizing (EN<u>F</u>P)	2. Perception by means of feeling	Making converts	Many projects	Squander energies on diversions	Brokering
Internally focused intuitives	Inspiration about what could be	Iconoclastic (I<u>N</u>TJ)	1. Judgment by means of thinking	New arrangements	Individualism	Commitment to constant change	Influencing
		Cooperative (IN<u>F</u>J)	2. Judgment by means of feeling	Eliciting cooperation toward goal	Getting peers to understand and approve	Internal compromise of innovation	Influencing

* The underlined letter indicates dominant decision style.

until the necessity for action arises. Many ITs are articulate, but they seldom use their verbal skills. They expect decisions to take root without much intervention. They use perception to read the situation and shy away from making judgments. The ISTP uses a secondary process of perception to search for facts, and the INTP seeks possibilities (see Table 7.2). Their perceptive and internal orientation leads to a tuning style of implementation.

The Ordered Style. Managers with an ISTP or ordered style seek decision principles to bring order and give meaning to data purposely collected to compare options. Managers with this style organize decision steps so that they can be specified in advance. As a result, people with an ordered style seem likely candidates to use the quantitative decision techniques taught by many business schools. Such managers use their perceptive powers to represent the situation they confront by applying quantitative techniques. To implement, they use reflection to bring out objections. ISTP managers examine the implications of these objections to find ways in which they can shape a preferred option without its losing its inherent advantages. For instance, managers who treat strategic planning as goal pro-gramming eliminate much of the ambiguity in strategic man-agement by creating specific trade-offs and comparisons by applying explicit criteria to compare options that depict busi-ness opportunities. Valued principles (the need to organize decision steps) are captured by the goal-programming model. A strength of managers with this style is realism that stems from the data collected purposefully to give order and meaning to a decision. A key weakness is the appearance of an economy of effort, such as oversimplifying decisions to quantify them. This trait can be seen as a lack of commitment when managers with an ordered style face difficult decisions (see Table 7.2).

The Intellectual Style. Managers with an INTP style use internally focused thinking, moving from the abstract (needs and opportunities) to specific ideas instead of beginning with specific solutions, as managers with an ordered style are prone to do. Decision makers with the INTP style use reflection in two ways. First, they use reflective thinking to identify principles on which to base a decision. INTPs then use these principles to derive possibilities, which often leads to innovation. Second, intellectual decision makers reflect to identify principles they believe are important to key constituencies to determine whether or not key ideas are likely to be acceptable to important stakeholders. These decision makers seek a synthesis position that overcomes objections to a course of action. For example, to select capital projects for a firm's capital investment package or plan, an INTP manager may recognize and balance the growth potential of organizational units against the return on investment of the projects pushed by these units. The strength of managers with an intellectual style lies in their ability to tease out unique and ingenious options that have both of these qualities. Managers with this style, however, often fail to see the limitations in their ideas. They may discount or ignore arguments made by other people that are based on principles that differ from their own, such as investment equity among organizational units as a decision rule in forming a capital expenditure plan.

Managers with an intellectual style attempt to develop a litany of all conceivable qualifications as they make decisions. For example, complex contingencies are derived on the basis of "if-thens" associated with how market factors and key actors may react to specific projects that are included or excluded from the capital plan. This trait makes the ideas of managers with an intellectual style very complex and leads to problems in communication. As a result, managers with this style act as if they expect their decisions to take root without much intervention. Many failed decisions can be predicted from these tendencies.

Externally Focused Feeling Types

Externally focused feeling type (EF) managers concentrate on eliciting value from people's opinions, attempting to reconcile all discordant views when making a decision. The EFs' personal views are often lost in this pervasive attempt to reconcile contradictions in what others believe to be true. EF managers often vocalize their reconciliation attempts as they make judgments about action. The EJ persuasion that results often seems clumsy to the T types because rationale takes shape during expression. Persuasion and the development of rationale often occur simultaneously. The secondary process focuses feeling by using either S (firsthand knowledge) or N (insight). Both styles rely on verbal skills and implement by persuasion.

The Political Style. ES̲F̲J managers see decision making in terms of people's tangible views, determining the merits of a case by drawing on various viewpoints. Decision rules stem from work group sentiments that give rise to these values and beliefs. A consultative process, such as that of groups, is preferred, because this tactic provides an efficient means to process and reconcile facts that give rise to sentiments. For example, as a group leader, an ES̲F̲J manager uses persuasion to restate viewpoints, hoping to shape the arguments used by others so that a consensus will emerge. The meandering groping for consensus, often seen in a group, is facilitated to promote mutual understanding. Persuasion is used to sell the ideas of others rather than to impose one's own views. Elected officials seeking a consensus to act frequently adopt this tactic.

Managers with this style tend to have an acute appreciation of the need for acceptance, and implement through the use of (often implicit) human relations skills. Weaknesses stem from concentrating on reconciliation at the expense of understanding issues and generating new ideas. Managers with a political style may appear indecisive and lacking in leadership skill because their own views often remain dormant and undeveloped. Political managers are prone to jump to conclusions by making faulty assumptions. For example, a group leader with this style may facilitate the ebb and flow of discussion as it moves from premise to premise without exploring any of the premises to the extent needed to permit in-depth understanding. A decision based on faulty premises can result. Groupthink (Janis and Mann, 1977) and focusing on traditional lines of inquiry that flow from interacting groups (Delbecq and Van de Ven, 1971) illustrate two types of faulty premises.

The Mediator Style. EN̲F̲J managers use their verbal skills to coax and cajole agreement, making persuasion a natural implementation style. The mediator concentrates on peers, in contrast to the more indiscriminate campaigning of a manager with the political style. Knowing what others think about a decision is a precursor to expressing personal views. Mediators are driven by a desire for approval and a desire to overcome indifference. Persuasion tactics are a natural outgrowth of a preference for oration about a decision. To make a decision, mediators attempt to create a dialogue with other key people, groping for an understanding of the "common good" by reconciling the ideas of these individuals. For example, a tax-deferred retirement program would be proposed as company policy when an executive with this style is persuaded that key actors in the organization believe that such a program is essential. The mediator is open to persuasion rather than its exercise and sets in place situations, such as informal gatherings, that permit dialogue to focus feeling by means of possibilities. Managers with a mediator style then "work the crowd," using persuasion to extract sentiments and ideas that pertain to the situation and to overcome indifference. Implementation flows from the shared values and understandings that emerge. This preoccupation with approval can delay action and make managers with this style seem to lack leadership skills, particularly to thinking types (ET and IT managers).

Internally Focused Feeling Types

IF-type managers rely on personal values that they view as crucially important. The action focus that is used to map these values into the decision situation is perceptive. Managers with this style must believe in a decision in order to implement it. They must see an action as making a contribution toward an important end before they advocate it. The secondary process uses perception to focus feeling by using S (realities) or N (possibilities). The internal and perceptive preferences of IF managers lead to a tuning style of implementation.

The Flexible Style. Managers with an ISFP or flexible style concentrate on the needs of the moment and modify decision procedures to fit perceived circumstances. As a result, flexible decision rules are used. This allows the dominant process of feeling to be focused by facts. Reconciliation and adaptation become an inherent part of the process. As a result, little overt intervention is required to implement a decision. For example, managers with a flexible style in the role of group leader strive to maintain harmony within the group as it makes a decision. A decision made by a group is thought to sell itself when there is agreement, because the group members will act as advocates. To get a consensus, ISFP managers constantly adjust disagreements within the group about facts or values to find regions of agreement. As disagreements arise, such leaders attempt to locate a common ground for differing points of view. As this example suggests, managers with a flexible style act to maintain positive interpersonal relationships among decision stakeholders, using a supportive style of leadership.

The Committed Style. Managers with an INFP or committed style are often slow to act because they must form personal dreams of what might be before action is possible. For instance, the INFP manager must come to a personal commitment to support affirmative action before action will be taken. After being convinced, managers with this style attempt to implement the affirmative action program, by describing the need to adopt the program to key people by using devices, such as a memorandum or a position paper, that set out personal views of what is believed to be right or desirable. Managers with a committed style envision who might object to the affirmative action program, sort stakeholders who might object to the program into importance categories, and estimate the intensity of views that key stakeholders hold. These managers develop modifications that overcome the objections of the key stakeholders, much as Churchman (1979) does when calling for the systems planner to anticipate the esthetic, ideological, political, and moral objections to a plan. Uncovering these objections serves as the vehicle for analysis. First, the manager reflects to identify objections. He or she then modifies the decision until it takes these objections into account. The key step is reflection, looking inward to identify the people who object and the intensity of the objections in order to discover the prospect of accommodating these key individuals. If these compromises can be folded into the decision, it is offered for public consumption.

Externally Focused Sensates

ES-type managers rely on testimony provided by their senses, making them particularly adept at seeing things as they are. An impending decision provokes a need to compile facts that describe the decision situation. Favored options have measurable and describable characteristics. Fanciful or hypothetical options are discounted or ignored. Perception is used as a secondary process to compile either logical consequences (the T preference) or the interests and values of people (the F preference). The external and perceptive preferences of ES managers call for a brokering implementation style.

The Traditional Style. Managers with an ESTP or traditional style attempt to grasp the underlying principles of practical options that are variations of procedures used by others inside or outside the organization. They stress firsthand knowledge, such as seeing the preferred system or procedure functioning in another organization, so that they can make a personal assessment of suitability. Such managers carry out implementation through negotiation. The basis for the barter is facts, with causal elements specified. For example, when managers with a traditional style debate with others, they attempt to draw out the others' facts. These new facts are blended with current facts to create a synthetic factual description acceptable to potential bargainers. Support is gathered by showing how the decision meets the synthetic fact set. The manager demonstrates the merits of the decisions on an individual basis, stressing criteria advocated by each individual.

The Relational Style. An inherent interest in people leads managers with an ESFP or relational style to make estimates of how individuals may react to a given decision. Managers with this style are particularly adept at seeing the social environment realistically, leading them to prefer practical options and to make accurate appraisals of the implementation prospects of these options. These managers use negotiation to gain approval. Because managers with this style emphasize tact, they are particularly at ease with people and dealings with people. For example, a manager with a relational style in the role of a group leader implements by building a supportive environment for the group and emphasizes external linkages. A utilization review committee in a hospital can be supported by pointing out its purpose (to identify questionable medical practices) to other key groups, such as the medical staff, and making commitments about who will be consulted as the committee nears a decision.

A key weakness of managers with this style is leniency. ESFP managers are often poor at analysis and may promote the selfish views of people without taking a hard look at the needs of the organization. Such managers may put aside tough choices in the interest of maintaining good relations. For example, relational-style managers who hope to avoid confrontations with stakeholders may delay implementing cutbacks required by the elimination of federal funding in mental health services. An overly optimistic assessment of the prospects for local levy support to fill a federal funding void can lead such managers to avoid drawing contingency plans with a worst-case scenario. This approach may allow a troublesome situation to drift into a crisis.

Internally Focused Sensates

IS-type managers amass a huge store of facts and impressions drawn from their experiences. They reconcile decisions against this fact store, making tradition important. The present is often compared to the past, so precedent is a crucial norm. This posture makes the internal sensate wary of change. Decisions are practicable, based on what internal sensate managers believe they can and cannot do. To focus data, IS managers use a secondary process of thinking or feeling. Their internal and judgmental orientations lead to an influencing implementation style.

The Empirical Style. Managers with an ISTJ or empirical style stress logical judgment when compiling their store of facts.

These managers delay action until they can make sense of options by applying these facts. Empiricists act only when an option emerges that can be logically reconciled with their senses. Once inwardly convinced, empirical managers take what *seems* to be decisive action (Simon, 1982). Note than an understanding of both behavior and cognition is necessary to account for this action. Empirical managers are excellent at reviewing bids because they will be certain that nothing has been overlooked and will make no assumptions about omissions. Managers with this style often catch the mistakes of others.

To implement plans, empirical managers use incentives and other mechanisms that employ nondirective *influence* mechanisms. They attempt to orchestrate a situation by seeking a commitment that the best-performing option will be adopted, lobbying for a rational-choice format to make the decision. Decision criteria are discussed and agreed upon before the analysis begins. For example, both criteria and criteria weights are specified for contract review in the U.S. Department of Health and Human Services prior to a review. Reviewers are asked to determine only the extent to which each criterion is met by each contract being reviewed. Reviewers are required to explain their decisions by using these criteria and weights. This approach limits the qualifications a reviewer may wish to offer, but it tightly controls the process.

The Anecdotal Style. Managers with an ISFJ or anecdotal style amass a fact store of incidents that emphasize interpersonal problems that occurred during action taking. These managers have an encyclopedic memory of anecdotes that they recount to make a decision. For such managers, a choice must square with anecdotes in the fact store thought to be relevant as determined by similarity of an anecdote to the current situation and by the way people reacted to a similar situation that led to success or failure. If these managers cannot find an appropriate precedent upon which to base action, they delay action.

Influence tactics that take these facts, viewed as "relevant" anecdotes, into account form the basis for implementation. Managers with an anecdotal style look for a mechanism that they can use as a vehicle to promote the "relevant" anecdote. For example, a person can manage the situation by forming a decision group made up of people who have experienced situations thought to be relevant or of people who support the manager's views. The group is delegated action-taking power only when it represents the desired viewpoints and experiences. These arrangements are used to manage the situation, giving the group authority to act because the group's views are likely to be congruent with the manager's.

Externally Focused Intuitives

EN-type managers use perception to uncover possibilities. They often act in sudden and unforeseen ways, promoting options no one would have predicted. To consider these possibilities, the secondary process applies either logic or concern for the views of peers to make choices. However, enthusiasm for ideas may not extend to forceful implementation. EP brokering tactics are not pursued with uniform energy. To create converts, the EN relies on personal enthusiasm in making possibilities visible in routine contacts that call for negotiation.

The Visionary Style. Managers with an ENTP or visionary style concentrate on emergent possibilities and test these possibilities by using intuitive logic to determine their value. A key trait is independence. For example, such managers who are engaged in subordinate selection search for job candidates who have new ideas for their "short list." Fit is determined by logical, impersonal analysis. Support is rallied by an assessment of how people can be affected by or can affect the decision. However, the focus of the analysis concerns which possibility (for example, job candidate) may be blocked. ENTP managers assess implementation prospects by raising objections that are logical and predictable from past experience, such as problems that they have experienced during brokering attempts, with individuals who would be affected by the decision.

To implement a decision, managers with a visionary style seek out exchanges with people to find out about their preferences. Negotiation with stakeholders focuses on the virtues of new ideas. For example, when selecting a new CEO, ENTPs expect bargaining to focus on which candidate offers the freshest perspective, the newest set of ideas, or the best plans for the organization. Other views of a candidate's merit (for example, experience) tend to be ignored. Bargaining with search committee members who have like views is lively, and negotiations with others much less effective.

The Proselytizing Style. Managers with an E_N_FP or proselytizing style have many concurrent projects for which they are seeking converts. These managers carry out decision making with missionary-like zeal by considering possibilities (the primary process) using feeling (the secondary process). Managers with this style have a tendency to squander energies, both in hopeless attempts to convert people and in competing activities. The proselytizer has more natural brokering skills than the visionary. Each has a fresh perspective, but proselytizers promote their perspective by using a person-centered approach. This leads the proselytizers to freewheel by generating enthusiasm for their preferred courses of action. Typical steps include marketing efforts that stress tangible and intangible benefits of the preferred alternative. For example, proselytizers hold meetings with key people to extol the virtues of an idea and to learn about objections. These meetings serve both to promote the idea and to appreciate the potential for dissent. Proselytizers also attempt to rationalize the decision in one-on-one meetings with people who object. If this fails and an objector has sufficient clout, proselytizers float a modified version of the idea to find an area of compromise. Discussions continue, periodically shaping the idea, until it is deemed acceptable by key parties to the decision, much like mutually adjustive adaptation (Lindblom, 1965).

Internally Focused Intuitives

IN-type managers have flashes of inspiration in which insights into relationships, meanings, or symbols provide a picture of what could be. IN managers are independent and individualistic and have good access to the resources of their unconscious mind. Action for the IN stems from judgments about consequences and requires the use of logic to determine the reactions of key stakeholders to possibilities. The internal and judgmental orientations of IN managers suggest influencing as an implementation style.

The Iconoclastic Style. Managers with an INTJ or icono-clastic style value change and innovation. Individualism can be quite extreme in iconoclastic managers. They often ignore venerated practices and tradition. The attitude that everything can be improved, made bigger, and reorganized makes decision making appear easy. Iconoclastic managers draw on their inherent creativity to identify ideas that seem superior to traditional arrangements and venerable procedures that make up current practice. The need for constant change reveals restless executives always on the move and seeking out new challenges. This commitment to constant change makes iconoclasts good candidates for the management of departments undergoing (or intended to undergo) major change.

Using influence tactics, iconoclasts attempt to organize the situation rather than confront it as those with the evaluative style (ENTJ) are prone to do. The notion that change is good seems so obvious that iconoclasts use only mild forms of influence to coax people into the "logical" posture of supporting a decision. For example, iconoclastic managers call for new norms to assess a situation in order to get protagonists to see that current procedures lack desirable levels of performance. Discrediting current practices opens the way for change. To implement a state-of-the-art MIS, the iconoclast attempts to demonstrate that the current information system's capacity, turnaround, and the like are inadequate and that new systems can be installed at less net cost.

The Cooperative Style. Managers with an INFJ or cooperative style attempt to enlist recruits and rally them to their position. They select action by using a broad-scale view that they think will inspire and move people. Acceptance in the movement toward a goal becomes the theme in this style of decision making, which satisfies cooperative managers' individualistic traits. Inspiration takes two forms: ideas and ways to handle opposition. Cooperative managers place considerable emphasis on mobilizing acceptance of preferred goals that will result in commitment. They use influence tactics with this aim in mind.

The cooperative manager attempts to implement decisions by getting key peers to understand, approve, and cooperate toward a goal, whereas an iconoclast promotes only goal understanding. This outward appearance of human relations skills is used to hide incentives and other influence tactics that are intended to coax adoption. Coalition building of like-minded influential executives to back the course of action believed to be in the best interests of the organization is a common tactic used by cooperative managers. For example, a hospital CEO seeking to expand a hospital's physical plant first consults with key groups in the community to solicit their support. Applications the CEO sends to regulatory agencies stress the nature and depth of this support. The threat that these power centers can be mobilized is implicit but recognizable to seasoned regulators. Managers with the cooperative style balance innovation with acceptance better than iconoclastic managers do, but the former may allocate much of their energy to setting up influence tactics, such as subtle incentive schemes, that result in a de-emphasis of discovery.

Using More Than One Style

Many managers use several decision-making styles. This trait stems from individuals who lack strong preferences for S, N, T, or F, the means of appreciation, or for I, E, J, or P, the means to take action, or have a strong internal orientation toward action. In these instances, subordinate or auxiliary styles provide optional ways of making decisions. When managers have strong preferences for modes of appreciation or means of taking action, the least preferred mode or means identifies what are called *shadow styles*. Shadow styles represent a manager's untapped potential to act.

Auxiliary and Shadow Styles

Managers who lack strong preferences for types of data, ways to process data, action foci, or action types are apt to use several styles. For instance, consider a manager with an INTP or intellectual style who has strong preferences except for the action focus and who prefers internal action only slightly more than external action. This manager uses both visionary (ENTP) and intellectual (INTP) styles, with the visionary as an auxiliary. The ESFJ or political style becomes the shadow style and identifies decision rules or warrants that are seldom, if ever, evoked. Similarly, managers with strong ST preferences who are indifferent to action types and action foci would use procedural (ESTJ), ordered (ISTP), traditional (ESTP), and empirical (ISFJ) decision styles and have mediator (ENFJ), committed (INFP), proselytizer (INTJ), and cooperative (INFJ) shadow styles. These managers stress factual analysis and tend to ignore or discount inferences based on people's sentiments, personal values, emergent possibilities, and inspiration. Managers with clear-cut preferences for an action type, action focus, data type, and data-processing option are not likely to use auxiliary styles. Such managers would tend to rely on their dominant style and would have shadows in the remaining fifteen styles.

A flexible style has preference equivocality on *each* of the four Jungian dimensions. Managers with an inflexible style have strong preferences and no auxiliary styles. Ramaprasad and Mitroff (1984) call the manager with a flexible style an ideal, suggesting that many auxiliaries have an advantage in decision making.

Hidden Styles

Managers who have a strong internal orientation, behaviorally expressed as introversion, and who also strongly prefer perception to judgment have no way to express their views. For instance, managers with ordered (ISTP), intellectual (INTP), flexible (ISFP), and committed (INFP) styles, which have a strong IP orientation, must switch to another style to make their wishes known. Two switches are possible: a movement to an external action focus or to a judgmental action type. For instance, individuals with a strong ordered style (ISTP) can adopt a traditional (ESTP) or an empirical (ISTJ) style, using brokering or influencing tactics to express their views. Using this logic, the intellectual (INTP) may use an ENTP (visionary) or INTJ (iconoclastic) style to express his or her views or take action; the flexible (ISFP) can use an ESFP (relational) or ISFJ (anecdotal) style; and the committed (INFP) can adopt an ENFP (proselytizer) or INFJ (cooperative) style.

These styles are not true auxiliaries because individuals who are internally oriented use the unspoken warrant of their dominant style to reach a decision, changing only how they must overtly act to express or implement the decision. Behavior in these situations is apt to be misleading, revealing little about how a decision was made.

Producing Self-Awareness

Decision style is a lens through which individuals determine the prospects for collaboration or conflict. For instance, in both social and work situations people can be observed gauging their desire to socialize or work with others by listening to discourse that sets out positions, applies logic, uses information, and displays or avoids dogmatism. Attractions identify potential collaborators, and repulsions identify individuals to avoid. Animosity among managers in an organization may have its roots in style-based conflicts. To manage these conflicts, such steps as structure and delegation can be taken to allow antagonistic individuals to coexist in an organization. Similarly, coalitions often arise in organizations made up of "like-minded" people. Like-mindedness may stem from compatible decision styles. Managers with the same style of decision making are likely to work well together.

Predictions of the potential for agreement among decision makers with each of the sixteen decision styles are summarized in Figure 7.1. To make the best use of these predictions, a manager should temper them with situational factors. The power relationships between individuals, such as superior-subordinate, may act to suppress or hide conflict. Strong personal ties among people can grow as the result of shared commitments in political campaigns, service clubs, volunteer activities, and the like. The strengths of such associations can moderate managers' views of decision-making activities, causing them to be seen in a more positive light than facts would warrant. In the same way, negative associations may limit what appears to be a potentially positive relationship among styles.

As a consequence, the predictions in Figure 7.1 must be viewed as a means to explore threats and opportunities, as groups and coalitions are formed and managed. These predictions help to augment but do not supplant person-specific knowledge about stakeholders and their relationships.

Types of Conflict

The action focus of potentially antagonistic individuals suggests the type of conflict that may occur. *Open conflicts* can result when members of a coalition or group share an external focus or when an externally focused member provokes an internally focused member. *Hidden conflicts* are predicted when members are focused internally. The following discussion of some of these conflicts highlights the origins and potentials for disagreement.

Open Conflicts. The external nature of persuasion and brokering implementation tactics can draw people with these styles into open conflict. People with evaluative and political styles seem particularly prone to confrontation because they both use *persuasion* in an attempt to rally support for their views. Evaluators stress consequences that flow from possibilities but are inclined to ignore advice, particularly advice based on how people feel. People with a political style are preoccupied with who thinks what about options and are blinded to logic traps. Evaluators often see people with a political style as preoccupied with the politics of the situation and slow to appreciate consequences that logic makes readily apparent. People with a political style view evaluators as naive because value-based constraints to rational action go unrecognized as evaluators uncover their action-taking imperatives by using logic. People with traditional and visionary styles share a *brokering* implementation style. Conflict may surface during their efforts to lobby

Figure 7.1. Potential for Agreement in Approaches to Decision Making.

Dominant Concern and Action Focus	Decision Style	Procedural	Evaluative	Ordered	Intellectual	Political	Mediator	Flexible	Committed	Traditional	Relational	Empirical	Anecdotal	Visionary	Proselytizing	Iconoclastic	Cooperative
Thinkers																	
External	Procedural	+				−			−	+		+	−	−		−	
	Evaluative		+	−	+	−				−				+			+
Internal	Ordered			+						+		+	−	−		−	
	Intellectual				+					+	−					−	
Feelers																	
External	Political					+	+	+	−		+			−	−	−	
	Mediator						+	+	+		+	−			+		+
Internal	Flexible							+	+		+					−	+
	Committed								+			−	−	−	−	−	−
Sensates																	
External	Traditional									+		+	+	−		−	
	Relational										+				+		+
Internal	Empirical											+	−	−		−	
	Anecdotal												+	−		−	
Intuitives																	
External	Visionary													+	−	+	
	Proselytizing														+	−	−
Internal	Iconoclastic															+	−
	Cooperative																+

Note: A box with a plus sign (+) indicates a positive relationship. A box with nothing in it indicates a neutral relationship. A box with a minus sign (−) indicates a negative relationship.

one another. Traditionalists are wedded to practical action, which is often based on variations of current practice. Visionaries are concerned with new ideas. In one case innovation is shunned, and in the other it is required; little room exists for negotiation. Conflict seems likely.

Externally (E) focused managers, using bargaining or persuasion, may goad internally (I) focused individuals to react because strongly held views are violated, producing open conflict. This type of conflict occurs infrequently but is often quite vehement, producing lasting animosities. For instance, an individual with an intellectual style may sit quietly as managers with a mediator style sort through possibilities or as managers with a relational style attempt to broker with a group. Individuals with an intellectual style rarely comment or take part, but they may react with suddenness and emotion if one of their principles is violated. Similarly, people with a committed style internalize strong views of what is right and may also react vociferously if mediators and relational managers ignore or dismiss their views. These reactions are difficult to predict because the internal action focus often keeps people with an intellectual style from disclosing their operant principles and keeps people with a committed style from sharing their views of what they believe is right.

People with iconoclastic and procedural styles are potentially antagonistic. Proceduralists are committed to current practices and venerated procedures, and iconoclasts see change as synonymous with the pulse of life. Change ideas for the iconoclast arrive with suddenness, and implementation follows a heavy-handed incentive-based schema that ignores dialogue. These tactics make life unbearable for the external orientation of managers with the procedural style. As a result, proceduralists may use organizational SOPs and a control perspective to create roadblocks in an attempt to stifle iconoclasts. Iconoclasts find persuasion attempts that rely on the tired rendition of logic, based on past practices of decision making, irrelevant and trivial and see proceduralists as ignoring strategic considerations, making organizational renewal difficult. Such views make conflict between people with these styles seem likely.

People with intellectual and traditional styles may also develop conflicts because of their fundamental differences in view. People with an intellectual style develop unique and ingenious ideas that may clash with traditionalist managers, who insist on practical action. Intellectuals stress imagination, and traditionalists rely on a matter-of-fact testimony of the senses. Managers with a proselytizing style may become offensive to people who rely on personal values. In particular, people with a committed style, who come to a decision through careful study and reflection, will be put off by conversion attempts.

Hidden Conflicts. When individuals have an internal action focus, they may not express their reservations. The shared internal action focus tends to keep the conflict covert. For example, iconoclasts may be seen as "irresponsible activists" by others with styles that also have an internal orientation. Managers with an intellectual style want to delay action until operant principles that support the action can be identified, managers with an empirical style want evidence before acting, managers with a flexible style need assurances that the social order will not be upset, and managers with a committed style want to determine if action is congruent with their values. To people with these styles, iconoclasts can seem cryptic and impulsive. To iconoclasts, people with intellectual, empirical, flexible, and committed styles seem incapable of taking action in a timely manner. People with ordered and anecdotal styles provide another example of hidden conflict. Anecdotes, relevant or not, appear silly compared to the operant principles that people with an ordered style believe they have discovered.

Hidden conflicts illustrate one of the barriers that keep team members from recognizing that the strengths of one style complement the weaknesses in another. People with mediator and empirical styles can be used to illustrate this point. People with an empirical style discount the value of human relations and verbal skills, which individuals with a mediator style are prone to use. Relationships seldom touch on empirically validated truisms in the empiricist's fact store. Furthermore, empiricists see verbalization as heading in unpredictable directions. A preoccupation with approval can conceal empirical truths. In contrast, empiricists' influence attempts seem misdirected to people with a mediation style because empiricists make no attempt to seek shared meaning. Resting change on empirical evidence makes change seem unlikely, whereas getting people to "buy in" through the creation of shared meaning is believed to be likely to succeed. These conflicts can obscure the obvious value of a synthesis of the decision approaches used by mediators and empiricists.

Compatible Styles

Managers with complementary decision-making tactics share views about how decisions should be made, which lowers the prospect of conflict. For example, managers with a relational style and managers who have a political style emphasize similar inferential systems in their decisions, as do iconoclasts and visionaries, political and relational styles, mediating and cooperative styles, evaluative and intellectual styles, procedural and traditional styles, and ordered and empirical styles. People with these styles seem likely to form informal coalitions to carry out much of the path clearing that precedes a major decision. However, these informal coalitions may lack sufficient diversity in points of view to appreciate the multiple perspectives needed in making tough decisions. To introduce these perspectives is apt to create conflict. Decision makers can manage this conflict by learning to appreciate what each perspective can offer and the need for multiple perspectives to cope with tough decisions.

Competing Values and Multiple Perspectives

A synthesis of views leads to development and learning, which are essential for decision making, as pointed out by Quinn (1983) in his competing values framework, by Argyris and Schön (1978) in their learning-to-learn arguments, by Wilber (1982) and Hampden-Turner (1981) in their mind-to-mind conversational heuristics, and in the creativity literature (for example, Gordon, 1971). A metaview that permits a careful examination of competing ways to make a decision seems necessary to promote the multiple perspectives that are required in tough decisions. These requirements pose two problems for self-reflection and team building. First, managers must become aware of the diversity in viable decision approaches, acquiring knowledge about such tactics as human relations, adaptation and innovation, planning, and control to the point that each can be effectively used. Second, merely having knowledge may not be sufficient to create a synthesis. However, a synthesis seems more likely when managers with a particular style select individuals with a style opposite as participants in decision making in order to promote a dialogue (Nutt and Backoff, 1986).

Key Points

1. The distinctive features of the sixteen decisions styles offer a means to anticipate conflicts so they can be mediated and a way for managers to appreciate styles that differ from their own.
2. People alter their styles in two ways. First, managers who lack clear-cut preferences shift among styles called auxiliaries. As a result, many managers have a range of styles that they unconsciously apply. Second, perceptively oriented managers with a strong internal focus have no means to implement their ideas and must shift to another style to take overt action. For these managers, behavior is misleading and does not signify how they arrived at a decision.
3. Shadow styles identify means of appreciation (S, N, T, or F) and taking action (I, E, J, or P) that a manager overlooks when making a decision. Managers who reflect on the means they seldom use can test their decisions in fresh ways, which will provide new insights that help to avert decision debacles, as described in Chapter Two.
4. Coalitions and groups are formed so that members have perspectives that complement the decision maker. If the coalition or group is well managed, superior decisions will result.

 Part Three

Decision-Making Processes

Part Three describes a procedure for decision making and outlines the steps in the process. The recommended decision process is organized into four stages, each with several steps. These stages and steps are offered to help managers cope with the behavioral problems encountered in making decisions, as described in Part Two, and to deal with the conflict, ambiguity, and uncertainty posed by tough decisions, as described in Part One. Chapter Eight outlines these steps and groups them into three types of decision processes, each with specific uses. By tailoring each process to these uses, the chapter introduces economics, simplifying and shortening the process while preserving the steps needed to deal with the specific kinds of conflict, ambiguity, and uncertainty posed by tough decisions. Chapter Nine links these three processes to three types of tough decisions, offering guidelines to help managers identify when each process can be used to its best advantage.

Decision-Making Processes

8

Analytical, Group, and Mixed-Mode Processes

Chapter Eight offers an outline of the steps needed to cope with tough decisions, drawing on all the ideas presented in this book for decision making. These steps are then organized into decision processes applicable to tough decisions. The processes are called analytical, group, and mixed-mode. The *analytical* decision process can be used by a single decision maker. The *group* decision process is essential when several stakeholders are affected by the decision. Finally, the *mixed-mode* process is developed for conditions in which there are many stakeholders with potentially conflicting aims.

The Decision Process

The process that a decision maker is encouraged to follow to make tough decisions is shown in Figure 8.1. The process calls for an iterative movement between stages, carrying out several steps to meet the requirements of each process stage, and backtracking as important insights are uncovered. A brief rationale for each stage is offered, and an outline of all steps needed to deal with conflict, ambiguity, and uncertainty is presented. Parts Three and Four of this book detail the rationale undergirding each step and provide specifics on how to carry out each step. The steps call for framing by problem identification, establishing intentions by setting objectives, applying analytical techniques (called *decision trees* and *sensitivity analysis*), and using groups adroitly. Decision makers facing tough decisions must

Figure 8.1. The Decision Process.

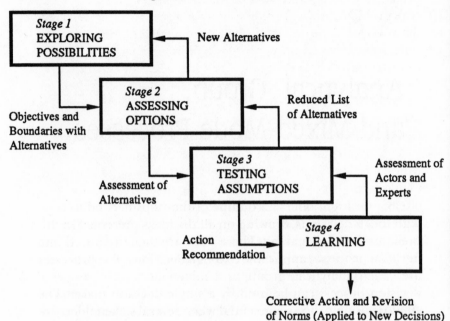

examine and reexamine their intentions, engage in coalition building and coalition management, use multiple perspectives, and seek to learn by reflecting on decision outcomes to improve their decisional capacity.

For tough decisions, a coalition of interests is formed by the titular decision maker. The coalition receives information from each step of the decision process and in doing so becomes gradually drawn into a full understanding of the implications of making a choice. A report on findings, followed by a description of activities needed to carry out the next step, makes up the typical agenda items in a meeting. This process is staffed by experts who are called on as needed by the decision maker, who in turn becomes the group leader.

Stage 1: Exploring Possibilities. The first and most important step in a decision process is to become immersed in the problem situation. The decision maker confronts the ambiguity and conflict in tough decisions by uncovering and exploring several problems before selecting a problem focus, assumed to be the core problem, that will guide subsequent activity. Once selected, the core problem indicates or implies a current and a desired state, such as confronting problems of increasing occupancy to industry norms or keeping expenditures below those of last year. The difference between existing and desired states is called the performance gap (Downs, 1967). Core problems also imply a solution domain, such as ways to increase occupancy or lower costs in the preceding example, defining the decision's "context."

Core problems give a decision its context, much the way a window frames what we see. Problems must be sought out and then carefully explored to avoid looking through a window that offers a misleading view. Tough decisions require careful framing. Several frames or windows are examined to determine what each implies the decision is and is not about, to see which offers the most advantages. Tactics that can be used to carry out framing are described in Chapter Eleven.

Exploration is also carried out by establishing objectives and identifying alternatives (Figure 8.1). Setting objectives produces two somewhat distinct benefits. First, attempts to clarify objectives often lead to a vastly different decision than the one that was initially contemplated. Second, all decisions must be *bounded* to focus subsequent inquiry. Objectives that provide this bounding can be too broad, producing unfocused inquiry, or too narrow, producing missed opportunity. Ways to develop and select decision objectives are discussed in Chapter Sixteen.

Alternatives pose a different set of problems and opportunities. A preliminary listing of alternatives provides a useful way to test an implicit decision boundary. Alternatives can be sorted into categories that seem to imply a particular problem or issue. The decision maker can reflect on what the decision is about by considering these groupings and the boundaries they imply. Grouping also points out the need to generate additional alternatives. Alternatives that stem from the pet ideas of key people, the practices of respected others, staff proposals, and the like can be expanded by means of problem solving, searching, and using creativity. The procedures described in Chapters Fifteen and Sixteen are used to expand the pool of alternatives.

The following steps are carried out by the decision maker to deal with tough decisions in stage 1.

1. *Identify a coalition.* Decision makers should explore problems and consequences from the vantage point of various stakeholders, using the decision seminar and the "5W" technique described in Chapter Eleven. Managers must identify coalitions whose interests seem congruent to those the titular decision makers are pledged to represent. Decision makers seek advice from many sources about whom to include and exclude, using problem analysis and problem exploration tactics.

2. *Explore attitudes toward ambiguity.* A coalition is often made up of individuals who have little tolerance for ambiguity. To deal with this tendency, coalition members are asked to fill out and self-score a form found in Appendix B, which measures their tolerance for ambiguity. The norms, also shown in Appendix B, help each coalition member come to terms with his or her views about ambiguity in an effort to head off premature closure in which core problems evade discovery.

3. *Present information.* The coalition leader (decision maker) introduces information gained by specific activities undertaken in steps 1 through 7 of the Decision Seminar (intelligence, promotion, invocation, prescription, application, termination, and valuation). (See Chapter Eleven.) This information may be trimmed or shaped, depending on the insights offered by coalition members.

4. *Identify problems.* The coalition uncovers problems, using one of the silent reflective group processes described in Chapter Fifteen. Problem analysis and exploration are repeated with the coalition, sorting problems into categories, applying the has/has not occurred in the 5W technique. The coalition speculates about root causes. The preferred group process technique is used to identify a consensus about the underlying issues that must be addressed (Chapter Fifteen).

5. *Identify objectives.* Objectives are identified, using the pre-

ferred group process, to deal with the priority problems that the coalition wants to address. Candidate objectives are tested for their semantic content and arrayed in a hierarchical fashion to encourage selection of an appropriate level of activity, as described in Chapter Sixteen.

6. *List preliminary alternatives.* A list of ways to meet the objective is constructed, again using a group process (Chapter Fifteen). The coalition decides whether to augment this list by seeking additional alternatives from such sources as the ideas and procedures used by others, staff proposals, consultant recommendations, internal planning, RFPs sent to vendors, innovation via research and development, and in still other ways. This step can be brief or extended, depending on the means used to uncover alternatives. These preliminary alternatives are pruned to identify those that merit further consideration. This list of potentially viable alternatives is examined to find how they affect stakeholders by making them possible winners and losers.

7. *Provide emotional inoculation.* Possible negative outcomes from the alternatives are identified and examined and ways to handle setbacks are proposed (Chapter Eleven), using one of the group processes in Chapter Fifteen.

8. *Encourage ethical considerations.* Ethics has a special form of rationality, just as economic and political considerations do. Unless steps are taken to encourage an open discussion of ethical concerns, they are often overlooked. Silent reflective group processes (Chapter Fifteen) are particularly useful in uncovering ethical questions about objections (ends) and ways to respond (means) that rule out some objectives and alternatives or pose criteria that capture these concerns as alternatives are being valued (Chapter Sixteen).

The decision maker, armed with an objective and a set of preliminary alternatives, is prepared to enter the next stage, in which information to assess the alternatives is sought.

Stages 2 and 3: Assessing Options and Testing Assumptions. The information required to assess options is obtained in stage 2.

Steps must be taken to firm up the list of relevant alternatives, determine criteria that these alternatives must satisfy, identify important future conditions, apply the criteria to the alternatives tied to future conditions, and determine the value of additional information as needs become apparent. Analytical frameworks incorporate objectives and subjective estimates of these factors to determine the merit of each alternative course of action.

Experiments with the framework are carried out to test key assumptions. These experiments yield two kinds of insight. First, opportunities to acquire additional information that can clarify chance outcomes often crop up as a decision process unfolds. The process becomes a series of choices, each dependent on the cost of acquiring additional information. The decision maker must decide whether to purchase additional information that clarifies the nature of chance outcomes that influence payoffs before proceeding. Chapter Eighteen offers procedures that can be used to determine when information purchases can be justified. Second, the likelihood of the future conditions can be treated as an unknown. The decision maker poses "what if" questions, using sensitivity analysis to determine when changes in preferences from one alternative to another would occur, considering the various sets of assumptions about future conditions. The same kind of analysis can be applied to any factor that has unreliable values, such as criteria weights and costs that are difficult to estimate. Various forms of sensitivity analysis are discussed in Chapters Thirteen, Eighteen, Nineteen, and Twenty.

The steps in the process for stages 2 and 3 are listed below.

9. *Use multiple perspectives.* The decision is profiled, using technical, personal, and organizational perspectives to uncover how each view can be played out in the decision, as described in Chapter Twelve.

10. *Identify criteria and norms.* The objective and the insights gained from the multiple-perspective assessment are used as a focus to identify criteria that the alternatives must satisfy (see Chapter Sixteen). The group process found to

be appropriate in previous steps is used to identify criteria and specify performance expectations for the criteria, called *norms*.

11. *Generate new alternatives.* The list of current alternatives is reviewed by asking if attempts to find additional alternatives are warranted. This activity is needed to avoid prematurely settling on ways to respond. This is particularly important in dealing with coalitions. The coalition decides how it will seek new alternatives, such as more self-generation using a group process, or by using one of the tactics noted in stage 1 to uncover alternatives. Often the search is conducted through the lens offered by the technical, personal, and organization perspectives.

12. *Clarify alternatives.* Alternatives are compared in terms of the criteria. The disaggregated criteria level for each alternative is presented for the coalition to appraise.

13. *Explore attitudes toward uncertainty.* Attitudes toward uncertainty are determined by having coalition members fill out and self-score the form shown in Appendix A to measure their views about uncertainty. The norms, also found in Appendix A, help to caution coalition members who have a very low tolerance for uncertainty.

14. *Identify future conditions.* The three perspectives offer three windows that can be used to look for future conditions suggested by contemporary events that are apt to arise in dealing with the priority problems selected by the coalition. A group process previously selected is used to help the coalition identify and select conditions that must be incorporated into the analysis. One of the techniques selected to make subjective estimates (see Chapter Nineteen) is used by the coalition to estimate the likelihood of events associated with each condition, such as the prospect of high or low demand.

15. *Explore decision rules.* Decision rules that depict various kinds of rationality are explored to see if there are any extreme conditions that warrant risk taking, risk aversion, and the like. If not, an "expected value" rule is used to determine the value of the alternatives under plausible

future conditions. Using expected values to measure pay-offs is a key step in managing the uncertainty inherent in tough decisions (see Chapters Thirteen and Eighteen).

16. *Use decision trees.* Assignments to staff are made to clarify alternatives, using decision trees applied with each perspective (see Chapters Twelve and Eighteen). The analysis is carried out by using each perspective to determine whether the preferred alternative is the same after incorporating the considerations identified from each perspective. These three decision trees are used to provide graphic displays. A combined analysis, merging criteria into a valuation index, can also be carried out by applying techniques described in Chapter Nineteen to merge the valuations of multiple criteria for an alternative.

17. *Weigh the merit of acquiring additional information.* In some decisions, the need for additional clarifying information becomes apparent at various points as assessments are made, such as follow-ups to market assessments that probe a particular market segment. The cost of acquiring this information is weighted against its benefits by means of the techniques described in Chapter Eighteen.

18. *Conduct sensitivity analysis.* Key assumptions are examined, using analytical and graphic techniques described in Chapters Thirteen, Eighteen, and Nineteen, called *sensitivity analysis.* This technique allows a coalition to see the risk inherent in various alternatives as they relax assumptions. Five types of "what if" questioning are discussed in this book. They allow decision makers to explore future conditions, estimate unknown payoffs, determine the impact of values implied by criteria weights, examine several future conditions at the same time, and determine the risk in acquiring more information.

19. *Conduct decision analysis as a policy exercise.* Criteria selected by the coalition are used to consider alternatives in the abstract. The exercise permits the coalition to see how alternatives fare when particular assumptions are made. Decision analysis, described in Chapter Twenty, is used to show members their values and the implications of these

values. Sensitivity analysis, changing the value of criteria weights, is carried out to identify the value change needed to produce a consensus. This analysis points out how much of a value change (measured by changes in criteria weights) must occur for the coalition to prefer one alternative over another.

20. *Choose and act.* The coalition makes a choice among alternatives by using consensus or majority rules (see Chapter Ten) after reviewing assessments from a decision tree and sensitivity analysis.

The information produced by these steps may clarify the decision by reducing ambiguity, or it may lead to new definitions of future conditions, new alternatives, or new criteria. The decision maker reverts to stage 2 to incorporate the new information into the analytical framework or implements the choice and moves to stage 4 to reflect on the process and its results.

Stage 4: Learning. After a choice has been made, the decision maker takes steps to determine the nature of the outcome produced by the decision and reflect on how the decision was made. Care must be taken to avoid hindsight bias and recognize shifting norms and their implications, as discussed in Chapter Five, when making such assessments. The precision of the information offered by experts in the decision process also can be assessed by keeping records of who had the best insight into future conditions and their prospects of occurring. In this way, the decision maker determines who provides the most useful assessments. Reflection is used by the decision maker to determine whether objectives were realistic and whether the decision was sensibly bounded.

Procedures that help a decision maker learn are discussed by Argyris and Schön (1978) and by Argyris, Putnam, and Smith (1985), who show how to avoid the double binds produced by "undiscussability." Decision makers who fear the consequences of failure make decisions undiscussable. Bad news is offset with irrelevant good news. There is a coverup and a coverup of the coverup, both of which are undiscussable. Decision outcomes are not accurately presented until the incentives that produce this behavior have been removed. This type of learning is discussed in Chapters Fourteen and Twenty.

The final steps in the decision process are presented below.

21. *Determine outcomes.* The results of the decision process are examined to measure observed performance against norms and the original needs articulated in stage 1.
22. *Reflect on outcomes and missed opportunities.* The coalition receives and considers feedback on the success of the decision process. The monitoring role of the coalition includes considering performance assessments, reflecting on the merits of the process and the precision of required forecasts, and considering the need to rethink and possibly alter the norms that guided the process.
23. *Conduct decision analysis.* For regularly recurring significant decisions, careful assessment of decision maker consistency is an essential component of the learning process. Such analyses uncover value differences among factions and compare the outcomes to performance norms. Procedures for decision analysis are described in Chapter Twenty.

These steps make up a decision process that explores the desirability of alternatives before implementation is attempted and then reflects on outcomes. The decision process is used to identify various constituencies to determine how each would be affected by the decision. The process recognizes that analytical information can be misleading, in part because of the multitude of interests and claims that must be considered. Premature closure is avoided by locating pockets of resistance and drawing out the reasons behind observed resistance. The process unfolds from this point in a step-by-step manner. The coalition experiments to determine the sensitivity of decisions to changes in values and other factors. The choice is based on a consensus of the coalition. Finally, the coalition explores the decision's outcome to determine the precision of key estimators, the appropriateness of norms, and the need for process steps that were used and not used.

Types of Decision Processes

Tough decisions are ambiguous because the locus of inquiry is unstable. This instability stems from the inability to specify core problems because these problems will shift, depending on whose interests are being considered. This shifting set of core problems makes aims that guide inquiry unknown or unstable.

Three types of situations that produce tough decisions can arise. In the first, there is a single decision maker who has been unable to identify the core problems that have provoked the need for action, making aims unclear or conflicting. The lack of clarity in aims makes any action contentious. Stage 1 (exploring possibilities) of the decision process attempts to clarify aims and find ways to organize a systematic search to identify alternatives that respond to those aims. This type of decision cannot be bounded until the decision maker decides on his or her aims.

The second type of situation stems from decisions that involve identifiable stakeholders whose views about core problems may differ. The arena or boundary of the decision is ambiguous because the interests of the stakeholders are unclear. During the exploring stage, the decision process involves these individuals in a group to uncover their interest and views of core problems provoking action. Aims are shaped by the group until a consensus emerges that is adopted to guide the decision process. Often the stakeholders must have a role in the remaining stages of the decision process or be allowed to monitor its progress.

A third type of situation arises when the key set of stakeholders is unknown or disputed. During the exploration stage, coalition building is carried out to identify whose interest must be managed as a decision is made. Two types of difficulties can result. In the first, competing groups of stakeholders, each with potentially conflicting aims, are known to exist. In the second, lists of stakeholders are hard to construct because the problems that have prompted action are too ill-defined for anyone to know whose interests are threatened.

Objectives, which indicate what the decision is about, can be hard to specify in each of these three situations, and this leads to tough decisions. For situations in which the decision maker is the dominant stakeholder, exploring calls for decision makers to sort out their aims as an aid in specifying objectives. When identifiable stakeholders are involved, a consensus must be built before an objective can be selected to guide action. When there are many stakeholders with potentially conflicting aims, an arena is defined by the formation of a coalition that is known to support the values of the organization for which the decision is to be made. Scenarios are used to explore aims that are apt to emerge from various groupings of stakeholders to determine which offers the most leverage to the organization.

The three types of tough decisions can be summarized as follows: Condition one has a dominant interest or single decision maker. Condition two has stakeholders with multiple interests. In condition three, the prospects of unknown stakeholders seem likely. A different decision process is used for each of these conditions. These processes, called *analytical, group*, and *mixed-mode*, all move through all of the four stages. Each stage can produce feedback to a previous stage or activate the stage that follows.

The Analytical Decision Process

The decision process for dealing with situations in which a dominant stakeholder acts as the decision maker is called *analytical* because much of the activity involves analysis. The analytical process differs in emphasis from the other processes to respond to the conditions it has been tailored to serve. For example, objectives and boundaries are easier to establish in condition one, resulting in relatively less emphasis on stage 1, exploring, than needed by the other processes. Process steps are summarized in Table 8.1.

Exploring Possibilities. In condition one, the dominant

Table 8.1. The Analytical Decision Process.

Exploring Stage

Step 1 Identify problem
Step 2 Explore problem
Step 3 Establish objectives
Step 4 Develop a list of alternatives
Step 5 Consider ethical concerns
Outcome: A bounded decision, with objectives and alternatives

Assessing Stage

Step 6 Use objectives to specify criteria
Step 7 Uncover future conditions, establish likelihoods, and select decision rule
Step 8 Organize with a decision tree
Step 9 Value alternatives, using criteria tied to future conditions
Step 10 Value additional information
Outcome: Assessment of the alternatives

Testing Stage

Step 11 Apply sensitivity analysis to future conditions
Step 12 Apply sensitivity analysis to criteria
Step 13 Select best alternative
Outcome: Action

Learning Stage

Step 14 Determine outcome
Step 15 Appraise performance and process
Step 16 Use decision analysis for recurring significant decisions
Outcome: Reflection on results and process used

stakeholder, the decision maker, must reflect to identify problems and conduct a problem analysis before establishing objectives. Core problems help to identify objectives. Objectives can be set by arranging candidates in a hierarchy of levels, which range from small to a sweeping scope of activity (Nadler, 1970, 1981). Objectives are tested for their semantic content, to delete means and blamefinding implications (Volkema, 1983). The decision maker then selects an appropriate scope of activity. Objectives bound the decision, specifying what it is and is not about. (Techniques for problem identification and analysis are discussed in Chapter Eleven, and techniques for setting objectives are discussed in Chapter Sixteen.) The objective is used to guide a search for alternatives that offer optional ways to respond to the core problem. The next step calls for a cataloguing of alternatives thought to be relevant given a particular objective. The decision maker expands the initial list of options, using various devices such as memory, observing the practices of others, vendors, searches with RFPs, soliciting ideas from subordinates and creativity. The problem analysis, objective setting, and search activities are often carried out with considerable staff support.

The purpose of the exploring stage is to establish boundaries for the decision. Alternatives are catalogued and new ones uncovered to fill the implied boundary. Several potentially usable alternatives should be provided. The decision maker consults with trusted colleagues, subordinates, and superiors, asking them to identify ethical questions posed by the options under active consideration. The information can be used to rule out certain options or to identify criteria to use in the valuation of alternatives. The next stage is activated by the list of alternatives generated in this first stage.

Assessing Options. In stage 2, the decision maker values alternatives by using a decision tree and related analytical approaches described in Chapters Thirteen and Eighteen. Steps call for identifying future conditions, estimating likelihoods for these conditions, specifying criteria that the alternatives must satisfy, using objectives as a guide, and applying the criteria to value payoffs for the alternatives tied to each set of future conditions. The decision tree organizes the decision, defining information that must be obtained and how it can be formatted for analysis. Finally, the decision maker determines the need for additional information. In sequential decisions, there can be several opportunities to purchase clarifying information, such as a market survey or a forecast, which may illuminate the payoffs produced by the alternatives. These choices help the decision maker prune the decision tree by discarding alternatives that are no longer relevant.

The outcome of this stage is an assessment of the alternatives. In some instances, new or hybrid alternatives crop up. Such alternatives may be assessed or they may force the process to move back to stage 1 so the decision maker can determine whether the boundary has shifted and what the implications of a shift might be, should one occur. The testing stage is activated by a set of competitive alternatives and their assessment.

Testing Assumptions. The testing stage examines key assumptions to determine the risk inherent in various choices. Risk is explored by examining factors, such as product demand, from both an optimistic and a pessimistic vantage point. Without such an assessment, decision makers will crimp their risk valuations away from extremes, making too low an estimate of high risk and too high an estimate of low risk (Edwards, 1968). Sensitivity analysis is carried out in this stage, to explore the assumptions in condition one decisions by asking "what if" questions about the value-laden criteria weights and the likelihood of future conditions. Criteria weights are explored to determine the implication of a shift in a weight. First, the impact of changes in weights is determined. The criteria can be weighted by various parties, or given equal importance, to see how the choice among alternatives would be altered. Second, the weights of key criteria are subjected to sensitivity analysis to find out how much the weights must change to produce a different decision. This step provides an appreciation of how values influence a decision. *Value-free* decisions occur when a choice using a particular decision rule is not influenced by any conceivable shift in the weights (see Chapters Nineteen and Twenty).

Changes in playoff produced by favorable and unfavorable assumptions about demand and other future conditions are also explored by using sensitivity analysis (Chapters Thirteen and Eighteen). This step provides an appreciation of the risk inherent in the decision. Various decision rules can be applied to see how conservative and aggressive attitudes toward risk would influence a decision. This step produces a recommended choice, which activates the final stage.

Learning. In the learning stage, the decision maker looks for missed opportunities and ways to improve decisional capacity. Learning can be inhibited by three factors: norms, the hindsight bias, and discussability. Many repeatable decisions are made by means of cutoffs on key criteria, such as exams that are

applied to select civil service executives. As norms are lowered —
which, for example, occurs in equal opportunity cases — the
predictive ability of the test seems to increase, overstating the
value of the test as a decision rule (Hogarth, 1980). The hindsight bias (Fischhoff, 1975) stems from creeping determinism.
In the aftermath of a decision, what happened seems inevitable
and clearly related to the *now* salient cues. Discussability is a key
barrier to learning (Argyris, Putnam, and Smith, 1985). Given
fear of the consequences of bad outcomes, bad news is offset by
good news. There is a coverup, and a coverup of the coverup, and
both are undiscussable. The information needed to learn will
not be accurately presented until the incentives that created this
behavior have been removed, making the decision discussable.

Learning can be delayed for some time, until some notion
of outcome is obtained. Outcome information specifies the
realized payoff (for example, profit) and allows the decision
maker to reflect on his or her predictions and those made by key
experts about future conditions, such as the level of demand.
The decision maker compares future conditions that have been
realized to estimates, to see how actual values differ from the
estimates. This step allows the decision maker to judge the
accuracy of estimates of demand and other future conditions
made by experts. It also allows for an assessment of the risk level
adopted during sensitivity analysis.

The decision maker notes other results, such as performance gap reduction (Nutt, 1979d), to monitor the need for
additional activity that may activate another decision. This type
of assessment allows decision makers to incrementally approach
their long-range aims (Rappaport, 1969) through a series of
choices that attempt to reduce the difference between objectives
and norms or expectations. It also allows decision makers to
catalogue what works, what does not, and why. Decision analysis
can be applied to recurring significant decisions, according to
the procedures presented in Chapter Twenty, to explore values
and measure consistency.

Learning can be transformational. In some cases, the
organization may have to establish new norms because a decision introduced new practices to the organization. In this situa-

tion, exporting current norms is inappropriate, and new norms are required to learn about whether a decision was or was not successful. The process calls for learning about learning, reflecting on the process as well as on the outcome and on how to judge the outcome (Argyris and Schön, 1978).

The Group Decision Process

The decision process for dealing with condition two situations, in which there are multiple stakeholders, is summarized in Table 8.2. Decisions can be rendered obscure when the interests or stakes of people who can affect or are affected by the decision are unclear. This situation arises when people with stakes have aims that are unknown. The decision process begins when a group made up of these stakeholders identifies its aims and resolves conflicts.

The dominant approach used in this type of situation is derived from group decision-making procedures, which are discussed in Chapters Ten and Fifteen. The process uses the group to promote "buy in" and moves through the usual stages but lingers in stage 1, exploration. The group explores core problem possibilities. All the activities in the analytical process are carried out, but they are conducted through the eyes of a group made up of key stakeholders. Analytical procedures are carried out in response to the premises established by the group. This sanctioning is the essential ingredient that makes analysis feasible.

Exploring Possibilities. Stakeholders are formed into a group that will guide the decision process. All process steps are carried out by using a silent reflective group process, following the guidelines provided in Chapter Fifteen. In stage 1, the group identifies priority problems. These problems are explored by using "5W" analysis (see Chapter Eleven). With this information as a guide, the group identifies objectives. Objectives are organized in a hierarchical fashion, as in the analytical process, according to procedures described in Chapter Sixteen. Next, the group attempts to discover new alternatives and then winnow the list to include only potentially viable alternatives. The

Table 8.2. The Group Decision Process.

Exploring Stage

Step 1   Form decision group
Step 2   Identify problem
Step 3   Explore problem
Step 4   Establish objectives
Step 5   Uncover and review alternatives
Step 6   Consider ethical concerns
Outcome: A bounded decision, with objectives and alternatives

Assessing Stage

Step 7   Group specifies criteria, considering objectives
Step 8   Group uncovers future conditions, establishes likelihoods, and selects decision rule
Step 9   Clarify alternatives, using criteria
Step 10   Organize, using decision tree
Step 11   Value alternatives, using criteria and future conditions
Step 12   Value additional information
Outcome: Assessment of alternatives

Testing Stage

Steps 13, 14   Apply sensitivity analysis to future conditions and criteria
Step 15   Group agrees to an action, group leader implements
Outcome: Action

Learning Stage

Step 16   Determine outcome
Step 17   Appraise performance and process
Step 18   Use decision analysis for recurring significant decisions
Outcome: Reflection on results and process used

group reviews priority problems and explores preliminary ways to respond to uncover ethical issues that merit consideration (Catron, 1983). The silent reflective group process is used to promote disclosure. Significant ethical concerns are factored into the decision by dropping alternatives or introducing ethically based criteria that will be used to value the alternatives in stage 2.

The exploring stage ends when a set of alternatives has been identified for assessment.

Assessing Options. The decision is organized in the same way as described for the analytical process except that the group makes all judgments called for in the assessment of options. The

group identifies the future conditions it wishes to explore, estimates likelihoods, and derives criteria from objectives, weights
them, and values the need to acquire additional information.
Staff support is often required to conduct the analyses that are
needed to value the payoffs associated with each alternative. The
payoffs are described graphically by means of a decision tree
representation (see Chapter Eighteen), to lay out the sequence
of events and the assumptions that have been made. The outcome of this stage is a preliminary assessment of alternatives,
which activates the next process stage.

Testing Assumptions. The group leader (titular decision
maker) commissions staff to carry out a sensitivity analysis. The
results are presented by the analysts to the group. The steps are
identical to those described for analytical decisions. These steps,
however, take longer in a group, to allow for the needed interpersonal adjustments and accommodations (see Chapter Ten). The
results of the analysis are used by the group leader to raise
questions for the group to contemplate.

Learning. To learn, the logic traps produced by norm
shifts, the hindsight bias, and problems of discussability must be
confronted, as in the analytical process. The group process faces
still another barrier to learning. Ad hoc groups quickly disband
and are seldom retained to monitor a decision. In this case,
feedback can be provided to individuals, but such information
can be avoided or relegated to a special-case category for the
reasons cited in Chapters Four and Five. Recommendations for
group control, described in Chapter Ten, provide one way to
deal with this difficulty.

Some of these problems can be overcome by getting an ad
hoc group to accept that an essential step in any decision process is being briefed about outcome. The group should consider
its success in reducing the performance gap, in making precise
estimates during the decision process, and in assessing the need
to alter norms it used to view outcomes. The norm discussion
can be particularly important because norms are often difficult
to change without considerable sentiment in the group that
supports this action (Argyris, Putnam, and Smith, 1985).

The cooptation produced by group action can help to

overcome barriers to organizational learning. Some of the coverups discussed in Chapter Fourteen are harder to sustain following an open discussion of double binds and incentives to
dress up a bad decision. Groups diffuse blame and offer an
excellent vehicle to own up to the need to take corrective action
and change the expectations of the organization regarding the
action provoked by a decision. Decision analysis (Chapter
Twenty) for recurring and significant group decisions is carried
out by staff to identify the impact of values held by factions in a
group and to measure consistency.

The Mixed-Mode Decision Process

The mixed-mode process (Nutt, 1976b, 1979c, 1981a) is
used for condition three, in which there are multiple stakeholders with conflicting aims. In this type of situation, it is not
clear who should have an interest or stake in the decision or
when disagreements about whose interests are paramount will
arise. The process steps to deal with this type of situation are
summarized in Table 8.3. The process is dubbed *mixed-mode*
because coalition building and group process are used to direct
analysis.

Many coalitions can be identified in tough decisions.
Some can be ruled out because they lack influence or coherence.
Other coalitions, however, offer reasonable ways to view the
decision. At the outset, it is not clear (nor are there any tests that
can be applied to determine) which of these views provides the
most advantage. The decision maker explores various ways to
frame the decision in terms of various interests. A coalition of
interests is formed whose values and beliefs are aligned with
those of the decision maker and the interests that the decision
maker is pledged to represent. Once mobilized, these interests
are managed so as to create a consensus in which exploration
can be carried out, sealed off from distractions to the extent
possible.

In the mixed-mode process, the key consideration is to
establish an arena of action that is both manageable and defensible. To be manageable, an arena must have stakeholders with

Table 8.3. The Mixed-Mode Decision Process.

Exploring Stage

Step   1 Identify possible constituencies
Step   2 Simulate values and select constituency
Step   3 Form coalition as a decision group
Step   4 Engage intelligence, promotion, invocation, prescription application, termination, and valuation steps of the Decision Seminar Procedures
Step   5 Explore attitudes toward ambiguity
Step   6 Identify and explore problem
Step   7 Coalition selects priority problem to address
Step   8 Coalition establishes objectives
Step   9 Uncover and review alternatives
Step 10 Provide emotional inoculation
Step 11 Pose ethical concerns
Outcome: A bounded decision, with objectives and alternatives

Assessing Stage

Step 12 Use multiple perspectives
Step 13 Identify criteria implied by objectives through each perspective
Step 14 Uncover more alternatives
Step 15 Clarify alternatives, using the criteria
Step 16 Explore attitudes toward uncertainty
Step 17 Identify future conditions, likelihoods, and decision rules, using each perspective
Step 18 Value alternatives from each perspective or merge criteria measures into a valuation index
Step 19 Value additional information
Step 20 Organize, using each perspective to present the results of the analyses
Outcome: Assessment of alternatives

Testing Stage

Step 21 Apply sensitivity analysis to future conditions and criteria
Step 22 Use policy exercises
Step 23 Coalition recommends an action, titular decision maker implements
Outcome: Action

Learning Stage

Step 24 Determine outcome
Step 25 Assess results and information provided by participants and support staff
Step 26 Use decision analysis for recurring significant decisions
Outcome: Reflection on results and process used

potentially homogeneous aims (March and Simon, 1958). Defensible arenas establish intentions that support the dominant values in the organization. Once the arena has been set, objectives can be established and alternatives sought.

Emphasis in the mixed-mode process is directed toward the exploring stage. Deciding what the decision is about has overriding importance. As a result, several kinds of precautions are taken. First, problems are identified and assessed by using various tactics. This step is essential because the confusion surrounding constituency identification can mislead. Dealing with several problems simultaneously leads to unnecessary arguments about alternatives. Arguments crop up because an alternative can be justified by one problem perspective but not another (see Chapters Eleven and Twelve). A shift away from a discussion of what action to take to what is prompting action is needed to uncover areas of potential agreement. Second, the decision maker uses multiple perspectives to open up the process. This step is essential because stakeholders must be exposed to several points of view as they focus on a given problem. Third, policy exercises are commissioned by the decision maker to uncover the diversity of views and allow for a careful discussion that explores values and their congruence to values called for by the organization. Finally, attitudes toward ambiguity are explored and setbacks anticipated and managed, to control the level of conflict and stress people often experience in this type of decision process.

The decision maker frames the decision by identifying possible coalitions in terms of the problem arena they are willing to confront and the aims that this arena implies. The coalition carries out subsequent inquiry, using group and analytical procedures. To permit a thoughtful exploration of alternatives in a tough decision, important centers of power are carefully managed by the decision maker. Valuation information must consider and attend to the needs of these centers as they emerge. A coalition that makes up these power centers is built, managed by group procedures, and informed by analysis. To carry out the mixed-mode approach, coalition identification and management are added to group and analytical procedures, discussed previously.

Exploring Possibilities. Before a coalition is formed, the titular decision maker becomes the coalition organizer and conducts a search that explores problems and consequences as they would be seen from the vantage point of various stakeholders. To expand the list of stakeholders, the titular decision maker draws inferences about who has stakes from various sources, such as subordinates and trusted peers (Mason and Mitroff, 1981; Freeman, 1983). Constituency identification and profiling take place at the same time. The coalition organizer considers various stakeholder groupings to determine which grouping identifies a coalition whose values appear aligned with those that he or she seeks to represent.

After the coalition has been identified, exploring takes place according to steps 6 through 9 in Table 8.3. The coalition members reflect on their attitudes toward ambiguity before proceeding with the self-assessment form and norms offered in Appendix B. Coalition management activities are guided by the Decision Seminar Procedures described in Chapter Eleven (Laswell, 1974). The titular leader moves the coalition through the seminar steps to anticipate and deal with value conflicts that are apt to emerge and derail the decision process. With these insights, the coalition begins to *bound* the decision. The coalition, acting as a decision-making group, identifies problems, participates in problem exploration, sets objectives, and suggests alternatives or ways to search for alternatives to meet the objective. Emotional inoculation (Janis and Mann, 1977) is used to diffuse the perceived threats that can be posed by the alternatives. This step is essential to ward off baseless fears and to deal with legitimate concerns that often crop up in coping with choices that involve multiple stakeholders.

The process moves to stage 2, to value the alternatives, or lingers in stage 1 until the threats posed by the alternatives can be reduced. To reduce threats, the process can be reframed by repeating steps 4 through 9 of Table 8.3, or the process can revert to steps 8 and 9 to uncover and shape alternatives to reduce their objectionable elements. Ethical considerations are introduced by the decision maker, acting as coalition leader and using the same procedures recommended for the group decision process.

Assessing Options. The decision tree format is applied to value the alternatives from stage 1 according to three perspectives: technical, personal, and organizational (Linstone, 1984). This allows issues to be raised in multiple contexts and identifies a choice that can cope with the values inspired by each. Different candidates for action that emerge from each perspective are identified and discussed. The coalition members reflect on their attitudes toward uncertainty, using the self-assessment form and norms offered in Appendix A. With these insights, the coalition makes judgments about future conditions, estimates likelihoods, derives criteria from objectives and weights them for each perspective, and considers the merits of acquiring more information. The valuation of options proceeds in the same manner as that described for group and analytical processes. If the same choice is identified by the decision tree analysis for each perspective, a strong candidate for action emerges. If the same choice is not identified, value conflicts are reviewed before the coalition moves to stage 3. Should value conflicts prove to be important, additional steps are taken by the coalition leader to find agreed-upon arenas in which to act. Reverting to stage 1 for reframing to identify more alternatives may be necessary.

Testing Assumptions. Sensitivity analyses are carried out as in the other decision processes. More care must be taken in exploring key assumptions because coalitions can be volatile, producing alternatives that have long-term negative consequences as interpersonal accommodations are carried out. In addition to sensitivity analysis, policy exercises (step 22) may be needed to uncover how much values must shift to influence a decision, which aids in consensus building. Important value differences identify factions (see Chapters Ten and Twenty) that must be accommodated by compromise alternatives or new ideas, causing a shift back to stage 1 or 2.

Learning. The barriers to learning for a coalition are similar to those for groups but can be more difficult to overcome. Coalitions are invariably ad hoc and expect to disband when a choice has been made. To ensure learning, the coalition must receive and consider the same types of feedback as called for in the group decision process. To allow learning to occur, the coalition organizer must make it clear at the outset of a decision process that the coalition has a role in decision monitoring and error correction.

Monitoring involves performance and process evaluations. Performance assessments, such as the reduction of performance gaps measured in traditional ways, are made by comparing outcomes (for example, costs) to norms that specify expectations. Monitoring also involves reflecting on the merits of the process, considering the precision of the estimates that were made and the need to alter norms. If the coalition members learn from these appraisals, organizational capacity grows. As with groups, insights that are produced from cooptation make it easier to take corrective action and diffuse recriminations. Decision analysis is used by coalitions in the same way as in the group decision-making process for repetitious and significant decisions.

Key Points

1. The decision procedure outlined in this chapter can help decision makers cope with ambiguity, uncertainty, and conflict in tough decisions and the behavioral factors that inhibit and mislead decision makers.
2. To introduce efficiencies, this procedure is tailored to three types of situations:
   a. dominant stakeholder or single decision maker
   b. multiple, known stakeholders
   c. multiple stakeholders with conflicting aims and the strong likelihood of unknown interest groups
3. Analytical, group, and mixed-mode decision processes have been formulated for the three situations, including the essential stages and steps in each process.
4. The reader is encouraged to do still more tailoring, selecting among the suggested process steps those that seem essential by appraising the decision being confronted.

꧁ 9

Matching
Decision Processes
to Types of Decisions

This chapter offers guidelines to match the analytical, group, and mixed-mode decision processes to types of tough decisions that often arise in organizations. Tailoring these decision processes to specific uses saves the manager time and effort while retaining steps needed to come to grips with various kinds of tough decisions. Cues are provided to help managers recognize the kind of conflict, ambiguity, and uncertainty that signals when to use a particular process. Matching decision process to decision type also helps managers overcome the habitual use of certain approaches to decision making that are prevalent in many organizations, as discussed in Chapters Six and Seven. Various decision approaches gain footholds in organizations and develop many persuasive advocates who claim that beneficial results can be obtained by the exclusive use of a favored approach. Advocates contend or imply that a particular approach should be used for most, if not all, decisions. The benefits that can be derived from using an appropriate decision process and the problems that are apt to stem from a mismatch are discussed to demonstrate the need for a balanced perspective in decision making. In this chapter the selective benefits of various decision processes are demonstrated and the dangers of using an inappropriate process are highlighted.

Table 9.1. Types of Decisions.

		Nature of Information	
		Rich	*Poor*
Procedure	*Well structured*	*Level 1* Representational decisions	*Level 2* Empirical decisions
	Poorly structured	*Level 3* Information decisions	*Level 4* Search decisions

Kinds of Decisions

Decisions can be defined in terms of information and ways to process information (Nutt, 1981a). Information for a decision can be known (or knowable) or unknown and hard to acquire. Information-rich decisions result when an inventory or list of needs can be drawn up. Decisions in which information is unknown or difficult to obtain can also arise (McKenney and Keen, 1974). Information-rich and information-poor conditions provide one way to classify decisions.

The second factor, ways to process information, considers the existence of a procedural base to process the information (Perrow, 1967; Van de Ven and Delbecq, 1974). Decisions amenable to some form of systematic appraisal have a known procedural base. Such a decision situation is referred to as "well structured." The procedural base is often accepted without question. When no set of procedures seems relevant, a "poorly structured" decision situation results.

Decisions as Types

The nature of information and means to manipulate it are used to identify four types of decisions, as shown in Table 9.1.

Representational Decisions

Decisions in which there are a rich informational base and a clear way to manipulate the information are called *representational*. To make a decision, managers arrange data according to the dictates of the preferred means of data processing. For example, decisions involving service capacity of an airport can be represented by means of a queuing model to capture trade-offs of cost and service time. Inventory policy can be set by models that identify the required data, such as the costs of ordering, stock outs, and holding inventory, and a way to arrange the data to permit analysis. The quality of the decision depends on the fit of the model to the decision situation, seldom on context, the specific application to which the model is applied. Good fits of models to assumptions provide an accurate representation of a decision and good results. Managers with an ST or systematic style are particularly good at dealing with representational decisions, as discussed in Chapter Six.

Representational decisions are *not* tough decisions. No ambiguity is recognized, conflict has been assumed away, and uncertainty, if considered at all, is captured by statistical distributions. The only difficulty is one of recognizing that the decision is amenable to a particular type of treatment. Techniques to deal with decisions of this type are widely available. They include mathematical models that rely on techniques such as operations research, cost-benefit analysis, Monte Carlo simulation, evaluation research, and other methods. This book does *not* consider representational decision problems or ways to deal with them.

Empirical Decisions

Decisions that are information-poor but have a clear means of processing information once it is obtained are called *empirical*. These decisions are tough because of their lack of information. There are both ambiguity and potential conflict over what information to acquire and how to make estimates of uncertain events. As a consequence, the acquisition of information becomes the primary task in decision making. Information tends to be content-specific: dependent on the nature of the situation being confronted and the decision maker's views, as well as on his or her knowledge of the situation.

Empirical decisions require deductive reasoning according to some known principle or framework to identify and format for analysis the information needed to make a decision. One type of empirical framework poses a causal model to suggest relationships so that data can be collected to weight the importance of explanatory factors in the model. Statistical techniques such as experimental designs and regression can be used to determine the importance of model factors. After parameters in the model have been empirically derived and validated, the decision maker can relax key assumptions to determine the sensitivity of alternatives to changes in use rates and the like. Managers with a speculative or NT style are often good at dealing with empirical decisions (Chapter Six).

Consider two examples. In the first, policymakers became concerned about nursing home costs. An explanatory model was developed to identify factors that might influence cost. The model was built to include cost factors such as the home's ownership (public or private), profit or nonprofit status, size, nurse-patient ratio, occupancy, and so on. Policy options, such as altering the size of the nursing home, were considered in light of possible changes in the environment, such as various growth rates for the elderly population. The impacts of high and low growth rates on cost were estimated according to the model, and various assumptions were made about nursing home size and other factors. The analysis was complex but understandable by the application of deductive reasoning.

In the second example, policymakers sought policy options regarding ways to deal with malpractice lawsuits aimed at hospitals. To detect the risk associated with malpractice lawsuits naming hospitals as defendants, a deductive study was applied by analysts to relate the size of the award to various factors. In this case the factors believed to influence the size of an award were the severity of the injury, a hospital's service intensity and size, time until settlement, type of alleged error, incident location, claimant factors (age and sex), and mode of disposition (trial, out-of-court settlement, arbitration). The analysts found that mode of disposition offered several policy options that were assessed by relating each option (by trial, arbitration, and other modes of settlement) with contextual factors (severity, time until settlement, claimant factors). The analysis was able to determine which option had desirable outcomes from a public perspective, such as lowering the payouts for nonsevere injuries (Nutt and Emswiler, 1979).

Information Decisions

Information-rich situations coupled with problematic or controversial means to process the information produce what are called *information decisions*. Conflict stems from the prospect of differing views about what information is diagnostic and needed to make assessments. An incomplete understanding of how key stakeholders may view the information produces a potentially volatile context in which a decision must be made. This prospect of conflict produces both ambiguity and uncertainty and leads to tough decisions.

This type of decision calls for induction. Facts and circumstances that surround the decision must be coherently assembled to isolate a preferred course of action or to serve as a basis from which to draw a conclusion. A synthesis is sought to reconcile the data into a pattern that suggests a preferred course of action. Managers with a judicial or SF style frequently deal skillfully with this type of decision (Chapter Six).

For instance, decisions in collective bargaining bring out information on safety, wages, productivity, grievances, profitability, and the like. Negotiations by a city with an AFSCME local show how each party makes selective interpretations of this information. Union and management stake out different positions and support their positions with some of the available information. The initial proposal brought by management to the table may call for cutbacks in vacation time, reductions in sick-leave allowances requiring reduced pay for sick time taken, the scrapping of a disability program, the cutting of birthday holidays, as well as the setting out of pay provisions for the next contract period. A union's response to these "takebacks" results from an interpretation of its strength, based in part on the size of its membership, its past relationships with the mayor, the recent success of other unions (bus drivers), potential media interest and position (pro- or anti-union), as well as the anti-union tone of the country in the 1980s. The decision to negotiate further, strike, or cave in is based on the union's assessment of its position. The union can also counter the contract proposal with one of its own that deals with new issues such as overtime pay and rates for buyout of unused sick time based on information drawn from a comparison of wages within similar organizations. Conflicting facts must be reconciled by the writing of a contract that can be endorsed by both union and management.

Analysis in information-rich decisions can be more controversial than helpful, as noted by the decision debacles in Chapter Two. The amount of available information frequently leads to conflict. This conflict stems from the selective use of available information with analysis to suggest diametrically different courses of action and from alternatives that address different underlying problems. Key parties must agree upon meaning before analysis is possible. Conflict over meaning makes informational decisions tough and context-dependent.

Search Decisions

A search decision occurs in situations that are information-poor and have no obvious or agreed-upon way to frame the decision to begin an information search. Such ambiguity makes it difficult to know where to start and creates fears that conflict will emerge because there is no way to anticipate potential objectives. Managers with a heuristic or NF style are often adept at coping with search decisions (Chapter Six).

To deal with search decisions, managers must apply both inductive and deductive tactics in a reciprocal fashion. They must use deductive reasoning to mount a search for cues and explanatory concepts to find contexts in which to operate. Managers must then apply deductive reasoning in order to use context to suggest alternatives and ways to judge the merits of alternatives. Search decisions are often strategic in nature, making predictions difficult and the consequences of action hard to tease out. For example, consider a community mental health center, with a windfall of tax support, choosing among adding new services, expanding current services, or maintaining the status quo. Decision makers know little about demand, revenues, and potential benefits (remission rates) for these options, so they must find ways to identify needed information before they can seek that information.

Search decisions are wholly dependent on context. Benefactors, power centers, and constituents can abruptly shift as the context changes. A search is mounted to *select* a context. The implications of viewing the decision from several vantage points are played out by bounding the decision in various ways. A comparison of these ways to frame suggests which one gives the most leverage in making a decision. In the mental health center example, the implicit context is *allocative*, which can be compared to other possible contexts. For example, the windfall could also be used to carry out strategic management, creating a *transformational* context, to mount training or hire new skills, by application of a *human capital* context, or to create a trust fund to cover anticipated shortfalls of federal support, producing a *preservation* context. Identifying a context for the decision is the key act in making a search decision.

Decisions As Levels

The decision types represent *level shifts* in which context becomes progressively more important. At level 1, representational decisions arise. Context can shift markedly without posing serious problems for the decision maker. Aims are fixed by the needs inherent in the decision to be made, aims that tend to be independent of shifts in context. For example, organizations with fixed production capacity that cannot change in the short term, such as steel mills and foundries that have firm contracts for their product, can seek to minimize their cost of operation (their aims), ignoring shifts in context, such as the acts of foreign producers and costs of raw material. Level 1 decisions are closed off from environmental influences that can create context shifts, such as changes in the market penetration of competitors.

At level 2, empirical decisions occur and context becomes important for the first time. Decision makers must reflect on their own aims and how these aims fit with those of the organization, which can be context-dependent. Aims may be in a state of flux, in part because environmental factors have become important. For example, if the steel mill loses key production contracts, raw material costs and innovations by competitors must be considered in any decision. Various objectives can be entertained, including profitability, utilization, and appearances, to head off troublesome queries from big clients during a period of transition. Managers can no longer assume that a minimal cost objective is appropriate no matter what decision is made, as in level 1 decisions.

At level 3, information decisions occur. Context can pose serious problems because it is given by the views of a group, which makes it subject to sudden shifts. Such shifts can occur when preferences are discovered or revealed and when preferences change unexpectedly. Before acting, decision makers must consider how stakeholders view a decision situation. These views often create surprise, in part because it is difficult to predict the range of responses that people will make to information-poor situations. For instance, a decision group in a steel mill made up of representatives from marketing and sales, production, engineering, cost accounting, and the like can have many different insights and ways to view an information-rich decision. Aims must remain fluid until these insights about markets, raw material, other suppliers, customers, innovation, and the like are sorted out. As a result, aims in information decisions become quite context-dependent.

Level 4 produces search decisions. Context at this level is the most difficult to handle because key parties to a decision have stakes that are unknown and may conflict. This makes level 4 decisions harder to deal with than level 3 decisions, in which stakeholders are all internal, so their views are often partially known by the interests they represent and positions they have taken. In level 4 decisions, agendas and aims can be hidden, revealed only to trip up the coalition leader. Aims must remain fluid until these interests and the insights are sorted out. For example, a steel mill in Chapter 11 reorganization must use a coalition of interests to make strategic decisions. The coalition includes insiders (marketing, engineering, production) *and* outsiders made up of court representatives, banks and lawyers representing creditors, members of its board of directors, and others. Each party has an interest in all major decisions of the company. These stakeholders share the goal of preserving the company but are likely to have different aims for a given decision, such as avoiding high-risk options (banks) or preserving jobs (management). Furthermore, stakeholders are apt to see environmental factors very differently, creating a complex and volatile context in which to make choices. Search is needed to capture these views and catalogue them to understand the context in which action must be taken. Level 4 decisions are complex because their steps are filled with the potential for conflict, which can be hard to manage.

Matching Decision Types to Decision Processes

The parties affected by a decision suggests which process to use. Guidelines for matching process and decision type are given by the number of stakeholders and the diversity of their views. Single decision makers can use the analytical process, multiple known stakeholders the group process, and coalitions the mixed-mode process. Situations that call for individual or group procedures, as well as decisions involving groups or coalitions, can be hard to differentiate. To help decision makers recognize when to use each process, additional clues are useful. These are offered in the form of guidelines that match decision processes to the decision types. When the match of a process to a decision type meets these guidelines, certain benefits can be expected; when it does not, problems can be anticipated. The tougher the decision, the more difficult it is to produce good outcomes. Nevertheless, good results are more likely when the decision process and decision type are matched.

Judging the Effectiveness of a Decision Process

Indicators that can be used to suggest the merits of a decision process are cost, timeliness, validity, reliability, and acceptance (Nutt, 1979c). Cost is incurred in both the development of decision aids and the carrying out of the decision-making process. Decision makers may adopt a low-cost decision-making process because they have few resources, beyond their own time, to underwrite their activities.

The delay between a recognition of the need to make a decision and a choice is a measure of timeliness. The time required to apply a decision-making process creates the delay. In decision making, speed may be a practical virtue because those with power in an organization may have a history of demanding short-fuse decisions.

Accuracy can be measured when a choice suggested by the process can be verified by events. Decision processes with a successful track record are strongly preferred. However, many decisions, such as capital budgeting and staffing, have no way to verify that a choice produced a desirable outcome. As a result, use of this indicator is limited to those decisions in which an outcome can be classified as desirable or undesirable.

A consistent decision-making process produces the same choice with repeated applications when conditions and information remain constant. To defend their actions, decision makers may have to demonstrate that they have responded in a consistent or reliable manner. For instance, regulatory decisions that approve rates or expansions under a particular set of justifications and needs and deny them under comparable conditions are capricious, making them subject to appeals in the courts.

Acceptance results when a decision process helps pave the way for the implementation of a decision. For example, acceptance is promoted when affected individuals can participate in the decision-making process.

Decision-making processes that seem best for each of the decision types are identified on the basis of how cost, timeliness, validity, reliability, and acceptance are influenced by the process-type match.

The Analytical Process Used for Empirical Decisions

The analytical decision process is recommended for empirical decisions to specify the information needed in information-poor situations. For instance, purchasing decisions can be based on the analysis of provisions in vendor agreements. The relationship between quality and delivery guaranties can be balanced against penalty clauses and quantity discounts. Information of this type is sought from vendors and assessments of options (vendors) can be made by applying the analytical decision process. The nature of the empirical decisions makes analytical approaches essential. For level 2 decisions, the analytical decision process can be consistent, timely, and potentially valid, although validity can be difficult to infer. Costs are lower with this process than with the others. Acceptance depends on the ability to demonstrate that a good decision has been made. Acceptance is, at best, neutral when the analytical decision process is used.

Poorer results are more apt to occur when either the group or mixed-mode decision process is applied to empirical decisions. Group procedures can be misused when applied to empirical decisions. For instance, public organizations tend to appoint task forces to settle questions of fact. Disputes over the productivity in local and state governmental agencies or the economic impact of a convention center on a community get sidetracked by committee rhetoric. The fact-finding committee seldom finds much in the way of facts or any new information, but it does create the aura of action. Decision cost, consistency, timeliness, and validity (when obtainable) are adversely affected when the group decision process is substituted for the analytical process for this type of decision, but acceptance is often enhanced.

Applying the mixed-mode decision process to empirical tasks creates even more confusion. For instance, decisions regarding technological systems such as electronic data processing (EDP) can be made by using accuracy, turnaround, capacity, and related performance features to compare EDP alternatives. The cost and timeliness of choosing among EDP systems can be adversely affected by the mixed-mode approach because coalitions take longer to act and involve several, often high-priced, organizational representatives. Reliability and validity can also be adversely affected. Involving a coalition can make it more difficult to compare systematically the attributes of candidate systems, although participation makes acceptance more likely.

The Group Decision Process Used for Information Decisions

The group decision process is ideally suited to information-rich decisions. This process allows stakeholders to develop a shared interpretation of the available information. Group methods are preferred because they promote acceptance and can be timely and relatively inexpensive given proper management. This type of decision has low consistency. Groups can act in unpredictable ways and are unlikely to respond in the same way to comparable decisions. Analyses can be used after the decision group frames the decision question if the group has the resources and patience to wait for an answer. Analysis, used to support a group process, can greatly improve decision consistency. Poor decisions may still result because the question may be framed obscurely, either intentionally or through ignorance. This, of course, makes validity a potential problem. For instance, a power-generating utility making a decision on whether to pursue the rehabilitation of a nuclear power plant can use a decision group to judge feasibility. The group involves key people sensitive to trends in nuclear power acceptance, attitudes of local regulators, the political climate, the difficulty and cost of meeting post-Chernobyl safety requirements, and the like. The group sorts this information and develops an appreciation of the pros and cons of acting. At this point, analysis can clarify the risks of action and prospects of success, following the group decision-making procedures described in the last chapter.

Applying the analytical or mixed-mode decision process to information-rich decisions would produce less desirable results. In information-rich decisions, several parties are potentially in conflict. This conflict must be managed by ensuring that pertinent information is first shared and then sorted according to importance. Until this sharing and sorting take place, analysis is apt to provoke conflict rather than provide the basis for a decision. For instance, the unilateral act of a utility president to reopen a nuclear power plant, closed before its completion because of alleged safety violations, can provoke controversy and resistance unless the views of interested parties are heard and their buy in is promoted via their participation. As a result, using the analytical decision process for information decisions often results in high decision cost and low decision acceptance. Cost is driven up by the refusal of key stakeholders to accept the results, which can lead to repeated attempts to conduct analysis in an acceptable manner. Acceptance is low because analysis is premature and displaces bargaining and compromise among stakeholders. Reliability may also be low because it is difficult to find agreed-upon core problems from which to derive a fact set to use in the analysis. Dealing with the wrong set of core problems with first-rate analysis produces the aura of validity when none is present. Analysis that creates illusions of validity produces a false sense of security that can be misleading and even dangerous.

The mixed-mode decision process applied to information decisions results in overkill. The steps of coalition identification can be costly and unnecessary when the stakeholders are well known. Going through these steps renders the coalition leader naive, lowering process credibility. Both decision cost and timeliness are adversely affected, as is decision acceptance.

The Mixed-Mode Decision Process Used for Search Decisions

The mixed-mode decision process is best for search decisions. Search decisions are open-system in nature. Causal relations are influenced by myriad environmental factors that make analysis both expensive and unlikely to produce usable results. For instance, hospitals judge the feasibility of mergers by announcing their intentions and monitoring the reactions of regulatory bodies, competitors, banks and other sources of venture capital, and the affected medical staffs, as well as power centers in the community. The prospects for success are judged by

simulating the formation of various coalitions to see if a coalition with shared interests emerges, one that can be used to
sanction the merger and has the power to successfully promote
it. Under these conditions, the mixed-mode decision process
(compared to the other processes) can be timely and consistent
and promotes acceptance. No decision process can ensure validity or have low cost when search decisions are involved.

Neither the group nor the analytical decision process can
cope with search decisions. When the organization fails to
search for stakeholders, a decision group made up of insiders
often results. Such a group is more apt to frame the decision in a
parochial manner and develop groupthink (Janis and Mann,
1977). Groupthink and parochialism limit the search for information and increase the chance of poor decisions. Decision cost
is lower and delays fewer when insider groups are used, but these
virtues are offset by low consistency and poor validity. A group
decision process has considerable risk of omission, which leads
to low consistency, and may prematurely terminate search,
which limits discovery. The advantages of a group decision
process (timeliness and low cost) are more than offset by the
advantages of the mixed-mode decision process when they are
applied to search decisions (increased acceptance, consistency,
and lower risk of omission).

Applying the analytical decision process to search problems can be disastrous. The context is shifting, making it impossible to bound the decision to give analysis a focus. When
assumptions are made to permit analysis in a search decision,
the results are often silly and can be widely off target unless a
coalition of interests is available to identify an arena. As a
consequence, analysis is misdirected. For instance, analysis applied to judge the performance of a mental health center could
frame the decision in terms of federal officials and their interest
in cost reduction and their emphasis on particular classes of
patients. The adoption of this approach would sweep aside the
interests of mental health treatment professionals in patients
with high cure rates, court-assigned evaluations of people con-
victed of substance abuse, the community and its concern with
the availability of service to the severely retarded, and still other

interests. In this type of decision, costs are inflated and time-liness declines. Consistency and validity are seldom, if ever, realized.

Matching Degree of Puzzlement to Decision Processes

Cues in how to select a process can also be derived from the puzzlement created by tough decisions. The degree and type of puzzlement in a decision can be used to suggest procedure. Following these cues has benefits similar to those described for decision types. Guidelines are offered to match processes to degrees of puzzlement, identifying additional conditions in which each process can be profitably used. As in matching processes to decision types, the match of a process to an appropriate degree of puzzlement produces benefits, and a mismatch creates problems. Decisions with no puzzlement, such as representational decisions, can be addressed by means of mathematics techniques, such as operations research approaches. A discussion of these decision approaches is beyond the scope of this book.

Indicators of Puzzlement

Puzzlement can be defined by a decision's novelty and procedural clarity, specifiability of the decision, and the stability and homogeneity of the decision environment (Nutt, 1979c). Decisions are classified as having high, moderate, low, or no puzzlement when one uses these factors, as shown in Table 9.2. Guidelines are offered to match processes to appropriate degrees of puzzlement and to illustrate how cost, timeliness, validity, reliability, and acceptance are influenced when each of the three decision processes is used under varying degrees of uncertainty.

Puzzles Due to Novelty and Procedural Obscurity. Important indicators of puzzlement stem from novelty and the clarity of the demands posed by a decision (Perrow, 1967). The term *analyzability* describes the difficulty of information search and the amount of thinking time that is required to decide how to go

Table 9.2. Indicators That Identify the Degree of Puzzlement in a Decision.

Indicators	Degree of Puzzlement			
	None	*Low*	*Moderate*	*High*
Novelty and procedural clarity	Frequent, with known procedures	Infrequent, with known procedures	Frequent, with unknown procedures	Unique, with unknown procedures
Specifiability	Criteria and causality known	Criteria known, cause-and-effect relations unknown	Criteria unknown, cause-and-effect relations known	Both criteria and cause-and-effect relations unknown
Environment	Stable and known demand or use rates	Forecasts for demand and use rates	Forecasts can be made in ranges	Demand or use rates impossible to estimate

about making a decision. The existence of a procedure to make a decision, no matter how complex, defines the "high" end of the continuum. Experience and intuition are used to derive procedure when analyzability is "low." The frequency with which similar types of decisions occur provides another indicator of puzzlement, called *variety* or *variability*. Variability identifies the number of occurrences for a particular kind of decision, which gives an indication of novelty.

When analyzability is low and the decision unique, decision makers have little to guide them in selecting among alternatives. A high degree of puzzlement can be expected. For example, a hospital administrator, attempting to strip privileges from a medical staff member, uses a one-time heuristic search for information. There is no puzzlement when decisions are recurring and clear-cut decision procedures are used, even if sophisticated techniques are applied. A recurring decision may permit the decision maker to "systematize" the decision through programming. Inventory control procedures that establish order points and order amounts for stock items are examples. This suggests that a low degree of puzzlement occurs when decisions are infrequent, but procedures can be found to deal with them. When faced with an expansion decision for the first time, a manager must search for ways to make the choice by consulting peers or the literature; thus procedure is unknown but discoverable. "Moderate" puzzlement is created when decisions are repeatable, making an investment in discovering decision procedures easy to justify. For instance, a strategic manager establishing a new product line must set premises to deal with hiring, marketing, and costing, thereby establishing performance norms and the like. However, the manager can use these premises in future product line decisions.

Specifiability Puzzles. Puzzlement can be identified by the amount of clarity in the criteria to be used and cause-and-effect relationships that appear to be at play (Thompson, 1967). For example, inventory control procedures for supply items have exploited the clarity of criteria (ordering and holding costs) and the ability to specify how the usage rates of supplies vary with sales rates and other factors to apply analysis and optimality tests. This type of decision offers no puzzlement to the decision maker.

When criteria are known but cause-effect relations are not, only satisficing decisions can be made (March and Simon, 1958). For example, compensatory education programs, such as Head Start, can be evaluated by comparing the Head Start participants' reading readiness test scores and the like to those of a comparison group (such as children exposed to a private preschool program) or merely to the performance of non-welfare children. The selection of a norm creates a bit more puzzlement in a decision than does the use of an optimality rule. For example, the choice between "private preschool" and "non-welfare" norms to evaluate a Head Start program will be controversial.

"Instrumentality" tests are used when criteria are unknown but cause-effect relationships are thought to be clear. Quality assessment programs in hospitals often use checklists to ensure that accepted procedures have been followed because desirable outcomes are undefined. The degree of puzzlement is greater than that with a satisficing test because criteria to measure an outcome are unavailable.

"Social" tests are applied when neither criteria nor cause-effect relations are known. For example, some universities mimic other universities thought to have prestige, adding educational programs and student services and adopting tactics for promotion and salary increases used by the high-prestige university. Puzzlement is greater than with an instrumental test because there is no procedural base one can use as a check.

Environment Puzzles. The environment is another factor that can create puzzlement in a decision (Thompson, 1967). Environmental puzzles can be depicted in terms of the demands for products or services. The "stability" of projections or forecasts required to estimate product sales or service usage provides a definition. To make a forecast, one must consider the demands for products or services, the laws or regulations that influence the products or services, and the key benefactors or customers who provide important sources of revenue.

When use or demand, benefactors, and regulations are

heterogeneous and subject to many changes, the environment becomes obscure. For example, state workfare programs in unemployment commissions have both shifting budgets and shifting mandates or objectives, causing decisions in this environment to be bewildering. Conservative governors are apt to call for employment increases and reduced budgets at the same time. More liberal governors may stress training and counseling and increase budgets. As a result, the environment is constantly shifting in a state employment agency as governors come and go. In clear environments, the puzzles evaporate. Decision making is deterministic because environmental attributes are known and can be understood. Well-endowed hospitals that have no competitors in their service area and are located in states that permit cost reimbursement and limit the state's regulatory power over expansion plans have a comparatively clear-cut decision environment. In such an environment, forecasts for demand or use take the form of point estimates. Decisions under certainty result. Forecasts can be made in ranges in moderately puzzling environments, producing decisions under risk. For obscure environments, use or demand rates can be enigmatic. Low forecast precision creates tough decisions.

The Analytical Process for Decisions with Low Puzzlement

The analytical decision process should be applied to decisions that have a low degree of puzzlement (Thompson, 1967). In these decisions, one can make forecasts, identify criteria, and come to know decision procedures. When used to address low degrees of puzzlement, the analytical decision process should be consistent and may be valid. Choices can be made with moderate timeliness and modest decisional cost. Acceptance will be neutral at best because analytical procedures seldom entice buy in by stakeholders. For example, a low degree of puzzlement occurs when utilities can forecast usage for their service area by projecting population growth in that area. If the industrial base is stable and not likely to change, extrapolation can be used to make relatively accurate forecasts. The puzzlement inherent in a decision to increase capacity to meet fore-

casted demand is manageable, and the analytical decision process can be effectively applied.

Applying an analytical process to decisions with moderate to high puzzlement, however, is apt to produce poor results.
The analytical process applied to decisions with substantial
puzzlement creates the aura of certainty when, in fact, the numbers produced are expected values at best and are biased estimates of the midpoint of a range of values at worst. For example,
behavioral modification centers use group decisions by treatment professionals to set reading, dress, and other behavioral
goals according to what they believe is attainable for each men-
tally retarded client. The expected behavior is clear, and various
treatment procedures are attempted until this behavior is obscure. Averages would be misleading and offer little guidance in
treatment selection decisions.

The Group Decision Process for Decisions with Moderate Puzzlement

In decisions with moderate puzzlement, procedures and
criteria must be discovered by applying known aspects of
causality and forecasts that can ecapture expected ranges of
usage or demand. Groups are useful because they provide multiple sources of insight into useful procedures and possible criteria. Such a decision occurs when a firm considers vertical integration through the purchase of key suppliers, such as the
purchase of a company that provides critical raw material. For
example, Eastman Kodak could vertically integrate by purchasing a silver mine, silver being a key component in producing
film emulsion. Eastman Kodak's management would be faced
with assessing each available silver mining company and finding
appropriate criteria to judge the merits of a buyout. A decision
of this type uses groups to manage the obscurity in unknown
aspects of the decision. Using such an approach can result in
modest reliability and cost and in timeliness and is much more
likely to be valid than using another approach. Acceptance can
be high because of the participation inherent in using a group.

Applying groups to low-puzzlement decisions produces
an overkill. As a result, decisions are apt to be costly and lack

timeliness. Reliability may be low if the group refuses to apply analysis or ignores the results of analysis. Acceptance, however, will be enhanced. Applying a group to decisions with a high degree of puzzlement can harm both reliability and validity unless key sources of expertise are included in the group and their views prove to be influential.

The Mixed-Mode Process for Decisions with
a High Degree of Puzzlement

Decisions can become obscure when they are one of a kind, involve unfamiliar procedures with unknown criteria and causal relationships, and must cope with inherently unreliable forecasts. The key concerns in decisions of this type are framing, exploring choice prospects from several vantage points, and managing an arena of interest. For example, charities such as Red Feather or United Way agencies face uncertain futures because they must serve many clients, each with service technologies that must be understood to appreciate the value of the services they offer and the implications of increases or decreases in support levels. Their level of support depends on projections of "giving," most of which is coerced from employees by the CEOs of large firms in a community. If the CEOs of local firms refuse to be coopted by participating in the coalition as fundraisers or give only token support, the level of giving can drop precipitately. Under this condition the Red Feather or United Way agencies are understandably reluctant to make long-term commitments. Coalition building and coalition maintenance involving key community leaders are crucial to the agencies' success. Whatever rates of giving local firms agree to, which can shift from year to year, stipulate budget and funding. Allocation decisions depend on agreements that are struck annually and are always subject to shifts due to local and/or national economic conditions and other factors. As a result, the funding decision for a given recipient, such as a suicide prevention center, is highly uncertain. With good coalition management, decisions of this type can be relatively timely and inexpensive and produce acceptance, but they are unlikely to be consistent.

Validity, defining a "correct" allocation, has no meaning to the decision makers because the needs of the recipient are often poorly understood, which makes priorities difficult to establish.

Applying analysis to decisions riddled with puzzlement can produce disastrous results. The loss of acceptance in using analysis makes coalition management difficult, leading to a loss of support. In the Red Feather example, funding through coercion arrangements may collapse or lose its grip, leading to lower agency budgets. Groups, made up of funding users, would improve the premises used to make allocations but would fail at fund-raising because they could not manage the crucial aspect of the fund-raising process: coercion.

Key Points

1. Most organizations face each of the types of decisions with varying degrees of puzzlement. Decision makers with a repertoire of decision processes, skills or staff support to apply them, and guidelines to match decisional tactics to decision types and degrees of puzzlement can improve their decision making practices. When a decision process fits a decision amenable to its procedures, a favorable effect on cost, timeliness, risk of omission, flexibility, acceptance, consistency, and validity should result.
2. The mixed-mode decision process is best for search decisions that are very puzzling and involve stakeholders with unknown interests. Wider use of the mixed-mode procedure under these conditions should improve both acceptance and consistency through coalition management.
3. The group decision process is recommended for information-rich decisions, moderately puzzling decisions, and decisions involving multiple stakeholders with known interests. When properly managed, groups can be timely, inexpensive, and flexible and can promote acceptance. Reliability, although difficult to achieve in a group setting, may be enhanced when the decision group sponsors analysis that uses a deductive tactic, such as a decision tree. The performance of decision groups should improve when the

decision group reconciles evaluation information generated by the analyses that it initiates.

4. The analytical decision process is recommended for empirical decisions, decisions with a low degree of puzzlement,
and decisions in which there is a single dominant decision
maker. Analytical processes stress deduction and help the
decision maker identify and organize the activities needed
in making tough choices.

 Part Four

Key Steps in Decision Making

Part Four offers the details managers need to carry out each of the three decision-making processes. Chapter Ten describes how to use groups for decision-making purposes. Chapter Eleven confronts the paradox of problems, offering ways to uncover and explore problems in an attempt to discover core concerns. Chapter Twelve describes ways to introduce multiple perspectives. Basic analytical procedures are introduced in Chapter Thirteen. Finally, in Chapter Fourteen, steps are offered to learn about missed opportunities.

10

Using Groups
for Decision Making

This chapter describes how groups are used to make decisions. Chapter Ten provides guidelines to aid managers in the organization, management, and control of groups used to develop ideas, exchange information, influence stakeholders, and make judgments for decision making. This step versus a function matrix is used to organize the group literature in a unique way. Chapter Ten covers material related to group formation, leadership, and control, offering ways to improve the performance of groups in each area. The chapter describes tactics that managers can use in an attempt to draw out the beneficial attributes of groups and to overcome some of their drawbacks. (Chapter Fifteen describes how groups can be managed by applying group process and how to select among process types for specific tasks.)

Formal Groups

Groups have been used throughout human history for decision making. The rationalization for them has moved from folklore to a widely accepted management tactic with the advent of the "human relations" (HR) approach to management theory. HR theory stems from research by Mayo (1933) and his associates, who found that positive group sentiments lead to impressive improvements in attitude and productivity. Using these findings, human relations advocates have proposed groups for a variety of purposes, including information exchange, influencing others, ideation or discovery, and judging. In each case, the use of groups assumes that people are motivated by fulfilling social and psychological needs and that participation is an ideal vehicle to use in managing these needs. Today formal groups, identified as committees, directorates, and task forces, are widely used in organizations hoping to evoke acceptance through participation. Such acceptance by members, which stems from group action, is called *cooptation*.

Problem with Groups

Managers spend much of their time in groups. Mintzberg (1973) found that a typical chief executive officer attends an average of eight meetings in a single day. Middle-level managers spend as much as 80 percent of their time in some form of grouplike conversation (Burns, 1984). In spite of their frequent use, groups and meetings are often regarded with dislike, if not outright contempt. Managers see groups as taking too much of their time, producing conformity, and being used by people to evade taking responsibility for action.

Groups can create many problems for managers. Decision groups can be costly, cantankerous, hard to dismantle, unpredictable, and difficult to control (Nutt, 1976c). Political considerations often dictate who must serve. Problems arise when the interests of a constituency represented in the group are threatened. Warring factions may disagree on a policy and delay important strategic choices until their interests are protected. For example, when decisions that seem to be in the best interest of a hospital threaten the members of the medical staff, key physicians often become obstructive (Nutt, 1979a). Problems often stem from managers who use groups inappropriately, negating their benefits and reinforcing their negative image. This chapter offers ways to overcome these problems and improve the performance of groups that are assigned decision-making tasks.

The Benefits of Groups

Decision groups are formed by managers who desire or see the necessity of collective action. Managers use groups to promote a mutuality of interest, prompting some members to buy into a decision and others to defer when the members acting as individuals would likely disagree. Extensive literature compares the performance of a group to the performance of its members acting individually. Groups invariably outperform individuals (Herbert and Yost, 1979). In particular, a group does the following things:

- Provides a summation of the contributions of individual members
- Rejects erroneous information, ideas, and suggestions by permitting the best-informed and most confident members to sway others
- Heightens the interest of group members in the task
- Creates a large pool of information
- Innovates, creating ideas that would not be thought of by members acting alone
- Improves the quality of results

Groups can be used for recurring or transformational decisions (Mohrman, 1979). Recurring decision groups are a part of the decision structure of an organization that makes judgments but is not permitted to raise new questions. Transformational decision groups are permitted to raise new issues. The latter groups can question premises and change the direction of a query. Such decision groups are more likely to stimulate trust in the organization and favorable intragroup relations.

Types of Participation

The scope of stakeholder involvement and the extent of delegation influence the degree to which a group's decision will be accepted by affected parties. Four types of participation have been defined according to the scope and extent of delegation (Nutt, 1986d). Fully representative groups involve all individuals affected by a decision. If such a group is delegated the authority to make a decision, "comprehensive" participation results. "Complete" participation stems from fully representative groups that have an advisory role, making recommendations or offering commentaries on a proposed action. This type of group can offer ideas but cannot set direction. Complete participation has been found to be less effective than comprehensive participation because the authority of the group is restricted. "Delegated" participation involves some of the key stakeholders and delegates the decision to this group. Buy in is typically limited to those directly involved. Delegated participation produces less buy in than complete participation because group members must persuade nonparticipants. As the scope of participation declines, as measured by the proportion of interested parties who participate in the group, so does acceptance of the decision. "Token" participation uses stakeholder representatives in an advisory role. Decision acceptance has been found to be hampered by the use of both representatives and role, making token participation the least effective form of participation.

What Groups Do

In group decision making, the group members attempt to agree on the meaning of evaluation information. When a properly formulated group comes to a decision, it is thought to be objective (Mason and Mitroff, 1973). Decision making becomes a learning process in a decision group. Individuals contribute their experiences (implicit valuations) and knowledge (explicit valuations), which the group attempts to apply to the decision task. For example, performance appraisals are often reviewed by a panel of supervisors who share their experiences with the subordinates, comparing their views of subordinates with similar performance ratings. Similarly, when a tissue committee in a hospital examines claims of unnecessary surgery, data are accumulated from several sources, including the findings in pathology reports and opinions about the surgeon's motives. Both quantitative and qualitative information are routinely provided in such reviews. A decision group can also commission special studies to explore particular aspects of a decision, such as requesting an in-depth evaluation of a particular subordinate or department.

Groups qualify, shape, and tune the evaluation information to fit their perceptions. Inconsistent information is pruned. Forecasts of qualitative information, such as the sentiments of key reference groups, are combined with quantitative information. The views of persuasive members often dictate what information is used and how it is combined to make a final judgment. A synthesis of this information can provide important new perspectives (Mason, 1969), and participation in a decision group promotes decision acceptance (Hall, 1972).

Decision-making groups are often the best way to secure accurate decisions when multiple sources of information are needed and acceptable decisions when powerful people are involved. For these reasons, group decision making is widely used in organizations.

Key Activities of Decision Groups

Formal groups, serving as temporary or permanent parts of an organization's structure, have been studied carrying out four key activities or functions: discovering, evaluating or judging, influencing, and exchanging information. All four functions have important roles in decision making. For instance, a group can be asked to come up with a new option (discovery), assess it (evaluation), point out locations of resistance (information exchange), and alter member views (influence). In other instances, a group may be used only to evaluate alternatives or exchange ideas. Research in group literature will be described in terms of each of these functions.

Discovering functions include the following:

1. Identifying new criteria and suggesting norms to compare alternatives
2. Laying out features of an alternative to identify useful attributes
3. Identifying attributes that make up criteria
4. Developing contingency plans to sway future decisions

Evaluating and judging functions include the following:

1. Accepting or rejecting an alternative
2. Determining the degree to which an alternative meets a criterion
3. Comparing alternatives using several criteria
4. Providing priorities or identifying high-ranking (feasible) alternatives

Groups' influencing functions include the following:

1. Laying out the needs of the proponents of an alternative
2. Pointing out the consequences of a pending decision, such as who is disadvantaged
3. Identifying the prospect of and problems with an appeal

Finally, groups may exchange information in the following ways:

1. Offering rationales
2. Using comparable decisions as a baseline
3. Anticipating demands from others if an alternative is selected

Development occurs, for instance, when a group is used to lay out the features of a new service, such as open-heart surgery in a hospital. Development can also occur when a group devises a decision plan. For instance, a strategic planning committee can provide decision premises that aid in evaluating the need for open-heart surgery in the hospital. These premises can be quantitative, such as standards for usage and cost, or qualitative, such as concerns about the reactions of community professionals, government regulators, and consumers. An organization can use groups to evaluate various proposals for open-heart surgery and other activities by applying criteria or comparing the proposals to similar activities internal and external to the organization. Influence attempts often occur during a decision process and may provide valuable information, such as consequences of a negative decision or internal problems that prompted protagonists to propose the open-heart program.

Exchanges of information will occur throughout a decision process.

Groups are used most often in organizations to exchange information and to sell ideas (Filley, House, and Kerr, 1976). In hospitals, decision groups are used for such tasks as utilization review, selecting and reviewing treatment, and reviewing postoperative tissue. In firms, decision groups are often called on to choose among capital plans, evaluate subordinates for wage increases, review performance data, resolve complaints and grievances in personnel departments, and serve as sounding boards for emergent ideas. Developmental groups are used less frequently but have a major role in strategic and project planning.

Rules for Group Management

Formation, cohesion, process, and control are essential phases in the establishment and management of effective decision groups. To provide guides in the management of groups for decision making, questions of power, influence, and the like are considered as they apply to the various functions of decision groups, such as information exchange, as shown in Figure 10.1. Each "phase-function" cell in Figure 10.1 is discussed to describe how to manage a group charged with carrying out a particular function, such as discovering. Pertinent research findings are synthesized to suggest tactics that can be used to initiate and manage groups effectively.

Group Formation

Research pertaining to group formation concerns how membership selection and size influence the effectiveness of a decision group.

Membership. Group members can be selected by appointment, by past and present group members and third parties, by volunteers, and by contract. Appointment by a third party usually involves delegation to some outside organization, such as permitting a bank to place its representative on a firm's board of directors. In some instances, membership guidelines take the form of a contract in which the group's organizer agrees to certain constraints in the selection of members. Also, suggestions for members often come from current or past members and those merely expressing an interest.

Membership is accepted for several reasons (Filley, House, and Kerr, 1976). Members can view the group as either a means or an end, where they can fulfill social or task needs, as shown in Figure 10.2. When the group serves as a means to achieve social needs, membership is accepted for *status* reasons. Participation can be socially satisfying, and some people accept membership with that end in mind. *Task*-oriented members seek control by manipulating the group's processes or by dictating choices. Mixing people with these diverse motivations creates tension in the group. In particular, those with task and social needs may clash because some members seek a pleasant atmosphere while other members must, on occasion, be contentious to achieve

Figure 10.1. The Phase-Function Classification of Groups.

	Discovering	Evaluating or Judging	Influencing	Exchanging Information
Formation				
Membership				
Size				
Cohesion				
Leadership				
Interpersonal relations				
Authority				
Power				
Aspirations				
Rules				
Roles				
Process (Chapter Fifteen)				
Survey				
Interacting				
Brainstorming				
Nominal				
Delphi				
Kiva				
Nominal-interactive				
Control				
Rewards, penalties				
Arrangement				

Figure 10.2. Group Members' Attitudes Toward Decision Groups.

Need to Be Fulfilled

		Social	Task
	Means	Status	Control
Use of Group			
	Ends	Participation	Action

Source: Adapted from Filley, House, and Kerr, 1976.

their goals. Means-ends clashes are signaled by members who stress procedural matters when other members are seeking action on important issues. Decision group members who seek prestige are careful not to antagonize others and thus risk losing their status (Bales, 1951). Such members contribute little to the process and therefore have little influence on the outcome.

Consortia and Buy In. Decision making often relies heavily on intragroup bargaining, which, properly managed, entices participants to buy in to the group's decision. To enhance the prospects of buy in, representatives of important organizations are permitted to make decisions for the group's sponsor. In theory, participation enhances the chance that a decision will be accepted and gives the sponsor some degree of control over the process through agenda setting. A consortium is a quasi-temporary body that is independent of its sponsor. Hospital-shared service corporations, kidney disease foundations, police review boards, and advisory boards for joint ventures by firms are examples.

Consortia are formed when a sponsor asks key stake-holders, such as leaders in a community, to select representatives for a controlling body. The term *cooptation* is often used to describe the process that promotes buy in. Cooptation in a consortium stems from absorbing people the sponsor hopes to influence into a policy-making group (Thompson, 1967). Cooptation makes acceptance more likely because of participation (Filley, House, and Kerr, 1976), wards off threats from potential adversaries (Thompson, 1967), and gathers support through legitimization of the decision process (Delbecq, Van de Ven, and Gustafson, 1986). For instance, the participation of organizations affected by the decision often enhances the prospects of decision acceptance.

Consortia are used because they provide needed information or represent centers of power that must be managed. Consortia are similar to "venture management" project teams used by defense contractors and firms to stimulate innovation (Galbraith, 1971). A team of experts, drawn from inside or outside the organization, is assembled to develop an idea or to select a course of action. The consortium is used when cooperation among several organizations or interests is needed. For instance, decisions made by a state kidney foundation cut across many organizational and disciplinary boundaries that have somewhat overlapping charters or mandates. Kidney foundation members are drawn from organizations that have (1) the resources that are needed (for example, tissue-typing laboratories), (2) leadership required to implement the decision (for example, nephrology professional societies), and (3) the mandate to deliver the services to be expanded (for instance, university hospitals). A consortium attempts to marshal the resources, leadership, and mandates of these organizations by offering representatives a chance to participate in decision making. Involvement is believed to enhance the quality and acceptance of the group's decisions. Experts from cooperating organizations are expected to bring fresh perspectives and new ideas to the decision process (Delbecq and Van de Ven, 1971).

In practice, such groups can be difficult to manage, making their benefits elusive. Organizations represented in a consortium often have conflicting objectives. Some consortium members may find that attending to these objectives keeps them from disclosing information useful in the decision process (Maier, 1970). Other members of the consortium may seek personal goals, such as prestige, while still others may seek advocacy of a personal viewpoint or the interests of a professional group (Collins and Guetzkow, 1964). As a result, some members actively support innovative ideas and others embrace a more traditional point of view (Utterback, 1971).

Studies show that consortia representing several organizations produced no more "new ideas" than conventional groups, but their ideas had significantly higher quality and were more acceptable than those of conventional groups (Nutt, 1979a). Thus, a consortium that represents several organizations or viewpoints seems likely to improve the developmental efforts of a group. This conclusion is particularly relevant for service organizations because of the multitude of jurisdictions, mandates, and disciplines they must consider in making decisions.

The cooptative benefits attributed to consortium decision groups are more difficult to secure. Member conflicts, rather than positive reinforcement by peers from another organization, are often prevalent. Conflict is likely when a decision group's members have status differentials, unique frames of reference, different views, or dissimilar objectives and beliefs (Collins and Guetzkow, 1964). Conflict among group members eliminates "participation effects" and leads to lower acceptance.

Cooptation can be effective when new members are solicited one at a time. Introducing a new member to a core group whose members are committed to the sponsor's point of view may subtly pressure the new member to conform to the standards, goals, and expectations of the sponsor. Thus, cooptation may occur only when a group gradually builds its power and influence with its members.

Comparisons of the merits of plans developed by consumer and provider groups offer important guidelines in the selection of consortium group members. User, client, or consumer group members were found to be much less effective than expert group members grappling with the same problem in a developmental task (Nutt, 1976c). This finding challenges the contention that users are in the best position to understand their own needs (Delbecq and Van de Ven, 1971; Parker, 1970). "Activist" consumer types were found to be innovative, but they created considerable friction when they participated in a decision-making process. Consumers who were direct service users were found to offer little to a decision group.

The participation of users, clients, or consumers in decision-making activities has little influence on the process (Nutt, 1976c). Consumers had no effect on the criteria or criteria weights applied in the process and thus had no impact on the judgments that were made. Experts systematically influenced the consumer members until they made decisions that were indistinguishable from the experts'. In summary, the effectiveness of group decision making can be improved by carefully reviewing membership criteria, using homogeneous groups whenever possible, limiting the use of cooptation as the dominant reason for forming a group, and having expert and consumer groups carry out separate evaluations.

Size. Small groups are best for evaluation and judging tasks. Generally, five is the preferred size. A small group encourages equal participation, which is important in making judgments and assessments. Similarly, influence attempts are harder in large groups because those being influenced must be gradually coaxed to go along, a process that cannot be rushed. Large groups are best for developmental tasks because innovation is an individual matter and benefits from exchanges of ideas that stem from many different viewpoints. Information exchange is limited by communication opportunities, so group structure rather than size inhibits information flow.

Four-person groups solve more problems than two-person groups, and groups of thirteen are superior to groups of six to eight members in solving problems (Faust, 1959). Solution quality increases with group size (Cummings, Huber, and Arndt, 1974). Both the amount of discussion and the quality of discussion among group members are important determinants of whether a group will provide a quality solution (Holloman and Hendrich, 1972).

Judgment, in contrast to problem solving, takes longer in large groups because of the additional time needed for compromises (Hinton and Reitz, 1971). Large groups require more person hours than do small groups. Small-group productivity is better for dealing with concrete problems, and large groups are better for abstract problems (Thibaut and Kelley, 1959). For instance, studies of subcommittees of the United States Senate have found that the mean size of action-taking committees is five, compared to nonaction committees, which had an average size of fourteen.

Member participation and reaction to the decision process are also related to size. As group size increases, so does tension, but the number of suggestions per member and the prospect of agreement falls (Hare, Bogatala, and Bales, 1955). Comparing the least and most active members, the least active member's participation declines rapidly as the group's size goes from three to ten members (Bales, 1951).

Elaborate patterns of interpersonal relationships are needed in large groups. Further, more information is lost in large groups because some group members are unable to assimilate it. Lost information causes errors and decisions that seem ill-advised to the better informed. Sensitivity to other points of view decreases as group size increases (Collins and Guetzkow, 1964). Delbecq (1968) finds that this is due to time constraint and to the "fact that in larger groups careful attention to many viewpoints calls for considerable computational ability, great psychological concentration, and empathy—in each case to a degree beyond the capacities of most individuals." As groups increase in size, a few high-status members tend to have more influence over group activities (Stogdill, 1969).

As group size increases, factions also tend to increase. In large groups, subgroups are inevitable. Typically, factions are undesirable. These subgroups formulate their own goals and have their own leaders, leading to a decrease in group participation (Filley, House, and Kerr, 1976). Factions form in an effort to change an opinion of the group before it reaches a decision. Factions usually stem from intragroup conflict and are generally temporary.

There is a greater tendency for groups of twelve to form factions than for groups of five to do so (Hare, 1962). As groups increased from three members to twenty members, an increase in cliques was observed. Larger groups with more factions experienced a decrease in group cohesiveness. Eight people are ideal for close associations to form. As group size increases beyond this limit, the chance for factions increases.

In summary, judging or assessing groups should be small. A small group introduces a wide range of options, eliminates inconsistency in judgments, and ferrets out inferior proposals better than a large group does. This finding creates problems for many organizations because committees with thirty or more members are common. For instance, boards of directors and trustees, long-range planning committees, and project planning groups often have a large membership. Small subcommittees to carry out review for decisions should be considered for such groups. In development, larger groups are desirable if their activities can be managed.

Cohesion in the Decision Group

The cohesion phase considers issues that must be managed to fuse members of the group into a viable decision body. Issues such as leadership, interpersonal relations, authority, power, aspirations, and rules of operation must be considered in this process.

Leadership. Leadership can be defined as the tactics used to exert control over a group (Filley, House, and Kerr, 1976). Studies of leadership have considered leader role in terms of the style of leadership used, the roles that a leader and the group can play, and the extent to which a decision group member can adopt multiple roles. A "socioemotional" leadership style provides social rewards, such as recognition, which create strong intragroup ties (Collins and Guetzkow, 1964). This style of leadership is best for decisions that stress acceptance. "Task" leaders provide more information in the decision-making process but create tension. Task leaders are best when a decision must be defended with a logical argument.

Stogdill and his colleagues (Stogdill and Coons, 1975), in their leadership studies, distinguish between leaders who offer "consideration" and leaders who offer "initiating structure." Consideration measures the leader's rapport with the group and the quality of the working relationship. Considerate leaders are willing to accept new ideas, show respect for the members of the group, and the like. Initiating structure details the specificity of work assignments, deadlines, work evaluations, and committee procedures designed to help deal with the group's task. Studies show that consideration and initiating structure are somewhat incompatible. A leader may have to stress one or the other (Fleishman, 1975; Halpin, 1954). Figure 10.3 lists some of the attributes of consideration and initiating structure.

Leadership in a group stems from the leader's skill in controlling the group and offering good ideas (Schlisinger, Jackson, and Butman, 1960). If the leader's control is not satisfactory, members will attempt to influence one another. Leadership has little to do with the leader's popularity. Groups often support a "take charge" chairman (Collins and Guetzkow, 1964).

Should the leader of a decision group offer both social support and structure? Considerable research has considered this question in the past two decades and tends to suggest that combined roles are desirable but hard to achieve. Typical of the prescriptions that have emerged is the Blake and Mouton (1964) "managerial grid," in which combinations of concern for production and concern for people are used to define styles that emphasize people, production, or some of both. An adaptation of the grid is shown in Figure 10.4. A type A approach to leadership is the opposite of a type E. A type A leader exerts minimal effort. The type E combines high amounts of task and people concerns, which often poses conflicting demands on the leader. Type B and type D leaders are also opposites. A type B style is dictated by task demands, and a type D by people demands. The type C style is a compromise leadership style that balances the demands of the task with the needs of people.

These styles have not been clearly tied to productivity. However, the Ohio State University studies led by Stogdill have found that leaders inherently high on both consideration and structure tended to be more effective leaders. Structure eliminates ambiguities in the group's task, facilitates discussion, and reduces stress, all desirable features (Filley, House, and Kerr, 1976). Acceptance of the decision is influenced by consideration.

Figure 10.3. Leadership Behavior When Consideration and
Initiating Structure Are Used as a Leadership Tactic.

The System of Categories Used in Observation
and Their Major Relations

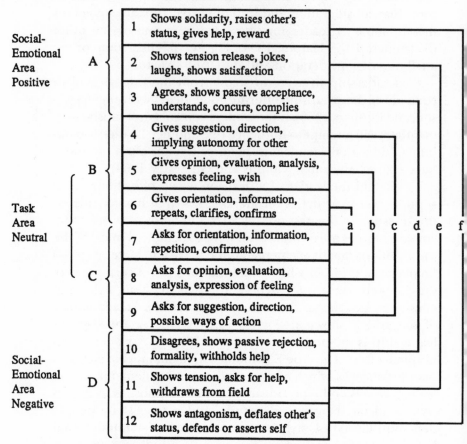

Social-
Emotional
Area
Positive

A

1 Shows solidarity, raises other's status, gives help, reward

2 Shows tension release, jokes, laughs, shows satisfaction

3 Agrees, shows passive acceptance, understands, concurs, complies

B

4 Gives suggestion, direction, implying autonomy for other

5 Gives opinion, evaluation, analysis, expresses feeling, wish

6 Gives orientation, information, repeats, clarifies, confirms

Task
Area
Neutral

C

7 Asks for orientation, information, repetition, confirmation

8 Asks for opinion, evaluation, analysis, expression of feeling

9 Asks for suggestion, direction, possible ways of action

Social-
Emotional
Area
Negative

D

10 Disagrees, shows passive rejection, formality, withholds help

11 Shows tension, asks for help, withdraws from field

12 Shows antagonism, deflates other's status, defends or asserts self

a   b   c   d   e   f

Key: A. Positive reactions   a. Problems of communication
      B. Attempted answers   b. Problems of evaluation
      C. Questions   c. Problems of control
      D. Negative reactions   d. Problems of decision
                                   e. Problems of tension reduction
                                   f. Problems of reintegration

Source: Bales, 1951.

Figure 10.4. Leadership Styles.

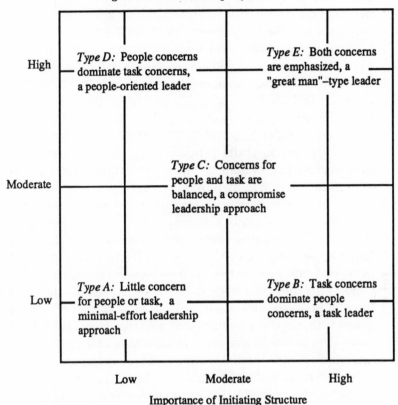

Source: Nutt, 1984b.

Intragroup relations can be cooperative or competitive. In studies that provide an incentive to adopt one of these postures and where the group behavior has been inferred, a cooperative posture is best. Cooperation is linked to members' liking one another, their involvement in the group, and their satisfaction (Deutsch, 1962).

Leader Selection. The leader of a group can be allowed to emerge or may be designated by someone in power (Delbecq, 1967). The emergent tactic is often avoided because power figures believe that they can (and should) select leadership for a group. Selecting a leader usually involves examining candidates' personal characteristics. Trait, behavioral, and contingency approaches have been proposed to identify potentially effective leaders (Filley, House, and Kerr, 1976). A trait is a distinctive physical or psychological characteristic of an individual. Traits can be intellectual, social, and emotional. Leader selection by traits is difficult because traits are never measured directly (Ghiselli, 1971). Traits can be merely an observer's conceptualizations, which may not be shared by others. For instance, people's physical traits (appearance) can be perceived as positive, negative, or neutral. Similarly, people often differ when identifying people thought to have charisma.

New developments in trait theory suggest some interesting links between traits and managerial success. Bennis, in a study of chief executive officers, found that leaders with competence, respect, *and* ego were far more effective than leaders who possessed only one or two of these factors (Bennis and Nanus, 1985). This study sets aside the widespread homily that leaders must contain or hide their ego. One's everyday observations confirm that ego is an important, perhaps even indispensable, ingredient in leadership. Bennis contends that ego is essential but must be augmented by respect and competence if a leader is to be effective. Leaders who lacked either respect or competence were found to be ineffective, but so were leaders who lacked ego. Big jobs call for leaders who have big egos, but big-ego leaders were ineffective unless they had equal amounts of competence and respect. A balance of ego, competence, and respect, for given leadership tasks, is one emerging prescription for leadership.

Quinn (1988) offers another trait-related description of leadership, called "competing values." In this framework (shown in Figure 10.5), the consideration-task tension (shown as the human relations and rational goal values in the Quinn formulation) is augmented by a "continuity" and "change" tension.

Instead of the two competing styles identified by Blake and Mouton (1964), Quinn offers four styles of leadership: human commitment, preservation, growth, and productivity. Quinn contends that leaders favor one or more of these styles,

Figure 10.5. Competing Values Framework.

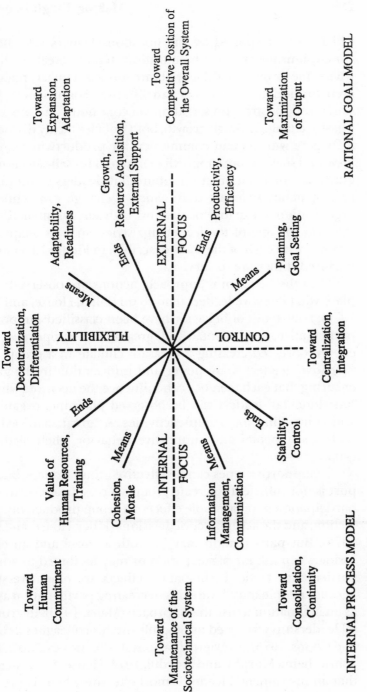

HUMAN RELATIONS MODEL

OPEN SYSTEMS MODEL

RATIONAL GOAL MODEL

INTERNAL PROCESS MODEL

Source: Quinn, 1988.

which can be spotted by the questions leaders ask and the conclusions they reach. Organizations tend to create a climate where one or more of these traits are rendered unacceptable, or even forbidden, and others can flourish. For instance, some organizations stress preservation via continuity, and others emphasize change through growth; both policies tacitly discourage managers with human commitment or productivity values to leave and seek a more supportive climate. This self-selection can gradually shape an organization until its leaders begin to have homogeneous styles or traits. Such a change can render an organization incapable of dealing with environmental shifts that call for one of the leadership styles, such as adaptation. Leaders with each of the traits described in Figure 10.5 must be nurtured if they are to survive.

In the behavioral approach, actions are observed to explain what effective leaders tend to do (Filley, House, and Kerr, 1976). Four types of behavior have been classified: supportive, participative, instrumental, and "great man." "Supportive" leaders are observed creating a pleasant climate in a group. "Participative" leaders share power and information in the group, ensuring that each member can influence the decision, whereas "instrumental" leaders can be observed planning, organizing, and controlling the group's activities. A "great man" exhibits both instrumental and supportive behavior when leading a group.

Supportive types can be effective group leaders, but support is not sufficient to create group success. Leaders stressing participation have favorable effects on group productivity, satisfaction, and the acceptance of decisions (Filley, House, and Kerr, 1976). But participation may be both a cause and an effect: Leaders can ask for participation or may be forced to adopt a participative tactic. Participation effects are often overstated because people must have skills in creating participation as well as an inclination to use this approach (Maier, 1970). Instrumental leadership was tested by Stogdill and his colleagues (Stogdill and Coons, 1975). A review of various studies (for example, Kerr, Schriesheim, Murphy, and Stogdill, 1974; House, 1974) suggests that an instrumental leader is most effective when (1) pressure for an answer is high, (2) members of the group need to share information to make a decision, (3) group members expect help in defining the task, (4) the task is poorly structured, and (5) members feel threats from outside the group.

"Great man" studies have linked instrumental and supportive behavior with success, finding that they are negatively correlated (Kerr, Schriesheim, Murphy, and Stogdill, 1974). Group leaders have a difficult time offering ways to solve problems while being supportive of the psychological needs of each member.

No single leadership style is universally effective (Schriesheim, Tolliver, and Behling, 1980). The relationship of leader behavior with group performance and member satisfaction changes with each situation. Not even leaders high in both consideration and initiating structure always produce the best result. This conclusion led researchers to the situational approach to leader selection, in which situational factors are matched to an ideal leader behavior for that situation. Fiedler (1965) devised one of the first contingency models. Consideration-oriented leaders are proposed for routine planning problems and the task-oriented leader, who offers an initiating structure, for ill-structured problems that are vague and only partially defined. Changing leaders (or styles) as the group moves from discovering to assessing and judging, influencing, and exchanging information may be warranted. Leaders may use up their "social credit" with a group in steering it through one of these phases. At this point, the leader may not be able to function effectively in drawing out group members. Also the task (initiating structure) leader approach seems best for discovering and exchanging information, and the consideration (socioemotional) style seems best for the other functions of group decision making (judging and influencing).

Power and Influence in a Group. Power and influence are crucial elements of a decision group. Power can be defined as the *right* to make a decision, whereas influence is the capacity to make a decision without applying formal sanctions (Filley, House, and Kerr, 1976). Groups may be powerful because they can apply sanctions but more often because their judgment bears the mark of legitimacy. It often takes considerable effort to reverse decisions stemming from a group that lacks sanctions. Thus, influence can be present even when power is not. For example, a board of directors may have the right to make decisions but lack the capacity to make changes in operations. This power is vested in CEOs and stems from their right to act within a prescribed arena. For example, H. Ross Perot's failure to get General Motors to drop executive bonuses as management was closing plants led to his departure from GM's board. From his position as a board member, Perot was unable to implement any of his ideas to humanize GM.

A power base can be expanded by the adoption of one of several tactics (Filley and Grimes, 1967). A group can extend the bureaucratic definitions of power by initiating investigations, making requests, making veiled threats, stating strong preferences or opinions, announcing a decision in advance and asking for support, and vigorously defending a preferred course of action.

When a group believes that an ideal course of action has been discovered, an *investigation* is likely to verify this view, so the group is wise to advocate this tactic. If those to be influenced lack expertise, this tactic often works. Groups can sway their sponsor with this approach. *Request* is used when the group has less power than the target of an influence attempt. Success depends on the predisposition of those being approached. For instance, an executive low in prestige is more likely to be influenced by veiled threats from a committee. *Threats* can work when compliance by the target of the influence attempt can avert a rebuke or when the target has less power than the influencing group. For instance, coequal groups can take public positions on project decisions, hoping to create a debate. The board of a utility company uses this tactic when it anticipates that state regulatory groups will disagree with its decision to hike rates, terminate service to certain types of nonpayers, or expand the company's capacity to generate power. Announcing a decision and vigorously defending it work best when the parties are independent, such as the utility company and the regulatory agency, or have comparable influence.

In summary, group influence may exist even when power and authority do not. By carefully structuring a group's base of power and by selecting appropriate tactics, a group can make its influence a viable substitute for power.

Managing Power and Influence. Power and influence often stem from subordinate-superior or peer relationships that have emerged between group members. Group members draw on the influence that has taken shape in these relationships when serving together in a group. Various tactics can be used by people in organizations to increase their influence, which often leads to a growth in their personal power. One set of tactics is based on reducing the influence of peers or supervisors, and the other set is based on increasing peer and subordinate influence.

Influence reduction tactics are based on reducing status, defining jobs, maintaining formal relationships, and promoting liking. A superior's status is reduced as pay, prerogatives for individual discretion, such as the use of personal time, and access to various types of recognitions and rewards become similar to a subordinate's. Another tactic calls for defining a superior's job. Job descriptions and the like are more constraining than liberating, providing a vehicle for a subordinate to raise questions about the legitimacy of supervisor actions. Similarly, licensure can be constraining because licensing implicitly precludes nonlicensed acts. For example, nurses found their jobs more tightly defined after the lobbying of state legislatures by their professional organizations during the past decade to produce licensing. Both physicians and administrators used the do's of nursing to limit their upward mobility and job discretion. Finally, interpersonal tactics can be used to reduce power. Subordinates who promote liking by peers and superiors while remaining detached, keeping relationships formal, can use liking as a source of influence. For example, superiors who frequently invite subordinates to their homes can be exploited by power-hungry subordinates who use such occasions for self-promotion by ascribing more significance to the invitations than the superiors intended. Some subordinates seek out invitations of various kinds merely to exploit them.

Another set of tactics focuses on increasing the power of

subordinates relative to supervisors and peers. *Influence enhancing* tactics include increasing status, controlling key resources, ensuring social support, increasing mobility, creating dependencies, and associating with the powerful. Status-enhancement tactics for subordinates stem from symbols they acquire and norms that these symbols imply. For example, elective positions in professional organizations give staff members special legitimacy that may result in leverage over their superiors because the positions imply the subordinates have competence the superior lacks. Other tactics include increasing the subordinate's pay, perceived job skills, or recognition relative to the supervisor. Controlling resources that people need is an effective way to equalize power between subordinate and superior or among peers. Subordinates can gain control over information, procedures, or interpersonal networks that a superior needs. Information can be controlled by both sharing and restriction. The authority to manage information, such as delaying cost analysis or claiming that computers cannot produce informational breakdowns that are needed, is often an important source of power in organizations. The threat to disseminate sensitive information, such as pay levels in a group, provides the information holder with an important source of power. Many organizations have "witch doctors," people who are effective at using means that are guarded or unknown. Power can be promoted by refusal (or failure) to train a potential replacement and by the parceling out of good advice when it is needed. Accountants in the health care industry play the role of witch doctor because their advice is thought to be essential. Others, such as industrial engineers, lose some of this leverage because their advice is not sought by administrators. Control over social support can be a source of power. When subordinates become skilled in getting peers to share their views and in creating special ties to perceived experts, they acquire leverage. With these carefully cultivated connections, such subordinates can ferment opposition among others and can imply that this influence will be used, undermining a supervisor who needs support to act and make change. Subordinates who have mobility, such as many job opportunities inside or outside an organization, can use the implicit or explicit threat to leave to undercut a superior's power (March and Simon, 1958). Subordinates who create dependencies enhance their influence. For example, a manager or consultant who acts as a gatekeeper, deflecting certain types of inquiries from subordinates, and makes decisions a supervisor avoids will acquire power. CEOs who spend most of their time on new ideas may allow their chief operating officers to make all important decisions on internal management. Some consultants and managers are often good listeners with these purposes in mind. Finally, subordinates who associate with the powerful can create an aura of power for themselves. Subordinates often create opportunities to mix with key people to build a personal power base. For example, a subordinate may do menial tasks, such as routinely delivering an analysis to an executive, in order to frequently meet the executive in the hope that these contacts will lead to a relationship that can be exploited.

Goal Specificity. Goals in a group can be implicitly or explicitly formulated. Nadler (1970) believes that all groups should carefully review their purpose and select a realm of action. Others believe that making goals explicit merely leads to exploitation (for example, Lindblom, 1965). Goal displacement, such as the replacement of ends with means, often occurs in groups (Kerr, 1975). For example, a group may select procedures to guide it, believing that an explicit process replaces the need to have a formal goal (Etzioni, 1964). Goals are also kept vague to avoid responsibility or to duck contentious issues. Goals are valuable because they link group members into an overall web of responsibility.

Clear goals have been found to improve group productivity and encourage cooperative efforts (Drucker, 1964). Many empirical studies verify these views (Locke, 1968). Nevertheless, overquantification also has dysfunctional features. Cyert and March (1963) claim that group members can be induced to adopt a goal but that adoption often has a price. Some members will embrace the goals, while others will adopt them for the sake of appearance. Conflicting views may be submerged only to percolate to the surface in some future group activity.

Decision Rules. Several studies have considered groups'

voting rules. Majority rule is more effective than veto (one person can block) and consensus (all must agree) when groups make judgments (Burnberg, Pondy, and Davis, 1970).

Polarization occurs in a group when member views after a decision tend to be more extreme but in the same direction as initial views. Polarization is more likely when a group is confronted with choices that are not compared by using criteria. In large groups, polarization can be avoided if the mode is used in place of the mean as a decision rule (Ziller, 1956).

In reviewing decisions made by groups such as regulatory bodies, researchers find that measurable criteria are seldom used (Grossman, 1978). Measurable criteria can reduce dependence on political solutions and lead to improved group decisions. The voting solidarity of regulatory groups suggests that consumers have considerable intragroup agreement, but experts do not. Both the consumer and expert factions seem to agree on the decision, but polarization creates intragroup conflict that has to be managed.

Building Group Relationships Conducive to Consensus. Agreement in a group is likely when the self-oriented needs of the members are suppressed, individual concerns are relaxed, the atmosphere remains pleasant, and the issues are orderly and focused (Collins and Guetzkow, 1964). Groups in *conflict over an issue* can be managed to promote agreement when the group associations are friendly and when facts are available and used by a leader who aids the group in penetrating the issue. In contrast, groups with *conflict among members* can be managed to promote agreement through simple agendas, considering one issue at a time. Agreement is promoted when members withdraw from discussion or when the issue is defined so that it has a lower level of interest to some members. This tactic has undesirable consequences because group relations remain poor. Building a cohesive group pays dividends in this situation.

Assessing the Roles of Members and Leaders. People can take one of several roles when they serve in a group. These roles can be sorted into supportive and nonsupportive categories. A key supportive role involves helping the group deal with the tasks that it must confront. This is called the group task role. Another supportive role deals with the maintenance of interpersonal relations within the group. This is called the group maintenance role. Some roles are discordant—for example, focusing on individual needs at the expense of the group and its needs—and are termed self-oriented roles.

Supportive Roles. Group task roles include contributor, information giver, opinion giver, information or opinion seeker, summarizer, elaborator, and evaluator (Hall, Bowen, Lewicki, and Hall, 1982). People taking the contributor role propose goals, ideas, and solutions. Individuals in this role often define problems or suggest procedures to attack a problem. An information giver offers relevant facts, information, or experiences. An opinion giver states beliefs about alternatives. The focus is on values rather than facts. The seeker of opinions and information asks for clarifications and suggestions, looks for facts and feelings, and solicits the ideas and values of other group members. Summarizers pull together ideas, opinions, and suggestions. They often restate to elicit agreement about what has transpired. Individuals who take this role often synthesize, tying together the contributions of others to offer conclusions. Elaborators provide interpretations, seeking to clarify. They give examples, define terms, and attempt to clear up confusion and ambiguity. Evaluators provide assessments of the product of the group. They help the group determine whether a conclusion has been reached or a consensus has emerged.

People who take *group maintenance roles* are concerned with the interpersonal relations within a group. Roles include encourager, harmonizer, expediter, normer, and follower. Individuals adopting an encourager role are supportive of others, using praise to recognize ideas and other kinds of useful efforts by group members. Such individuals are particularly willing to accept the contributions of others. Harmonizers try to reduce conflict. When tension emerges individuals adopting this role attempt to reconcile differences, often by showing areas of agreement among people seemingly in conflict. Harmonizers use tactics such as humor to reduce tension when it emerges. Expediters attempt to maintain open communication among all members. Individuals adopting this role seek out opportunities for all members to contribute and offer ways for isolates to participate. Normers offer standards or expectations. Individuals adopting this role remind the group of its performance expectations or may offer procedures that enhance the prospects of being successful. Finally, followers go along. They can be identified by their willingness to accept the ideas of others and to compromise for the sake of group consensus.

Discordant roles. Individuals who take self-oriented roles in a group can produce dissension, contention, and strife. Such people promote differences of opinion, arguments, and the need to win among members. Blocker, recognition seeker, dominator, and avoider roles can produce these discordant outcomes. Blockers distract. They interfere with group progress by getting discussion off target. Their behavior is often focused on personal concerns instead of the group's problem. Blockers' actions include persistent arguing, resistance, and disagreement beyond reasonable limits. *Recognition seekers* attempt to draw attention to themselves. Their behavior often involves boasting, excessive talking, and other attention-getting devices. *Dominators* also control much of the discussion, but their purpose is different from that of the recognition seeker. They attempt to control the group's decision without any regard for the views of others. Dominators often see themselves as superior to the other group members and may let this view become apparent. Finally, *avoiders* appear to be indifferent. They may withdraw from discussion and seem to daydream, or they may engage in nonproductive activities such as excessively talking to others who are also avoiders.

Making Leader and Member Assessments. A useful exercise in self-awareness calls for each group member to self-rate his or her behavior relative to the supportive and discordant roles, with reference to a particular group in which the member has served. Table 10.1 provides a form that can be used for this purpose. The self-rating scale extends from 1 (rarely behave in this way) to 5 (behave in this way most of the time) for each of the group task and group maintenance roles, dysfunction roles, and leadership roles.

A useful extension has each member (the number will

Table 10.1. Role Rating Form.

Use a rating scale of 1 through 5 for each role (1 means never act(s) this way; 5 means always act(s) this way).

	Self-Rating	Member A	Member B	Member C	Member D	Member E
Functional Roles						
Group Task Roles						
1. Contributor						
2. Information giver						
3. Opinion giver						
4. Information or opinion seeker						
5. Summarizer						
6. Elaborator						
7. Evaluator						
Group Maintenance Roles						
1. Encourager						
2. Harmonizer						
3. Expediter						
4. Normer						
5. Follower						
Dysfunctional Roles						
1. Blocker						
2. Recognition seeker						
3. Dominator						
4. Avoider						
Leadership Roles						
1. Task						
2. Socioemotional						
3. Self-oriented						

Source: Adapted from Benne and Sheats, 1948.

vary among groups) rate every other member in the same way. Comparing self-ratings with the ratings provided by others in a group provides a contrast of personal perceptions with those of coworkers. (Average ratings and the range of variance in the ratings of group members provide useful forms of feedback.) Discrepancies between self-ratings and the ratings of others offer useful areas for self-reflection, potentially improving one's self-awareness and personal effectiveness in a group.

Similarly, leaders can use self- and group ratings to determine whether their behavior fits a socioemotional or task style or seems to others to be self-oriented (focused on personal needs). When there are rotating or shifting leadership opportunities in a group, self-ratings can also be contrasted with ratings by other group members to denote self-perceptions that can be compared to the perceptions of others.

A more detailed approach to leader behavior assessment is shown in Table 10.2. Scores are tabulated by summing of the response indexes of 5 ("always") to 1 ("never") in the table. High scores for questions 1, 4, 7, 8, 10, 13, and 14 signify a task leader and high scores for questions 2, 3, 5, 6, 9, 11, 12, and 15 indicate a socioemotional style. The average difference between these scores, as shown by ratings by group members, provides an interval scale that measures the dominance of one of these leadership styles over the other.

Group Control

Rewards and Penalties. Control of group performance may be achieved by the manipulation of rewards and penalties. Rewards can be financial, in-kind, or social. Financial rewards have the greatest effect. For example, firms often pay their boards of directors. Nursing homes also pay their boards, typically, according to the number of meetings members attend, to encourage participation. An exchange of resources (pay for ideas) results in creating expectations for the nursing home trustee to make substantive contributions to nursing home operation. Hospital trustees, in contrast, are seldom (if ever) paid. This same situation can be found in most third-sector (private, nonprofit) organizations. Trustees who are not paid are coaxed to see their contributions as "community service" and are likely to place fewer restraints on their behavior and may limit the quality of their contributions. One might ask why directors of some organizations are paid but not the trustees in third-sector organizations. Pay is unlikely to diminish a trustee's fiduciary

Table 10.2. Leader Behavior Questionnaire.

	Ratings	
Person described _____	*Ideal*	*Actual*

For each statement, enter the number which best describes your perceptions of the person, using the following response code:

5 = *Always*   4 = *Often*   3 = *Occasionally*   2 = *Seldom*   1 = *Never*

_____ 1. Lets group members know what is expected of them.

_____ 2. Is friendly and approachable.

_____ 3. When faced with a problem, consults with others in the group.

_____ 4. Decides what shall be done and how it shall be done.

_____ 5. Does little things to make it pleasant to be a member of the group.

_____ 6. Before making decision, gives serious consideration to what others in the group have to say.

_____ 7. Makes sure that leader's part in the group is understood.

_____ 8. Puts suggestions made by the group into operation.

_____ 9. Asks members for their suggestions concerning how to carry out assignments.

_____ 10. Schedules the work to be done.

_____ 11. Treats all group members as equals.

_____ 12. Before taking action, consults with others in the group.

_____ 13. Maintains definite standards of performance.

_____ 14. Gives advance notice of changes.

_____ 15. Asks others in the group for suggestions on what assignments should be made.

Source: Adapted from Hall, Bowen, Lewicki, and Hall, 1982.

role and may enhance one's commitment to improve the organization.

In-kind rewards are unwise if conflicts of interest can arise. Charges of logrolling are inevitable when factions or groups help each other in substantive ways, such as providing services to each other or social support in the face of criticism. In-kind rewards create obligations that lower a group member's perceived objectiveness, which, in turn, limits his or her influence and power.

Social rewards (praise, ceremony, and other forms of recognition) can be used effectively by organizations that rely on volunteers as group members. Rewarding the entire group provides a greater task emphasis but will fail to recognize important individual contributions (Collins and Guetzkow, 1964). However, the group can divide some rewards according to its beliefs about each member's contributions. For instance, various kinds of awards, such as a plaque or memento, can be used to signify an individual's contributions.

Many group sponsors act as though a decision group member is rewarded by his or her mere participation or task accomplishment. There is some merit to this view, assuming that satisfaction with group accomplishments creates a reward (Collins and Guetzkow, 1964). For instance, perceived accomplishment, such as percent of the agenda completed, creates satisfaction. The longer it takes to resolve a problem, the lower the satisfaction, thereby diminishing this type of social reward. A meeting that is orderly, efficient, and fast-paced creates satisfaction. Similarly, dealing with interpersonal problems and creating a congruence of aims among the members are sources of satisfaction. Members who have a stake in the outcome have higher satisfaction when the problem is resolved than those who have no stake. Cliques (factions) in the group lower satisfaction, as do conflict and frustration. On the other hand, a perception of power and/or freedom to act increases satisfaction.

A leader who can modify a person's behavior has power over that individual (Collins and Guetzkow, 1964). For example, the leaders of community planning groups have little power because they have few rewards other than praise to dispense.

Hence, social rewards must be used with considerable care. Friendly interactions among members and association with high-status peers are sources of power that a leader can use. In contrast, punishment (verbal rebukes) will lower friendly relations and inhibit interpersonal attraction. These findings again dramatize the importance of selecting a leader with good leadership skills.

A useful form for rating group performance is provided in Table 10.3. This form can be used to compare groups or to trace changes in the views of group members about the group and its accomplishments.

Spatial Arrangement. Another way to exercise control over a group is through spatial arrangement. Spatial relations influence the pattern of participation by group members and the behavior of the leader (Sommers, 1965; Howell and Becker, 1962). Group members tend to communicate with people facing them across a table rather than with people sitting adjacent to them. Consequently, round tables should stimulate discussion.

Individuals seated at the ends of a rectangular table tend to participate more in group discussion and have more influence over the group's decision than people situated elsewhere at the table. As a group increases in size, the group leader (elected or appointed) tends to assume a position at the end of the table and the other group members sit as close as they can to the leader (Sommers, 1965). For groups of three to five, the spatial arrangement seems to have no effect (Cummings, Huber, and Arndt, 1974). Formal leadership also reduces the effect of spatial arrangement (Hearn, 1957).

Risky Group Behavior. A "risky shift" often accompanies group decision making. Group decisions tend to be riskier than the average risk preference of individuals who make up the group. The risky shift has been attributed to diffusion of responsibility, familiarization, and a view of risk as a value. The diffusion-of-responsibility view, which is supported by Kogan and Wallach (1967), contends that groups pool risk, which lowers their resistance to act. People are more apt to act in groups because the group spreads responsibility. The famil-

Table 10.3. Measuring Group Effectiveness.

Through these scales, it is possible to get a general picture of the perceptions that various members have about the group and how it is growing. It is also possible to pick up areas in which there may be difficulties blocking progress.

1. How clear are the group goals?

1	2	3	4	5
No apparent goals	Goal confusion, uncertainty, or conflict	Average goal clarity	Goals mostly clear	Goals very clear

2. How much trust and openness in the group?

1	2	3	4	5
Distrust, a closed group	Little trust, defensiveness	Average trust and openness	Considerable trust and openness	Remarkable trust and openness

3. How sensitive and perceptive are group members?

1	2	3	4	5
No awareness or listening in the group	Most members self-absorbed	Average sensitivity and listening	Better than usual listening	Outstanding sensitivity to others

4. How much attention was paid to process (the way the group was working)?

1	2	3	4	5
No attention to process	Little attention to process	Some concern with group process	A fair balance between content and process	Very concerned with process

5. How were group leadership needs met?

1	2	3	4	5
Not met, drifting	Leadership concentrated in one person	Some leadership sharing	Leadership functions distributed	Leadership needs met creatively and flexibly

6. How were group decisions made?

1	2	3	4	5
No decisions could be reached	Made by a few	Majority vote	Attempts at integrating minority vote	Full participation and tested consensus

7. How well were group resources used?

1	2	3	4	5
One or two contributed, but deviants silent	Several tried to contribute but were discouraged	Average use of group resources	Group resources well used and encouraged	Group resources fully and effectively used

8. How much loyalty and sense of belonging to the group?

1	2	3	4	5
Members had no group loyalty or sense of belonging	Members not close, but some friendly relations	About average sense of belonging	Some warm sense of belonging	Strong sense of belonging among members

Source: Adapted from Hall, Bowen, Lewicki, and Hall, 1982.

iarization explanation contends that discussion reduces the uncertainty inherent in a new task, permitting more risky stands to be adopted as the issue is resolved. Still others advocate risk as a value and take the position that there is a pervasive cultural value favoring risk. These distinctions are important because the diffusion-of-responsibility explanation suggests that a group provides a mechanism for innovation or adventurousness and an evasion of responsibility. The other explanations argue that the risky shift is a natural process and risky behavior is not provoked. No clear choice among these explanations can be made. Policy guides are likewise murky. Nevertheless, organizations should anticipate a movement toward a risky posture in their decision groups.

Key Points

Several tactics can improve the performance of groups. In particular, organizations that stress participation emphasize the formulation and cohesion stages and tend to ignore the process (which is discussed in Chapter Fifteen) and control stages. This practice reduces the effectiveness of groups. Carefully considering each phase is the key to successful group performance.

Several guides that can improve the performance of a group are summarized below:

1. Many groups use consumers to define service problems, administrators from sister institutions to sensitize the group to political and resource constraints, and experts such as physicians to supply technical information. However, homogeneous decision groups with moderate status differentials are best. Mixing members who satisfy political constraints with members who are expected to provide information in a group is unwise.

2. Group members who serve because of a need to participate should not be mixed with those who seek to influence results.

3. Large groups are best for development and information-generation tasks, whereas small groups are superior in

influencing and making judgments. A subcommittee strategy can be used for decisions that must be made by a large,
unwieldy group.

4. Cooptation, selecting a group that represents centers of
power the sponsor hopes to manage, is a vastly overused
tactic. The benefits of cooptation (acceptance and innovation) are not realized when intragroup conflicts are present and unmanaged. Moving away from a power focus to
one of expertise will improve a group's performance.

5. Group leaders can take on various leadership styles. A
socioemotional style provides social rewards, such as recognition and tension release, which is best for decision
tasks because this style elicits information and enhances
acceptance of a decision. Task leaders contribute more
information but create tension. Task leaders are best for
developmental tasks or highly uncertain decisions because actions must be defended by logical arguments.

6. A group can enhance its base of power by using such
tactics as initiating investigations, making requests or
threats, stating views, announcing a decision to monitor
reactions, asking for support, and vigorously defending a
decision once it is made. Groups often select a tactic that is
unlikely to work in enhancing their power.

7. Concrete goals are preferred. They hold a group responsible for a result and make good performance more likely.

8. Consensus building must be carried out differently with a
group in conflict over issues than with a group that has
conflict among its members. Issue conflicts are best handled through leadership in defining the issue and getting
relevant information. Interpersonal conflict is managed
by framing clear-cut choices that do not exaggerate the
conflict among the group's members.

9. Group control is often limited to social rewards. Organizations can use formal presentations and other recognitions
as sources of reward for committee work.

10. Making the task accomplishment an intrinsic reward assumes that favorable aspects of the process (quick resolution, good relationships, and the like) are possible,

whereas unfavorable aspects of the process (conflict, frustration, and cliques) can be eliminated or minimized. Relying solely on task accomplishment as a source of satisfaction can be a poor strategy unless the unfavorable aspects of participation can be managed and ameliorated.

11

Uncovering Core Problems

The first stage of the decision process explores possibilities. This exploration is designed to uncover problems provoking the need to act before irrevocable commitments are made. This chapter provides ways to search for core problems. It offers procedures that can be used by individual decision makers and decision-making bodies. First, techniques are suggested to help decision makers deal with "the problem with problems." Next, these ideas are extended to decision groups. Finally, the process of coalition building is discussed, showing how to create and manage a coalition capable of uncovering and exploring problems before committing to action.

Figure 11.1 highlights the topic to be discussed in Chapter Eleven. This form of highlighting will be used throughout Parts Three and Four to identify the topic or topics to be treated in each chapter and to show how these topics relate to the decision process.

The Importance of Problem Finding

Determining the most pertinent problem to work on is the single most important act in decision making (Kolb, 1983). Problems establish a window that frames all subsequent activity, establishing and justifying an arena of action. If the wrong arena is selected, both objectives, which direct inquiry, and alternative courses of action, which provide ways to respond, will fail to deal with core issues. As a result, misleading problems are the primary source of bad decisions.

As discussed in Chapter Three, the problems that

Figure 11.1. The Decision Process.

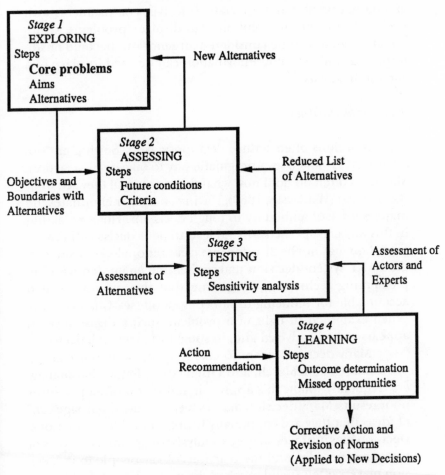

Note: Boldface type indicates the topic addressed in this chapter.

provoke action are often taken for granted. Stating problems eliminates a key source of conflict and ambiguity in tough decisions, so decision makers feel considerable pressure to specify a problem quickly and forcefully (Nutt, 1984b). This leads decision makers to make premature commitments to action without a clear notion of what is provoking the need to act. These commitments stem from dealing only with solutions and by being misled by problems that are more apparent than real and more urgent than important. Four types of "problems with problems" can occur. Solutions can displace problems, symptomatic signals can be considered, urgency can become misinterpreted, and available information can be used in place of a careful diagnosis.

Solutions as Problems

Solutions often seduce decision makers. Seizing an "opportunity" is viewed as a pragmatic way to take decisive action. Managers often do not know what they want until they see what they can get (Wildavsky, 1969). Having an answer eliminates the major source of ambiguity in tough decisions. However, acting in this way can also be rash and lead to poor decisions because the action may not be directed by a clear rationale. For example, the BART system decision makers became enamored with implementing technology, forgetting that they would be held accountable for reducing urban congestion (see Chapter Two). When examined in light of a problem, such a decision often appears to be ill-advised and, in some instances, a debacle.

Many decisions seem to take shape as solutions chasing problems. Cohen, March, and Olsen (1976) found that managers frequently follow this approach and that it often produces poor results. Many decision makers seem to have a "garbage can" of ideas that they are continually fitting to problem situations. Decision making takes shape as analysis to explore the virtues of someone's pet idea and the reactions of key people to it. Decision makers often spend much of their time defending a hastily selected opportunity instead of searching for core concerns and ways to respond to them, as pointed out by the failed decisions described in Chapter Two.

Another manifestation of the seductive solution occurs when managers define problems in terms of solutions. For example, consider this statement: "The problem with this department is low motivation." Such a problem statement implicitly limits the search to solutions dealing with motivation. However, treating the problem as one of "low productivity" would not limit the search to motivation-related responses. As this example suggests, even problem definitions that include implied solution characteristics can seriously limit the search for alternatives in a decision process.

Symptoms as Problems

Another danger stems from settling on a problem that is symptomatic of deeper concerns, which could have emerged with careful probing. Experienced decision makers know that bad decisions often stem from dealing with superficial issues that keep them from looking for core concerns. Core problems are often shrouded in ambiguity that eludes quick specification. For example, grievances from unionized hourly employees can signal real or imagined concerns due to autocratic supervisors, poor working conditions, rumors, and the like. Probing at the grievance signal uncovers several issues that can be tested to see which offers the most illuminating way to view the decision.

Misplaced Urgency

Urgent pressures that trigger action often contain misleading signals. Every experienced manager knows that decision situations contain a range of problems and opportunities that vary in urgency and importance (Kolb, 1983). Some are obvious and some are not. Urgency can provide a poor basis for action because urgent signals can divert attention from more important, but less pressing, concerns. Urgency may cause decision makers to miss hidden or disguised problems that also require attention because they offer crucial opportunities or identify long-term needs. When urgency is misread, it can cause artificial time pressure, such as occurred in the ITT and RCA decisions (Chapter Two). Even when urgency is real, as in the Iranian hostage rescue decision, it can divert attention from less pressing but important long-term problems. For instance, long-term hostage problems have become a reality in the Middle East, a reality provoked by Iranian radicals who saw the failed hostage rescue attempt as a victory for Iran. Hostage taking has become a viable way to exert continuing pressure on the United States and the West for decades of meddling in Iranian affairs. Misplaced urgency often signals deeper problems. For example, the immediate problem of replacing key people who resign can displace the exploration of inequitable reward systems and bureaucratic managers that lie behind the resignations.

Available Information

When available information is used to frame a decision, more diagnostic information can be overlooked. As discussed in Chapter Four, decision makers give too much weight to information that is recognized first, particularly vivid, consistent with their past experience, and provided by individuals or situations with whom they have a sense of kinship. Decision makers who find it hard to set this information aside establish problems by using incomplete and potentially misleading information. Problems in information handling that give available information salience allow solutions, symptoms, and urgency to become translated into problems.

Problem Situations

Problem situations stem from managers' perceptions about the clarity of the problem they confront, their expectations, and ways to respond. Using this approach, managers can see the nature of problems in one of eight ways, each offering particular kinds of insights and constraints that influence subsequent decision-making activity.

In this section, the following eight types of problem situations are discussed.

Situation 1: Tasks, in which the problem, expectations, and ways to respond are all known
Situation 2: Structured problems, in which the problem and expectations are known but ways to respond are unknown
Situation 3: Unstructured problems, in which the problem

and ways to respond are unknown but expectations are known

Situation 4: Structured opportunities, in which the problem and ways to respond are known but expectations are unknown

Situation 5: Unstructured opportunities, in which the problem is known but expectation and ways to respond are unknown

Situation 6: Solutions searching for uses, in which problems and expectations are unknown, but a potentially useful idea exists

Situation 7: Idea searches, in which the problem is unknown but expectations and ways to respond are known

Situation 8: Undefined opportunities, in which the problem, expectations, and ways to respond are all unknown

Problems as Tasks

In situation 1, the decision maker responds to the stimuli as a "task" in which problems, expectations or norms, and alternative courses of action that stipulate ways to respond are known. The task is to select an alternative and apply it, measuring the extent to which expectations are met. An even simpler version of the task situation occurs when there is but one alternative. In this case, the task is one of taking action and determining results. The task problem contains minimal insights and provides maximum constraints on decision making. If perceptions match reality, treating a decision as a task is both sensible and efficient. However, decision makers often misread problem situations, making perceptions differ from reality. Biases that stem from symptomatic signals, misplaced urgency, and available but incomplete information are apt to mislead the decision maker. Unless there is convincing evidence for a particular action, careful problem exploration is essential, shifting most task situations (situation 1) to situations in which problems are unknown (situation 2). Tactics for problem exploration are discussed in subsequent sections of this chapter.

Structured Problems

In situation 2, problems and expectations or norms are thought to be known, but alternative courses of action are not. The standard "structured problem" results (Kolb, 1983); a search is conducted for ways to respond. In systems terms (Nutt, 1984c), the decision maker searches for "conversions" in which the performance shortfalls defined by problems (the need to improve profit) and norms (profit expectations) are addressed. The notion of conversion stems from searching for a way to respond to the performance expectations given by problems and norms, which can convert a problem to a solution. If the situation has been correctly diagnosed, the decision maker can move directly to generating alternatives (discussed in Chapter Sixteen). The biases noted above often make problems suspect. What seems to be a structured problem (situation 2) shifts to an unstructured problem (situation 3), in which problems are *not* known and a different approach is required.

Unstructured Problems

The "unstructured problem" arises when problems and ways to respond are unknown but norms, which identify expectations, are thought to be clear. A correct diagnosis leads to a "production problem" (Nutt, 1984c). Problem solving with clear-cut goals is carried out to find both problems and ways to respond. In a production problem, norms must be clear. For example, consider a state legislature deciding whether to underwrite the costs of a substance abuse program. The desired outcome, abstinence, is clear, but the nature and scope of problems leading to substance abuse are unknown, and ways to respond (Alcoholics Anonymous and Synanon models) can be argumentative, each with many staunch proponents. Decision makers facing unstructured problems must engage in problem identification (discussed in this chapter) and generate alternative ways to respond (Chapter Sixteen).

In some instances, norms can be elusive. Consider a firm that uses targets based on industry averages to make decisions.

The specific situation of the firm can make these targets unrealistic. For example, when General Motors emerged from a substantial loss of market share in the late 1980s, recovery to its prior market share in the short term was unrealistic. Similarly, an expectation of abstinence implies a 100 percent success rate for substance abuse programs, which can be an unrealistic norm for certain kinds of client groups. In such situations, treating the norm as unknown would shift the unstructured problem (situation 3) to an unstructured opportunity (situation 5). Norm identification activities (see Chapter Sixteen) are added to problem identification and solution generation.

Structured Opportunities

A "structured opportunity" (situation 4) arises when problems are thought to be clear and ways to respond to the problems seem available. The task is to identify expectations. For example, unused capacity in a firm or a service organization has a clear problem (fill the capacity), and often many proposals for products (franchise, rent the space, and the like). But the target profit can be unknown if prior experience offers no way to judge profit prospects when idle capacity is used. Norms are very important and require thoughtful reflection so that managers are clear about targets that are used. The targets establish expectations that help managers select among alternatives, using the "elimination by aspects" decision rule (Chapter Nineteen), and guide the search for new alternatives, under a "satisficing" decision rule (Chapter Thirteen).

Managers can misread the problems provoking action for the reasons discussed previously, making situation 4 give misleading cues in some decisions. For example, unfilled capacity may stem from poor management, which, if left unaddressed, will render all attempts to fill the capacity ineffectual. Dealing with this situation as an unstructured opportunity (situation 5) would permit problem exploration, which offers at least some hope of finding the core problem.

Unstructured Opportunities

An "unstructured opportunity" (situation 5) arises when problems are viewed as known but norms and solutions are not. A search is made for both expectations and ways to respond, with the known situation providing direction to these activities. The decision maker's first step is to structure the opportunity by identifying targets and then using these targets to search for ways to respond (see Chapter Sixteen). For example, to deal with morale problems, a manager must explore the meaning of good morale before searching for ways to improve morale.

The prospects of symptomatic signals, misplaced urgency, and available information can make problems appear to be clear when they are not. Dealing with less significant problems can render the unstructured opportunity unstable. Problem exploration in such a situation is essential, again shifting the situation to an undefined opportunity (situation 8).

Solutions Searching for Uses

In situation 6, a protagonist hopes to get the organization to adopt a seemingly viable idea. The protagonist's motivations are often valid. Such a situation occurs when organizations are unaware of innovations, technological advances, or merely better ways of doing things. Ideas crop up in many ways, such as through continuing education, new peers, literature reviews, and plant trips, in which the prospect for significant payoffs captures a decision maker's attention. Becoming aware makes both problems and norms clear. For instance, a new software package can offer ways to improve performance, and this new level of performance becomes a new norm for the organization. This situation also arises when a process provides a by-product, or a new use for waste is discovered. Eastman Kodak washed silver from negatives and flushed the residue into the Genesee River for decades before it realized that the silver could be reclaimed.

Solutions seeking uses can lead to disastrous decisions for situations in which the protagonists are motivated by selfish goals and in which the solution keeps decision makers from exploring problems, as discussed above. In both instances, problem exploration is essential. The solution is held in abeyance until problems are understood, making the situation become an undefined opportunity (situation 8).

Idea Searches

In situation 7, unknown problems with known solutions and performance expectations arise as a special case of solutions seeking uses. In this case, a need is proposed that has been explored to the point where performance expectations are clearcut. The situation is managed by encouraging salespeople looking for clients to demonstrate their products and services. Managers need periodic exposure to vendors selling their wares to keep abreast of new technology and business practices. However, this exposure needs to be selective, stressing demonstrable benefits. Vendors will absorb all of a manager's available time if they are allowed to. In most instances, a vendor's idea should create a shift to situation 8, undefined opportunity, in which the idea becomes one of several responses the organization will consider in a decision process. Such a shift is often beneficial because there may be vendors with better ideas and, more fundamentally, more significant problems that merit attention than those implied by the original idea.

Undefined Opportunities

Situation 8 arises when the nature of the problem is undefined. All tough decisions have this characteristic because the absence of a definition creates ambiguity and uncertainty and can produce conflict. For many of the foregoing situations, a shift to situation 8 is desirable because it makes a manager realize the "opportunity" inherent in keeping one's options open. Premature closure on problems, norms, or ways to respond is a key source of bad decisions.

To deal with undefined opportunities, managers need to take three steps. They must uncover core problems. They must employ tactics useful in problem exploration as discussed in the remaining sections of this chapter. Managers must also set norms and uncover alternatives. Tactics for norm development and the generation of alternatives are discussed in Chapter Sixteen.

Determining Core Problems

The biases that stem from seductive solutions, persuasive vendors, symptomatic signals, misplaced urgency, or available information can draw a decision maker away from a problem focus, which is essential in tough decisions. The level of ambiguity, uncertainty, and conflict makes untested assumptions about problems, norms, or ways to respond dangerous. For tough decisions, problem identification and exploration are essential.

To carry out identification and exploration, the decision maker must gather information about various ways to view a decision so that problems from several perspectives can emerge. Each of these problems is then subjected to careful analysis in order to sort relevant problems from the irrelevant and decide which of the problems or problem hybrids seems to represent core concerns. In tough decisions, there is no test that can be applied to ensure that the right problem has been selected. However, staying problem-centered by looking at the situation from several vantage points increases the likelihood that core concerns will emerge. As ambiguity and conflict increase, so should the care and time the decision maker devotes to problem identification and exploration.

The first step in uncovering problems calls for the decision maker to confront the possibility that information emerging early in the decision process is potentially misleading and that readily available solutions are often ill-advised. Problems are uncovered and explored in different ways for each process. For the *analytical decision process*, the decision maker uses the "5W" procedure, discussed below, to identify and explore possible problems. The decision maker consults with colleagues and others as this step is carried out, as described in Chapter Eight.

For the *group decision process*, the decision maker carries out the "5W" procedure to establish a preliminary arena and to aid in the selection of the stakeholders who will become members of the decision group. The decision group uses a silent reflective group process (Chapter Fifteen) to uncover problems and then repeats the "5W" process to explore problems and designate one as the core problem meriting attention.

The *mixed-mode decision process* lingers even longer in the problem exploration step. The decision maker frames the decision by identifying possible coalitions in terms of the arena that each coalition would be willing to confront, using the "5W" procedure, and the goals that each of these arenas implies. The coalition carries out subsequent steps, using group process procedures. Many coalitions can be identified in tough decisions. Some can be ruled out because they lack influence or coherence. Other coalitions, however, offer reasonable ways to view the decision. At the outset in tough decisions, it is not clear, nor are there tests that can be applied to determine, which of these views provides the most advantage. The decision maker explores various ways to frame the decision in terms of various interests. A coalition of interests is formed whose values and beliefs are aligned with those of the decision maker and the interests that the decision maker is pledged to represent. Once mobilized, these interests are managed to create a consensus in which exploration can be carried out, sealed off from distractions to the extent possible.

The most complex form of problem identification, that involving coalitions, is described in the remaining sections of this chapter. Simplifications outlined above, which follow the steps required for the analytical and group decision processes as outlined in Chapter Eight, should be readily apparent.

Sources of Conflict in Coalitions

Conflict is typically expressed in terms of potential or actual disagreements among stakeholders about problems, salient future conditions, objectives, viable alternatives, and criteria to assess the alternatives. Tough decisions can produce undesirable and often irreversible consequences for an organization if choices turn out to be ill-advised. Differences in how to approach a decision and the threat inherent in making a poor choice produce stress that can make systematic search and processing of information impossible. Deliberations involve many sensitive, value-laden issues, which lead to what Janis and Mann (1977) call "hot cognitive" processes. Hot cognitions produce a level of arousal that can produce irrational choices. For example, in 1988 a U.S. warship in the Persian Gulf was unable to identify a radar image, and so the captain ordered the firing of a missile that killed several hundred civilians who were passengers in a commercial airplane that had wandered off its course. Stress simultaneously creates a strong need to take action, to relieve the stress, and a fear that any action will produce undesirable consequences.

The decision procedures presented in Chapter Eight call on decision makers to be systematic information processors (Simon, 1977). When stress is intense, it can seriously disrupt the capacity of decision makers to be "vigilant" in their processing. Stress stems in part from the prospect that a choice will produce winners and losers. Stakeholders who believe that they can become losers have incentives to thwart the decision process and impose core problems and the responses they imply, which serve their vested interests. These competing notions held by stakeholders can lead to a clash between power centers that often provokes conflict. Following a fruitless search for alternatives that can offer a compromise, a pattern of behavior called *defensive avoidance* emerges. Warning signals are distorted, and the decision maker engages in wishful rationalizations (Janis and Mann, 1977). The decision maker in this bind blindly gropes for an alternative that can end the conflict, as discussed in Chapter One.

During this process of groping, time horizons seem to shrink because of repeated failures to find an acceptable choice. These conditions produce "hypervigilance" (Janis and Mann, 1977, p. 51). When time seems short and there is no way to escape making a choice, decision makers can act irrationally. Analytical techniques seem unrealistic, and the decision maker resorts to simplistic ways of thinking, as described in Chapter Four. In this situation, a decision maker is likely to feel panic. Hypervigilance produces a frantic search that is apt to overlook alternatives and fail to adequately assess available alternatives. This behavior leads decision makers to contrive a solution that provides immediate relief but often leads to postdecisional regret, as in the Persian Gulf airliner disaster.

Managing Conflict

To manage conflict, decision makers must take steps to foster vigilant information processing. Some of these steps deal with understanding the origin of the conflict, and others are concerned with identifying problems to sweep away some of the ambiguity surrounding a tough decision. People with a stake in the decision, the stakeholders, are a major source of conflict in tough decisions.

Conflict is often provoked by stakeholders, inside and outside the organization, who take or stake out positions that prohibit or limit the resolution of a problem or issue. For instance, federal regulators, in the wake of the Three Mile Island accident, now require power-generating utilities to invest in extensive modifications of nuclear power plants that make them cost-ineffective. To deal with an anticipated demand for power, as predicted by patterns of housing and industrial development in its service area, a utility would be forced to choose among several undesirable alternatives. Management can elect to make the modifications in nuclear power plants under construction and hope that another set of regulators will allow them to increase utility rates to cover their costs. The nuclear plants can be abandoned if power can be purchased from a neighboring utility by means of a contract. This option is troublesome because of its high costs and the short-term provisions other utilities can impose, such as "take or pay" provisions that guarantee a price to be paid over the contract period. The nuclear plants can be modified to make them coal-burning plants. Costs for this can be uncertain because of the state legislatures' impending decisions on pollution-abatement devices and requirements to support a local coal industry. If this industry produces only soft coal, with a high sulfur content, it is certain to produce high levels of acid rain and other pollutants. Environmental groups may form and vow to fight all new coal plants that burn soft coal, no matter what precautions are taken.

A utility facing these choices must also contend with internal stakeholders. For example, some of the managers inside the organization may have "gone public" in support of the coal option and others in support of nuclear power. After taking a position, each group must contend with dedicated critics. Coal advocates have to deal with the hazards in coal mining and may appear to be tolerating the loss of life and health problems for miners by promoting increased coal use. Nuclear advocates must cope with public hysteria about the safety of nuclear power following the Three Mile Island and Chernobyl accidents. In their attempts to fend off these critics, the two positions tend to harden. Neither group can back away from its position without loss of face. The choice between coal and nuclear power seems to ruin the careers of managers whose interests are abandoned. Furthermore, a large group of junior executives who have been enticed to support the prevailing views of their superiors may leave the utility if these views are not emphasized. The exit of these junior executives would strip the utility of people being groomed for major management responsibility.

The utility's capacity decision in this scenario eventually produces losers and creates dependencies on the uncertain acts of regulators (future conditions). The conflict that results is likely to produce hot cognitive processes and hypervigilance. A frantic, panic-ridden search for a way out of the capacity-choice dilemma can lead to hasty choices, such as signing gas transmission contracts with utilities in another state that tie the utility to gas prices pegged above the market. Postdecisional regret may occur if gas prices fall but rates cannot because of the contract. Local regulators can go public with the utility's "poor decision" and call for rate cutbacks, insisting that the utility, not its customers, bear the cost of its poor decision.

In such a situation, politics is impossible to avoid. The decision maker must choose between stakeholders and form a coalition that best serves the interests of the organization. For example, the utility may have to choose between internal stakeholders (the coal and nuclear divisions) and take steps to salvage the junior executives damaged by the choice. Coalition formation and management become a key consideration in making tough decisions.

Perspectives from Which to View a Decision

Problem identification calls for a multifaceted version of Janusian thinking, nicely captured by the famous picture of a head with two faces, which signifies more than one way to view a situation. The problem that is selected becomes a frame, like the picture window in a house. By changing position, one finds that new views providing new perspectives come into focus. A change in one's position changes the frame and gives a different view. Problems are analogous to windows because each provides a specific view of a decision. Multiple views of problems are essential in tough decisions to make one appreciate foreground and background and thus the focal issues and their context.

The problems the decision maker selects for attention provide a frame that indicates what the decision is and is not about. The frame is stakeholder-dependent because the problems stakeholders in one coalition think are important are apt to be different from those perceived as important by another coalition. Once stakeholders are identified, problems can be identified and the decision process can move forward. The selected coalition settles on problems to be addressed and, by doing so, stipulates the nature of the choices to be made and sweeps away some types of ambiguity and uncertainty. For instance, the coal alternative mentioned above eliminates the need for further discussions with nuclear regulatory commissions. Supporting the nuclear option eliminates the need to worry about acid rain legislation.

Problem Identification

At the start of a decision process, decision makers often have information, which may or may not be diagnostic, and the opportunity to extend their knowledge by expanding their in-formation base. To collect information, they can use a variety of devices that poll staff, users, peers, and experts by applying surveys and formal group processes (see Chapter Fifteen). With the assistance of peers, subordinates, or a group, augmented by reflection, the decision maker attempts to collect three types of insight to search for core problems. These include problem specification, factors that contribute to the problem, and root cause speculations (Kepner and Tregoe, 1965).

Preliminary Problem Listing

Five types of queries are useful in problem listing. The decision maker uses reflection to lay out problem and non-problem areas, which helps to rule out inconsequential issues. (Groups can also be used in problem listing when the decision maker can disclose factors motivating action.) Cues that can be used to elicit problems include deviations from expected per-formance (called *performance gaps*), disagreements inside or outside the organization, policy positions of stakeholders, tech-nological advances that pose opportunities or threats, and un-satisfied claims of customers or clients (Nutt, 1984c). Using these cues, the decision maker lists conditions under which salient problems have and have not occurred. For instance, nuclear power may not have been publicly opposed by state regulators when utilities emphasized the number of jobs to be created. The coal option may not have provoked opposition when assurances of "local coal first" were widely publicized by utilities.

Sorting

Problem listing is followed by a sorting into categories that identify when a problem has arisen and when it has not, and to what extent the problem has or has not occurred. For in-stance, lobbying with legislatures or special-interest groups may have softened opposition. The effects of lobbying can be studied to identify the proportion of time it has produced useful results, sorting according to intervening factors such as favorable or unfavorable economic conditions. Finally, a list of stakeholders is produced for problems, indicating who stands to gain and who stands to lose.

The "5W" Procedure

The decision maker next seeks contributing factors. The "5Ws," who, what, where, when, and why, provide a useful way to assess each problem. An array of the "W" questions along one axis and problems along the other provides a way to systematically record what is known about the decision situation. A hypothetical example showing how a utility could use this analysis is provided in Table 11.1. Note that the three problems of maintaining cash for investment, meeting forecast demand, and making the best use of capacity result in very different appraisals when the 5Ws are applied to these three problems. Alternatives will shift as the focus of the decision changes, time frames move from past to present to future, and different rationales are used. Conflict, disguised as different positions on alternatives, can be diffused by showing how these alternatives address different problems. Uncovering these problems helps to resolve the conflict, lowering stress and the prospect of losers.

The decision maker next looks for root causes and seeks patterns and relationships within the list of contributing factors. For instance, a dispute over a policy of service shutoffs for nonpayers in a utility may have angered organizations designated to regulate public utilities. The regulator may be determined to "win" the next dispute to demonstrate that it is an effective consumer advocate. The decision maker ponders whether a concession on shutoffs might soften the regulator's views on pollution, nuclear safety, and the like, or at least create a positive attitude toward the utility in external stakeholders, such as politicians. The decision maker explores a list of causes in an attempt to find those that explain the majority of the problem dilemmas, to identify a core set of problems that must be addressed. The 5W procedure helps to open up the decision process so that a search for new ideas and expanded information that describes the ideas is possible.

Table 11.1. Illustrating the "5Ws."

5Ws	Problems of a Utility Company		
	Maintaining Cash Reserves	Meeting Forecast Demand	Making Best Use of Generating Capacity
Who	List of stakeholders who share position	Stakeholder list	Stakeholder list
What	Finding ways to increase income within limitations set by regulations	Finding ways to meet the expected demand	Finding ways to use or sell the capacity
When	Currently	Forecasted to occur in two years	Historically
Where	Corporate level	A few key subsidiaries	Companywide
Why	Future dividends and investment capacity will be eroded	Future service commitments and implicit franchise to provide service will be questioned	Power-generating capacity has lowest unit cost in the industry

To explore the issues posed by a set of problems, the decision maker reflects on a series of questions posed for each problem that seems significant. These reflective queries are listed below.

1. List the objectives of stakeholders thought to be in conflict. How are they alike and how do they differ? Test views with trusted peers and subordinates (see Chapter Sixteen).

2. What are the merits of current alternatives? Consider ways to pose new alternatives by soliciting the views of peers or subordinates, using groups, RFPs, vendors, the practices of competitors, and innovation through research and development (see Chapter Sixteen).

3. List the positive and negative consequences associated with each alternative. What information is missing?

4. What criteria are implied by the objectives of stakeholders? Seek information that elaborates the merit of alternatives,

using criteria implied by the stakeholders in conflict (see Chapter Sixteen).

5. What sources of expertise can be used to augment existing information?

6. Does the implementation of the alternatives create any special problems?

Using information acquired from trusted peers and subordinates, the decision maker considers these questions to play out what is known and not known about the decision. The decision maker identifies objectives, alternatives, consequences, criteria, expertise, and implementation barriers that seem to be implied by each problem. These steps reduce the effects of hypervigilance and defensive avoidance.

An illustration is provided in Table 11.2. Conflict in this example stems from the distinctly different problems that lie behind the alternatives offered by various stakeholders. The positions of stakeholders differ, in part, because their problem perceptions are different. The criteria and implementation barriers that are implied allow the decision maker to explore these actions, looking for a win-win solution that caters to the needs of all parties. Experts in each area implied by the problem illustrations would be summoned to help the decision maker make realistic appraisals.

Becoming a multistate operation is an example of a win-win option that deals with internal conflict in the utility company example in Table 11.2. The coal-nuclear confrontation is averted by dealing with the problem as one of cash reserves. Finding ways to stockpile cash reserves provides funds to purchase power if needed, managing the service obligation objective. Capacity enhancement is also possible when there is a favorable cash position, dealing with the industry leadership objective. However, the negative consequences of the multistate-operation option must also be explored. For example, an explosive situation may arise if regulators sniff out the policy of shifting costs to cover profits in excess of those permitted by the regulatory policy of a given state.

Table 11.2. Applying the Reflective Queries: Problems of a Utility Company.

Reflective Queries	Maintaining Cash Reserves	Meeting Forecast Demand	Making Best Use of Generating Capacity
Objectives	Improve profitability	Meet obligations for services	Maintain industry leadership
Alternatives	1. Divestiture of low-profit companies 2. Purchase nonregulated businesses 3. Become a multistate operation to frustrate control by regulators 4. Etc.	1. Increase capacity to meet consumer demand 2. Make power purchase arrangements to ensure reserves 3. Etc.	1. Market unused capacity 2. Invest in maintaining technological leadership 3. Etc.
Consequences (Pro/Con)	1. Regulators see utilities as dumping needy users and hold up approval of rates, etc. 2. High profits in some subsidiaries can be masked by allocating corporate overhead	1. Investment directed toward low-profit subsidiaries 2. Use leverage from positive image of service orientation to argue for rate hikes	1. Full use of capacity quite profitable (high volume means low unit costs) 2. Marketing, used by a regulated company with capacity shortfalls, creates bad press
Criteria Implied	Profit and return on investment	Reserves to meet needs	Maintain status as industry leader
Expertise	Financial	Forecasting	Engineering and marketing
Implementation Barriers	Regulatory power	Volatile needs, forecast precision	Resistance to engineering mentality

Problem Exploration as Diagnosis

Problem exploration helps to develop an intellectual understanding of a decision (Susman, 1983). A decision can be viewed as influencing technical and social systems. The need to act stems from mismatches between technical and social systems or either of these systems and the environment. For instance, technical systems in a utility company include its power-generating capability, and the social system includes people's commitment to it and to the organization that produced this capability. The environment is made up of regulators and special-interest groups, among others. The utility company's commitment to superior performance in its power-generating system, in cost-effectiveness terms, may be in conflict with the aims of environmental groups that wish to halt the damming of wild rivers that produce cheap hydroelectric power. The utility company's dependence on environmentalists, the availability of information about the utility company's plans, and the values and roles of key actors suggest system-environment mismatches. Moreover, technical-system advocates, guided by instrumental values, may be in conflict with social systems in which people seek personal aims, such as job security and advancement.

The boundaries that separate the utility company from its environment can be vague. For instance, regulators that have an advisory role in rate setting and the location of power-generating plants are treated differently than regulators with direct oversight responsibility. Decisions in which regulators have oversight call for a crossing of the system-environment boundaries. Including regulators as stakeholders enlarges the social system. For instance, when regulators are treated as stakeholders, a cooperative relationship becomes essential. To develop such a relationship, decision makers must explore the views of regulators and how those views may change. Assessment identifies the degree of regulatory consensus and how that consensus may change through outside pressure and the turnover of commissioners. An understanding of how a consensus guides position taking and the means available to the regulators to resolve conflicts, such as whether rule making is public and whether hearings must operate as a court of law does, is required to forge a relationship. This expanded social system calls for considerable time and effort to be expended in acquiring the information needed for stakeholder management.

The decision maker ponders the values that emerge from this analysis, such as whether rewards in the organization seem sufficient to get internal stakeholders to respond to performance gaps. In other cases, incentives may be found in challenges and responsibilities. Mismatches between incentives and the required leverage serve as guides to predict problems or issues.

Coalition Building

To build a coalition, two sets of activity are recommended. The decision maker takes steps to cope with conflict, considering various coalitions to determine which is best for the organization, and attempts to lower the level of stress in the coalition.

The steps to this point in the decision process have identified core problems, explored options, and identified the worst that can happen. With these factors set aside for the moment, the titular decision maker forms a coalition of interests that must be managed by listing those who have key interests or stakes in the core problems to be confronted.

Tactics that help people cope with stress in a coalition are essential if participants are to be vigilant, to the extent demanded by analytical decision approaches, or patient enough to use decision groups. Stress management tactics are needed to save time and effort and prevent emotional burnout. Problem and situational assessments are carried out to allow alternatives to be enumerated, to play out consequences for the alternatives, and to anticipate and cope with possible setbacks.

Coalition Identification

The core problems the decision maker uncovers in the initial steps of framing will suggest several sets of stakeholders. Each core problem defines an arena in terms of stakeholders associated with the problem. One of these arenas is selected to provide a set of people whose values are similar to the interests the decision maker must represent. This coalition is made a formal entity and managed; the other people are ignored. There is no attempt to choose between core problems. Each has its own rationality. The decision maker searches for a powerful set of allies to deal with the organization's interests (March and Simon, 1958).

The coalition's membership is skewed to include people known to be sympathetic to the aims that must be represented. Most successful coalitions, such as kidney foundations and shared service corporations, go through this type of organizational phase. Various factions are monitored to see if their agendas are compatible with those of the emerging coalition. If so, the membership of the coalition is expanded to incorporate these potentially powerful allies. After the *arena* stabilizes, bargaining is used to select objectives acceptable to the coalition. Some guides for the selection of coalition members are discussed in Chapter Ten.

Group processes (Chapter Fifteen) are used to help the coalition explore problems. Group process tactics are also used to help the coalition identify objectives, uncover alternatives, specify criteria, and isolate future conditions, as discussed in Chapters Sixteen and Seventeen. Finally, analysis is applied to the arena produced by these negotiations. The decision maker frames the decision by selecting core problems, identifies and selects a coalition, uses group techniques to uncover information, and applies decision trees and sensitivity analysis (Chapter Eighteen) to extract implications. The mixed-mode procedure shuttles back and forth among these activities, responding to inquiries as they take shape, as described in Chapter Eight.

Emotional Inoculation

Conflict-filled situations call for emotional inoculation. For instance, children's hospitals prepare youngsters for surgery by having them attend a puppet show a week prior to the surgery. The puppet show and hospital visit eliminate the uncertainty that provokes unwarranted fear in children and prepares them to make realistic projections of the pain and discomfort they may suffer. The children get a head start at working through their natural fears and prepare to cope with what will come. Recovery is speedier when appraisals of this type are realistic. Similarly, a realistic appraisal of possible consequences by decision makers in organizations increases their tolerance for postdecisional setbacks that result from making good decisions and experiencing bad outcomes. Bad outcomes can be minimized by good procedure, but not eliminated.

Emotional inoculation calls for three steps: identify possible negative consequences, determine how stakeholders can lose, and offer ways to handle the setbacks of stakeholders. First, key parties are prepared for undesirable chance occurrences. Worst-case scenarios are posed to explore what might happen. To gain realistic outlooks, parties to a decision think through the chance factors that can lead to this type of outcome for each alternative that seems viable. For example, to meet the forecast demand shortfall problem, key parties can explore the coal alternative by considering the most restrictive legislation imaginable and the costs implied, as well as the lowest price hike to offset the costs that seem likely given the attitude of the regulators.

When key parties confront aspects of the decision that cannot be controlled, they reduce surprise. The emotionally inoculated stakeholder has thought about the worst-case scenario and played out personal options to form contingency plans. Recriminations are minimized by these tactics (Janis and Mann, 1977, p. 155).

Useful devices that allow key people to explore the worst-case scenario include role playing, in which each party to the decision lays out his or her fears. Suggestions that deal with these fears can be sought to provide useful coping mechanisms. Assurances can be helpful in eliminating or reducing the stress in unwarranted assumptions about possible consequences. For instance, the junior executives in the nuclear division of a utility company that is abandoning nuclear power could be offered employment continuity, training, and/or assurances of leadership positions when they become available. Such action reduces defensive avoidance.

Coalition Management with the Decision Seminar

The "Decision Seminar" (Laswell, 1960) provides a framework that can be adapted to coalition management. In a Decision Seminar, potential stakeholders are assumed to function as both value shapers and value sharers. As *value shapers*, they point out the desires (requirements) of power centers and what they regard as "enlightened" views. Power stems from the authority to act or to regulate. Enlightenment takes a different course. For instance, tissue typing and organ procurement are vital activities in a renal disease program. However, to "harvest" kidneys, both state laws and prevailing attitudes had to change through enlightenment. Firms anticipating the toxic waste disposal problems associated with a new line of business can ask legislators for tax relief in return for locating plants in low-income areas and assurances that steps will be taken to reduce toxicity in the waste. Enlightenment stems from the joining of several interests to reduce, if not eliminate, social problems. Value shapers can also possess special expertise, prestige, or resources. The power of expertise is exercised through special knowledge. For example, physicians control the process of selecting among alternatives in many hospitals by merely pointing out which alternative is consistent with the "best" medical practice. Waste management experts have a similar impact when they label tax incentives "useful in dealing with social problems." The highly influential can shape values by merely announcing their preferences, as can those who control needed resources.

Stakeholders are also *value sharers*. Those with power gain by thinking through enlightened views, as well as the views stemming from people with expertise, special visibility, or control over resources. The Decision Seminar is designed to promote this type of give and take.

The Social Process Model

The social process model provides the basic underpinning of the Decision Seminar (Laswell, 1974, p. 15). Social processes are made up of person-to-person or person-to-resource interactions. People are predisposed to select alternatives that benefit them. Their preferences are based on how they perceive options as well as on the options' objective features.

Impulse often governs behavior. If organizational participants do not see a proposal for reorganization as offering them opportunity, they may resist it. Impulse leads to a subjective phase in which people form perceptions; this in turn leads to an expression of opinion or to overt behavior. The sequence implies that impulses are activated by events (for example, the reorganization plan) and the messages that events suggest. The inference may or may not be reasonable, but the perceiver often does not wait to corroborate it.

Reactions. Social processes create many reactions. Interactions of various kinds lead to webs of actions and reactions, which make up the social fabric of a decision. Some webs create trails. Following these trails, people will uncover views that they must understand, so they can identify attempts to exploit or counter. Typically, the results of a decision process make its supporters and dissidents easy to spot. Finding them at the outset is the trick. Cues stem from specialized and nonspecialized reactions. A nonspecialized reaction can be cultural, where machismo or similar motifs are transmitted from one generation to another. Specialized reactions hinge on the specifics of the decision and are more difficult to predict.

Perspectives and Myths as Causes. Perspectives in the reaction to an alternative stem from identity, demand, and expectations. Identity deals with self-perception. For example, people often identify with their ancestry (Irish) or their discipline (engineering). Identity may also stem from those excluded from participation or membership, such as male-only athletic clubs. Demand concerns volition. People's desires and aspirations dictate much of their behavior. Expectation deals with illusions about the future and concrete goals. Key stakeholders may believe that the problems provoked by nuclear power are not manageable, making service obligations difficult to meet.

A specialized reaction may also stem from myths. Myths

are relatively fixed patterns of belief that lack empirical foundation. Myths contain doctrine, norms, and active elements. Doctrine describes abstract ideals or a philosophy that guides a person, such as the sanctity of life or business has the right to make profits. Norms dictate rules of conduct, how a person tends to react. Active elements of an individual's personal myth are all the concrete views that he or she expresses on a variety of subjects.

Value Groupings. Values are determined by power, enlightenment, expertise, prestige, and resources. Value shapers act in their own self-interest, expressed in terms of their ability to control the situation. *Value outcomes* represent the positions taken, or likely to be taken, by certain groups or factions on the merit of alternatives considered in a decision process as support is given or taken away. Enlightenment stems from insights and is often based on information. Stakeholders seek to maximize their position, creating gains and avoiding losses. The flow of events, or their anticipation, prior to a reaction or an alternative triggers the value-shaping process. The decision seminar probes these values, hoping that participants will understand and manage them.

Seminar Procedure

The Decision Seminar provides a map that guides the decision maker in dealing with stakeholders who make up a coalition. Laswell (1956) envisioned the seminar as following a seven-step procedure.

1. Gathering and processing information
2. Exploring alternatives
3. Promoting specific recommendations (for example, combined options)
4. Developing general rules
5. Applying the rules to conduct a valuation of alternatives
6. Appraising the alternatives and recommendations
7. Providing the framework for choice

These steps are sequential and somewhat interrelated, and they can be called intelligence, promotion, invocation, prescription, application, termination, and valuation, respectively.

Intelligence. The term *intelligence* is borrowed from Simon (1977), who saw information gathering as both data accumulation and the acquisition of logic to support the data. Defined in this way, intelligence includes the gathering of viewpoints, along with associated justifications and rationalizations, that provides various diagnoses and offers various remedies. The decision maker should gather tangible and intangible as well as explicit and implicit information and reconcile it to initiate the decision process.

Promotion. In the second step of the seminar, the decision maker collects information concerning the agitation for change or resistance to it. Alternatives can have both protagonists and antagonists. The decision maker must measure the force of these feelings to predict the behavior of groups who may support or block implementation. Traditional and Delphi surveys (Chapter Fifteen) may be needed to measure the force of views when many alternatives, each affecting many parties, must be considered.

Invocation. The support or resistance measured in the second step may be rooted in norms or standards that stakeholders apply. Decision makers attempt to identify these norms and how they are applied, to identify offensive or supportive features. For instance, community health centers as an alternative to traditional health care delivery can be controversial because they offer an abortion service. Right-to-life groups would oppose the health centers and free-choice groups would support them because of the implicit support of abortion, not because of the centers' larger purpose of service to the poor. One can oppose a coal alternative for a utility company because it appears to create problems of acid rain; the same alternative can be supported because it seems to help a depressed local economy by providing jobs.

Prescription. In step 4, decision makers compare each alternative to the objectionable or preferred norms uncovered in step 3. The court system does this in a public setting. In decision making, exploration is carried out to find how, for example, the abortion norm can be diffused by treating it as a nonessential service in each alternative health care delivery system under consideration. In another example, opposition to the coal alternative may be softened by a utility's agreeing to use scrubbers to remove pollutants in coal-burning plants.

Application. In the application step, decision makers determine the circumstances that sum up the adoptability of alternatives and propose countermeasures.

Termination. Termination publicizes the new norms to be evoked and how norms were modified because they were found to be objectionable. This step deals with the good-faith claims made by those supporting or objecting to each alternative. Those who would suffer loss of face are acknowledged for their "aid in stimulating a thoughtful debate." A compromise solution is offered when possible. For example, "abortion on demand," a code phrase that creates heavy resistance by some groups, can be modified to "pregnancy counseling," thus softening the community health center's position toward these services. "Acid rain" can also be a code word, one likely to set off environmental groups. An emphasis on pollution-control steps and local job prospects may soften objections to the construction of a coal-burning plant.

Valuation. The coalition becomes a consortium (see Chapter Ten) formed to represent the key power centers whose views must be managed. This group can be multiorganizational in nature but is typically drawn from key interest groups within an organization. The consortium now becomes the dominant force in the decision process. Extending the ideas proposed by Laswell (1965), the consortium is provided with information describing alternatives, level of acceptance by others, the new norms created, and the responses to efforts to ameliorate resistance by reshaping the objectionable alternatives.

Key Points

1. Problem identification and exploration procedures can be used in the analytical, group, and mixed-mode decision

processes. These procedures are applied by a decision maker in the analytical process and by a group in the group process.

2. The mixed-mode process calls for more elaborate procedures to deal with the stress-induced conflict in tough decisions. For these decisions, both core problems and stakeholders can be unclear and potentially in conflict.

    a. Careful exploration of problems provides different frames or windows that offer different ways to explore possibilities as a decision maker attempts to separate symptomatic from core problems. Procedures were offered to identify and explore core problems. The problem perspectives give decision makers a Janusian representation of the decision to play out various implications, using the "5W" analysis, before acting.

    b. Using the insights gained from the problem assessment steps, decision makers define a coalition consistent with interests that they are pledged to represent. This coalition, using an appropriate group process, examines the decision and selects a problem that it will use to guide the decision process.

    c. To deal with the coalition, decision makers need tactics for conflict management. Key steps call for emotional inoculation, exploration of the effects of bad outcomes, and precautionary corrective actions that prepare stakeholders for possible setbacks.

12

Providing
Balanced Viewpoints

Behavioral factors that inhibit decision makers stem in part
from their preferred decision style, as discussed in Chapters Six
and Seven. As a result, managers frequently approach decision
making from either an analytical or a people-oriented perspective, tending to ignore one or the other even though both are
important. This chapter describes a procedure called *multiple
perspectives*, which helps decision makers broaden their views to
cope with these biases and provides a way to examine key
aspects of a decision by applying several perspectives. Figure
12.1 highlights decision steps in which multiple perspectives is
used.

Multiple Perspectives

The concept of multiple perspectives was derived from
Allison's (1971) study of choices made by the Kennedy administration during the Cuban Missile Crisis. Allison's work and that
of Cyert and March (1963) challenge the prevailing economic
theories and contend that decisions must also adhere to the
dominant perspectives that reside within an organization.

Linstone (1984) adapted Allison's work, calling for multiple perspectives to be used for what this book calls tough decisions. Three perspectives are applied: technical, personal, and
organizational. They provide a means to examine the decision
from different angles, illuminating different views of the decision. Each perspective offers unique insights. Tough decisions

Figure 12.1. The Decision Process.

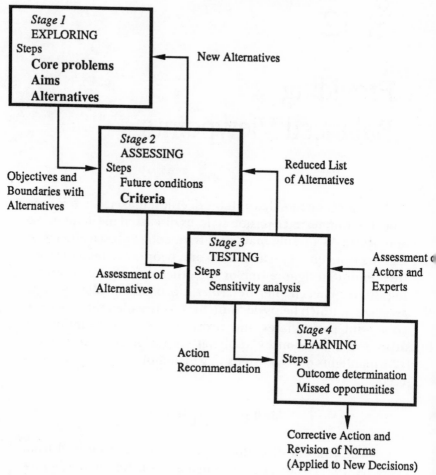

Stage 1
EXPLORING
Steps
  Core problems
  Aims
  Alternatives

New Alternatives

Objectives and
Boundaries with
Alternatives

Stage 2
ASSESSING
Steps
  Future conditions
  Criteria

Reduced List
of Alternatives

Assessment of
Alternatives

Stage 3
TESTING
Steps
  Sensitivity analysis

Assessment of
Actors and
Experts

Action
Recommendation

Stage 4
LEARNING
Steps
  Outcome determination
  Missed opportunities

Corrective Action and
Revision of Norms
(Applied to New Decisions)

Note: Boldface type indicates the topics addressed in this chapter.

call for multiple insights to expose complex considerations that may otherwise go unattended. The technical, personal, and organizational perspectives are treated as mutually supportive because they reveal different but complementary aspects of a decision.

The Technical Perspective. The technical (T) perspective stresses the economic realities of a decision. Questions are posed and answered in terms of statistical comparisons, quantitative measures, and countable attributes. Emphasis is placed on measures such as the amount saved, projected profit, or level of quality achieved. Other measures commonly applied in the T perspective include adherence to preset specifications, such as army ordnance judging a rifle in terms of its bullet speed, cost to manufacture, and reliability. This perspective may dominate in some types of decisions unless the other types are given a legitimate place in the decision process. The analytical procedures discussed in Chapters Thirteen, Eighteen, and Nineteen provide examples of how this perspective is used in decision making.

The Personal Perspective. To use this perspective, the decision maker attempts to see the decision through the eyes of those who are affected. The personal (P) perspective brings to bear individual concerns such as job security, opportunities to demonstrate competence, or means for advancement. Because the perspective can be highly idiosyncratic, it can be elusive. The P perspective calls for speculations about how individuals will be benefactors and victims, doers or users, and the like, as well as what Linstone and others (1981) call "hidden movers." A hidden mover has power in an organization, power that can allow or retard, or even prohibit, a decision from becoming a reality. A hidden mover tries to tease out the views of both gatekeepers and power brokers, as well as individuals with stakes in what is to be done. Power brokers can be identified as individuals who prepare policy statements and SOPs that set the tone of the organization. People who occupy such a position over long periods of time acquire considerable influence. Individuals who are frequently contacted to get around rules and procedures also have this type of power.

The P perspective offers the following kinds of insights (Linstone and others, 1981):

1. Political activity can be predicted by knowing the motives of individual players and their stakes.
2. Aspects of the organizational perspective can be illumi-

nated through the motives of power brokers and gate-keepers. These motives may not surface in a group.
3. Key people can make a difference. Consulting them offers the decision maker ideas and provides a means to implement.
4. Personal concerns and complex problems emerge through individual perspectives that can be swamped by the organizational perspective.

The Organizational Perspective. The organizational (O) perspective views the decision as affecting an entity prone to in-fighting among a collection of power centers whose leaders are poised to fight off competitors and whose staff members maneuver to claim credit. The actors in this system have goals as well as strengths and weaknesses that lead to shifting alliances and coalitions to push their interests.

Seen from the O perspective, decisions move an organization from one state to another. Organizational rules and unwritten treaties are used to guide this process of movement over periods of questioning and controversy. It is this process, rather than the end result, that must be maintained. Rules, codes, agreements, and policy must be followed to ensure that the checks and balances in the organization have had a chance to function. Like the legal and medical systems, the O perspective assumes that the outcome will be correct if the proper procedure is used.

The argument for this perspective stems from the realization that rational and technical information often ignores social interests and questions of value. Seen from the O perspective, rational analysis frequently creates problems in the organization. Rational arguments can disturb the status quo and become a disharmonious voice that breaks down cohesion carefully constructed in accord with the treaties negotiated to take care of the business of an organization. The views of a historian or a political scientist have more salience than those of an economist, in the O perspective. Group procedures discussed in Chapters Ten and Fifteen are often used to develop the organizational perspective.

According to Linstone and others (1981), the O perspective offers the following insights into a decision process:

1. Uncovering pockets of support and opposition and their
   stakes or interests
2. Determining how to absorb the change to be imposed
3. Understanding how to gain support from key power centers
4. Teasing out impacts inherent in the O view, such as organizational costs expressed as delay and turnover

Using the Perspectives. The multiple perspectives concept
has been effectively applied to a variety of decisions in business
and government, dealing with topics ranging from the use of
technology to complex systems. For example, Linstone and
others (1981) describe the army's decision to introduce an improved combat rifle. Army ordnance preferred the M-16 rifle
because it was smaller, had faster bullets, and used a plastic
stock, which reduced its weight. The T perspective was based on
field tests of combat conditions. The tests showed that most
soldiers fire at targets 300 yards or closer, which suggests that
bullet speed is more important than caliber size. In addition, the
M-16 was found to be durable and easy to maintain and could be
manufactured at less cost than its predecessor, the M-14. The O
perspective highlighted significant opposition to the M-16,
which stemmed from the army's tradition of marksmanship. In
competition, large heavy rounds are needed to minimize the
effects of wind resistance. The P perspective included the views
of U.S. Secretary of Defense Robert McNamara, who had been
pushing for cost-effective procurement throughout the military
establishment. The M-16 was purchased, in part, because of the
agreement found in the P and T perspectives. Nevertheless,
army brass had the M-16 modified, reducing its effectiveness as a
combat weapon and increasing its cost, to reassert the marksmanship traditions they embraced. Caliber size was increased,
rifling was used to increase accuracy, and a bolt was introduced
to hold the modified bullets, all of which led to repeated jam-
ming and other malfunctions during combat in Vietnam. Rec-

ognizing and dealing with the O perspective might have kept army personnel from sabotaging the rifle.

Risk assessment applied to a utility company that is deciding between coal and nuclear power options illustrates how multiple perspectives illuminates different aspects of risk. The T perspective raises issues in actuarial and probabilistic terms. Fail-safe ideas and margins of safety could be used to make expected value calculations of risk for varous types of plants and procedures. Through use of the O perspective, different concerns would emerge, such as company image, threats to product lines, avoidance of negative publicity, prospects of litigation, extent of responsibility (ease of assigning blame and anonymity), and difficulty in altering a decision. The P perspective would uncover perceptions about the dangers of nuclear power on the basis of media presentations and personal experiences with nuclear accidents. Such representations and images suggest that a crisis would leave people no time to escape from the potentially devastating and largely unknown consequences of nuclear accidents.

Applying Multiple Perspectives to Tough Decisions

Several cases are presented to illustrate the value of multiple perspectives in tough decisions and to demonstrate how to develop each perspective. Three cases, in which one of the three perspectives dominated, illustrate the benefits of multiple viewing.

The Dominant O Perspective. The deregulation of the banking industry in 1980 caused many savings and loan institutions (S&Ls) to lose their competitive position. Prior to deregulation, S&Ls were allowed to pay a quarter of a percent more interest on savings than could banks. Deregulation allowed banks to use the same rate structure as S&Ls. Soon both banks and S&Ls pegged interest rates to within a quarter of a percent of U.S. Treasury issues.

To retain its customers and remain competitive, a small savings and loan institution (called Mutual) in a medium-sized city elected to offer the top interest rates allowed by law, as well as competitive mortgage rates. This led to Mutual's paying out more in interest than it was yielding from its mortgage business. Mutual needed its strong reserves to offset the deficit. After several loss-plagued years, Mutual's board began to search for a partner with whom the S&L could merge before its reserves were depleted. Other reasons behind the merger decision were the need to acquire management expertise in commercial and consumer lending, which Mutual could not afford, and to offer services provided by larger lending institutions. Mutual's current financial position and economics of scale made this expertise and expanded service impossible.

Mutual's board of directors voted unanimously to pursue a merger with a larger savings and loan institution (Northwest). The *technical* perspective was based on Mutual's profit shortfalls and the perceived need to acquire technology and services that a larger institution could offer. The *organizational* perspective was concerned with preserving Mutual as an entity. Mutual's board thought that more aggressive management would be able to make better use of Mutual's reduced reserves, provide better staffing, and expand services to the community to improve market share. The *personal* perspective was expressed by the views of key actors. The president of Mutual openly opposed the merger, anticipating a loss of prestige if not of his position. A major redefinition of authority was anticipated. To deal with employees' fears of job loss, Mutual secured an agreement from Northwest that guaranteed job security. The agreement ensured that no employee would lose his or her job as a result of the merger, but it did not guarantee employees their current positions.

In this decision, the O perspective dominated. Mutual's board took action to ensure the bank's survival and to meet its perception of the needs of the institution. Northwest took several steps that eventually led to profitability but also led to unrest and low morale, which delayed the impact of its actions.

According to Northwest's standards, the salaries of Mutual's employees were excessive, so those salaries were frozen. Morale was damaged when Northwest replaced Mutual's computer system with its own. Mutual's computer capability was one of the S&L's few distinctive competencies, and its elimination led to the resignation of key employees and the loss of customers. There was no attempt to adapt Mutual's capabilities into Northwest's system. More attention to the T perspective might have salvaged Mutual's computer capability. Many of Mutual's service departments, such as accounting, were eliminated, with their services subsequently provided by Northwest. Morale was further eroded when the transfers due to departmental elimination were presented as a "take it or leave it" offer to which people had to commit within forty-eight hours. More attention to the P perspective would have helped the merged institution deal with these morale problems. For instance, the automated teller network, which was expanded from three to thirteen units, and the new branch offices that were being planned could have been used to offer job prospects to displaced Mutual employees.

The Dominant T Perspective. The decision summarized in Table 12.1 was carried out in 1984 in a major division of a U.S. steel company located in a small city. The company had to shut down one of its three blast furnaces for a "reline" that would require four months to complete. Sales forecasts revealed that customer needs could not be met by the steel ingots produced in other divisions of the company during the reline period. Because high-quality ingots were not available at competitive prices from domestic firms, the company initiated negotiations with foreign producers.

The announcement of impending foreign steel purchases produced an outcry from both employees and the community. The union had just finished a bitter contract negotiation, having accepted both wage cuts and benefit "take backs" in response to the company's plea that it had been severely hurt by competition from foreign steel producers. Some top officials in the division were also upset because top management had made the foreign steel purchase announcement without consulting them. Top management was reminded that it had promulgated a practice prohibiting its employees from buying foreign cars because they were made of foreign steel. The community reacted to the steel company's marketing, which included billboard ads that de-

Table 12.1. Multiple Perspectives Analysis Applied to a Steel Company.

Decision: Select a way to deal with lost capacity during four-month blast furnace reline period.

Options	Perspective	Positive Considerations	Negative Considerations
1. Purchase domestic steel	Technical	None	Inferior ingots at high cost lower product quality and increase cost
	Organizational	Buying "American"	None
	Personal	Top management seen as loyal to union and domestic business	None
2. Shut down temporarily and lay off employees	Technical	Decrease in costs	Decrease in revenues
	Organizational	None	Poor customer relations from canceled orders, poor employee relations due to layoffs
	Personal	None	Top management seen as passive and reactive, unable to plan for predictable events
3. Purchase foreign steel	Technical	Decrease cost, maintain quality	None
	Organizational	None	Potential loss of community prestige and credibility
	Personal	None	Credibility of managers suffers both inside and outside the organization
4. Produce steel internally	Technical	Maintain quality	Modest cost increase
	Organizational	Challenge offered to workers requiring teamwork and responsibility may lead to motivation and positive attitude	None
	Personal	Top management retains credibility, willing to take risks for employees	If plan fails, VP may lose job and take others down with him

scribed the plight of the company and attributed it to foreign competition.

The steel purchase decision was made from the T perspective, drawing on information cited in Table 12.1. However, top management was unable to sustain the decision to purchase foreign steel, even by noting that the purchase was a one-time proposition and that only foreign ingots were both high-quality steel and inexpensive. This defense provoked key people to note that Hondas were of high quality and inexpensive and a one-shot decision as well. Pressure from employees and the community forced top management to revise its decision. At this point, the fourth option in Table 12.1 turned up from an employee quality circle. The proposal identified a way to increase production in the division's remaining blast furnaces. The proposal would increase production but called for production levels never before reached in the division. This option was adopted to avoid the problems of the other options. The decision was clarified by the P-and O perspectives, and the risks to management were specified so the division could take steps to lower them. For instance, if the plan failed, a smaller amount of foreign steel would be purchased as a stopgap measure.

The Dominant P Perspective. H Clothing Stores is a chain of stores that caters to big and tall men. The corporate office of the chain is in a small town in Ohio. Top managers all had winter homes in Florida and for some time had toyed with the idea of a Florida operation to write off personal travel to these homes. In 1979, H expanded into south and central Florida by opening three new stores. Seventy percent of H's merchandise was centrally purchased, which resulted in merchandise geared for a midwestern market and northern climate being sent to the Florida stores. Winter clothes face a hard sell in Florida, and H experienced severe financial losses for the first time in its high-profit history.

Three options were identified by the top executives: close the Florida stores, sell the Florida stores to another chain, or try to revitalize the Florida stores. Because the inventory could not be absorbed by the other stores and the Florida stores' fixtures would have to be written off, the first option would have created a huge loss. Selling the Florida stores would have produced a smaller loss because store property was leased. Only the inventory, fixtures, and location were available for sale. Although the close and sell options could have been ruled out by cost considerations, the P perspective of the company president was dominant in the decision to adopt the option of resurrecting the stores. No data were presented to support the resurrection option. The president of H was committed to the Florida locations and determined to make them work.

Using the Multiple Perspective Approach

Table 12.2 illustrates one way to use multiple perspectives when making tough decisions. For this type of decision, perspective can be crucial. There is no test to ensure that core problems have been uncovered, let alone understood. Multiple perspectives are applied to explore the decision in three explicit ways. This step exposes the decision process to different modes of viewing, offering insights from several perspectives.

H Clothing Stores. The H Clothing Stores case is used to illustrate how the multiple perspective approach can work. Table 12.2 summarizes how this decision of dealing with losses in the Florida stores could have been addressed by using information that was available when the decision was made. Market research had revealed that Florida was one of the best and most rapidly growing markets in the nation. Natives are middle aged and older, a clientele that H had long served, and they are wealthy. Florida has a large tourist population with discretionary money to spend. Business conventions often choose Florida, and H specializes in business attire.

The analysis in Table 12.2 has several implications. First, different core problems emerged from each perspective and led to different objectives and thus to the application of unique criteria. The conflict in the decision could have been avoided had the president made his objectives clear. This step would have allowed managers to make a broader search for alternatives to revitalize the stores, including changing (temporarily or permanently) the scale of store operations, trying new locations, hiring

Table 12.2. The H Clothing Stores Decision Based on Multiple Perspectives.

Decision: Find a way to deal with losses in the Florida stores.

	Technical	*Organizational*	*Personal*
Core Problems	The economy was bad because of a recession; most businesses were contracting The Florida stores had very poor financials and very few customers	Florida managers were poorly trained in H's procedures, but distances called for extensive delegation; merchandise that sells in Florida outside company buyer's area of expertise; to close stores would look bad in eyes of suppliers and public Other stores cannot offset losses in Florida stores	President saw Florida stores as way to smooth Midwest recession problems that hurt other stores; had been with company twenty years and never closed a store Chairman of board had supported Florida stores and would experience loss of face if they closed Top management wanted stores to permit the write-off of trips to their winter homes in Florida
Objectives	Make profit comparable to that of other stores	Have company stretch from Michigan to Florida	Seek stores that complement existing stores with market potential
Criteria	Profit	Growth	Stability and growth
Alternatives	1. Close stores: sell fixtures and inventory 2. Sell stores to a competitor	1. Use store comanagers 2. Use close supervision by regional managers 3. Train or fire personnel	Revitalize the stores (seven-point plan involving new advertising, new merchandise, and consideration of customer age, climate, tourism, and convention clientele)
Consequences of Alternatives	Selling stores opens door for competitors in a viable market; closing stores creates a large projected loss	Travel to fix problems costly and debilitating for regional manager; comanager idea never worked when tried before	No way to assess prospect for success
Implementation Barriers	Family-owned company opposes all "close store" alternatives	Limits to double-duty managing	Lack of personnel and expertise to run the stores

people with expertise in Florida men's clothing tastes, or employing people with experience in Florida store operation who would be aware of customers' preferences and habits.

PBB Contamination. A second example of the use of multiple perspectives can be found in Table 12.3. The decision involved a PBB incident that occurred in Michigan. At its St. Louis plant, the Michigan Chemical Company was manufacturing polybrominated biphenyl (PBB) as a fire retardant (called Firemaster) and magnesium oxide, which improves the fat test in milk (marketed as Nutrimaster). In the summer of 1973, these two products were inadvertently switched. Firemaster (made of PBB) was sent to a feed mill in Battle Creek, where it was mixed with feed and distributed to farmers throughout the state of Michigan by the Michigan Farm Bureau. By August, a wave of cattle ailments spread across the state, including changes in food consumption and milk production, abnormal growths of hoofs, stillborn calves, and difficulties in breeding. In 1974, analysis of the feed mix revealed PBB contamination, which was confirmed by the detection of PBB in the milk of affected cattle, and the error was discovered.

Livestock were quarantined for testing, and guidelines were established. As a result, 181 farms were designated as having contaminated herds. Thirty thousand contaminated cattle were taken to remote Kaekaska County by state veterinarians and killed and buried on state-owned land in the county without any public notice. In 1974, the FDA established more rigid standards, which placed several hundred more herds under quarantine. After considerable bickering, the governor of Michigan signed an executive order calling for these cattle to be treated in the same way as the more heavily contaminated herds. The governor's action received nationwide media attention. Residents of Oscoda County, the county selected for the second burial, protested loudly and subsequently took legal action.

The lawsuits pointed out that there had been no research on the environmental effects of PBB. The same properties that made PBB an excellent fire retardant (stable, persistent, nonflammable, and only slightly toxic) seemed to pose environmental risks. Environmentalists in the Department of Natural Re-

Table 12.3. The PBB-Contaminated Cattle Disposal Decision
Based on the Use of Multiple Perspectives.

Decision: Find a way to deal with PBB-contaminated cattle.

	Technical	*Organizational*	*Personal*
Core Problems	Standards that specified contamination were unclear Effects of low levels of PBB contamination were obscure Precautionary geological tests found little recontamination of food supplies; test wells were proposed to monitor groundwater Media attention made herd useless despite MSU's progress in restoring some of the animals Some animals were dead and decomposing, and immediate site selection for disposal was required	Michigan Farm Bureau sought to act quickly to moderate public opinion of incompetence stemming from the incident Department of Agriculture wanted to restore good name of Michigan products	No public notification of first burial attempt Second burial announcement enraged residents in selected area; suit was filed with EPA to block burial Farmers were losing money as politicians debated
Objectives	Arrange prompt and safe burial	Satisfy politicians and put issue to rest	Protect local area
Criteria	Unknown PBB toxicity cost and prospect of groundwater contamination	Dire straits of state livestock industry and prospect of public protest	Safety margin must be ensured
Alternatives	1. Mass burial in 20-foot clay-lined pit in remote and sparsely populated area 2. Mass burial in one-foot clay pit 3. Burial on private farms 4. Shipment out of state	Fastest means available	Incineration
Consequences of Alternatives	People unwilling to accept assurances that PBB level was nontoxic (private burial and out-of-state shipment costly and time-consuming)	Environmental impact ignored	Delays
Implementation Barriers	Civil court action	Prerogatives to act blocked by legal action	Process to burn carcasses would take six months to carry out

sources claimed that precautionary geological tests found little chance of food chain contamination and suggested that test wells could be installed to monitor groundwater. The total amount of PBB in the second quarantined herd of cattle was estimated to be less than the toxicity in one pack of cigarettes. The total quantity of PBB to be put in the burial pit was less than two ounces, which, if put into a river in pure form, would produce no measurable environmental effect. These facts were available but not reported by the media.

Oscoda residents were not placated by assurances from state officials. They formed a legal action committee, raised money, and filed suit against the state. The suit claimed that the contaminated livestock would pollute the environment, in direct violation of the Environmental Protection Act. It claimed that the proposed clay pit could develop faults and result in the contamination of groundwater. An incineration alternative was proposed because exposure for two seconds at 2000°F rendered PBB nontoxic. The court ruled against the incineration option despite its long-term benefits and its ability to appease the county residents. Incineration would take six months, and some animals had died and were already decomposing, which made immediate disposal necessary. The court ruled that the animals already dead should be buried in Oscoda County and the remaining livestock sent to Utah to be killed and buried.

The technical perspective suggests that the hysteria, produced by media coverage, and the state's previous covert burials made it impossible to salvage the quarantined herd after the second testing, even though a university veterinary school found that the animals could be restored to health. However, the T perspective also pointed out that there was no danger in adopting the cheapest option (a one-foot-deep lined clay pit). More attention to the P and T perspectives by the O perspective could have averted this comedy of errors.

Building a Museum. Fort Leavenworth, Kansas, claims to have the oldest continually occupied military post west of the Mississippi. Established in 1835, the post was home to cavalry and dragoon units and the starting point for wagon trains on their way to the Santa Fe and Oregon trails to colonize the

American West. Subsequently, the fort became the infamous Leavenworth penitentiary. More recently, it served as the home of the Command and General Staff College, a postgraduate school for military affairs and tactical research. The barracks, offices, and prison are considered national historical landmarks and must meet stringent repair and renovation requirements. A World War II hangar was used to house the military and pioneer history collection, and plans to create a more fitting site were being discussed. Before final arrangements for the collection could be made, the Reagan administration, in its token slashing of military spending during the 1980s, banned the use of military funds to construct museums. In response, local citizens organized an association to raise money to construct the museum on land donated by the military prior to the ban. The decision considered here is the selection of an architectural design team to design and build the museum.

Representatives of the association interviewed seventy-five architectural firms. Large firms were screened out, leaving only local firms, with or without museum experience. The remaining firms were asked to submit a statement of interest and illustrations of their work. After three months, a list of seventeen firms was submitted to the association's board of directors. Some of these firms were eliminated and others added by the association's board of directors. The executive director contacted each firm, producing a short list of seven firms after two more months of work. The seven firms were asked to prepare written responses to questions and make a presentation to the fundraising committee. At this point, four firms were ruled out. Conflict developed over the remaining three. Some members of the board and the entire fund-raising committee, who favored one firm, clashed with other board members who favored either of the other two firms. The board took several votes before a firm was finally selected. Compromise was achieved when an adviser, who had worked for the U.S. Army Corps of Engineers and served as the fort's engineering adviser, offered his views to the board. Full and half votes were parceled out by the board's chairman, ensuring that the firm favored by the board would be selected.

The museum case provides yet another illustration of problems that arise when managers deal with architectural matters, as pointed out in the opera house decision (Chapter Two). The criteria implied by form and function are invariably difficult for a decision maker to deal with. The architect offers a "picture" or model of a building (form) that seemingly provides a solution because it appears to be a tangible alternative that sweeps away ambiguity. The decision maker has something specific to contemplate and show to donors, which puts decision making on what appears to be a tangible basis. This bias toward form eventually creates problems with function. The technical perspective often uncovers functional considerations, such as the needs of users, interpreted in terms of space and expansion, and the more mundane issues of building access, storage, and the like.

The interests of donors arise in the organizational perspective in which a model or picture can be used to capture the imagination of people during fund-raising. When decision makers consider both technical and organizational perspectives, form and function become two integral parts of the overall decision. Neither gets emphasized at the expense of the other.

The personal perspective arises in the selection of which form or the trade-off of demands of various users to keep a building within budget. Decision makers must address the question of whose interests are to be served. By making these interests explicit, in both form and function, decision makers are more likely to uncover needed compromises.

Debates about form (which design) often cover up vested interests, which, if made public, would harm fund-raising. Conflicts of interest, both large and small, are present in most decisions of this type. They cannot be ignored and must be carefully managed to keep the conflict under control. These problems often arise in the selection of an architect. To manage the process of architect selection, a selection committee that represents the T, P, and O interests should be named. Working out these interests articulates requirements posed from each viewpoint. For instance, catering to the interests of individuals in visionary, realist, promoter, and operator roles is possible

Table 12.4. Selecting an Architect for a Military Pioneer Museum
by Means of Multiple Perspectives.

Decision: Select design for museum.

	Technical	*Organizational*	*Personal*
Core Problems	Missouri River's flood plain City traffic patterns Future and current space needs	Make defensible decision and minimize conflict that could undermine fund-raising	The perspectives of individuals acting as visionaries, realists, promoters, obstructionists, and operators
Objectives	Identify what constitutes a good firm by interviewing historical societies, U.S. Army Corps of Engineers, American Institute of Architects, etc.	1. Select a well-qualified local architect 2. Follow preset rules and procedures 3. Ensure board members' satisfaction 4. Show progress toward goal	Self-interest of key people
Criteria	Fees and capability of firm	1. Reasons for or against a particular firm 2. Board acceptance	1. Gut reaction to firms 2. Self-interest in power, pleasure, prestige, or personal gain
Alternatives	Favored firms	Favored firms	Favored firms
Consequences of Alternatives	Best firms were not well connected	Best firm and compromise firm produced different choices	Best firms did not meet personal interest of power broker
Implementation Barriers	Paying more and getting less	Disclosure that best firm was not selected	Disclosure of personal interests

while preserving the unified front needed for fund-raising and capturing the technical demands posed by site and building, as shown in Table 12.4. Adapting these steps could have shortened the museum decision process and heightened satisfaction of those involved in the outcome.

Key Points

1. Applying technical, personal, and organizational perspectives to a decision provides a way to broaden the perspec-

tives of a decision maker and deal with the biases inherent in the decision styles of participants.

2. Each of the technical, personal, and organizational perspectives offers a valid and complementary way to look at a decision.

3. A synthesis of the T, P, and O perspectives provides a superior way to carry out a decision process by incorporating the T, P, and O values as objectives, alternative courses of action, and criteria by which to judge the alternatives that are uncovered.

❧ 13

Comparing
the Value of Alternatives
and "What If" Questioning

This chapter presents analytical procedures to deal with people's information-processing problems, discussed in Chapters Four and Five. These procedures merge subjective and objective information and show how managers can use analysis to supplement judgment. Analytical procedures are offered to support the informal reasoning preferred by decision makers, not to supplant this reasoning with analysis. The analytical framework defines the information needed to value alternatives, provides a way to deal with uncertainty, and helps to build a vocabulary. The analytical procedures identify information that is essential and, by omission, information that is superfluous, thus simplifying and focusing information acquisition. These steps permit decision makers to cope with uncertainty about future conditions by systematically exploring the impact of plausible conditions. Decision makers can then relax assumptions by asking "what if" questions to determine whether a choice is sensitive to assumptions made about key conditions, such as demand. Finally, a set of terms that make up a vocabulary of decision making is offered to sharpen the reader's thinking about how to make decisions.

These procedures are useful because they extend managers' memory and help them cope with the frustration and anxiety often provoked by tough decisions. The analytical framework shows how to store needed information for future use to help overcome short-term memory problems that can lead managers to make poor decisions. Most decision makers fear situations that are filled with conflict, uncertainty, and ambiguity about choices. The need to act and, at the same time, protect themselves coaxes decision makers to use their energy defensively in situations that could benefit the most from their insight and other kinds of intuitive skills. The analytical procedures help to organize the decision, which reduces anxiety and allows decision makers to probe and learn, directing their energies in productive directions.

Analysis, however, can do more harm than good when it is carried out without the focus provided by a response to core problems. Recall the cost analysis in the BART decision, discussed in Chapter Two. The appearance of analytical sophistication gave decision makers a false sense of confidence, which discredited the legitimate questions about the runaway cost of the BART system and its ability to reduce traffic problems that were raised by thoughtful critics. Analysis is useful only when it is directed by objectives and alternatives that offer ways to respond to core problems. For example, in the BART decision an objective of reducing urban congestion in a cost-effective manner would have called for the comparison of high-speed urban transit and fast-lane buses as well as other alternatives, in terms of how each could reduce congestion and at what cost.

The material in this chapter deals with the steps called for in stages 2 and 3 of the decision process, as highlighted in Figure 13.1.

Information Management

After bounding a decision by clarifying its objective, alternatives are sought. A decision maker faced with choosing among these alternatives can be distracted by what Simon (1977) calls the "limits of rationality." As demonstrated in Chapters Four and Five, a manager's information-processing capabilities are frequently unable to cope with some of the demands of decision making. Such limitations make it impossible for the decision maker to deal with all of the available pertinent information in

Figure 13.1. The Decision Process.

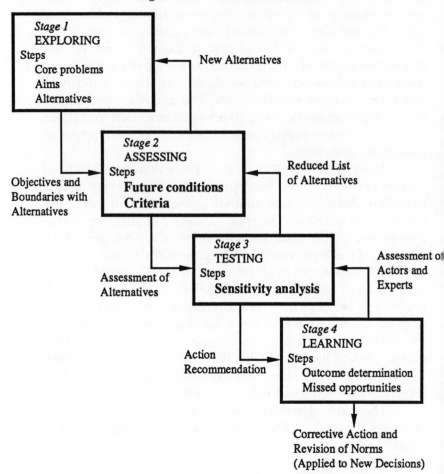

Note: Boldface type indicates topics addressed in this chapter.

order to describe and value alternatives, let alone to explore their more subtle consequences. This situation is made worse by time constraints and distractions that demand the decision maker's attention (Downs, 1967). The amount of objective information available may be but a small portion of what is potentially available if one conducts a careful search. This additional information, however, can be costly, and its acquisition may cause delays in decision making. Finally, some types of information are not available, no matter what the cost or delay, and other types can be obtained only as subjective estimates. Predicting future conditions, such as demand or utilization, and shifts in preferences provide examples.

Information-processing limitations entice decision makers to engage in behavior that can lead to poor decisions. First, choices are often made by managers without the full use of available information. The complexity of the task overwhelms them. As a result, decision makers make a snap judgment, using simplistic approaches, such as rules of thumb and heuristics, as described in Chapters Four and Five. Second, decision makers fail to tease out some of the consequences of alternatives they believe to be viable. Third, decision makers seldom look beyond conspicuous alternatives (Cyert and March, 1963) to find new and potentially better ones. They have enough trouble processing the information that they have without seeking more. Stress creates situations that produce fatigue, and frequent interruptions intensify these reactions, reducing the processing of available information even further, as described in Chapter Eleven.

These difficulties lead to decision rules that simplify a choice in order to make it manageable. Two such rules are satisficing and incrementalism. A satisficing (March and Simon, 1958) decision rule is used when decision makers adopt the first alternative they find that meets their expectations. Incrementalism (Lindblom, 1965) is applied when decision makers minimize their commitment by adopting the alternative most like current practices. Both of these decision rules allow a decision maker to make choices with very little information in short-fuse situations. In the long term, however, such behavior leads to missed opportunity and a hodgepodge of choices that are hard to defend when viewed as a stream of commitments.

The key to improving decision making lies in overcoming these limitations by improving the information search. The first step in a search is to recognize crucial types of information and ways that they can be identified and organized for future use.

Some Examples

The analytical framework presented in this chapter can be applied to many diverse decisions. Examples include staffing, bidding, new products or services, job selection, managerial succession, office location, inventory investment, real estate investment, and lobbying.

Staffing decisions must often deal with increased work load during periods of heavy demand, such as sales and Christmas. A department store can have several alternatives to deal with the anticipated increase in demands. It can use temporary help, restrict vacations and use overtime, or ignore the situation. These alternatives can be described as temporary employees, regular staff, and do nothing. The future conditions under which these alternatives must be evaluated depict the amount of business the store anticipates during the peak period. Suppose these conditions are assumed to be either a 25 percent or a 75 percent increase in sales volume during the peak period. The criterion used to evaluate the options is profit. Other criteria can be relevant, such as lost future sales due to customer dissatisfaction and employee resistance to a policy of increased work hours during a holiday, which might cause good salespeople to resign. Ways to handle multicriteria decisions are discussed in Chapter Nineteen.

The framework just described for the department store organizes the decision situation by specifying what the decision maker needs to find out. For instance, time lost in the training of temporary employees would have to be added to the cost of recruiting or paying an agency to recruit. However, the cost of these temporary employees would be less than overtime paid to current employees. The current employees might be more adept at making sales and more efficient with the paperwork, making them more productive. However, during a period of long working hours and heavy demand, current employees might lose some of their effectiveness as fatigue set in. The do-nothing option might result in lost sales due to long customer lines. These and related considerations are swept into profit estimates made for each of six outcomes (the three alternatives times the 25 and 75 percent future-condition projections).

Analytical Framework

The framework used to value alternatives is normative decision theory (NDT). This approach, first proposed by Von

Figure 13.2. Components of the Normative Decision Model.

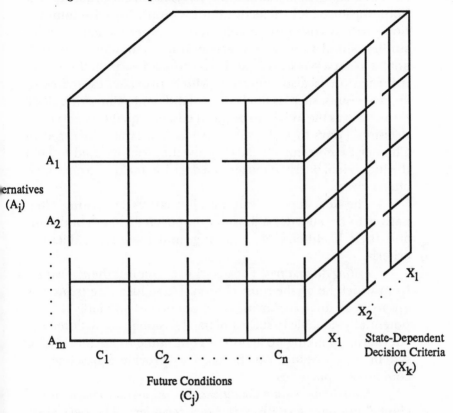

Neuman and Morgenstern (1947), provides a way to link future conditions to the value of alternatives, thus merging the analytical and judgmental aspects of making a choice. To carry out an analysis, one must specify alternatives, future conditions, the likelihood of future conditions, and criteria, as shown in Figure 13.2.

The decision maker, supported by staff members, describes the alternatives under consideration, identifies future conditions that could occur, estimates the likelihood that each condition will occur, and examines objectives to derive criteria that can be used to evaluate each alternative, considering its intrinsic merit and how merit is influenced by future conditions, such as level of demand. The analysis calls for the acquisition of both objective and subjective information. Objective information, such as cost, can be collected by experimentation, pilot studies, simulation, survey, accounting techniques, statistical analysis, survey research, and operations research. Subjective information is also required, which provides estimates of chance events, such as levels of demand, and value-laden situations, such as the weight to be given cost and quality criteria in a decision. (Ways to make subjective estimates are discussed in Chapter Seventeen.) The NDT procedure can be used to help the individual decision maker or a decision-making group value alternatives.

The key steps in valuing alternatives are listing alternatives to be valued, establishing important future conditions and their likelihood of occurring, and identifying decision criteria.

Listing Alternatives. The decision maker lists the *alternatives* from which he or she must choose. These ideas are treated as givens in an analysis, having been uncovered and judged to be potentially valuable in stage 1 of the decision process. Often the alternative of taking no action or continuing to use an existing system or procedure can be used to provide a baseline for comparison purposes.

Establishing Future Conditions. An important factor in the choice among alternatives is *future conditions*. The best alternative under one set of conditions may not be best under different conditions. These conditions are beyond the manager's control but offer important opportunities to manage their effect. For example, to exert a degree of control over the environment, the manager uses marketing programs designed to increase the level of demand for a hospital's services or a firm's products. The tactics people use to influence future conditions differ in profit-making, public, and third-sector (nonprofit, private) organizations. For-profit organizations focus on potential customers who may purchase products. Public organizations must define their "market" in terms of entitlements stemming from legislative oversight or rule making. Third-sector organizations, such as a nonprofit hospital, can market to physicians (the consumers of their services) but must also define their market in terms of the interests of key members of their oversight body, such as endowers who serve on the board of trustees. Each of these types of markets can be managed to an extent by the organization through tactics such as lobbying or promotional action.

Some future conditions are imposed by the actions of third parties and function as constraints. Governmental regulation limits capacity expansion in utilities, hospitals, and other types of organizations. Plant expansions in for-profit organizations can become infeasible when tax incentives or interest rates change. Lobbying and promotion often are dysfunctional in this type of situation. Decision making must be organized to manage the acquisition of information that describes future conditions, such as marketing prospects and the likelihood that constraints will be imposed.

Future conditions describe states of nature that can influence the value of an alternative. The analysis must consider how key future conditions can alter the alternative's value. For instance, consider Boeing's decision *not* to build an airplane to compete against the Concorde, which was to be built by a consortium of Common Market countries. This decision was influenced by uncertainties about future conditions, including forecasts of environmental impact, demand for the airplane as a function of price, the prospects of legislation allowing a supersonic aircraft to be flown across the United States, and the airplane's potential value as a military aircraft. When deciding on the desirability of competing, Boeing used these future conditions to consider the potential demand for the aircraft. A more favorable assessment of the future conditions would have suggested higher numbers of potential aircraft sales, which might have made the "competing" alternative more desirable.

Each future condition can be described in various ways as long as the description represents all conditions that are conceivable, such as the range of product sales possibilities.

Estimating the Likelihood of Future Conditions. Future conditions are made up of plausible levels of the conditions, such as various levels of demand. Estimates are made to attach a likelihood to each condition (for example, demand levels). For instance, forecasts of "hospital patient days," a measure of demand used by hospitals, can be linked to experience in the field. The data can be used to establish the likelihood of two conditions, one that assumes demand will be high (say, 150 percent of the projection) and the other that assumes demand will be low (50 percent of the projection). To collect this information, several comparable hospitals could be surveyed to detect their volumes, creating a frequency distribution that would describe their composite demand. Subjective information can also be used to estimate demand likelihoods when relevant forecasts cannot be made. Subjective probabilities are estimated by experts who are knowledgeable about the future condition and aided by tools for subjective estimation described in Chapter Seventeen. The probabilities are assumed to be independent of the alternatives selected. When the distribution of probabilities is continuous rather than discrete, a more complicated formulation is required.

Identifying Criteria. Criteria provide the basis for making a choice. Criteria are derived from the intent implied by the decision maker's objectives by applying the procedures described in Chapter Sixteen. The intersection of a future condition and an alternative in Figure 13.2 produces an outcome. This outcome is valued by criteria, such as cost or profit, that link each alternative to each future condition to determine the alternative's value.

Several criteria are often needed to characterize value. For example, an emergency medical service's dispatch service can be valued according to its cost, response time, and capacity under various levels of demand. The capacity criterion may be important for a condition that has a very high level of demand. Some patients may not be served, should this condition occur. Cost illustrates a criterion that varies with demand. Response time is not influenced by demand, assuming that queuing is prohibited. The relative importance of these decision criteria is subjective, reflecting the values of the decision maker. The outcome describing the value or merit of each alternative is made up of objective information, such as the cost and level of satisfaction in a given state, and subjective information depicting criteria weights and the likelihood of the future conditions. To simplify the discussion, examples in this chapter use a single criterion. (Ways to handle decisions involving multiple criteria are discussed in Chapters Nineteen and Twenty.)

Collecting this information often reveals defects in the objectives thought to be important or the alternatives that respond to these objectives. When this occurs, the decision maker recycles to stage 1. Steps are taken to expand or contract the decision boundary and review the core problem. A different boundary may emerge, one that appears to have more salience, thus producing a new set of alternatives to be valued in stage 2.

Types of Decisions

Choice problems are classified by what is known about future conditions. If only one condition can occur, a *choice under certainty* results. Such a situation can arise when the level of demand or expected usage can be predicted with a high degree of precision. For example, the managers of captive operations, such as an organization's computer system, can often predict future demands by using past trends. Similarly, firms in stable environments can assume that demands for their products can be predicted by a forecast that relies on historical patterns of consumption. For example, firms making fuel-efficient cars during the gas crisis caused by the oil embargoes of OPEC knew they could run their production lines at full capacity throughout the crisis.

A *choice under uncertainty* occurs when several conditions exist but neither objective nor subjective probabilities can be assigned to indicate the likelihood that any given condition will occur. This situation can result when decisions are made in a turbulent environment. For example, a decision under uncertainty may develop when a manager is deciding whether to market a new concept for a fuel-efficient car as ambiguous signals about another oil shortage appear. Decisions under uncertainty and certainty are treated in the same way. When the level of demand is predicted or when likelihoods cannot be assigned to levels of demand that may occur, the decision is made on the basis of information that values each alternative. The alternative with the highest value is selected.

A *choice under risk* occurs when probabilities for future conditions, such as demand or usage, can be estimated using the subjective estimates of experts or by drawing information from a comparable situation. For example, a choice under risk can arise when a firm's marketing staff has been reading environmental signals and believes it understands shifts in preference and other factors that influence demand. It can also arise when analogies can be drawn to the organization's history or to another organization's experiences. For example, a frequency distribution of responses to past new-product offerings can be used to estimate demand likelihoods. Both types of decisions are illustrated in the examples that follow.

Example of a Choice Under Certainty

Assume that a planning process has recommended the purchase of word processors to replace old-style typewriters. The word processors' initial cost may be offset by lower operating cost. The alternatives are (1) retain the typewriters and (2) purchase the word processors.

The following data have been collected:

	Typewriters Alternative	Word-Processors Alternative
Purchase cost	0	$40,000
Operating cost	$20,000	$10,000
Salvage value	$ 4,000	0
Expected life	—	5 years

The present-worth technique can be used to evaluate each alternative. This approach determines the time-discounted present value of all savings and compares it to the capital outlay for each alternative. If the discounted savings exceed the capital requirements, the purchase of word processors is desirable. The option with the largest amount of "savings less outlays" would be selected.

The present worth of the word processors is as follows:

$$\begin{array}{llll} \text{Present worth} = & \text{Salvage} + & \text{Annual} & \times \text{Present} \\ & \text{value} & \text{operating} & \text{worth} \\ & & \text{cost} & \text{factor} \\ & & \text{savings} & \end{array}$$

The present worth factor is calculated in this way:

$$PWF = [(1 + i)^{n-1}]/i(1 + i)^n$$

where PWF = present worth factor
i = interest rate
n = number of years

or it is determined by consulting tables (see, for example, Grant, 1960). Assume the organization has been receiving a 10 percent return on investment but believes a more aggressive strategy would yield 15 percent. Applying this assumption, the present worth (Pw) of the new equipment alternative is

$$Pw = \$4,000 + (\$20,000 - \$10,000)(3.352) = \$37,520$$

The cost savings associated with each alternative would be

$$\begin{array}{l} A_1 \text{ (retain)} = \$0 \\ A_2 \text{ (purchase)} = \text{discounted return} - \text{purchase cost} \\ \qquad\qquad = \$37,520 - \$40,000 \\ \qquad\qquad = -\$2,480 \end{array}$$

Word processors would not be purchased, as indicated by the operating cost savings for the alternatives.

A_1 (retain) $0

A_2 (purchase) $- \$2,480$

Note that the alternatives are valued by projected savings in operating costs.

The same logic would be used for decisions under uncertainty because, using the example described above, usage factors would be unknown and thus cannot be tied to the criterion of cost savings.

Example of a Choice Under Risk

Using the same example, assume that the organization is concerned about its internal capacity if an unlikely event, estimated to have a one-in-ten chance of occurring, increased the demands placed on its typing pool by 50 percent. In this situation there would be two states: one reflecting the current volume ($P_1 = .90$) and the other a 50 percent increase ($P_2 = .10$). Each alternative must now be valued under the increased-volume condition to compare with the current-volume condition that was valued in the previous example.

The change in volume can influence the operating cost of both the replace and retain alternatives. Under this assumption, all typewriters would be fully occupied and no additional typing capacity could be created with the current system. Assume that the only feasible way to increase capacity is to contract out work at a 50 percent increase in cost. This would result in an increase in operating cost of $15,000 and a total operating cost of $35,000. (A 50 percent increase in activity would increase costs from $20,000 to $30,000, and a 50 percent increase in cost for this $10,000 increase would add another $5,000, for a total of $35,000.) The word-processor option could deal with the increased volume with a 25 percent increase in operating cost, resulting in an operating cost of $12,500. Present worth would be computed in the same way as in the previous example, altering operating costs to reflect the increases caused by the higher level of volume. The present worth of the cost savings of the new equipment would be

$$Pw = \$4,000 + (\$35,000 - \$12,500)(3.352) = \$79,420$$

The discounted cost savings of each alternative under this condition (a 50 percent increase in demand) would be

A_1 (retain) = increase in operating cost
= $(15,000)
A_2 (purchase) = Discounted return – purchase cost
= $79,420 – $40,000
= $39,420

The decision is captured in Table 13.1. Selecting the alternative with the greatest value is no longer clear-cut. A significant increase in cost can occur for each alternative. The retain alternative results in a $15,000 increase in cost when volume is high, but the purchase alternative results in a $2,480 cost increase under a current volume assumption.

Table 13.1. Example of a Choice Under Risk.

	C_1 Current Demand	C_2 50% Increase in Demand
Alternatives	$P_1 = .90$	$P_2 = .10$
A_1 (Retain)	$0[a]	– $15,000
A_2 (Purchase)	– $2,480	$39,420

[a] Value measured as *saving* in operating cost.

Decision Rules for Choosing Among Alternatives

In the previous example, the value of the two alternatives was determined by average cost savings for each future condition, weighted according to the likelihood that these conditions would occur. This should seem reasonable. The estimated savings in cost for each alternative is the weighted average of cost savings that could be realized under the relevant future conditions of current and increased volume. This calculation applies what is called an expected-value decision rule. The expected-value rule is considered to be the best way to handle uncertainty because the traps posed by people's information-handling limitations, discussed in Chapters Four and Five, are avoided and because all of the available information is used to value alternatives.

In this section, several other decision rules are discussed and compared with the expected-value rule. This discussion has several purposes. A decision rule can be used to indicate the way a decision maker's values can be imposed, both intentionally and inadvertently, on the decision-making process. Decision rules also point out shortcuts that managers often take to assume away uncertainty about future conditions. Finally, a review of decision rules shows why the expected-value rule is the best way to deal with uncertainty for most decisions by describing limitations in other decision rules. However, each decision rule has some useful applications, which will be pointed out with examples.

A decision that calls for a manager to choose among several new products, as shown in Table 13.2, will be used to illustrate the decision rules. (The outcomes for these alternatives were selected to illustrate each of the decision rules and may not represent outcomes likely in practice.) The same formulation can be used to capture a choice among services. The choice among five new products (or services) must be made under three assumptions about future conditions. Payoffs can be expressed as annual profit (revenue less cost) for favorable, neutral, and unfavorable assumptions about next year's economic conditions (the future conditions).

Which product produces the best payoff, greatest profit, in this example? Products 1, 3, and 5 avoid losses, no matter what economic conditions occur. Product 1 provides a net profit under all economic conditions that could develop. However, products 3, 4, and 5 realize very large profits under particular conditions. A cursory review of the information in Table 13.2 suggests that the choice is ambiguous and that intuitive hunches about which product to select are likely to be misleading.

Table 13.2. A New Product Decision.

Economic Conditions		C_1 Unfavorable	C_2 Neutral	C_3 Favorable
Probabilities[a]		$P_1 = .10$	$P_2 = .60$	$P_3 = .30$
Alternatives	Product 1	$ 1,000,000[b]	$ 1,000,000	$ 1,000,000
	Product 2	$ 1,000,000	0	– $1,000,000
	Product 3	0	$ 1,000,000	$10,000,000
	Product 4	– $1,000,000	$10,000,000	$ 1,000,000
	Product 5	$10,000,000	$ 1,000,000	0

[a] Probabilities for future conditions must sum to 1 to adhere to requirements that conditions be mutually exclusive and exhaustive.

[b] Payoff valued in terms of annual profit under unfavorable economic conditions for new product 1.

Several decision rules have been suggested for making a choice among alternatives:

1. Uncertainty
2. Sure-thing principle
3. Pessimism
4. Optimism
5. Regret
6. Satisficing
7. Expected value

Each of these decision rules will be illustrated with numerical examples to point out the values they embrace and how they clarify the nature of various types of decision situations.

Uncertainty

When nothing is known about the likelihood of future conditions, a LaPlace, or uncertainty, rule can be used. If nothing is known about likelihoods, equal likelihoods for the future conditions can be assumed $(P_1 = P_2 = \ldots = P_n)$. The alternative with the highest average payoff is selected. Applying this rule to the word-processing decision (Table 13.1) results in

$$A_1 \text{ (retain)} = (0 - \$15,000)/2 = -\$7,500$$
$$A_2 \text{ (purchase)} = (-\$2,480 + \$39,420)/2 = \$18,470$$

The purchase alternative would be adopted.

To compute the outcome of the product alternatives in Table 13.2, the profits for each option are averaged:

$$\text{Product 1} = (\$1,000,000 + \$1,000,000 + \$1,000,000)/3$$
$$= \$1,000,000$$
$$\text{Product 2} = (\$1,000,000 + 0 - \$1,000,000)/3 = 0$$
$$\text{Product 3} = (0 + \$1,000,000 + \$10,000,000)/3$$
$$= \$3,666,666$$
$$\text{Product 4} = (-\$1,000,000 + \$10,000,000 + \$1,000,000)/3$$
$$= \$3,333,333$$
$$\text{Product 5} = (\$10,000,000 + \$1,000,000 + 0)/3$$
$$= \$3,666,666$$

All products except 3 and 5 are eliminated by the uncertainty rule, but there is no basis for choosing between these two products. To make a choice in this situation, the manager must formulate a subsidiary decision rule, such as choosing between products 3 and 5 according to which has the smallest capital outlay.

Sure-Thing Principle

The principle of dominance can sometimes be used to eliminate alternatives. Note that product 5 produces higher profit than product 2, no matter what economic condition occurs (Table 13.2). Product 2 can be ruled out because there is a better choice for all possible future conditions. Eliminating the dominated alternative (product 2) simplifies the choice. In a few instances, one alternative will emerge that is clearly superior at this point, eliminating the need for further analysis. In other situations, this rule will not work. For instance, the word-processor decision cannot be made by using this rule because neither option dominates the other by producing better payoffs, no matter what level of volume is realized (see Table 13.1). In those instances in which the dominance rule works, it is easy to apply and results in an unambiguous choice.

The sure-thing or dominance rule will fail to work in two types of situations. First, some decisions are too complex to consider all the combinations. The task of enumeration becomes tedious and leads to errors. For example, to make pairwise comparisons in the relatively simple example in Table 13.2 requires that each of the five products be compared two at a time, under three economic conditions, yielding thirty comparisons. (Five things taken two at a time yields ten combinations in each of three states for a total of thirty comparisons.) Adding multiple criteria, more states, and more alternatives creates a tangled situation that can be difficult to sort out. Second, the sure-thing or dominance rule will not produce a clear-cut choice when some of the alternatives work well under some future conditions and poorly under others. For instance, in Table 13.2, four products do not clearly dominate one another.

Pessimism

Decision makers who are risk avoiders prefer decision rules that are risk-averse. Such decision rules are useful because, under certain extreme conditions, decision makers may want to avoid risk. For example, ask yourself if you would toss a coin to determine whether your salary would be doubled or reduced to zero (Matheson and Howard, 1972).

The pessimism rule is often used under conditions of high conflict in which conservative choices are required to avoid provoking factions that refuse to compromise. The pessimism rule can also be useful for decision making under hostile conditions. Such conditions arise when an organization faces a hostile environment emanating from price cutting and easy market entry by competitors, well-informed customers, and the frequent failure of competing firms. A single bad strategic decision can have disastrous consequences. Decision makers in this environment are worried more about potential losses than possible gains. A *maximin* decision rule can be used in this situation. The decision maker looks for the worst outcomes and avoids alternatives that can produce those outcomes.

To apply a maximin rule, the decision maker finds the poorest payoff for each alternative and selects the alternative that has the highest minimum payoff. Applying this reasoning to the alternatives in Table 13.2, the decision maker would select product 1. At least a $1 million profit would be realized, no matter what state occurred. The same logic applied to the word-processing decision (Table 13.1) would favor the "purchase" alternative because losses are minimal, no matter what future condition occurs. This type of analysis will usually identify a single favored alternative. If not, the decision maker must use a subsidiary rule.

Optimism

An optimism rule is used when a decision maker attempts to find big payoffs. Several types of searches can be conducted. One version uses a *maximax* rule. The decision maker finds the best payoff for each alternative and selects the alternative with the greatest payoff. The likelihood of future conditions is ignored.

The maximax rule applied to the word-processor decision would result in the purchase of the new system (Table 13.1). In the new-product example (Table 13.2), no single choice can be made because products 3, 4, and 5 each have $10 million profits under different economic conditions. A subsidiary rule is needed to break the tie. Note that it is not logical to select product 3 or 5 because they realize large gains only under unlikely circumstances. In other decisions, there may be a single alternative with a big payoff that occurs only in an unlikely future condition. Selection of this alternative signals a risk-taking "go for it" posture toward decision making.

A more conservative approach to the maximax decision rule finds the most likely state and selects the alternative with the best payoff in that state. Using this rule, a decision maker would select product 3. Note, however, that product 3 would result in a $1 million loss if the unfavorable condition actually occurred (Table 13.2). This future condition, however, is quite unlikely.

Regret

The regret rule incorporates the notion of postdecisional dissatisfaction, should a less than optimal choice be made. Managers may wish to exercise caution in making choices because they have experienced regret when past decisions failed to produce hoped-for outcomes. The regret-minimax decision rule can be used under such conditions.

The regret-minimax decision rule allows the decision maker to incorporate the notion of outcome dissatisfaction into decision-making procedures. Regret is determined by the difference between outcomes that would have occurred, with perfect foresight about future conditions, and the outcome that occurs if a particular alternative is adopted. To calculate regret, a particular state is assumed to have occurred. Regret is made up of foregone gains combined with gains or losses that would be realized.

To compute a regret, the observed outcome is subtracted from the best outcome that can occur for a given state. For example, assume that unfavorable conditions occur and that product 1 has been selected (Table 13.2). The regret is the unrealized profit of $9 million: the $10 million profit foregone had product 5 been selected (the best choice under unfavorable conditions), less the $1 million profit that would have been realized by selecting product 1. The regret for product 4, under unfavorable conditions, is the $10 million foregone profit, plus the $1 million loss, for a total of $11 million. A regret for each alternative is determined in this way, to produce the regret matrix shown in Table 13.3.

The same logic can be applied to the typewriter decision. Assume that current demand occurs and that the retain alternative is adopted. The regret is zero, because the best outcome

Table 13.3. The Regret Minimax Decision Rule.

New-Product Decision	Future Conditions		
Alternatives	Unfavorable	Neutral	Favorable
Product 1	$ 9,000,000	$ 9,000,000	$ 9,000,000
Product 2	$ 9,000,000	$10,000,000	$11,000,000
Product 3	$10,000,000	$ 9,000,000	0
Product 4	$11,000,000	0	$ 9,000,000
Product 5	0	$ 9,000,000	$10,000,000

Word-Processor Decision		
Alternatives	Current Demand	50% Increase in Demand
Retain	0	$54,420
Purchase	$2,480	0

has been realized. The regret for the purchase alternative, with current demand, is the best outcome (zero savings), plus the loss that occurs by adopting the retain alternative, or $0 - (-\$2,480)$, or $2,480. For increased demand, the regret for the retain alternative is $39,420 - (-\$15,000)$, or $54,420, and the regret for the purchase alternative is zero, because no savings have been foregone.

To make a choice, the decision maker applies a minimax rule. Locate the maximum regret for each alternative by scanning the rows in Table 13.3. Choose the alternative with the smallest maximum regret. You would select product 1 if you were applying this rule to the new-product decision. The purchase choice would be preferred in the word-processor decision.

The regret computation can render this decision rule hard to use in practice. The difference in profit under a specific set of future conditions may not approximate a decision maker's true regret. Lost opportunity may be reasonable for some criteria but not for others, such as satisfaction. Regret may not be fully captured by the "loss in satisfaction" measured by some scale in a questionnaire.

Satisficing

A satisficing decision rule captures the way that people cope with their information-processing limitations and unstable preferences (Simon, 1977). Experiences in purchasing expensive items, such as a car, suggest that preferences shift according to what is known about the alternatives. Each auto that we look at has new features that can change what we want, as well as how we imagine context (future conditions). Learning is inherent in the search for alternatives, which creates this instability in preferences. Aspirations create a target, but aspirations are often in a state of flux. A rational search under this set of conditions is terminated when an alternative that meets the target is found. However, targets are lowered when a search is unsuccessful and raised when many viable alternatives are found (March and Simon, 1958).

Initially, the decision maker has no alternatives and thus no information to describe them. A search is mounted that produces an alternative, such as a location for a warehouse. The location is valued under all pertinent states. If the location is found to be satisfactory, the search is terminated and a choice is made. If the location is not satisfactory, the search is continued until aspiration shifts, allowing an initially unacceptable alternative to be selected because one with better features has not been found and thus seems unavailable. Aspirations change according to the ease with which alternatives are uncovered, implying the likelihood of finding a better one. Also, the valuation of the alternative can be difficult or easy. If it is easy, more options are likely to be sought.

Satisficing, like all of the decision rules discussed thus far, does not require state probability estimates of future conditions, which can be an advantage. Moreover, under a satisficing rule, the time and cost of valuing options can be minimized if a satisfactory alternative is found early in the search. Finally, the task of assessing whether a target has been met is simplified. If an option has a bad outcome in one state, it can be abandoned without further valuation. As a result, satisficing is viewed as pragmatic by decision makers because the time and costs of search and assessment can be reduced. The value of satisficing is limited by its inability to deal with trade-offs and its appearance of being capricious. Satisficing works well in certain types of multicriteria decision situations, which are discussed in Chapter Nineteen.

Expected Value

The expected-value rule formally recognizes trade-offs that can balance possible gains against losses, considering the likelihood of a future condition and the payoff for that condition. For instance, some of the products in Table 13.2 may have low fixed costs that allow a cutback in production to minimize losses when conditions unfavorable to sales occur. Other products may have a manufacturing capability that can rapidly adjust to increases in demand. The costs of meeting unexpected demands may be large in some cases and small in others.

A "maximum expected value," or MEV, rule is used to capture compensatory aspects of possible payoffs, which are called outcomes. To apply the rule, a decision maker discounts the payoff of each product alternative in each future condition according to the likelihood of its occurrence. For example,

$$\text{Product 1 expected payoff} = P_1 O_{11} + P_2 O_{12} + P_3 O_{13}$$

P_1 is the probability of the first condition and O_{11} is the outcome, expressed in this example as profit, for product 1 in condition 1. The computations for product 2 (see Table 13.2) are shown below:

$$\text{Product 2 expected payoff} = \$1,000,000(.1) + 0(.6) - \$1,000,000(.3)$$
$$= \$100,000 - \$300,000 = -\$200,000$$

The expected payoff for product 2 is a $200,000 loss, considering the payoffs expected under the likelihoods of future conditions in Table 13.2. The remaining payoffs are as follows:

Product 1 expected payoff = $1,000,000
Product 3 expected payoff = $3,600,000
Product 4 expected payoff = $6,200,000
Product 5 expected payoff = $1,600,000

This analysis suggests that product 4 should be selected.

Applying the expected-value rule to the retain and purchase alternatives for the word-processor example shown in Table 13.1 provides a second illustration. The MEV rule adjusts the cost savings by the likelihood that each will occur. The calculations are shown below:

$$A_1 \text{ (retain)} = .9(0) + .1(-\$15,000)$$
$$= -\$1,500$$
$$A_2 \text{ (purchase)} = .9(-\$2,480) + .1(\$39,420)$$
$$= -\$2,232 + \$3,942$$
$$= \$1,710$$

According to the MEV rule, the purchase alternative has the best payoff, expressed in this example as savings in operating cost.

Drawbacks to the MEV rule stem from two sources: data availability and notions of utility. Obtaining estimates for data like those shown in Tables 13.1 and 13.2 can be difficult for some types of decisions. For instance, valuing outcomes in bidding decisions according to future conditions, such as what competitors are doing, can be either educated or uneducated guessing. Future conditions are defined by whether a competitor will bid in a certain way, as shown in Table 13.4. Consider a firm bidding on a government subcontract or a hospital bidding with a state to provide health care services for prisoners in correctional institutions. Feasible bids by the organization (bids that can make money) become the alternatives. Bid costs can be estimated. In this example, assume that bid costs are $10,000 in each case where a bid is made. Assume further that the costs to do the work are estimated to be $9,000,000. A low bid would produce a $990,000 profit (the bid of $10,000,000 less the bid and work costs of $9,010,000) in the third state. The high bid would produce a $5,990,000 profit (the $15,000,000 bid less costs of $9,010,000) in the third state. A no bid would produce a zero payoff, and bids above competitors' would result in a $10,000 loss, the bid cost. If all of the competitors made a $10,000,000 bid, both the state probabilities and payoffs would be hard to estimate.

Some decisions call for more concern about losses than gains (Kahneman and Tversky, 1982). For these decisions, the decision maker is more concerned about avoiding a product that can have a large loss under certain future conditions. The "utility" of the payoffs of possible gains and losses is not symmetrical. More value is attached to avoiding a loss than to making a gain. Other examples include outcomes such as satisfaction or compliance. Satisfaction and compliance (attending to all the details) above a certain level may not have any impact on outcomes such as productivity. However, low levels of compliance can lead to failure to complete work assignments, and very low levels of satisfaction can lead to significant absenteeism and turnover. Patients with low levels of compliance can create serious outcome problems in a patient care process. Ways to deal with these problems are discussed in Chapter Nineteen.

Comparing the Choices Under Each Decision Rule

A comparison of the preferred alternative under each decision rule for the new-product and word-processor examples

Table 13.4. The Bidding Decision.

	Future Conditions (Competitors' Bids)		
	Less Than $10,000,000	*At $10,000,000*	*More Than $15,000,000*
Likelihoods	$P_1 = ?$	$P_2 = ?$	$P_3 = ?$
Alternatives			
Do Not Bid	0	0	0
Bid Low ($10,000,000)	– $10,000	?	$990,000
Bid High ($15,000,000)	– $10,000	– $10,000	$5,990,000

Table 13.5. Preferred Alternatives and Decision Rules.

Decision Rules	The New-Product Example	The Word-Processor Example
Uncertainty (LaPlace Rule)	Products 3 or 5	Purchase
Sure Thing (dominance)	Rule out product 2	No decision
Pessimism (maximin)	Product 1	Purchase
Optimism (maximax)	Products 3, 4, or 5	Purchase
Regret (minimax)	Product 1	Purchase
Expected Value	Product 4	Purchase

is now possible. Decision makers who used any of the rules except the dominance rule would purchase the word processors. The dominance rule failed to identify a clear-cut winner. When this rule is used, a no decision frequently results because of the rule's stringent nature. Only a rule that looks for the best alternative under the most favorable future conditions would favor the retain alternative because the current level of demand is thought to be more likely and the retain alternative has the greatest payoff under the most likely future condition.

The decision rules applied to the new-product decision were able to rule out only one alternative. Product 2 was eliminated by the dominance rule. Depending on the values of the decision maker and the situation faced by the organization, any of the remaining alternatives could be selected (see Table 13.5). The expected-value rule, however, is preferred in all but extreme situations.

Note that the expected-value rule produced a different product choice than any other rule. This tends to occur because of the compensatory nature of the expected-value rule, which systematically considers trade-offs. The pessimism and regret rules tended to produce similar outcomes because they use similar logic. These rules emphasize the notion of a potential loss. The uncertainty rule produced markedly different choices because key information describing state probabilities was ignored, leading to payoffs in unlikely states having undue influence. This situation may also arise in practice, illustrating the need to encode whatever is known about states to support the decision process. Failure to use information about future conditions often leads to bad choices, such as those described in Chapter Two.

Sensitivity Analysis

When the decision maker is unsure about the likelihood of future conditions, it is desirable to make the best possible estimates and then treat these estimates as assumptions. Using sensitivity analysis, the decision maker can pose "what if" questions to determine the implications of making various assumptions about future conditions.

Sensitivity analysis is a technique that progressively relaxes important assumptions to determine how the assumption influences a decision. It is applied to all subjective information and to objective information that is apt to have large measurement errors. Using the examples considered thus far, the decision maker determines the magnitude of a change in the likelihood of future conditions that would lead to a different decision. The subjective estimate is treated as an assumption because its value cannot be known with precision. A small change in the estimate may change a decision. Sensitivity analysis is used to determine ranges in likelihood estimates that favor the adoption of particular alternatives. Sensitivity analysis can also be used to estimate the value of unknown payoffs, given assumptions about future conditions that a decision maker is prepared to make. This information helps decision makers overcome information-processing problems and organize their intuition to reflect on conditions that favor each alternative.

Using Sensitivity Analysis to Deal with Assumptions About Future Conditions

The example of a new word-processing system (Table 13.1) will be used to illustrate how to use sensitivity analysis to apply "what if" questioning to assumptions about future conditions. To use sensitivity analysis, the decision maker values each alternative by treating the likelihood of the future conditions as an unknown. This type of analysis is limited to two conditions. A collapse of the data, merging conditions to create just two future conditions, is required when there are three or more conditions to be considered.

In the word-processing example, there were two alternatives, retain and purchase. The likelihood of increased volume is represented by an unknown, designated as P in the expected-value format, as shown below:

$$A_1 = -15,000P$$
$$A_2 = -2,480 + P(36,940)$$

The payoffs can be plotted by having P take on values of 0 and 1 (see Figure 13.3).

	$P = 0$	$P = 1$
A_1	0	$-15,000$
A_2	$-2,480$	34,460

The break-even point value of P, where operating cost savings are the same for both alternatives, is found by setting the equations equal and solving for P.

$$-15,000P = -2,480 + P(36,940)$$
$$2,480 = P(36,940 + 15,000)$$
$$P = 2,480/51,940 = .048$$

This computation shows that the purchase decision is the safer of the two alternatives. Even if one assumes that the prospects of increased volume are very unlikely (for example, $P < .10$), the purchase decision has a greater payoff (operating cost savings). The plot of the linear relationship in Figure 13.3 provides visual appreciation. Note that the purchase payoff is above the retain payoff for nearly all assumptions that can be made above increases in volume. This set of assumptions makes the purchase decision easy to defend.

Using Sensitivity Analysis to Deal with Unknown Payoffs

A form of sensitivity analysis can also be used to estimate unknown payoffs, such as the amount of insurance to purchase, given various assumptions about the prospects of a loss. This type of analysis can be applied to installing safety equipment in a for-profit organization or assessing the decision to purchase an automobile with airbags as a safety device. Decision makers must consider the cost of the safety equipment and an unknown,

**Figure 13.3. Sensitivity Analysis for the
Word-Processing Purchase Decision.**

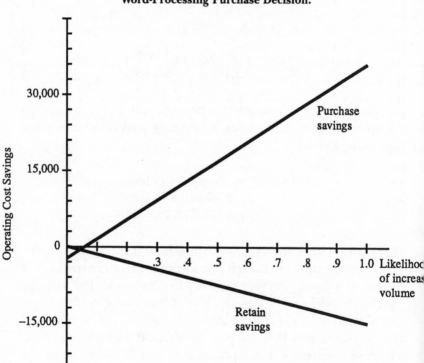

Table 13.6. The Malpractice Software Investment Decision.

Alternatives	C_1 No Crisis	C_2 At Least One Crisis
A_1 (Purchase)	$100,000	$100,000
A_2 (Delay)	0	$100,000 + X[a]

[a] X = the cost of a crisis including the cost of litigation and the cost of a successful claim.

depicting the loss should an accident occur. Future conditions are accident and no-accident events.

To illustrate the procedure, assume that a hospital is considering the adoption of a malpractice program made up of data-processing support to record and classify information relating to incidents that may produce litigation. This hospital has decided to self-insure for malpractice because of the exorbitant premiums insurance carriers impose on hospitals that have had no history of large, or indeed any, claims. The hospital would have to pay for a claim, should one occur, with its reserves. Assume that the American Hospital Association (AHA) is selling the software for $100,000, including all needed assistance to put the system into operation. The AHA contends that reviewing its reports has negligible cost in terms of management time and can head off a malpractice crisis. Assume further that if such a crisis occurs, the hospital will have to adopt the system in order to show its board of trustees and others that it is taking action to head off future litigation problems. The unknowns are the prospect of at least one malpractice crisis and the cost of such a crisis. Most hospitals have no way to estimate these values.

The data shown in Table 13.6 provide an example. The alternatives can be described as follows:

A_1 = purchase the software
A_2 = delay purchase until a crisis occurs

The future conditions are:

$$C_1 = \text{no crisis}$$
$$C_2 = \text{at least one crisis}$$

The states are treated as unknowns, as in the previous example, with the likelihood of avoiding a crisis designated P, the likelihood of a crisis is $1 - P$. Note that the state probabilities sum to zero. The alternatives are valued according to the expected-value rule, as follows:

$$A_1 \ (\text{purchase}) = (P)100{,}000 + (1 - P)(100{,}000)$$
$$= 100{,}000$$
$$A_2 \ (\text{delay}) = (P)(0) + (1 - P)(100{,}000 + X)$$
$$= (1 - P)(100{,}000 + X)$$

The cost of a malpractice incident is designated as X and includes the cost of litigation plus the amount of the claim to be paid. The purchase decision is preferred when the cost for A_2 (delay) is greater than A_1 (purchase). This can be represented as follows:

$$A_2 > A_1$$

Substituting payoffs for each alternative yields

$$(1 - P)(100{,}000 + X) > 100{,}000$$

Solving for X yields

$$X > \frac{P}{1 - P}(\$100{,}000)$$

Assigning a value of zero to P represents a pessimistic view, assuming that there is no chance of avoiding crisis. Substituting $P = 0$ reduces the equation to $X > 0$. The occurrence of any loss will make the software seem justifiable. The optimistic or risk-taking view assigns P a value of 1, taking the position that there is no chance that a crisis will occur. Letting $P = 1$ in the equation above reduces the equation to $X > \infty$. The cost of a claim would have to be infinitely large before an investment in the software would be made.

These extremes bracket postures that can be adopted. If the prospect of a loss is thought to be 50 percent, as determined by contending that one hospital in two experiences a claim, investment in the system will create a break-even payoff [$X = (.5/1 - .5)\$100,000 = \$100,000$]. If the prospect of a loss is greater than 50/50, an investment is justified. However, studies show that most malpractice settlements are small, in the range of $10,000 to $20,000 (Nutt and Emswiler, 1979). These data suggest that waiting to install the system may be desirable from a cost perspective. However, the negative publicity stemming from litigation poses a second criterion, which can alter the decision. (Multicriteria decision situations are considered in Chapter Nineteen.)

Key Points

1. Analysis poses a paradox for decision makers. Directed toward using objectives to compare various ways to respond to core problems, it can offer many valuable insights. However, when analysis is used without this perspective, it can do more harm than good, inhibiting legitimate questions about the merit of current alternatives.

2. Various kinds of rationality are expressed in decision rules. These rules illustrate ways to act out preferences that call for risk aversion, risk taking, satisficing, and the like. Decision rules capture the preferences, expressed as behavior, of some decision makers but can be suboptimal because they do not consider trade-offs. Ways to measure the payoff of alternatives under various future conditions capture trade-offs, providing a compensatory decision rule. The "maximum expected value," or MEV, rule shows how simple computations can cut through the uncertainty that often leads to bad decisions and capture these trade-offs.

3. "What if" questioning that relies on sensitivity analysis provides one way to relax assumptions about future conditions

to identify conditions that favor an alternative. When key assumptions about demand are relaxed, risks in the decision become clear. Sensitivity analysis can also be used to estimate the magnitude of unknown payoffs, such as the magnitude of possible litigation costs that prompt the adoption of several precautionary measures, such as insurance.

🖋 14

Learning from
Success and Failure

This chapter explores barriers to learning that apply to decision making and suggests ways to overcome these barriers. Learning in decision making is inhibited by the coverups of decision makers and ambiguities in determining and interpreting the results of a decision. Coverups can become routine when unrealistic expectations are imposed on decision makers. Viewed from the vantage point of hindsight, chance events seem more likely once they have occurred, making bad outcomes seem like bad decisions, as discussed in Chapter Three. Managers who seek scapegoats when bad outcomes occur act as if tough decisions contain no factors that are governed by chance. This behavior produces a fear of failure that creates considerable incentive to color or bury information that is essential for learning to occur.

Learning can also be inhibited by decisions in which outcomes are difficult to determine or interpret. Some decisions produce results that are hard to measure, and others produce results in some distant future, making them poor candidates for helping managers learn about the merits of decision procedures. Some types of norms used to interpret the results of a decision can create logic traps that make outcomes seem more desirable or beneficial than a cold appraisal of the facts would warrant, as presented in Chapter Five.

Together, the effects of coverups and ambiguities in interpreting outcomes create significant distractions that must be confronted if learning is to occur. The first step in such a

confrontation is awareness. The manager who is aware of incentives to cover up bad outcomes can take steps to eliminate the
incentives and offer inducements that encourage frank appraisals. Similarly, knowing the origin of biases in making interpretations provides managers the perspective they need to
judge outcomes realistically. Managers can then conduct a reflective review of decision processes in an atmosphere of trust,
making realistic appraisals by following the procedures offered
in this chapter. Figure 14.1 shows how the material in this
chapter supports the decision process.

Determining Outcomes

Managers learn from what they observe. Not all decisions
produce readily observable outcomes. The alternative *not*
adopted might have been a better way to act. Often there is no
way to know. For example, applicants *not* selected for a job go
elsewhere, and their accomplishments are seldom available to
make comparisons with people who were selected for the job. In
other instances, however, rejected applicants can provide a baseline. For example, university faculty members interview nationally and compete nationally, offering a way to compare
people who were selected for a position to those who were not.
When such comparisons are available, they can provide persuasive evidence to assess a decision process. However, this
evidence is often rationalized away because of the threat implied by a postdecisional review.

Some decisions produce outcomes that are difficult to
observe because they occur in a distant future. Decisions leading
to acquisitions, mergers, and new product development provide
examples. These decisions are difficult to assess because the
means used to make them are often shrouded by the departure
of key players. These constraints are real and many cannot be
managed, making learning difficult. Other decisions have outcomes that are hard to observe or measure. For example, the
effects of sensitivity training in dealing with people can be hard
to detect, and measures of the outcome difficult to specify.
Feeling better after such an experience does not guarantee

Figure 14.1. The Decision Process.

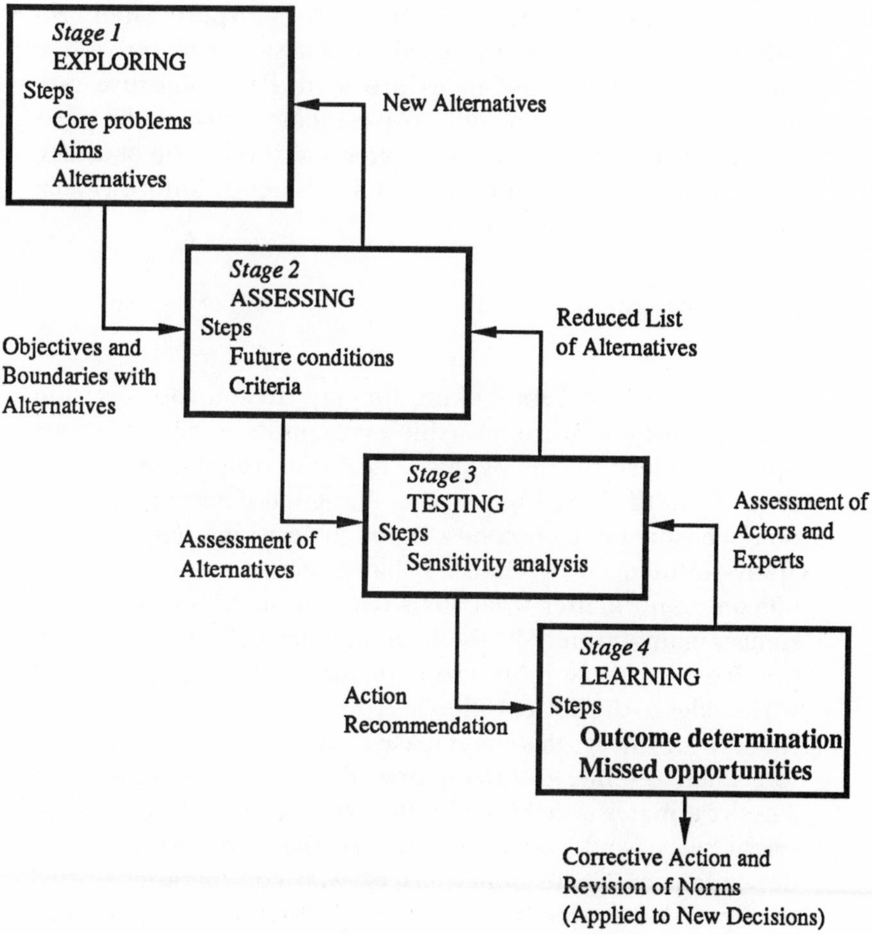

Stage 1
EXPLORING
Steps
  Core problems
  Aims
  Alternatives

New Alternatives

Stage 2
ASSESSING
Steps
  Future conditions
  Criteria

Objectives and
Boundaries with
Alternatives

Reduced List
of Alternatives

Stage 3
TESTING
Steps
  Sensitivity analysis

Assessment of
Alternatives

Assessment of
Actors and
Experts

Stage 4
LEARNING
Steps
  Outcome determination
  Missed opportunities

Action
Recommendation

Corrective Action and
Revision of Norms
(Applied to New Decisions)

Note: Boldface type indicates topics addressed in this chapter.

improved work performance, and changes in work performance may have nothing to do with the sensitivity training.

Many decisions, however, produce outcomes that can be
examined and compared to the process used to make them to
provide a basis for learning. For these decisions, the learner is
encouraged to reflect on predictions about future conditions
and other chance events to explore how values, expressed as

criteria weights, tilted a decision one way or the other and how risk was handled during sensitivity analysis. Experts often provide key estimates, and this step allows decision makers to judge the precision of the estimates provided. Both objective estimates, such as cost, and subjective estimates, such as the prospect of strong product demand, often merit this type of assessment. Two key factors inhibit such assessments: unforeseeable events and the hindsight bias.

Unforeseeable Events

Decision makers looking for ways to improve decision making must wade through a thicket of contradictory and sometimes counterintuitive signals. The most troublesome signal stems from the seeming paradox that good decision practices do not ensure good outcomes. In tough decisions, outcomes are always influenced by chance. Chance events can lead to bad outcomes, no matter what steps decision makers take. For instance, many farmers in the United States debt-financed land purchases to grow more crops in the wake of governmental wheat sales to the Soviet Union and others in the 1970s, thinking that export wheat sales could make them rich. Entire farms were lost when revenue estimates proved to be overly optimistic. These estimates were based on the expectation that the foreign wheat sales would continue. In fact, the sales proved to be dependent on fickle policymakers, who continuously shifted their position to accommodate the objections of each new interest group as they arose. The ensuing delays resulted in huge stockpiles of wheat, which depressed the price and made farmers' revenue unable to support their debt service obligations. Hundreds of farms were lost in this way.

The OPEC oil embargo had disastrous and hard-to-predict ripple effects on the raw material costs of many products. Many firms that decided to expand product lines or initiate new products that were dependent on raw materials derived from oil were faced with product line failure or the loss of market share to foreign competitors. Note that the farmers and firms could have made good decisions and experienced poor outcomes.

To make good decisions, decision makers explore *foresee-able* future conditions and use sound procedures to acquire and process information that informs their choices. To sort decisions into good and bad categories, decision makers must explore the procedures and information to find *foreseeable* defects.

The Hindsight Bias

A particularly insidious bias that inhibits learning stems from "creeping determinism," termed the *hindsight bias* in Chapter Five. After a decision has occurred and its outcome falls below expectations, people find it hard to believe that the now apparent warning signals were not recognized. Following a decision, one's memory of what happened becomes distorted. Events are consolidated to permit recall. A chance event, once it *has* occurred, seems more likely than an objective appraisal would suggest when the decision was made. The shuttle disaster and product expansions doomed by the Arab oil embargo seem inevitable today but must be judged according to the facts available when each decision was made.

Assessing Decisions

Managers can review decisions by using simulations and by posing alternative explanations. Each procedure offers a quick, insightful way to manage the effects of hindsight biases in assessing decisions.

Simulation

A simulation tactic recreates the decision. To assess the process, a reviewer(s) explores the facts available when decisions were made. Simulations can be formal or informal.

Informal Simulations. To deal with the biases of hindsight, managers must review decisions as they were made. The same ambiguities and uncertainties about information and events must be present to make a realistic appraisal of the decision process. A useful way to conduct such a review is to disguise key aspects of a decision. Admissions processes, medical diagnoses and treatment, and parole board decisions can delete the parties involved and the outcome and review according to the facts available when these decisions were made. Disguising outcomes is essential. People are remarkably adept at gathering facts that are consistent with a known outcome, suggesting that decision makers knew all of the risks they were taking in admitting a student, releasing a prisoner, or treating a patient. The review body is given all information, except cues that would give away parties involved and the outcome, and asked to make a decision. Comparing these decisions to those of the decision maker or decision body provides a quick and useful way to review a decision. After this review, the outcome is introduced. These steps deftly separate chance events from those that were foreseeable.

The following illustration of a graduate school admission decision shows how to apply the informal simulation approach. Students known to be "stars" or "admission mistakes" are identified on the basis of job and academic success measures. The information used to make the admission decision (for example, test scores, grade point average, and other key indicators), describing the "stars" and "mistakes," is provided to a decision-making body, which is asked whether the students should be admitted. The track record of members of an admissions committee can be assessed according to the precision with which they can identify the disguised "stars" and "admission mistakes" as students with or without potential.

Grant review agencies use similar tactics in a prospective manner. The ratings of individuals serving on review panels are tabulated. Averages of rank scores are compared to the scores of each member to identify people who tend to rank high or low. The results of a particular panel can be examined in light of members' tendencies to be harsh or lenient. Panels can be constructed to meet particular aims of the sponsor, such as stringent reviews, because of anticipated budget cuts.

Formal Simulations. Learning exercises can be useful for

very important and repeatable decisions, such as medical diagnoses. The analytical procedures used in formal simulations
and called *decision analysis* are described in Chapter Twenty.
Decision analysis applies the same principles used in informal
simulations to produce systematic appraisals of a decision
maker's skills. These appraisals are useful in improving skills by
pointing out areas in which analytical decision aiding is
essential.

Alternative Explanations

As pointed out in Chapter Five, easily constructed explanations of what went wrong in a decision are often misleading.
For example, some managers are quick to attribute success to
their own acts and fail to find equally plausible explanations for
the acts of their dedicated and hardworking staff; this leads to
disillusioned subordinates and missed learning opportunities.
By searching for other, equally plausible explanations, using a
group process described in Chapter Fifteen, managers can
avoid premature and often unfounded criticism. This step recreates the needed level of surprise, which is often assumed away
because of the hindsight bias. A careful review of several plausible explanations provides a more penetrating view of the decision and how to set things right.

Applying Norms to Outcomes

Norms that are selected to measure the desirability of
outcomes can shift because of aspiration changes (Chapter
Thirteen), as the search for alternatives reveals realistic expectations. As pointed out in Chapter Five, the probabilistic nature of
outcomes for repeatable decisions, such as graduate school
admissions, can bias the way in which outcomes are interpreted.
Norms determined by cutoff values applied to criteria, such as
standardized test scores in a graduate school admission decision, can subtly shift performance expectations by changing the
likely ratio of successes and failures. These changes, produced
by the chance nature of outcomes, should be understood before

success rates are used to assess a decision process. The same kind of logic must be used to understand success rates for a variety of decisions, such as physicians making diagnosis and treatment choices, stockbrokers recommending stocks, and the credit ratings made by Moody's and Standard & Poor's for municipal bonds.

Another kind of bias is produced when a decision carries with it "enhancements" that improve the prospects of a good outcome. People hired for management trainee positions get enhancements through training that improves their job performance, making the selection something of a self-fulfilling prophecy. The discussion of enhancements in Chapter Five should be reviewed as part of the steps needed to learn about success and failure.

Learning to Learn

The concept of learning is an important part of a decision-making process, but it is often ignored or treated superficially. The reality of organizational life makes it difficult to own up to failures. Managers often refuse to collect information that may expose a failure, fearing that such information can be potentially damaging. Onlookers may not separate good outcomes from good decisions. Because good decisions can produce bad outcomes and bad decisions good outcomes, information essential for learning can be difficult to acquire.

There is considerable incentive to reveal bad outcomes in carefully measured doses. Affected parties continue to speak glowingly of the decision, fearing that to do otherwise would expose them to sanctions. This continual refusal to face reality is often viewed with alarm by subordinates, who see no one willing to deal with crucial problems. For example, as indicated in Chapter Twelve, the H Clothing Stores in Florida continued to operate at losses, the Michigan Farm Bureau insisted on rapid burial of carcasses, and the selected architect's obvious connections to interested parties in the museum decision were ignored. Breaking through this veil of fear calls for strong management that removes the threat inherent in conducting a postmortem on a decision.

Changing values that have led to a decision can be even harder to carry out. Argyris, Putnam, and Smith (1985) call error detection combined with value assessment *double-loop learning*, or learning to learn. Single-loop learning involves error detection and correction that consider a decision to achieve current objectives. Double-loop learning occurs when error detection and correction lead to a *change* in underlying norms that allow for a change in the decision's objectives. Probing decisions can lead to the questioning of values and policies to which the organization is deeply committed. To avoid this questioning, bad news is offset with good news. The coverup has two tiers: the distorted good news and a sequestering of the process used to produce and disseminate the good news. This behavior is quite rational but often produces a lose-lose situation (Argyris and Schön, 1978). To expose errors, decision makers must call into question norms and values they are expected to protect and defend. However, not exposing errors prohibits organizational learning. The games of deception individuals play become undiscussable because to discuss them would reveal the lose-lose position created for the organization.

Ritti and Funkhouser (1986) offer a good illustration of how this kind of situation can develop. Divisions in a company manufacturing various components of an airframe had considerable incentive to overdesign their component to minimize the chance that it would fail. The cumulative effects of each division's overdesign caused the airframe to become too heavy, and the U.S. Air Force refused delivery. Management was unable to find the root cause of the excess weight because each division had engaged in the same behavior, which was undiscussable.

An accounting department in a major university had a chairman who, as a cover for his lack of research productivity, volunteered for all administrative tasks. By doing so over a long period of time, the chairman ingratiated himself with various centers of power. His contacts and accumulated favors created a substantial power base, which the chairman learned to use to wield control over all aspects of the department, including new faculty recruitment. Faculty members did not make changes they generally believed to be desirable and long overdue because they all owed the chairman, which was undiscussable.

When facts and issues become undiscussable, gaps and inconsistencies in reasoning and how the reasoning applies to action go undetected. For instance, a CEO of a major organization claimed that all well-run organizations must "have a vision." The CEO became irked when told that his line managers had no idea what he was talking about. When the CEO was asked to identify the properties of a vision and how to recognize it, the dilemma facing the line managers became apparent to the CEO, and thus manageable (Argyris, Putnam, and Smith, 1985). This step forced the CEO to see the logic being applied by others and made the undiscussable discussable. Discussability is the linchpin of learning.

Distinctions Between Individual and Organizational Learning

Organizations often know less than their key members. The individuals involved in a coverup know or have insight into what has gone wrong. However, they are not likely to share these insights without incentives to do so. For an organization to learn, it must apply what its individual decision makers have learned. Often organizations behave in one way and claim to act in another. This gap is caused by organizations that espouse one thing and act in ways that are incongruous. Recall the decision to purchase foreign steel, described in Chapter Twelve. The steel company attempted to purchase foreign steel while advocating "buy American," going so far as to require employees to drive American-made cars. This illustrates how espoused values and acts can provoke conflict in tough decisions.

Single-Loop Learning

Decisions produce outcomes that have consequences expressed as cost, profit, volume, and in other ways. To identify a performance gap, feedback loops connect outcomes to what was intended. Corrective action is taken, and the performance of key actors is assessed. Learning falls into two categories: actor and action.

Learning About Key Actors. There are various roles to be played in a decision process. Some key roles include those played by experts, group members, and coalition constituents. Experts provide much of the quantitative data used in decision making and many of the subjective estimates of future events. It is crucial to evaluate the precision of this information. The accuracy of cost estimates provided by accountants, for example, can determine who provides the most precise sources of quantitative data.

Errors in subjective estimates can create even more important biases. Comparisons of predictions to actual values for stochastic factors provide a way to assess subjective estimates. For example, Royal Dutch Shell executives found that company geologists who were 90 percent sure where to drill for oil were correct only 50 percent of the time. Norms are needed to interpret this seeming bias toward optimism by the geologists. For instance, unrealistic expectations by Royal Dutch management may have coaxed the geologists to make overly optimistic estimates. If so, management must relax these incentives before confronting the geologists to ask for more realistic assessments. Similar information is needed for investors to assess the suggestions of investment managers and stock analysts, such as T. Rowe Price and Kidder Peabody. Records that retain this information are essential to avoid the biases inherent in impressionistic recall, discussed in Chapter Five, by applying tactics discussed earlier in this chapter.

Learning About Actions. Outcomes are deemed undesirable when they fail to meet expectations. Monitoring to detect a performance gap can be misleading if certain kinds of referents are used. For instance, decision makers who persistently adopt low-gain/low-risk options have track records that seem successful when viewed in terms of success rates. They seem to continually produce things of value. Lost opportunity provides another norm, which may offer a different assessment. This norm may be seen in erosion of market share, failure to innovate, and en-

Table 14.1. Focusing Assessments of Decisions to Take Corrective Action.

		Decision Outcome	
		Good	Bad
Decision Process	Appropriate	Type 1 Context[a]	Type 2 Forecasts
	Inappropriate	Type 3 Process	Type 4 Process and Forecasts

[a] Focus of assessment.

vironmental warning signals that were disregarded. To learn, individuals must put their decisions in several contexts to see them realistically.

Learning Tactics

The organization learns when its individual decision makers carry out an open inquiry that produces discoveries, assessments, and explanations of decision outcomes. These explanations become informed when both individuals and the organization, through their actions, distinguish between good decisions and good outcomes. As shown in Table 14.1, these distinctions lead to four types of learning. When process is appropriate and outcome good, a focus on *context* is essential. Learning must contextuate, denoting the time, topic, situation, and other aspects of the situation in which good results were obtained. Failing to appreciate context can lead to exporting a good process to a situation or task that is ill-suited to this approach. This type of learning can be difficult because decision makers flushed with success tend to repeat the tactics they used to produce the success.

Good outcomes can be realized from poor process when, for example, demand estimates exceed expectations. In such cases, success is independent of the acts of the decision makers and, indeed, out of their control. This situation is hard to detect without careful recall of the estimates that were made for key factors. There is considerable danger that a serendipitous event will be misunderstood and lead to an endorsement of the decision makers or the process they applied. For example, a Blue Cross plan developed a formula that allowed up to 30 percent of a hospital's reimbursement rate to be based on debt service payments. The CEO of a university hospital covered by the plan made a verbal agreement with the executive director of the Blue Cross plan not to ask for the full rate because the hospital had no debt and a full increase would produce a 30 percent windfall profit. The understanding was exploited by a new university hospital CEO after the Blue Cross executive retired. As a result, the hospital CEO was regarded as a very adept decision maker, and his overt processes of decision making were widely emulated. When demand exceeds expectations, a recognition that actors provided overly pessimistic estimates is often needed. However, a desirable outcome can keep decision makers from a critical appraisal of their decision process. Cues that the decision process may be defective stem from failures to see or deal with important stakeholders and a mismatch of process to situation, discussed in Chapter Nine.

When decisions are good (a correct process was used) and the outcome bad, making more realistic forecasts of future conditions becomes the focus of inquiry. Learning stems from assessing forecasting abilities to detect when poor forecasts have occurred. For example, in the 1970s, economic downturns caused a recession that greatly reduced state revenues. Even the most pessimistic revenue forecasts were far above actual receipts. The shortfall reached devastating proportions in several states. In Oregon, revenues were one-third of those needed to support state budget appropriations. Nearly all states experienced huge shortfalls that forced major cutbacks in state funding. After more than a decade, publicly assisted universities have not been able to restore the funds lost in these cutbacks.

Finally, both process and forecast assessments are needed in some instances. This type of situation can be difficult to recognize because either process or forecasts could have been root cause of a bad outcome. Addressing one without the other leads to incomplete learning. Both forecast precision and process appropriateness must be checked if one is to avoid making an incorrect assessment by selecting the wrong type of correct action.

Double-Loop Learning

In some cases, a recognition of the need to alter norms is required. This can arise in the wake of decisions that set in place innovations, such as a new technology, that require new patterns of operation. A departure from familiar procedures to adopt new ones may call for new norms by which to judge materials, manufacture, distribution, marketing, and the like. Growth and predictability become conflicting aims: One must be sacrificed to obtain the other. To reflect on a decision that resulted in innovation, this conflict must be confronted by the manager. For instance, a decision to adopt innovative ideas may seem to result in operating inefficiencies. However, it is incumbent upon the organization to rethink its norms for efficiency in light of the new conditions provoked by the ripple effects of a new technology. This rethinking requires a change in values about efficiency.

Superconducting ceramics that allow electricity to flow without resistance, which causes power loss, provide an example. Organizations operating utilities, high-speed trains, and hospitals, among others, must consider how to use this breakthrough. For instance, power companies must consider rewiring transmission systems, such as their hanging and buried cables. Magnetic resonators, used in medical X-ray, may need to be redesigned. High-speed electric trains can become a reality. Computer manufacturers can use resistance-free circuits to create smaller, faster, and cooler operating machines. In each case, the organization is confronted with the need to understand new norms as it shifts from familiar to unfamiliar practices. Exporting old understandings leads organizations to be conservative, failing to take advantage of new technology and the benefits brought by innovation. Transitions, on the other hand, frequently lead to opportunity, which, when capitalized upon, creates new business prospects. Organizations that fail to deal with innovation can become moribund.

New ideas offer many important competitive advantages (Foster, 1986). Organizations adopting innovations have been successful in bringing competitors to their knees and, in doing so, have grabbed a vastly larger market share. Michelin increased its market share 11 percent by introducing radial tires. Boeing became the leader in aircraft manufacturing by introducing the swept-wing 707. Xerox doomed carbon paper manufacturers to extinction when it introduced Xerography for photocopying. In these and related examples, new norms were needed understand and exploit a new competitive advantage. New norms are also needed as firms shift from growth, geared to emerging businesses, to cost consciousness in mature businesses. For instance, during its growth phase, Xerox ignored widely accepted cost-based manufacturing practices and made getting its copiers to customers the dominant concern. Management reasoned that efficiency could wait until after the company saturated the market. Second-generation copiers could have a ready-made market, and efficiency would then dominate growth as a norm for decision making. Another tactic is to balance the new objective (growth) with the old (efficiency). Targets can represent norms for efficiency linked to norms about growth. The trade-off allows high growth and low efficiency to be regarded the same as moderate growth and high efficiency.

If practiced well, the steps in double-loop learning can produce a perspective that allows for "learning about learning." Strategic management that allows the organization to learn how to exploit new opportunities, produced internally or externally, is an example of learning to learn. Decision makers reflect on and inquire about prior contexts and previous decisions in which there was a learning failure. They find out what facilitated and inhibited learning and offer evidence to promote change that sets in place a new view of needs.

Key Points

1. Good decisions can lead to bad outcomes because chance events are never fully predictable in tough decisions.

2. Simulation and group-process tactics provide a way to deal with the creeping determinism inherent in the hindsight bias.

3. Expectations can shift during a decision process, and this creates problems in interpreting outcomes, such as rates of success.

4. Double-loop learning permits the decision maker to deal with coverups prompted by fear of failure and shift norms to account for new circumstances.

5. Actor and process assessments must be separated if one is to reflect on the process and its outcome in order to find needed process steps and improve forecasts in decision making.

 Part Five

Techniques That Support the Decision Process

Part Five provides techniques that are needed to support a decision-making process. In Chapter Fifteen several types of group process options are presented, along with guidelines for selecting an option for the decision process steps identified in Chapter Eight. Chapter Sixteen provides techniques that can be used to set objectives, identify alternative courses of action, and uncover criteria by drawing on group process insights. Ethical concerns that often arise in a decision-making process are also considered in Chapter Sixteen. Chapter Seventeen presents techniques with which to make subjective estimates. Chapters Eighteen, Nineteen, and Twenty present analytical techniques for dealing with several future conditions, multiple criteria, and "what if" questioning to explore key assumptions made to estimate criteria weights and likelihoods for future conditions.

Techniques That Support the Decision Process

15

Managing
Decision-Making Groups

This chapter presents several processes that can be used to manage group decision making and guidelines to help a decision maker select a process that is best for various aspects of decision making. The term *group process* refers to a set of steps that a group follows as it engages in decision-making activities. Several group processes with distinctive features have been developed. Group processes can be classified as synthetic, interactive, and silent reflective. Each of these process types contains several process options. Survey, Delphi, nominal, brainwriting, nominal interacting, kiva, and brainstorming are described and compared to show how each process option can be used and to point out their comparative benefits. These benefits suggest that some group processes are best to help a group develop ideas, and others are best for making judgments, bringing forward information, and exchanging views.

Process options are discussed for three reasons. First, to get the best results, groups engaged in discovering, making judgments, exchanging information, and bargaining should use a process that is best suited to carry out each of these activities. Each activity has different outcome expectations. For example, an ill-defined decision lacks information and calls for discovery to uncover new ways to frame the decision. In other decisions, feelings can be particularly important and may be volatile as judgments are made; these decisions call for careful management of the interpersonal relations in the group. These conflicting aims suggest that no single group process is best for all kinds of decisions. Both situational conditions and outcome expectations form a basis for process selection. Second, it is wise to avoid overusing a particular group process. A repertoire of processes within an ideal type are offered to provide options. Finally, problems in group operation that stem from leadership and give rise to "groupthink" are discussed. Process becomes a substitute for leadership and deals with the stereotyped actions produced by groupthink.

Kinds of Group Processes

Group processes can be classified as synthetic, interactive, and silent reflective types. Within these categories there are several types of process options that have comparable benefits, so they can be used somewhat interchangeably.

Synthetic Group Processes

A synthetic group pools the judgments of people without a face-to-face meeting. Two ways of creating a synthetic group are discussed in this chapter: survey approaches and the Delphi technique.

Survey Approaches. Pooling responses from a survey is one way to create a synthetic group. Two types of surveys are often conducted by decision makers or their staff. The first targets a specific set of individuals who have a certain attribute, such as expertise or leverage. The survey determines how centers of expertise or power, inside and outside the organization, view issues such as the need to act or action options. Second, surveys can be used to provide a barometer of opinion that describes a general reaction to various decision-related issues. Respondents are selected by means of a random sample. In both cases, an analysis of respondent views provides a starting point for discussion. Because techniques for survey research are widely available (for example, Sudman and Bradburn, 1982), they will not be discussed in detail in this chapter.

The Delphi Technique. This technique is whimsically drawn from the mythological Greek oracle of Delphi. A Delphi survey (Dalky, 1967) systematically solicits and collates judgments. A series of questionnaires are used. The first questionnaire solicits ideas, information, opinions, or viewpoints and asks group members to state the rationale behind their ideas, and so on. Subsequent questionnaires consolidate and feed back the ideas and associated rationales to the group. The initial Delphi questionnaire asks broad questions, and subsequent questionnaires are built on responses to the preceding questionnaire. Each group member can review the logic behind the arguments of others, which is thought to stimulate consensus. The process continues until a consensus is reached or sufficient information has been obtained or until the process is terminated by a participant vote, which offers members a chance to prioritize (Delbecq, Van de Ven, and Gustafson, 1986).

Delphi was devised to do technological forecasting. The Department of Defense used it to provide up-to-date technological information not readily available in a literature search. It also has value when used prior to a meeting by providing members of a decision group with an opportunity to clarify and share views without the clutter of interpersonal relations.

Time, skill, and motivation are essential ingredients in a successful Delphi survey. Delphi participants must have writing skills and the motivation to carefully set out their views. Staff competence is also essential because the Delphi survey places a heavy burden on staff members, who must interpret the survey responses. Time limitations can make a full compilation of the survey results difficult. A period of about forty-five days is usually required. The process has four steps: development of a Delphi question, participant selection, survey development and its analysis and feedback, and prioritization.

1. *The Delphi question.* The Delphi question specifies the query that the group will consider. For example: (1) What are the criteria for the selection of a new chief executive officer? (2) What are the strengths and weaknesses of various options, such as retirement programs or CEO candidates? and (3) What barriers are there to implementing a new internal operation, such as an information system? Each type of question elicits somewhat different information. The first

question noted above concentrates on one aspect of a decision, criterion development. The second deals with evaluation of options. The third seeks information on social and political factors that can block a decision. The Delphi question must be formulated with care to ensure a proper focus for the group.

2. *Participant selection.* Both expertise and motivation are key criteria in the selection of participants. Often, motivation can be ensured only by some form of payment or by a personal interest in the outcome of the decision. The feeling of personal involvement may offset the lack of monetary rewards, particularly when members also have views they wish to share. The needed expertise for the participants is usually suggested by the content of the Delphi question. For example, key stakeholders in a CEO selection decision suggest membership requirements for a group asked to screen candidates. A process of selection begins with information about prospective members. Nominations by others are solicited by the decision maker. The list is then pruned, and the participation of prospective panelists is solicited. The process should be fully explained, including the number of steps and time requirements, before a potential participant is asked to serve. Between ten and fifteen members is a manageable panel size.

3. *The survey instrument and its analysis and feedback.* The survey instrument is developed and pretested to eliminate possible biases. The Delphi question is usually posed succinctly, and plenty of space is allowed for a detailed response. A sample first-round form is shown in Table 15.1. The participants are told when the next questionnaire will arrive and given a deadline within which to respond (usually a week). A week may be required to analyze the initial responses. Either decision makers or their staff interpret and summarize the responses, such as strengths and weaknesses. This interpretation and summary is returned and comprises the next questionnaire. A minimum of three days is usually required to summarize the results and return them.

In the second round, members are asked to critique

Table 15.1. A Sample Delphi First-Round Questionnaire.

Name _____

Please indicate the strengths and weaknesses of our retirement program.

Strengths	Weaknesses

each response, adding still other strengths or weaknesses they may think of. The process is repeated until the critiques and new ideas stop or until a predesignated number of rounds is completed. Staff analysis consolidates areas of agreement and disagreement and items needing verification. Subsequent questionnaires may take the form of lists of strengths and weaknesses (barriers or problems), with a consolidated commentary of the panel under each.

4. *Prioritization.* Prioritization can be done by voting. Voting usually accompanies the third and all subsequent surveys. Each participant is asked to score the list of responses, such as strengths and weaknesses. Average scores are fed back for reconsideration by the participants in the final round of the survey. The final votes are taken to elicit the views of the Delphi panel. In some cases, no final vote is needed. The process is merely stopped when no new information is obtained.

Table 15.2 illustrates responses to an intermediate round of a Delphi questionnaire dealing with barriers to implementing a particular MIS for all the subsidiaries and divisions of a corporation spread across the United States. Participants are key people in the subsidiaries and divisions who have never met. The current vote tally is shown in the second column. The vote represents the average panel ranking from the previous round. The list of barriers taken from the first round and added to in subsequent rounds is shown in the third column. The last column lists the comments made by panelists in the previous rounds. Some take the form of questions, which one or more panel members are encouraged to answer. Other comments take a position on the merits of a barrier. The next round may provoke still further questions or new barriers to which the panelists will respond. Another survey that abstracts these issues is then prepared.

One form of a final-round survey is shown in Table 15.3. In this survey, issues, not barriers, have been abstracted and voted on. The last vote keeps the members aware of each barrier's importance to aid in the final ranking of each issue. The comments often become heavily annotated, indicating the way to deal with objections and answers to questions about feasibility. The final vote is then taken in the last survey.

Five surveys are minimal in the Delphi technique, one to get a listing and the others to get comments on the issues that have been *abstracted* by staff, as well as rankings of the issues. When new questions arise they must be summarized and sent out for the panelists' commentary, drawing out the process. For the simple form of Delphi pro-con analysis, three surveys are minimal: one to list and two to react and prioritize.

Delphi is an excellent information dredge. It is also useful when confidentiality is essential, because group members can remain anonymous, and when meetings are too costly because of travel distances. But Delphi can be cumbersome, time-consuming, and arbitrary. There are no generally accepted rules for summarizing results. The individual doing the summaries must have (or acquire) considerable knowledge to reduce the information derived to manageable proportions. During information reduction, unconscious staff views and preconceived notions can creep in to bias or manipulate the results. A large number of surveys may be needed before disagreements become apparent. Finally, closure forced by a vote can be artificial.

Table 15.2. An Intermediate-Round Delphi Questionnaire.

Instructions:	1. Review all items on list.	
	2. Select the top five priority barriers to implementing a management information system.	
	3. Give the most important barrier a score of 10 and the least important a score of 1, with other scores reflecting the relative importance of each barrier.	
	4. Return by _____to: _____.	

New Vote	Old Vote	Barriers to MIS Adoption	Comments
___	10	1. My budget will not stand the user charges to be imposed.	a. Is this true? b. For all types of services?
___	8	2. Why do we need a system for the entire organization? Aren't local control and decision making valuable?	a. We need uniform reporting because of federal regulations. b. Some local control is possible by electing the services you want.
___	7	3. This system is not cost-effective.	a. Cost studies were done and were convincing. b.
___	2	4. I heard that the CEO's brother-in-law sold him this mess.	a. This is not true. b. There was competitive bidding. c. The system was tailored to our needs.
___	___	5.	
___	___	6.	

Interactive Group Processes

An interacting group meets face-to-face and conducts an open-ended discussion. Rules or procedures that are used to guide this discussion are minimal. Two types of interacting groups are called *traditional* and *brainstorming*.

Traditional Face-to-Face Groups. Traditional decision groups have a conventional discussion format. Discussion is free-flowing and open-ended, and little in the way of process is used. Structure stems from the agenda and from the leader, who maintains a focus on the issue.

Table 15.3. A Final-Round Delphi Survey.

Instructions: 1. Review issues and comment.
2. Select the five most important issues.
3. Voting (see Table 15.2).
4. Return (see Table 15.2).

Barrier Vote	Issue Vote		Barriers to MIS Adoption Issues	Comments[a]
8	10	1. User charges	1. Equity	a. Budgets can reflect increases because of justifiable projection of MIS use. b. Etc.
	8		2. Coercion to use	a. This part can be budgeted. b. Etc.
7	7	2. Systemwide application	1. Uniformity	a. Participation in the core program is mandated. b. Etc.
	6		2. Improved capability	a. We improved service during the pilot phase.
3	8	3. Cost	1. System workability	a. Evidence... b. Etc.
	10		2. Cost-effectiveness	a. Evidence... b. Etc.
___	___	4.	1.	.
___	___		2.	.
___	___	5.	1.	
___			2.	
___			3.	
.		.	.	
.		.	.	
.		.	.	

[a] Under each comment, answers to the question are summarized to aid the ranking. The rejoinders are provided by panelists and summarized by staff members along with other information that the sponsor believes to be necessary.

Groups with complex interpersonal relationships work best in an open discussion environment (Guetzkow and Simon, 1950; Guetzkow and Dill, 1957; and Guetzkow, 1960). An individual in an interacting group is profoundly influenced by other group members. As a result, group members will divide their time between the task and the social environment. A well-defined issue, such as approving or disapproving a project, permits the group to attend to personal considerations that flow from the decision, promoting needed information exchanges and acceptance of the decision that is reached. This process promotes consensus, a feature that makes interacting groups a superior means of judging and/or choosing.

The performance of an interacting group can be improved by dealing with the interpersonal obstacles that crop up in a group. These obstacles and ways to deal with them are listed here.

1. Members of a group will withhold information they know to be relevant. To some extent, social rewards like praise and solicitous requests for their contributions will overcome the inhibition to share information.
2. Inferior group members have a depressing effect on the quality of a group's judgment. A group *can* come to grips with a difficult choice, where some members of the group will lose something, when all members view each other as competent. Demonstrations of competence (for example, a chairman who cites the past accomplishments of each member) are useful when group members are not acquainted.
3. Group members experience participation penalties when their views are not readily accepted or are rejected outright. A socioemotional leadership style reduces these penalties, suggesting that leaders with consideration skills are best to lead judging groups.
4. Groups become inhibited by large status distinctions. Those members who perceive themselves as "high power" will talk with "low power" members until their status is clear, and then they restrict their communication to other "high power" members. This behavior creates tension and conflict in the group.
5. The behavior of some members can be inhibiting to the group. Nonparticipants have a chilling effect, as do isolates (people without a clear role). Again, the socioemotional

style of leadership is useful to draw out nonparticipants and seek ways for the isolate to participate.

6. A group member seeking personal power (gratification from serving) and one seeking issue power (changing the course of events) are incompatible and should not serve in the same group.

7. The members of a decision group who support their views with logical arguments and show how their views are consistent with past experiences of the other group members have the most influence.

Brainstorming Groups. Brainstorming groups are interacting groups that are used to develop ideas. In brainstorming, the leader challenges the group into a rapid-fire generation of ideas, inviting new and modified ideas. Brainstorming works best when the fact-finding and problem-finding activities are separated (Osborn, 1963). Facts highlight issues. New ways to define problems are based on integrating and extrapolating known facts. Premature evaluation keeps the integrative and extrapolative steps from occurring, so early criticism is ruled out. These requirements lead to the two principles of brainstorming: "deferment of judgment" and "quantity breeds quality." These principles are valuable for any situation in which innovation is desirable.

The need for deferment stems from the distinction between the judicial and the creative mind. The judicial mind carries out analysis and comparisons that are required to make a choice. The creative mind makes forecasts to visualize new ideas. These mental processes are incompatible. Making judgments is not compatible with the free association one needs to be creative. The judicial mind tends to dominate. As a result, all forms of judgment are deferred in a brainstorming group. The leader must create an environment in which group members will verbalize their ideas without any concern for their acceptability or importance.

The second dictum is that many ideas are needed. The notion that quantity breeds quality stems from the view that a person's thoughts have a hierarchical structure. The dominant thoughts in the hierarchy are conventional. To transcend these conventional notions of problem definitions, considerable effort is needed to create new associations. The quantity dictum forces the members to exhaust their conventional notions to get at the creative ones.

The deferment and quantity-quality principles suggest four rules for a brainstorming group: no criticism, wild ideas, many ideas, and integration (Stein, 1975).

1. *Elimination of criticism.* All criticism is ruled out. Group members are told that a subsequent discussion will be used to evaluate. When criticism occurs, the leader can become self-critical (attempting to deflect the judgmental effects) or use a device, such as a bell. The leader gets the group to agree that he or she can ring the bell when one member is critical of another's contributions.

2. *Promotion of unconventional ideas.* The members of the group are made to feel that they are expected to offer unconventional ideas. This gives the adventuresome members the sanction they need to participate and helps the more inhibited relax. A plant or two — people prepared with unconventional ideas — can help get the session moving.

3. *Many ideas.* Participants are told that they should come up with as many ideas as they can. Encouraging quantity increases the chance that later suggestions will be original.

4. *Integration of ideas.* Ideas should be combined and improved whenever possible. When a member shows how integration can be achieved, the leader should reinforce this behavior. If it does not occur early in the session, the leader can give an illustration. This rule also helps those who contribute later in the session to mark out a distinct role for themselves. The notion of "hitchhiking," in which a member gives a variation on a theme of a previous idea, encourages both integration and refinement.

Several steps are needed to establish and manage a brainstorming group for decision making (Stein, 1975). First, a group size of about twelve members who have needed knowledge or experience is recommended. People who tend not to see each other in their day-to-day activities are also preferable as members. Second, the leader should be committed to the technique and be familiar with its steps and the rationale behind the steps. The leader should have an outgoing, gregarious personality. Third, steps should be taken to maintain a record. Tapes, chalkboards, flip charts, and many other devices can be used.

The leader begins with a "warm-up session," using a sample problem. Strategies for a mythic organization, such as the Bloom County *Beacon* or Bloom County boarding house, can be sought. The humor and good feeling derived from this provide a good springboard for tackling the more substantive problem.

To begin a session, the leader states the problem and spells out the technique's steps. A rapid-fire list of suggestions is encouraged, but members are limited to one idea each time they are recognized. The leader must be careful to let everyone participate. During slow periods, the leader can offer his or her ideas and call for hitchhiking. The typical session lasts between thirty minutes and an hour.

There are several ways that a brainstorming group can fail (Bristol, 1958). The most common way is failing to get sanction. For brainstorming to work, its participants must believe that the session is needed and that the process is approved by upper management. A second pitfall is preparing poorly. Expectations should be reasonable, and the participants should be indoctrinated into the technique's steps. Finally, follow-up is often a problem. Most forms of ideation that fail do so because the decision process was left incomplete. Management blames the most visible step (brainstorming) for the failure, not recognizing that the process was stopped prematurely.

Silent Reflective Group Processes

The process of silent reflection has been advocated to overcome barriers to group participation and to encourage thoughtful consideration of the decision task. During the silent reflection phase, the group members feel a certain tension, which promotes a form of competition for good solutions. This helps the group avoid superficial arguments, tired diagnoses, and pet ideas that stifle innovation. Several group processes use silent reflection, including the nominal group technique (Delbecq and Van de Ven, 1971), brainwriting (Gueschka, Shaude, and Schlicksupp, 1975), the nominal-interacting (or NI) technique (Souder, 1980), and the kiva technique.

The Nominal Group Technique. Nominal groups work silently to encourage reflection (Delbecq and Van de Ven, 1971). Group activity can be used to identify criteria or to specify norms, to elicit information, and to determine solution options. In the nominal group technique (NGT), four steps are used: silently recording ideas; listing ideas, giving each member a turn, one at a time, until the ideas are exhausted; discussing the ideas to consolidate the list and share information about the merits of each idea; and voting to select a priority list.

The nominal group technique was derived from behavioral science literature tempered by experience. Most groups have an ideation phase and an evaluative phase. Ideation provides a search for ideas, and evaluation screens and merges ideas into a coherent picture. Different steps are best for each phase: silent reflection for ideation, and interaction for evaluation. NGT can also control "rhetoric" leaders, who often try to dominate the group, which lowers both productivity and satisfaction. The NGT steps control this behavior by ensuring equal participation.

The NGT group should be small, composed of seven to ten members who are seated so each can view the others. The leader introduces the group and outlines all steps in the process. It is important that each group member understand the steps and agree to follow them. When the leader is unknown to the group members, an outside source of authority is often essential to get process acceptance (see Table 15.4).

The nominal group technique has the decision group initially work without discussion to encourage reflection. This reflective phase is followed by a systematic consideration of ideas. The leader begins by stating the purpose of each step in the nominal group technique. Next, the problem stipulation is provided. Each member is asked to write his or her ideas on a pad of paper, *without discussion.* Those who wish to talk during

Table 15.4. Leader Guides for NGT Meetings.

Step 1. Silent Recording
    1. Present a written problem statement and a written outline of all
       process steps.
    2. Resist all but process clarifications.
    3. Maintain atmosphere by also writing in silence.
    4. Discourage members who attempt to talk to others.
Step 2. Round-Robin Recording
    1. Indicate the purpose of step 2 (to create a record of the
       meeting).
    2. Ask members to present their problems briefly and clearly.
    3. Accept variations on a theme, but discourage duplicate items.
    4. Ask if an idea has been correctly recorded to gain approval
       before proceeding.
    5. Keep the list visible to all members by taping it on the wall.
Step 3. Interactive Discussion
    1. Indicate this step's purpose (to explain and consolidate).
    2. Skirt arguments, but accept both opinions when a difference
       arises.
    3. Give all items some consideration.
    4. Encourage elaborations from everyone without reference to
       who proposed them.
    5. Gain the group's agreement to merge similar ideas, keeping the
       ideas separate when the group objects.
Step 4. Prioritization
    1. Indicate the purpose of step 4 (to set priorities).
    2. Explain the procedure.

Source: Adapted from Delbecq, Van de Ven, and Gustafson, 1986.

this phase should be discouraged in a friendly but firm manner. The silent-listing phase proceeds until all of the members have stopped writing or until a given time period has elapsed, preferably the former. The leader should resist all but process questions and work silently to create a role model for the group.

In step 2, the leader solicits and records the ideas of each member. This phase is useful in depersonalizing the ideas and allowing each member equal time to present his or her views. It also provides a written record. Each individual is asked to give one idea from his or her list, which the leader then records on a flip chart. The leader should be sure the member agrees with the written version of the problem before proceeding. The leader rotates among the members, getting their ideas one at a time and recording each on the flip chart so all can see, until members confirm that their ideas are exhausted. At this point, several sheets should be taped to the wall in full view of the members. Between twenty and twenty-five items are usually listed in an NGT group.

In step 3, each idea is discussed. The leader asks first for clarification and then for the merits and demerits of each idea. Considerable discussion may result, and the leader should make notes on the flip chart, indicating significant elaborations. The leader should avoid focusing on one idea and should tease out the logic in each idea by asking for clarification and recording differences of opinion. Consolidation attempts follow; here the leader merges similar ideas, asking for consent of the members. The leader must avoid arguments, leaving both options when a consensus to merge them does not develop.

In step 4, the group is asked to create a consensus by selecting the most important problems. Several voting techniques that can be used for this purpose are explained in Chapter Seventeen.

The Brainwriting Technique. Brainwriting (Gueschka, Shaude, and Schlicksupp, 1975) is another technique that uses silent reflection. In the "cued" variation (Nutt, 1984c) of brainwriting, the leader initiates a group decision-making session by placing sheets of paper that contain several written cues (for example, ideas that focus the group's attention) in the center of the table. The participants are asked to take a sheet, read it, and silently add their ideas. When members run out of ideas, or want the stimulation of another's ideas, they exchange their current list with one in the center of the table. After reviewing the new list, ideas are added and the procedure continues until ideas are exhausted.

A variation called "structural brainwriting" induces more synthesis (Nutt, 1984c). Members are asked to list their ideas on several sheets. Each sheet has cues for a particular theme, such as criteria, people affected, stakeholders, and constraints. After two ideas have been added in a particular category, this sheet is exchanged for another member's sheet in the center of the table.

This process continues without discussion, with members exchanging their sheets until ideas are exhausted or time is called. The "structured" brainwriting approach creates synthesis around the themes initially selected and allows members to sort out themes within theme options, creating a second form of synthesis. These steps improve the quality of ideas without harming innovation.

The round-robin recording step of NGT can be used to list ideas. (In the structured form of brainwriting, several listing steps are required.) Each member is asked to describe one item on his or her current list. The leader records the ideas one at a time, moving from one member to the next. This listing continues until all members pass. A discussion phase follows; this phase permits members to comment and elaborate on their ideas or the ideas of others. Prioritizing is the final step.

The Nominal-Interacting Technique. An adaptation of the nominal-interacting (NI) technique (Souder, 1980) is particularly useful in providing a forum for "anteroom lobbying" during a group process (Nutt, 1984c). Group meetings are held using the NGT or brainwriting steps. The procedure is truncated at several points to allow lobbying. A special room is provided with refreshments, ostensibly for a break. Between thirty and forty-five minutes are allocated for members to share views and lobby each other. The process, adapted from Souder, is shown below:

> Round 1. Step 1: Silent reflective listing (NGT or
> brainwriting)
> Step 2: Round-robin recording
> Step 3: Anteroom lobbying
> Step 4: Group discussion
> Step 5: Anteroom lobbying
> Step 6: Initial prioritization
> Step 7: Anteroom discussion
> Step 8: Final prioritization
> Round 2. Repeat steps 3 through 8 on another day.

During each of the anteroom sessions, members are encouraged to share opinions, exchange facts, challenge another's views, and bargain. While votes are confidential, members can ask for one another's ranking and its justification. Out of these informal exchanges, greater mutual understanding is created and premature closure avoided. Typically, three lobbying sessions are needed. The first session identifies the diversity of opinions. In the second, members begin to adopt or reject others' ideas. After the third, final judgments can emerge.

This approach is particularly useful for ill-structured and obscure decisions in which little precedent can be used as a guide. The anteroom discussion teases out the information that can lead to the group's making thoughtful judgments.

The Kiva Technique. The kiva process was devised by the Hopi Indians to make important tribal decisions. The name *kiva* is drawn from the structures in which these deliberations took place.

A kiva process begins with the key decision body, such as the tribal elders, conducting an open discussion that leads to its making preliminary decisions. This key body is surrounded by several rings of tribal members who listen to the discussion. The ring adjacent to the tribal elders is made up of individuals who have status just below that of the inner ring. The rings terminate with adolescents. After discussion, the tribal council moves to the outer ring and all the other groups move one ring toward the center. The group now in the center discusses what the members of this circle think they heard, with all other groups listening as before. This process repeats itself until the tribal council is again in the center ring. The tribal elders, aided by reflections on the reflections of others, then reconsider their decisions in light of their reflections on what they proposed.

Management decision making can profitably use this type of process when decisions cut across several levels in the organization's structure. A kiva arrangement allows representatives of various levels to reflect on what management proposes. The process permits management to gain an in-depth appreciation of reactions, and reactions to reactions, before a final decision is made. Each circle can follow NGT, brainwriting, or NI steps or use an interactive discussion to uncover its own views and the views of every other circle.

Managing a Decision-Making Group

Groups, regardless of their structure, require an appropriate introduction to pose the question to be resolved by the group and to give the leader legitimacy in regulating the group's efforts. This introduction should define the issue, provide a procedural orientation, and serve to introduce the leader.

The first step provides sanction. To provide sanction, an organizational representative with the power to make the decision should introduce the group leader. The introduction should stress the leader's skills and accomplishments to give the leader legitimacy. The leader describes the procedures to be used in managing the group's activities and seeks agreement to follow the proposed steps.

Next, the leader thanks members for attending this meeting, pointing out that each person's participation and ideas are essential for success. The purpose of the meeting is defined as providing or exchanging information, getting the members' recommendations and ideas, or making a decision. The leader describes the decision task and its origins and indicates the expected outcome. The leader then indicates that the group was assembled because its members are thought to have information and knowledge crucial to dealing with the problem. This gives the members a responsibility and provides a general expectation for each member's individual contribution. Finally, the leader describes how the information provided by the group will be used. For instance, recommendations could be given to boards of directors for further study.

Benefits of Process Types

Concrete guidelines in the use of process types are beginning to emerge from the extensive group process studies conducted in the past four decades. These studies find that no single group process is best for all applications. For example, Collins and Guetzkow (1964), in their summary of research, find that interacting face-to-face groups promote innovation and acceptance and make formal groups better than synthetic groups for most aspects of decision making. However, synthetic groups serve as useful sources of information for both developmental and judgmental tasks when all affected people would make an interacting group too large and unwieldy.

Studies of the merits of brainstorming rules have been instrumental in evolving improved group processes. For example, people in one study were asked to compose clever titles for stories, with and without evaluation. The titles composed by the "without evaluation" group were both more novel and more appropriate than those of the "with evaluation" group (Christensen, Guilford, and Wilson, 1957). This study is typical of many that find that deferred judgment increases the quality of a group's efforts.

The link between quality and quantity has been studied in "Eureka"-like tasks, such as exploring various uses for hangers and brooms. As the number of ideas increases, the quality of ideas also increases (Parnes and Meadow, 1959). People are more likely to make clever observations when they are *asked* (Maier, 1970). The mere act of telling people to be creative has been found to promote more novel ideas. Implicit in the quantity argument is that better ideas will result from integration, which tends to occur later in the session. Generally, the quality of ideas has been found to be higher in the second half of a meeting (Parnes, 1961).

Brainstorming has been used for nearly half a century. Although there is a decided bias toward reporting successful and not unsuccessful applications, a large number of studies do cite impressive results. For instance, Bell Telephone found ways to increase the demand for long-distance phone calls by using brainstorming (Stein, 1975). The National Association of Social Workers implemented a large number of ideas that came from a brainstorming session. Other successful applications range from improving a city's bus service to making a community more livable. Secondary effects of improved morale and attitudes of group members are also widely reported.

Brainstorming groups are better than a synthetic group for developmental tasks (Herbert and Yost, 1979). But many researchers (for example, Bouchard and Hare, 1970; Vroom,

Grant, and Cotton, 1969) also find that both brainstorming and interacting groups can inhibit creative thinking. Members' inhibitions and hasty evaluations shut off valuable lines of inquiry. This reduces innovativeness and the acceptance of new ideas. Furthermore, people in both interacting and brainstorming groups prefer to react to someone else's idea rather than offering one of their own (Delbecq and Van de Ven, 1971). This is called the "focus effect," which inhibits creativity.

Nominal groups are superior to interacting groups for creative tasks (Van de Ven and Delbecq, 1974). These benefits persist after accounting for the effects of leader skill (Nutt, 1976a, 1977). In these studies, NGT groups were clearly superior to interacting groups in terms of innovation, acceptance, and quality of results. NGT conducts a broad search for information that stimulates new ideas.

Both NGT and Delphi provide twice as many ideas as an interacting group does. The silent reflection phase in NGT and similar group processes overcome some of the barriers to creative thinking, making these group processes quite useful in developmental tasks. Compared to an interacting group, the silent reflection format produces more ideas and better-quality ideas, as well as more candor, member acceptance, and innovation (Nutt, 1977). The silent reflective processes are clearly superior to other group processes for developmental tasks and the generation of information.

The effectiveness of NGT and Delphi has been compared in several studies. Recall that both have a form of silent reflection, a means to systematically expose members to the views of others to stimulate synthesis and pooled judgments. Delphi has the advantage of anonymity but lacks timeliness. An NGT session can be completed in one evening, whereas Delphi takes up to two months. NGT has more spontaneous feedback, which can help or hinder a group. Groups under extreme stress find that NGT promotes conflict.

Studies that controlled leadership, which can have a decisive effect on the performance of an interacting group, also found NGT groups to be superior to interacting groups in terms of innovation, acceptance, and quality of results for planning tasks (Nutt, 1976a). The silent reflection portion of the process permits a member to conduct a broad search for information that has been found to stimulate new ideas. NGT is clearly superior to other group processes in its ability to generate new information.

The relative merits of NGT and Delphi are less clear. According to Van de Ven and Delbecq (1974), NGT (and probably the other silent reflection approaches) provide more alternatives than Delphi but have a comparable level of satisfaction. However, when NGT and Delphi were used to develop criteria to evaluate emergency room care, comparable levels of innovation were observed.

Research in altering attitudes and conformity finds that interaction seems to coax members to go along, converging on similar opinions and conclusions (Vroom and Yetton, 1973). Conflict resolution is more likely when an interacting group is used. Delphi and nominal groups restrict, at least to a degree, the amount of discussion among members. By limiting face-to-face questioning, which often leads to agreement, the silent reflective processes may increase conflict. Delphi ignores conflict.

Basis for Process Selection

To improve the effectiveness of decision groups, process types are matched to demands posed by the decision and the situation. Managers consider their requirements, the group's intended use (information exchange and the like, as discussed in Chapter Ten), and situational factors to select the group's members and a group process (Strumpf, Zand, and Freeman, 1979; Nutt, 1982b). These factors are used to match particular kinds of decisions to types of members and group process.

Specifying Expectations

A group can be asked to seek quality, acceptance, or originality or to adhere to preservation requirements when discovering, judging, influencing, or exchanging information to make a decision. Quality decisions call for choices that have desirable performance features, such as cost benefit. Acceptance deals with the subjective views of people who can block or covertly subvert both the decision and the decision process. A decision with high acceptance has the support of key stakeholders. An innovative decision adopts ideas not previously recognized or attempted, in the hope that some of the ideas will offer a decisive advantage. Finally, some decisions have important constraints that must be adopted.

An emphasis on quality calls for selection of the best alternative. The group is called upon to select an alternative or option that best meets present criteria, such as revenue or profit (Nutt, 1977). For example, a group could be charged with finding ways to overcome delays in parcel delivery that meet the service demands of customers at an acceptable level of cost. Participants are coaxed to search for ideas that are better than what is currently preferred or being used. Another example is a group charged with discovering a cost-effective practice plan that has the best prospect of producing revenue for a university college of medicine. (A practice plan specifies how revenue produced by physician faculty members in the treatment of patients will be shared by the university. Plans range from 100 percent with physicians salaried to 0 percent when physicians are paid on a fee-for-service basis. The priority attached to research and teaching by the university declines as the proportion of salary based on fee for service increases.)

Quality is sought in many but not all instances. When people's feelings are intense and several equally acceptable options exist, buy in, or the acceptance of key stakeholders, is the dominant concern. For example, Maier (1970) shows how the assignment of repair trucks to crews, after the oldest truck has been replaced by a new one, makes little difference to the organization but can be seen as a status symbol and perceived as a reward by the crews. If the crews believe that their assignment to trucks is arbitrary or unfair, that belief could ferment dissatisfaction among the repair personnel and lower job performance. In this case, acceptance is the dominant concern. To ensure high acceptance, the assignment decision can be delegated to the repair crews. Vroom and Yetton (1973) also stress acceptance, noting that feelings about a decision group's activities can become so intense that both overt acts of sabotage and covert work slowdowns occur. In such situations, a decision group can be used merely to facilitate acceptance.

Innovation may also be a desired outcome. The group can be asked to discover a *new way* to create revenue in a practice plan, reduce delays in parcel delivery, coax people, or show people new technology. An innovative outcome provides a different, but not *necessarily* better, approach to deal with, for example, revenue generation, delivery, coaxing, or demonstration. (Note that a new idea may or may not be a better one. To be innovative, an idea must have been previously unrecognized by the organization. Some management scientists apply a stronger test, limiting the use of innovation to ideas that have never before been recognized by anyone.)

Preservation recognizes that requirements to maintain current arrangements and to work within them are often imposed on decision making. Examples include sacrosanct procedures, policies, programs, or status, as depicted by an organization chart, that the organization does not want to challenge. These commitments become real values that the organization commits to, not merely constraints, and thus become performance expectations in their own right. They set out an arena in which people can assume there will be order and continuity and act to preserve certain values.

Each decision assigned to a group will possess a particular combination of these requirements. For instance, a discovery task often calls for both quality and innovation. To devise a new management information system, it is important to consider new ideas as well as costs and benefits. Other discovery tasks, such as uncovering decision objectives or criteria, also call for both quality and originality in the group's work. Some decisions stress acceptance and quality. Selecting an original idea is not required because originality is subordinated to quality and acceptance in the judgment to be rendered. Influencing often stresses preservation and acceptance, and most information exchange seeks acceptance.

As a result, it is important to carefully consider expectations for decisions to be made. All combinations of high or low importance accorded to quality, acceptance, innovation, and preservation are used to identify key types of decisions (Figure 15.1).

Assessing the Decision Situation

Decisions are often made in a complex environment that is laced with politics and a loose set of internal and external stakeholders who must be managed. As a result, the selection of a group process must also take into account characteristics of the situation facing the group. These characteristics or features pose a second set of factors one can use in the selection of a group process. Strumpf, Zand, and Freeman (1979) offer three features: expertise, span, and conflict. They represent key features in a set of many that are potentially important.

Membership. The rationale behind the selection of experts and users or consumers as members of a group was discussed in Chapter Ten. Strumpf, Zand, and Freeman (1979) define consumers as representatives and add the category *co-worker*. A co-worker group has membership drawn from a particular work unit, such as the medical technologists in the pathology department of a hospital or employees in the quality-control department of a firm. Thus, a co-worker group is made up of members drawn entirely from a single reference group, such as a department. Such groups are homogeneous, often sharing similar opinions and attitudes. However, some co-workers may have long-standing conflicts. In such a situation, members are selected to avoid the historical conflict, as discussed in Chapter Eight. Each type of group is managed to produce a convergence of attitude and opinion to promote agreement.

Expertise. Appropriate knowledge and information are critical to the success of a group. These requirements and the need for special skills in the group call for expertise. Expertise is required, for example, when a hospital board considers the purchase of a linear accelerator or a firm takes steps to revise its benefit programs. Experts are needed to point out why the

Figure 15.1. Selecting Group Process and Membership.

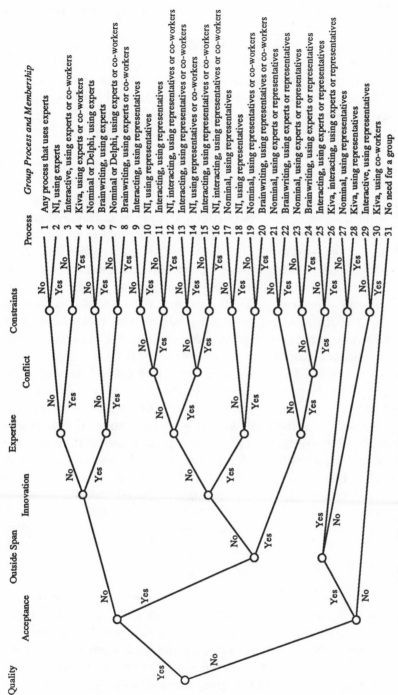

Source: Adapted from Strumpf, Zand, and Freeman, 1979, pp. 589–600; Nutt, 1982b, pp. 442–454.

equipment or change in benefit program is needed and to identify the merits of various types of equipment and benefit programs. If this type of expertise is not available, "quality" decisions may not be possible. When not available in co-workers, expertise must be solicited (Vroom and Yetton, 1973).

Span. Decisions can cut across departmental, divisional, or even organizational lines of authority. When lines of authority are cut, the group's membership is expanded to include representatives from each area affected by the arena of action. Span gives clues as to group membership, indicating whether departmental or multidepartmental representatives are needed. A broad span makes co-workers less desirable as group members. They tend to be familiar with only local values and interests and are less likely to represent and understand values that lie beyond their department or work group. Acceptance will increase if representation is appropriate to the span of the task (Bass, 1970). However, if the task is narrow — for instance, limited to a department — the participation of outside experts reduces acceptance (Collaros and Anderson, 1974).

Conflict. Some decisions are more likely than others to promote disagreement over the preferred action (Vroom and Yetton, 1973). For example, differences may crop up among members of a medical staff in a hospital about the merits of types of body scanners or among administrators about the desirability of various fringe benefit packages for employees. Each could lead to conflict. Conflict can be helpful when it is managed because it helps to promote novel insights. However, unmanaged conflict can lead to acrimonious debates and lasting animosities. Group process is one way to manage conflict.

Description of Process Options

The three types of group members — expert, representative, and co-worker — can be used with each of the three types of group process. Each of the resulting nine possibilities can be a clearly viable option for a given group task. Even a Delphi with co-workers can be used in some situations. For example, a hospital medical staff could be put into such a group if attending a meeting at the hospital posed hardships because of travel time or problems in scheduling.

How to Select a Group Process Option

The group process for applications defined by expectations, task span, conflict, and the need for expertise is selected according to a decision tree, as shown in Figure 15.1. The decision tree allows a manager to ask yes-no questions to elicit expectations and identify context to select an appropriate group process type. Moving from left to right in Figure 15.1, the questions are as follows:

1. Is quality required?
2. Is acceptance by those affected required to ensure adoption?
3. Does the task extend beyond the group initiator's control?
4. Should innovation be sought?
5. Are there people under the leader's jurisdiction with adequate expertise?
6. Is conflict among the group members likely?
7. Are there important constraints?

By answering each of the questions, one can identify the preferred type of group process.

Specific types of decisions can pose different requirements. The search for alternatives may call for innovation but not acceptance. For example, which crew gets the new truck calls for acceptance, not innovation. The group process preferred in each task is quite different, as the decision tree in Figure 15.1 illustrates. Several examples will be used to illustrate how to apply the decision rules to select a group process.

Consider, for example, the decisions involved in a search for a new leader. The stakes in leader selection are quite high. Poor leaders can cause considerable havoc and are hard to dislodge. This is due, in part, to the unwillingness of those involved in leader selection to admit an error.

Decisions of this type are typically initiated by forming a

search committee that is charged with identifying candidates. In one recent case, the search committee was charged with recommending candidates for a new CEO of a large university hospital whose previous CEO had been eased out. The search committee used an interacting group format for all aspects of the decision, including identifying and selecting criteria, uncovering the names of candidates, exchanging information about prospective candidates, and narrowing the list to select three viable candidates to be recommended to the university president. The search committee was made up of representatives of key university departments, such as pharmacy, but had no key members of the medical staff, involving only the medical director as a representative of physician views. Also excluded were members of a voluntary board of trustees and representatives of the business function of the university.

The committee produced four short lists of candidates before a new CEO was finally selected. The new CEO violated several of the criteria initially set (for example, had never held a CEO position and had no university hospital experience) and was not well received in several sections of the university community.

What went wrong? First, the search committee used a single process for all of its activities. Criterion development, for example, calls for a different process and a different set of participants than those that were used. Imagine that you are the chief operating officer in this organization and that the board of trustees asks you to form a committee to recommend criteria to select a new CEO. This decision calls for both quality and acceptance. The choice of criteria is beyond the COO's span of control. It is not likely that people under the COO's control possess all the information needed to identify criteria to select a CEO. Constraints in the actual case included a salary limit: the CEO had to be paid less than the governor of the state. This constraint remained implicit until the first short list emerged. The salary constraint conflicted with the requirement that candidates had to have had CEO experience at a major university hospital. Such experience called for a salary twice as high as that being paid to the state governor. The decision tree suggests process 22 (Figure 15.1), which calls for brainwriting by either experts or representatives. In this case, a combination would have been desirable, inviting members of the board of trustees and outside experts (for example, other CEOs and academics) to serve on a group to identify criteria. This group process would have been more apt to recognize and resolve the conflicting criteria of experience and salary limitations.

A second problem stems from the unrecognized conflict that was inherent in the selection process. Consider the same situation, with the university president asking the chief operating officer to create a search committee that will interview and screen candidates for the CEO position. Quality and acceptance remain important, and the choice remains outside the university president's span of control. Expertise is available. A search must produce a person who will fit in, so innovation is not critical. Also conflict and constraints seem likely, and this calls for process 25 in Figure 15.1. A kiva group with experts and representatives (formed as described above) is recommended. This process is more apt to uncover compromises that must be made to form a short list of CEO candidates acceptable to various factions of the university community.

Note that the processes recommended differ markedly from those that were actually used. Several conclusions are implied. First, interactive groups are overused. They tend to be adopted without much thought unless the group leader takes the initiative to alter the process, using a rationale such as that shown in Figure 15.1. Second, the members of a group are often not well suited to the task because pertinent information sources, points of view, or reference group representatives are missing. Subcommittees can be used to circumvent constraints imposed when an appointed group contains ill-advised members or lacks key individuals. Third, a decision process must be staged to deal with discovery, information exchange, bargaining, and making judgments. Subcommittees can be used to deal with some of these activities, or they can be dealt with in sequence by changing the process as required.

The reader should visualize a group task with which he or she is familiar and compare the process used to the one recommended, asking if the group's efforts could have been approved. Process mismatches often cause poor outcomes.

Leadership and Group Process

Selecting a group process simplifies the problems of using an appropriate style of leadership. The impact of group process is so strong that organizational behaviorists call it a substitute for leadership. Delphi groups need only good staff support in the development and summary of the surveys. Leadership is not a relevant concern in directing activity. Silent reflective processes use leadership principles in the discussion and voting stages but not in the early stages. However, the effectiveness of an interaction group can be quite leader-dependent.

In each case where the style of leadership is important, such as the NGT discussion phase and in interacting groups, the demands of the situation have been clarified. For instance, an interacting group is often used for a judging task, which calls for acceptance and a "considerate" or socioemotional style. The same style is used in the NGT discussion stages. As a result, the problems of selecting a style of leadership have been clarified by means of an appropriate group process. The socioemotional style can be used when needed.

Groupthink

Janis (1972) discovered that groups can have an invulnerability illusion, which he termed *groupthink*. This phenomenon can occur in an interacting group and in the discussion and influencing phases of all group processes. As a result, the influence of groupthink is limited to evaluating and judging tasks, if a proper group process has been selected.

The invulnerability illusion stems from one of the benefits groups create: cohesion and goodwill among members. This cohesion can be beneficial because it leads to agreement and consensus. But agreement and consensus can be helped along when a group has shared stereotypes, creates the same rationalizations, shares beliefs about the morality of its position, and engages in self-censorship. When this occurs, members and others who take opposing views are seen as deviates. Their views are censored. For example, during the decisions that preceded the Bay of Pigs disaster, Secretary of State Dean Rusk brushed aside the objections of his policy adviser, Chester Bowles. Rusk would not let Bowles discuss his objections with President Kennedy or with Kennedy's key advisers (Janis, 1980). The State Department is expected to take the lead in coordinating various committees charged with overseeing nuclear arms limitations talks with the Soviet Union ("Playing Nuclear Poker," 1983, p. 23). According to officials, meetings with these committees were rarely productive because committee members were afraid to contradict the Reagan administration's "zero-based" position for nuclear arms limitations, which was staked out in the early 1980s.

Seeing the danger in premature consensus, Alfred Sloan, former chairman of General Motors Corporation, delayed decisions whenever there was complete agreement, proposing "that we postpone further discussion . . . to give ourselves time to develop some disagreement and perhaps gain an understanding of what the decision is all about" (Janis, 1972, p. 378).

A key benefit of a group decision, acceptance, requires agreement in basic values and mutual respect. The members subordinate their own desires to serve the interests of the group. By giving up ego gratification stemming from outdoing other group members, in which they are seen as rivals to be defeated, a group can give up its best defense against massive mistakes.

Several prescriptions that can help prevent groupthink are summarized below:

1. *Critical evaluator.* The leader of a group can assign the role of critical evaluator to a group member. This individual, operating with the sanction of the leader, can prompt critical inquiry and head off premature agreement. The role of critical evaluator is rotated to avoid labeling any given member as a deviate.

   When an internal evaluator is not used, group members can discuss the decision with outsiders to get their reaction. Inviting experts to meetings on a rotating basis can interject new views. The expert is encouraged to challenge the views being expressed by members of the group during the discussion phase.

2. *Impartial leader.* Leaders can sway a group when their opinions are made clear. Rather than stating preferences at the outset, a leader should avoid advocating a particular position and listen to the unfettered views of the members. This recommendation is particularly important when the leader has much more authority than the group's members. Following this practice keeps a group from merely conforming with the leader's views. A variation on this role, which allows the leader more control, introduces conflicting information that the group is asked to consider before discussing options.

3. *Multiple groups.* When decisions have considerable importance, several groups with different leaders and group members are asked to consider options and make a recommendation. A variation calls for a group to break into several subgroups that meet separately under different leaders. Another tactic is "second chance" sessions, where group members are asked to rethink the decision and bring out residual doubts. The second-chance meeting can be promoted in a relaxed atmosphere. The Roman senate had a custom of arriving at a decision and then reconsidering it after consuming some wine. Second thoughts flow more freely under relaxed conditions.

Each of these tactics has drawbacks rooted in the behavior that critics, nondirective leadership, and multiple groups create. A critic can become the odd man out, even if he or she is protected by the group. For example, Robert Kennedy was assigned the role of devil's advocate during the Cuban Missile Crisis to break up premature consensus (Janis, 1980). The president's brother's role cost him popularity and created a reputation that haunted him throughout his political career. The rotating devil's advocate has little effect when a favorable image among the members and/or leader must be projected. For example, the Johnson administration had its "hawks" and "doves," but their debate had little effect on the decision to intensify the air war against North Vietnam (Janis, 1980). Johnson encouraged dissent, but his behavior suggested that the bounds of permissible dissent were quite narrow. When the devil's-advocate tactic is ritualized, nothing much is accomplished.

Nondirective leaders may have difficulty capturing control of the process. Divisive power struggles between points of view and overturning a popular group decision that is unacceptable to the leader both have negative consequences. Even when no cleavage in the group emerges, lack of progress may prompt the leader to become assertive, leading to a more domineering image than the leader would otherwise convey. Leaders must be willing to accept a consensus that emerges from a group to retain the benefits of acceptance.

Independent policy groups lead to leaks and require more time and cost. Efficiency and morale can fall when groups become aware of their joint task. Finally, with many people involved, there is a greater chance for pressure groups to form and push on groups with members thought to be sympathetic to their views. The result can be radically different decisions from the groups and no clear-cut way to rationalize them.

The best way to control the effects of groupthink is through a group process. The process forces a wide consideration of views that makes stereotyped responses harder to maintain. Processes are far more effective than critical evaluation tactics and can be used to make multiple groups and impartial leaders more effective.

Key Points

1. A group process is used to manage the activities of a decision group. The process helps a decision group create new ideas, bring forward information, exchange views, and make judgments. Survey, interacting, nominal, Delphi, brainwriting, nominal-interactive, and kiva procedures are viable options that can be effectively used.

2. A way to match process options to the demands of the
    decision task was presented. An interacting process is best
    for influencing and judging, and a silent reflective process
    is best for information generation and developmental tasks.
    Process can be a substitute for leadership and can eliminate
    the problems of groupthink as well as improve other aspects
    of a group's effectiveness and efficiency.
3. The best way to control the effects of groupthink is through
    a group process. The process forces a wide consideration of
    views, which makes stereotyped responses harder to main-
    tain. Group process is far more effective than critical eval-
    uator tactics and can be used to make multiple groups and
    impartial leaders more effective. Finally, group process per-
    mits the use of a socioemotional leadership style in guiding
    the discussion and judging aspects of a group. This, in turn,
    allows a group to grapple with conflict-ridden decisions
    that demand member acceptance.

16

How to Set Objectives, Identify Criteria, Uncover Alternatives, and Confront Ethical Concerns

This chapter deals with several closely related aspects of decision making: objectives, criteria, and alternative courses of action, as well as the ethical considerations that each raises. Each aspect is dependent on the core problems identified according to the procedures noted in Chapter Eleven. Problems and objectives have both similarities and differences. Similarities stem from the direction that problems and objectives provide that set out an arena in which a search for possible actions is conducted. Problems differ from objectives in the type of action they call for. Problems identify what is wrong, and objectives specify what is wanted. It is important to translate problems into objectives to capture the more positive nature of a search based on filling expectations instead of overcoming dysfunctions. Criteria and alternatives flow from objectives. Alternatives suggest ways to respond in order to meet an objective, and criteria identify performance expectations implied by the objective that can be used to determine the merits of the alternatives. Procedures useful in setting objectives, identifying criteria, and uncovering alternatives are described in this chapter. Selection among objectives, criteria, and alternatives may pose ethical questions. Thus, ways to deal with ethical considerations are also presented

Figure 16.1. The Decision Process.

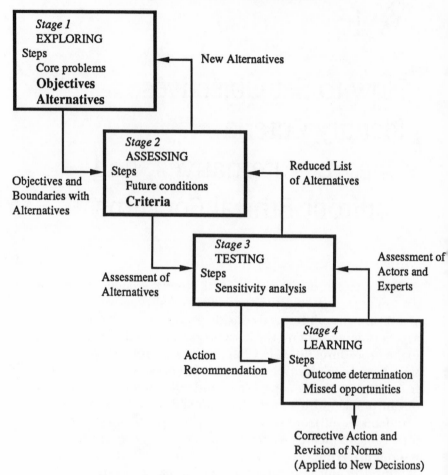

Note: Boldface type indicates topics addressed in this chapter.

in this chapter. Figure 16.1 indicates how these activities support the decision process.

Setting Objectives

Clarifying objectives is a key requirement in making a decision. A decision objective defines directions or aims that guide the search for alternatives and decision criteria to value them. The objective sets out an arena for search. Unclear decision objectives imply that several arenas are being considered at the same time, which leads to unfocused inquiry. Objectives that deal with problems and issues tangential to the factors motivating a decision can also misdirect inquiry. When decision makers seek alternatives and apply criteria to symptoms instead of underlying causes, two consequences result. Without a clear arena for inquiry, alternatives are hard to identify. Wrong arenas lead to alternatives that have little to do with the core problems prompting a decision. A second consequence stems from criteria inferred from objectives that are used to judge the alternatives. Criteria in an unfocused arena can be fuzzy or contradictory, making them hard to specify. Focusing on symptoms leads decision makers to apply nondiagnostic criteria to measure the value of alternatives.

Consider, for example, the decisions necessary to develop an alcoholism treatment program. A decision focused on the objective "to make people aware of alcoholism problems" is substantially different from one "to ameliorate alcoholism problems." An objective of making people aware implies case finding. Alternatives could be sought that deal with motivating self-assessment acts by at-risk individuals. Criteria to judge the merit of these alternatives would measure costs and the extent to which at-risk individuals have been reached by the program. In contrast, treatment objectives to ameliorate alcoholism problems call for alternatives that one can derive by adapting AA substance abuse programs and for alternatives from other sources. Criteria that measure an individual's abstinence, recovery rates, changes in the level of family tension, and job problems, as well as cost, would be used to judge the merits of alternatives.

Decisions for a state's capital budgeting program provide another example. Capital budgeting decisions can have a variety of objectives, such as determining the state's fiscal status, letting contracts, and prohibiting budget overruns. Alternatives for fiscal status, contracting, and budget control objectives include forecasting approaches, contractors with good records, and information systems, respectively. Criteria used to judge fore-casts, such as after-the-fact prediction accuracy, differ from those used to judge contractors (history of being on time and within budget) and budget control (budget variance).

These examples illustrate the importance of setting objectives to clarify intentions for decision making. Identifying the scope of a decision is the key consideration. For instance, decisions concerning people's alcoholism awareness (case finding) are subordinate to and precede treatment. Knowing fiscal status precedes letting contracts, which precedes steps to prohibit cost overruns.

The Structure and Semantics of Objectives

Objectives contain statements calling for action that have a particular structure (Nadler, 1970). Note that objectives in the examples considered thus far have an infinitive-action-verb form, immediately followed by a direct object. Recall the objectives "to make people aware" in the alcoholism decision and "to prohibit budget overruns" in the state budgeting decision. Sometimes this form is extended to add qualifiers, such as "to prohibit budget overruns within 10 percent" or "to make more/most people aware" (Warfield, 1976). The qualifiers can become complex, laying out a host of probable causes, consequences, contingencies, conditions, and targets. Such an objective could take the form of "to make unserved people aware by removing barriers to getting care, caused by ignorance and fear, thereby improving people's prospects of seeking care, within budget and time constraints and the limitations imposed by work-force turnover." The simpler and less qualified form for an objective is preferred because it has more focus and less clutter, leading to fewer restrictions that overly focus subsequent inquiry (Nutt, 1984c). Also, note that the qualifiers may include means. To avoid a premature choice, an objective lays out ends, not means.

The semantics of an objective are also important. The words used can bring meaning or take it away (Volkema, 1983). *Qualifiers* can be changed and thus add or take away constraints that set boundaries. Altering the objective "to reduce budget overruns by 10 percent" by dropping the qualifier (by 10 percent) has a similar effect. The response to an unqualified objective elicits a search for the broadest possible range of alternatives. (Qualifiers are treated as norms in the next section of this chapter.)

Alterations in the *verb* can also have important effects (Volkema, 1983). The action "maintain" is quite different from "enhance" or "maximize." Within an implied action type, semantics can have subtle effects that alter how objectives are interpreted. For instance, stakeholders may view "maintain competence" and "keep competence" differently, perhaps giving the former a neutral interpretation and the latter an interpretation that competence is slipping.

The *object* has the greatest potential to focus inquiry. A change in object can create very different impressions of needed action, ranging from very narrow to very broad searches for ways to resolve problems that the organization is confronting. For example, the objective "to get new budget forecasts" points to looking for a specific set of techniques compared with "to improve budgeting," which opens up inquiry into the entire budgeting process, thus allowing the decision process to consider a wider range of responses. Experienced managers are aware that bad decisions often stem from dealing with lower-level objectives at the expense of more pertinent higher-level objectives (Huber, 1980). Finally, changing from a negative to a positive context is desirable, as discussed in Chapter Four. For example, changing "to eliminate budget problems" to "to improve the budget system" moves inquiry from attaching blame to finding productive responses.

The Scope of an Objective

Objectives for all decisions have a hierarchical relationship in which one objective provides the means to accomplish another. For example, the alcoholism decision could embrace an objective "to make people aware" or "to motivate people needing help." Awareness is a means to motivate. Broad-scope objectives lead to expanded lists of alternatives that consider wider courses of action, unless the objective becomes grandiose (Volkema, 1983). For example, the objective "to engender growth and development" may not be helpful in stimulating ideas for decisions about alcoholism programs.

The arena of search is set by the scope of the objective in a hierarchy that is adopted to guide the decision process. The scope of the intended decision is crucial, and decision makers are encouraged to explore the implications of several objectives before selecting one to guide the decision process. To help the decision maker identify an appropriate scope for a decision, a three-step procedure is recommended: (1) identify possible objectives, (2) arrange objectives in a hierarchy, and (3) select an objective that will guide the decision process (Nadler, 1981). Either a group or a decision maker working alone can use the technique. (Group process techniques that can be used to set objectives were discussed in previous chapters.)

Objective-Setting Procedure

Step 1: Identify Possible Objectives. To initiate the session, the decision maker or leader of a group reviews problems that have prompted the need for a decision. This listing can include background about the core problem, imperatives for change, and support from key leaders that make a change possible. The decision maker (or group leader) then reviews an example of the outcome of this technique, which provides a hierarchy of objectives. An example of a hierarchy for an alcoholism decision (Nutt, 1984b, p. 137) follows:

To provide operational definitions of alcoholism
↓
To identify persons suffering from alcoholism
↓
To make person aware of alcoholism problem in
   general
↓
To make person aware of own alcoholism problem
↓

To motivate person
↓
To take some form of positive action
↓
To assist person's recovery
↓
To assist person to ameliorate or eliminate alcoholism problem
↓
To assist person in dealing constructively with problems associated with alcoholism
↓
To meet person's needs
↓
To meet person's needs for social, vocational, and personal adjustment

A hierarchy for a capital budgeting decision in a state department of transportation (see Nadler, 1970, p. 629) follows:

To estimate fiscal year funding needs for each project
↓
To identify funding requirements for all projects
↓
To determine state's fiscal status
↓
To fund commitments and obligations
↓
To let contracts for projects
↓
To keep spending within budget
↓
To allocate funds as commitments arise
↓
To maintain good contractor relations
↓
To create viable road-building capacity in state
↓

To complete road program
↓
To provide transportation

After the orientation, the decision maker identifies possible objectives for dealing with the perceived problem. For example, in dealing with the capital budgeting decision, someone may suggest an objective "to estimate fiscal year project costs." The "verb-object" form should be noted. The verb is "estimate" and the object is "fiscal year project costs." Objectives that have this format are sought. As they are suggested or uncovered, they are recorded.

Next, the objectives are reviewed. Limited or qualified objectives are deleted. For example, "to treat alcoholics within budget constraints" is trimmed to "to treat alcoholics." Statements such as "reduce costs" are disregarded because they suggest a criterion to measure an objective rather than offering direction.

Step 2: Arrange Objectives in a Hierarchy. In step 2, the pruned list of objectives from step 1 is ordered in a hierarchy. First, a search is conducted for the most immediate, direct, and irreducible objective in the list. This objective in the alcoholism decision is "to provide operational definitions of alcoholism." For the capital budgeting decision, this objective is "to estimate fiscal year funding needs for each project." The intended result is a vertical arrangement of possible objectives in which each higher-level objective encompasses all other objectives that are lower in the hierarchy.

As the expansion proceeds, objectives are sought that result in the smallest possible increase in scope. Decision makers can elicit levels by asking the following two types of questions: The first type asks what the objective of the last objective stated is. For example, what is the objective of defining alcoholism? The answer could be to identify people with alcoholism problems. Or one could ask what the objective of identifying people with an alcoholism problem is. An answer could be to make people aware. A second type of question asks what one gains by defining alcoholism, or what a definition of alcoholism permits us to do. A possible answer is to identify people with an alcoholism problem.

If a jump between objectives is too large, the gap is filled. Small increments are sought, for example, by asking in the capital budgeting example what we identify fiscal status for. This can trigger the next objective: to fund commitments and obligations (see hierarchy). Before each new objective is added to the hierarchy, it should be checked to ensure that it is larger in scope than the one immediately lower in the hierarchy. For example, in the alcoholism example, two objectives could be to identify alcoholics and to provide alcoholism treatment. However, "to identify alcoholics" is a part of treatment; therefore, it is a smaller objective and would be listed first. When two or more objectives seem to deal with the same issue, the objective that seems best is selected.

The highest-scope objective should appear so grandiose and expansive as to have little value. For example, the objective to meet personal adjustment needs of alcoholics may require more than traditional treatment services. These objectives are retained to illustrate the magnitude of the problem and to ensure that the decision maker's thinking about the nature of the decision to be made is sufficiently broad.

Step 3: Select an Objective. In the final step, the decision maker selects an objective. The objective with the largest feasible scope is preferred because most decisions take an overly restrictive view of possible arenas, which reduces the benefits of searching for alternatives. Selection should be preceded by a full consideration of the implications of adopting an objective with a broad or a narrow scope. The selection process can be carried out by applying one of the ranking techniques discussed in Chapter Seventeen.

Identifying Criteria

Criteria have two roles in decision making. In the first, they specify domains in which performance should be measured, such as employee satisfaction, revenue, and the like. The performance domain identifies information that will be used to make comparisons. The second role is to specify performance expectations, which provide norms. Norms are used as targets that guide the search for alternatives and decision rules in which expectations for each criterion are applied to rule out alternatives, such as "elimination by aspects" discussed in Chapter Nineteen. The qualifiers that emerge during objective setting often take shape as norms.

Two separate procedures are used to deal with criteria. First, criteria are identified and priority criteria are selected. This step is followed by the identification of expected performance levels for criteria, called norms, for structured problems, unstructured problems, unstructured opportunities, solutions seeking problems, and undefined opportunities, discussed as problem situations 2, 3, 5, 6, and 8 in Chapter Eleven.

Procedures to Identify Criteria

Objectives provide the dominant point of reference to select criteria, as discussed above. However, there are several other sources of criteria that should not be ignored. These include the expectations of key people, long-term organizational goals, and attributes or special features of the alternatives. A variety of individuals have a stake in decisions, including the system users, experts, and administrators. Each should be consulted as the decision maker applies the steps of listing and pruning to uncover and validate criteria. For instance, a bank's policy toward dealing with customer complaints may suggest criteria that measure customer acceptance. The bank's implicit goal of cost consciousness calls for criteria that reveal excess cost or cost reduction possibilities. The impetus to modify credit practices in a bank could stem from billing errors. In this example, criteria used to judge candidate practices would be based on the precision of billing information in the options considered.

Criteria Listing. The criteria listing step should be carried out for various types of stakeholders to get the unique perspective that each has to offer. For example, experts will often stress technology, users acceptance measures, and managers cost concerns. Experts tend to suggest measures that are alternative specific. Vendors offer MIS programs that have unique features, such as speed or precision, that can help in the choice among the alternatives. A merger of these interests provides a balanced set of criteria with which to judge the alternatives.

Users, experts, administrators, and others can be polled by survey or by group process techniques discussed in Chapter Fifteen.

Criteria Pruning. The listing step typically provides an unwieldy set of criteria that must be merged and winnowed. Discussion and voting are used to integrate and cull the candidate criteria. The group process techniques in Chapter Fifteen can be used for this purpose. In some instances, decision maker/staff discussion may be sufficient to select a workable set of criteria.

The prerogatives of users, experts, and administrators suggest which tactic(s) should be used. For example, a decision in which a particular manager is empowered to make the choice among alternatives would be dominated by the manager's criteria. When power is diffuse, involving several power centers that can influence the implementation of the alternative, groups are essential. A group process is used to manage the selection of a parsimonious set of mutually exclusive or independent criteria. The techniques presented in Chapter Seventeen can be used to prune the list or to weight the criteria. The "elimination by aspects" tactic can be used when many criteria must be considered, and the utility models can be used when a few criteria, with varying importance, emerge from this step, as discussed in Chapter Nineteen.

Identifying Norms

For many decisions, norms or expectations must be determined to guide the search for alternatives. Limits imposed on what can be spent or what benefits should be obtained are required in most decisions. These targets establish parameters that specify conditions to which alternative courses of action must fit. Fit is used to find potentially viable alternatives. Fit is also used to structure search, so alternatives with no prospect of being adopted can be quickly ruled out.

Deriving Norms. Norms can be derived from three sources by applying optimality, satisficing, or empirical logic (Thompson, 1967). Optimality logic stems from formal mathematical models that specify what is attainable. The models are manipulated to reveal optimum performance. For instance, linear programming has been developed for institutional menu planning, giving very precise norms regarding costs and other factors (Nutt, 1984c). Theoretical models available for production planning establish cost norms for manufacturing in which various schedules are required. As discussed in Chapter Nine, tough decisions can seldom use optimality logic, and norms must be sought from other sources.

Reference Groups. Decision makers can apply a satisficing norm that identifies a reference group to select a target or derive expectations. Properly selected, the performance of an industry group offers a way to estimate what should be attainable. Hospitals routinely compare their cost per patient day and other indicators to those of comparable hospitals. Firms make comparisons with their competitors to set targets for market penetration, profit, quality, customer complaints, employee morale, and the like. Public schools set reading readiness expectations on the basis of average scores attained by students in other, similar schools. Reference groups offer a quick and convenient way to elicit useful norms.

Empirical Tests. An empirical norm is extracted from analysis of pertinent data. Statistical techniques can be used to relate cost and many other quantifiable factors to situational effects. For example, nursing home costs per patient day can be linked to factors such as ownership (public, private), location (urban, rural), and region (South, North) to find average costs that fit particular combinations of these factors. Selecting the pertinent combination of factors establishes a cost norm or, more generally, a norm that meets these conditions. (A more complete discussion of this approach can be found in Chapter Nine.) The empirical test is more time-consuming to carry out than the reference group approach but is often essential if reference groups are ambiguous or information describing them is not readily available.

Norms Using Group Process. Norms for criteria can be uncovered by group processes using the same approaches that were applied to generate criteria. Group process techniques appropriate for norm identification are described in Chapter Fifteen. A group process should be used when reference groups are unavailable and empirical tests unfeasible because of time constraints or an inability to acquire the needed information.

Norms in Flux

The satisficing decision rule (Chapter Thirteen) shows that norms may have to shift as a decision process unfolds. Some expectations can become so stringent that the search for alternatives is drawn out to the point that success is in doubt. The need to revise norms and recycle back to an earlier stage of the decision process can occur, following the logic outlined in Chapter Thirteen and the learning dicta presented in Chapter Fourteen.

Uncovering Alternatives

Alternatives represent actions that can be taken in response to the objectives and norms. There is a tendency to mix the uncovering of alternatives with their assessment. Too often, alternatives are assessed as they are being identified. As pointed out in Chapter Ten, new ideas are quickly killed off by this type of premature evaluation. Separating the generation of alternatives from their assessment is essential if new ideas are to be encouraged. The search for alternative courses of action is guided by the objective selected by the decision maker, group, or coalition. This search can be conducted in several ways. Search can seek existing practices and ideas, or it can be directed both inside and outside the decision process.

Existing or Known Practices as Alternatives

Potentially useful alternatives can emerge from existing practices. Key sources include the practices of competitors, staff proposals, consultant recommendations, and other ideas devised previously but not yet used (Nutt, 1984b). This search can be short or extended, depending on the number of staff members and managers to be polled.

Alternatives Generated Outside the Decision Process

Decision makers can search for alternatives in a more formal way by seeking vendor proposals and using RFPs, internal planning, innovation via research and development, and so on. Each search approach represents another type of process that has distinct stages and steps, which can take extended periods of time to carry out (Nutt, 1984c). Typically some form of creativity or innovation enhancement is required in this type of process (Gordon, 1971).

Alternatives Generated Inside the Decision Process

Expertise is essential in the search for alternatives. In carrying out the analytical decision process, the decision maker can select a group of experts and poll them for ideas by using the Delphi technique, described in Chapter Fifteen. For the group and mixed-mode decision processes, one of the silent reflective group management processes would be used by the group or coalition to generate alternatives. This step should be carried out with considerable care to ensure that good ways to respond to the objective have been uncovered.

Confronting Ethical Considerations

Ethics must be considered in all tough decisions because no decision can be ethically neutral. For instance, decision makers in the BART case (Chapter Two) could have made a choice among alternatives by considering high-speed buses and other options along with urban transit to deal with the objective of relieving urban congestion. Because these options were ignored, the questions of who pays and who benefits posed serious ethical questions in the BART decision.

Ethical concerns crop up in many tough decisions. Single-source contracting with one's brother-in-law, dumping toxic waste into rivers, knowingly selling defective products, marketing products with health hazards known to be habit-forming (for example, cigarettes), and conflicts of interest are universally regarded as ethical problems. Other ethical situations can be more subtle. Because they are less apt to be discovered, the subtle ethical concern poses more serious problems for the decision-making process.

Consider, for example, that more than 70 percent of CEOs in U.S. companies use the impact on next quarter's earnings and tomorrow's stock prices to guide their decisions (Nussbaum, 1987). This pressure to focus on short-term profits stems from security analysts for 65 percent of the CEOs and from institutional shareholders for 58 percent of the CEOs. These same CEOs acknowledge that the competitive position of the United States is being undermined by these pressures for short-term profits, but the CEOs are unwilling to confront the issue. As a consequence, foreign firms continue to erode the market share of domestic firms, threatening the long-term viability of many companies with the attendant attrition of jobs and industrial capacity. Treating long-term profits as an ethical concern puts a new light on the urgency to confront the issue and take action.

Ethical considerations, such as the pressure for short-term profits, are often overlooked in decision making. Ethics frequently creates a paradox. Individuals easily recognize a lack of ethics in decisions made by others but not by themselves. Richard Nixon's Watergate coverup and Beechnut's routine mislabeling of the contents of its baby food products are condemned by most people. These same people, however, tolerate and even applaud deception, manipulation, exploitation, espionage, veiled truths or outright lies, and cheating in the workplace when these actions are directed toward competitors, suppliers, funding agents, oversight bodies, and subordinates (Catron, 1983).

Actions that seem wrong by personal standards seem not to apply to many of the decisions made in organizations. For instance, public and private sector managers routinely misrepresent the effectiveness of their programs in legislative and budget hearings, reasoning that they must be program advocates. For example, honesty in conceding that a 20 percent cut would do no harm to one's own program or department would surely result in a 20 percent cut but would *not* entice others to come forward with similar admissions.

Managers in firms routinely overstate the accomplishments of their subordinates, thinking that rewards can be used to create obligations, a form of slack, which can be stockpiled to be exploited when the going gets tough. In the military, anything below a 97 percent efficiency rating will damage a military career. This crimping of the evaluation scale makes it impossible to distinguish among officers who have made significant as opposed to routine accomplishments. Similarly, letters of recommendation are expected to exaggerate a person's accomplishments. Deciphering such letters becomes a discounting game. Readers may try to figure out what is being said (for example, by looking for cues of "damning with faint praise") or they may just read into the letter their biases about a candidate (see Chapter Five). Such expectations make it difficult for anyone to be honest because people would be damaged, thus perpetuating these practices.

Selectivity in reporting accomplishments and needs such as those cited above puts on a "best face." Advocacy is a part of the role that many people are expected to adopt when they join an organization. According to this view, organizations have a "special ethics." The objectives of an organization are treated as "higher values" in which the ends justify the means. This view has been expressed in various ways, perhaps beginning with Machiavelli (1952), who claimed that the mores and standards of justice applied to one's personal life should have no bearing on work behavior. One must be ruthless in the pursuit of objectives that serve an organization and use deceit and guile as instruments of action. To do otherwise would betray one's employer, whom one is pledged to represent.

A more recent justification was advanced by Carr (1978), who attempts to reconcile personal and business integrity by noting the "practical requirements" of business. A double standard of morality is viewed as a practical necessity. How, for example, can one be honest with a competitor or an accreditation review body? Decision makers are allowed to distance themselves from deceptive practices (or lying) by treating the situations as games. In a game, strategies are carried out to expose what is good for the organization, which allows one to ignore personal responsibility.

Catron (1983) draws on Machiavelli to advance the "dirty hands" explanation for decisions that ignore ethics. Those in power are thought to have dirty, or at least tarnished, hands because they must deal with unsavory issues. Those who serve (the people in power) need support because they are trapped by this situation. "Dirty hands" now becomes "many hands," as subordinates scamper to support the boss (or — a less charitable explanation — to posture for organization spoils). Implicitly, subordinates are obliged to use whatever means are necessary to help those in positions above them.

Suspending Ethics

There are several situations in which superiors and subordinates suspend personal ethics and substitute the ethic to serve the organization. They involve self-indulgence, self-protection, self-righteousness, and self-deception (Catron, 1983).

Self-Indulgence. Personal gain can produce choices that are sadly lacking in ethics. The insider stock trading scandals of the late 1980s and ex-administration officials who lobby their former colleagues are examples. Dean's (1976) description of corrupted values in the Nixon administration deftly lays out how the lust for power and greed corrupted people sworn to a higher standard of conduct.

Self-Protection. Many decision makers in organizations get caught up in buck passing. "Going along to get along" persuades people to adopt choices they would otherwise oppose. People fear that opposition would be costly to career and future effectiveness. Organizational life reinforces the notion that compromise and accommodation are expected—indeed, often demanded. As a result, people who keep faith with their personal ethics become a rarity. Data are fudged to make them support the boss's idea, and people line up to tell higher-ups what they think they want to hear. Even consulting firms, such as the "beltway bandits" located on the beltway that circles Washington, D.C., have acquired such a reputation. Carried to extremes, this behavior can bring on whistle blowers, who expose ethically questionable practices and cause serious long-term problems for an organization.

Self-Righteousness. Organizations often have zealots (Nutt and Backoff, 1986) who have been seduced by the "rightness" of their cause. This often results in solutions looking for problems, described in Chapter Eleven. Carried to extremes, zealots will use any means they can get away with to carry out what they believe is right, desirable, or needed. For instance, in the Iran/ Contra affair, during the Reagan administration, public officials ignored laws passed by Congress that prohibited trade with Iran, in the wake of the Iranian taking of hostages (Chapter Two), and prohibited aid to the Contras fighting to overthrow the Marxist government established in Nicaragua. The profits from the arms sold to Iran, in violation of statute, were sent to the Contras, also in violation of statute, because the Contras' cause was "right." According to this view, one gets power to use it, which often leads to what J. William Fulbright called the arrogance of power.

Self-Deception. The notion of an "advocate role" or buying into a superior's agenda leads to many small steps until a belief in the role or agenda has taken root. This type of deception occurs quite often and can be hard to deal with. To the individual involved, such behavior is not unethical but is justified or justifiable. Every situation is thought to have mixed motives in which both communal and personal interests are served. The "best face" choice is rationalized because of one's obligation to advocate a particular set of interests in a mixed-interest situation. Others are expected to do the same, and some higher body must sort it all out. The justifications include everyone does it, it's implicitly condoned by higher authority, the consequences are too remote to worry about, and it's only done under special circumstances, such as dire urgency.

The Issue Posed by Ethics

The erosion of ethics in decision making can be a serious problem that must be confronted. Catron (1983) uses the analogy of a play to point out the need for ethics. The drama of a decision reveals character because the decision maker becomes the play's author and director. Seen in this way, the organizational game becomes an elaborate pretense in which decisions are conveniently compartmentalized so decision makers can evade responsibility for the ethical aspects of their actions. The game may offer one an untroubled mind and a secure position in the organization, but it also leads to a gradual erosion of personal ethics, no matter how these actions are rationalized. Catron (1983) likens the untroubled mind to a self-inflicted lobotomy, pointing out that diminished responsibility can win verdicts of not guilty, but only by reason of insanity.

Inserting Ethics into Decision Making

The decision-making process described to this point may appear to take an amoral posture, seemingly ignoring ethical questions. For example, in Chapter Eleven, decision makers are admonished to form a collection of interests that align with the interests of the organization and to ignore other interests. Objectives (ends) and ways to respond (means) that the coalition identifies may or may not be ethically neutral. The criteria applied to judge means can include or exclude ethical concerns.

To insert ethical considerations into a decision process, they must be given status equal to that accorded economic and political rationality. If analysis searches for a belief warranted by fact, and politics searches for reactions warranted by self-interest, then ethics searches for actions warranted by mores and standards of justice.

Two kinds of steps can be taken to introduce ethics into decision making. In the first step, the decision maker searches for responses to neutralize the various interests noted above. In the second step, the decision maker confronts ethics as a step in the decision process, as noted in Chapters Eight and Nine.

Countering Vested Interests. Remedies lie in neutralizing or eliminating incentives that encourage stakeholders and subordinates to ignore ethical issues. Self-indulgent behavior can be met by fraud-proof systems. Examples include tamper-resistant systems and auditing procedures such as those used in financial systems. Analogies to the inspector general function in the federal government and the "ethics in government" act can also provide safeguards for many organizations. Making it clear that unethical behavior is wrong and will not be tolerated, by actions as well as words, may be the most important step a manager can take.

Ethics-evading motives of self-protection pose a more difficult management problem. Pointing out that people who raise ethical questions are very rarely subjected to any form of penalty or harassment is a needed first step. Demonstrating this as a policy is necessary to reinforce this view. For example, federal agencies have established a "designated ethics official" to act as a mediator and to provide an outlet for ethical concerns. Organizations could adopt this tactic or they could choose to vest the responsibility in all decision makers, holding them accountable for dealing with ethical as well as economic and political concerns. Dispute channels have the added advantage of eliminating whistle blowers because other means are available to express concerns. With such channels in place, those who continue to blow the whistle can be targeted as dissidents and managed effectively in the organization's postincident damage control activities.

Exposing vested interests helps to neutralize zealots, forcing their ideas on the firmer ground of justifying a need as well as a response. Self-deception can be headed off by noting that the ability to give reasons for one's choices is not the same as choosing right. For instance, when people push their own pro-grams by selectively including what will support their case and leaving out everything else, they create deception. Thus, letters of recommendation, fitness reports, the dire threat of collapse in capital budget requests, and the need for increased budgets are routinely discounted. Everyone asks for more than he or she needs and expects cuts. The pattern of deceit makes it impossi-ble to get a fix on the true magnitude of needs in an organiza-tion. Encouraging less game playing by dealing with exaggera-tions pays many dividends. Most significantly, true measures of need can be identified, allowing more persuasive cases for true needs to emerge in legislative hearings, budget meetings, and similar forums.

Confronting Ethical Issues. To introduce ethics, the decision maker reviews the objectives selected, as well as alternatives under serious consideration, to uncover ethical considerations. For groups and coalitions, a silent reflective process is used to encourage candor and disclosure by allowing people to express their concerns. To aid in the search for questionable actions, the billboard and moral code tests are applied. In the billboard test, members of groups are asked to imagine their reaction if a favored alternative and its rationale were to appear in the *Wash-ington Post* or the *Columbus Despair*. This tone can be set by titular leaders who introduce search activities (objectives, alternatives, and criteria) by telling group members to "propose only actions that conform with your sense of morality and object to actions that raise ethical questions in your mind." Introducing a moral cause is tricky business, as there are no moral absolutes. How-ever, providing a moral tone will allow questions to be raised that bring important borderline actions into focus.

There are no tests in tough decisions that can label one set of actions as more ethical than another. All decisions, to one degree or another, call for rule following, collusion, and obliga-tions that bring out possible ethical problems. By subjecting key actions (objectives, alternatives, and criteria) to an ethical re-view, managers can ensure that the rigidity and dogmatism that lead to self-protection and self-deception have a better chance of being set aside.

Properly managed, groups create a "mutuality" relationship which is substituted for self-orientation, in which ethical concerns can be suspended. A dialogue among the community of stakeholders about the notion of ethical action is
initiated. This dialogue centers on the management of relationships, where ethics is invariably located. When stakeholders
who make up a decision body become sensitive to ethical concerns, these concerns are less apt to be set side to satisfy implicit
organizational obligations. The discourse sets out what is acceptable according to the highest common denominator, not
the lowest. Even advocacy is seen in a new light when conven-
tionalized traps are highlighted for what they are: demands to
abandon personal ethics. The process of decision making becomes self-reflective and thus self-conscious by a consideration
of "what is right." Stakeholders who confront the way in which
they want to be regarded are less apt to advocate nonethical
actions.

Key Points

1.   Objectives are set to direct the search for alternatives and
     criteria to assess the alternatives.
2.   The scope of an objective is a key consideration in decision
     making. The objective-setting technique points out the
     means-ends linkage among objectives in a hierarchical rela-
     tionship. Decision makers should select the broadest possi-
     ble objective to avoid unnecessarily restricting the search
     for responses in the form of alternatives.
3.   Group processes, described in Chapter Fifteen, provide a
     way to carry out objective setting, criteria selection, norm
     identification, and the generation of alternatives.
4.   Ethical issues can arise as objectives are set, criteria identi-
     fied, and alternatives uncovered. Treating ethical concerns
     as a legitimate rationality in decision making, having equal
     standing with economic and political rationality, creates
     the opportunity to raise and deal with ethics. Using group
     process provides a way to raise the discussion from the
     lowest to the highest common denominator, to help deci-
     sion makers deal with ethical concerns.

17

Weighting Criteria and Estimating the Likelihood of Future Conditions

This chapter provides several easy-to-apply techniques for making subjective estimates. The chapter also offers ways to select among these techniques on the basis of how the needed information is to be collected (for example, in person or by survey, as discussed in Chapter Fifteen).

Two kinds of subjective estimates are required in the valuation of alternatives, as described in Chapters Thirteen and Eighteen. First, criteria weights must be specified to reflect the values of key participants about the relative importance of decision criteria, such as cost and quality. Second, the likelihood of future conditions deemed to be important must be estimated. These estimates of criteria weights and the likelihood of future conditions are essential components in the valuation of alternatives. The subjective nature of the values used often calls for the use of sensitivity analysis to assess the impact of risk, for future conditions, and the influence of values, for criteria weights, as described in Chapters Thirteen, Eighteen, Nineteen, and Twenty.

Figure 17.1 shows how these topics tie into the decision process.

Making Subjective Estimates

Approaches that can be used to estimate the likelihood of future conditions and criteria weights can be categorized as

Figure 17.1. The Decision Process.

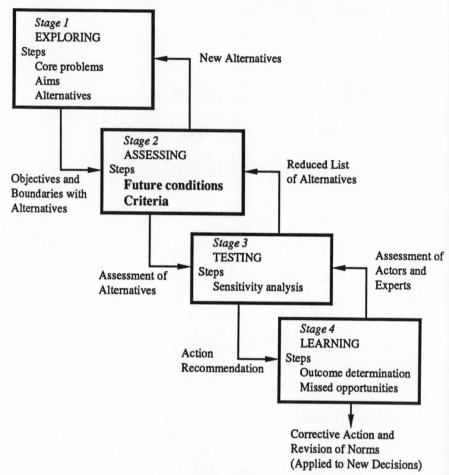

Note: Boldface type indicates topics addressed in this chapter.

betting and scaling. Betting approaches ask the participant (decision maker or expert) to respond like a gambler (Keeney and Raiffa, 1976). Decision makers play a game that has two outcomes, each associated with payoffs and the likelihood of attaining each payoff. Decision makers are given three of these values and asked to indicate the fourth that would make the choices seem identical.

Betting approaches are not used in this book because they are influenced by people's risk-aversion and risk-preference views, as described in Chapter One. The hypothetical gamble may have little relationship to the way decision makers deal with risk in actual decisions. Furthermore, decision makers do not like to imagine their decisions as gambles. They prefer more direct approaches. Such approaches call on the decision maker to deal directly with making subjective estimates and are known as scaling approaches.

Several scaling techniques can be used to make subjective estimates of criteria weights and the likelihood of future conditions. They include anchored rating scales, paired comparisons, rank-weight, direct assignment, and Q-Sort (Nutt, 1984b).

How to Weight Decision Criteria

This section shows how scaling techniques can be used to make subjective estimates of criteria weights.

Anchored Rating Scales. The anchored rating scale (ARS) approach uses a continuous scale with descriptors that elaborate the scale and help to define its increments and end points (Nutt, 1980c). The annotations help the decision maker visualize the meaning of scale intervals and scale end points. A variety of scale sizes can be used, including 0 to 100, minus to plus infinity, and 0 to infinity. A scale anchored with a 0 is used for criteria that have natural zero points, such as cost. A negative infinity end point can be used for criteria in which negative values are possible, such as profit. A positive infinity end point conveys the notion of no theoretical upper limit to criteria values. A log scale is used to capture increments on a scale with positive and/ or negative infinity as end points. To simplify the scale, linear increments with -100 to $+100$ end points are used for applications in which criteria values can be very large or very small. In most cases, a 0 to 100 linear scale can be used.

To illustrate the ARS scale, criteria that would be used to select among types of personal computers would be presented to decision makers in the format shown in Table 17.1. Criteria are listed alphabetically or randomly to avoid placement biases.

Table 17.1. The Anchored Rating Scale Technique for Weighting Criteria.

Criteria		Descriptors
Cost	1.00	Specifies all aspects of a decision
Dependability	.75	Dictates most aspects of a decision
Graphics	.50	Dictates some aspects of a decision
Printing speed	.25	Dictates a few aspects of a decision
Space requirements	.00	Ignored in making a decision

Each participant draws an arrow from each of the criteria to a point on the scale that indicates his or her view of its importance. These scale values are normalized to convert them to percents. For example, if a line were drawn from the cost criterion to .80 and from the dependability criterion to .60, cost would be weighted as .80/(.80 + .60) = .57, and dependability as .60/(.80 + .60) = .43. This computational tactic establishes a weight that can be used to estimate the relative importance of the criteria.

Paired Comparisons. Considering criteria in pairs permits the decision maker to concentrate on the differences between any two criteria, reducing the information-processing demands (see Chapter Four). Using the previous example, assume that the decision maker is presented with all criteria combinations in the personal computer illustration. Comparing the criteria, the decision maker indicates which is more important. Assume the decision maker made the following choices:

Pairs	*Choice*
Cost vs. dependability	Cost
Cost vs. graphics	Graphics
Cost vs. printing speed	Cost
Cost vs. space	Cost
Dependability vs. graphics	Graphics
Dependability vs. printing speed	Speed
Dependability vs. space	Dependability
Graphics vs. printing speed	Speed
Graphics vs. space	Graphics
Printing speed vs. space	Speed

The chart shown in Figure 17.2 is used to tabulate a weight for each criterion. Initially, the first column and first row are used. Cost is rated as more important than printing speed and space requirements, so a *1* is entered next to printing speed and space requirements in the first column. Cost is found to be more important than dependability, so a *1* is entered in the cost column adjacent to dependability. Cost is less important than graphics, so a *1* is entered in the first row under the graphics criterion. Zeros are entered in the remaining cells of the first row and column. The cells in the second row and second column are considered next, and each cell is scored in the same manner. The process is repeated for the remaining columns and rows. The totals in each column are normalized to define a weight for each criterion, as shown in Figure 17.2.

Rank-Weight Techniques. The rank-weight approach has decision makers first rank each criterion and then specify its importance. Ordering the criteria in terms of their importance and then weighting them eases the information-processing demands of the task (Chapter Four). Each criterion is placed on an index card. The decision maker first orders the criteria and then weights them. One of several approaches can be used to carry out the weighting. The odds procedure (Gustafson, Pai, and Kramer, 1971) has the decision maker compare the criteria, one at a time, to the top-ranked criterion, recording how many times more important one is than the other. The most important

Figure 17.2. Paired Comparisons for Weighting Criteria.

	Cost	Dependability	Graphics	Printing Speed	Space Requirements
Cost		0	1	0	0
Dependability	1		1	1	0
Graphics	0	0		1	0
Printing Speed	1	0	1		0
Space Requirements	1	1	1	1	
Raw Score	3	1	4	3	0
Normalized Score	3/11	1/11	4/11	3/11	0/11
Percent	27	9	36	27	0

criterion is given a value of one. If the first criterion is thought to be twice as important as the second, a value of one-half is assigned to the second criterion. The odd ratios are normalized to convert to percents. Weights can also be assigned according to linear scales of – 100 to + 100 or 0 to 100, log scales, or index numbers.

Direct Assignment. Direct assignment is useful in the weighting of large numbers of criteria to screen or sort out important criteria from the rest (Eckenrode, 1965). The procedure has three simple steps. First, labels and values are assigned as shown below:

Label	Value
Most desirable	10
Highly desirable	8
Desirable	6
Somewhat desirable	4
Marginally desirable	2
Undesirable	0

As the number of intervals increases, precision increases but the ease of designation declines, leading to blurred discriminations. Six to eight intervals is a good compromise. Second, criterion names are placed on index cards. The decision maker sorts the cards into piles associated with each label. Third, the sorts are repeated several times. This step ensures that the criteria allocated to each pile have stabilized.

Direct assignment can also be used to establish weights. In this case, the integers can be associated with descriptors, such as 10 = most important and 1 = least important, and assigned to each criterion to describe its importance. These values, when normalized, give a weight to criteria in terms of a percent.

Q-Sort. A broad search using a group process, survey, or public hearing often produces many candidate criteria. Because of their sheer number, these criteria are difficult to weight. The situation can be complicated by the value-laden, complex, and partially overlapping nature of criteria obtained from several sources. The Q-Sort technique provides a structure to screen criteria (Stephenson, 1953). Its procedure reduces the information-processing demands, which improves the reliability of criteria screening (Brown, 1980). See Figure 17.3.

Three steps are required to weight large numbers of criteria. In the Q-Sort procedure, important criteria are identified first. The second step repeats the first to ensure that the rankings can be reproducible, creating reliability. The final step weights these criteria according to a second Q-Sort or any of the weighting procedures previously discussed.

The Q-Sort technique can be used for item pools ranging from 30 to 130. With fewer than 30 and more than 130 criteria, reliability drops (Kerlinger, 1967). When fewer than 30 criteria are screened, the direct assignment technique can be used because the information-processing demands are manageable. When there are more than 130 criteria, the task becomes tedious and items tend to be overlooked in the sorting process.

The first step in using a Q-Sort for criteria screening calls for each criterion to be written on an index card, along with a brief definition. To begin a sort, an individual or the members of a group will read through the criteria to be ranked. The simplest sort consists of dividing the criteria into three categories of importance, such as "important" criteria, "unimportant" criteria, and the residual. The residual will be made up of criteria that have an intermediate level of importance.

To understand the procedure more clearly, consider a decision with fifty-five criteria that must be ranked (Brown and Coke, 1977). The rater selects the three most important criteria from the fifty-five and enters a code number for each item under the + 4 column in a scoring sheet. (An example of such a sheet follows the next paragraph.) The rater then selects the three least important criteria and enters them under the – 4 column. The rater then finds a second set of important criteria from those that remain and selects four. These criteria are listed under the + 3 column. Four unimportant criteria are selected next and put under the – 3 column. The rater continues, adding one criterion with each pass until seven criteria remain. These remaining criteria are listed under the 0 column. The sorts are

Figure 17.3. Q-Sort Record Sheet.

After sorting, insert the category number for each card in the appropriate box below. Be sure each category contains the specified number of cards.

Subject: _____ Sorter: _____

Information Source: _____ Date: _____

1	2	3	4	5	6	7	8	9	10	11	12	13	14	15	16	17	18	19	20

21	22	23	24	25	26	27	28	29	30	31	32	33	34	35	36	37	38	39	40

41	42	43	44	45	46	47	48	49	50	51	52	53	54	55	56	57	58	59	60

61	62	63	64	65	66	67	68	69	70	71	72	73	74	75	76	77	78	79	80

81	82	83	84	85	86	87	88	89	90	91	92	93	94	95	96	97	98	99	100	101

Category Value	1	2	3	4	5	6	7	8	9
Number of Items in Category	5	8	12	16	19	16	12	8	5

Source: Adapted from Nutt, 1984b.
Note: A value of 9 indicates most important; a value of 1 indicates least important.

repeated until the same sets of criteria appear in each category. This type of ranking takes from one-half to three-quarters of an hour the first time the procedure is used and considerably less time thereafter (Brown and Coke, 1977).

Different scoring schemes are needed for different-sized item pools. The distributions should be normal, or as close to a normal distribution as possible, to impose desirable statistical properties on the sort. Below are scoring schemes that use a ± 5 and a ± 4 scale. For eighty items, with a ± 5 scale, two items are initially selected; with the ± 4 scale, four items are selected in the first sort. Any other scoring scheme with frequencies similar to the classic bell-shaped curve of a normal distribution can be used. To set up a scoring system, the analyst creates a set of index numbers that specify each category's value to create a scale. For instance, a ± 5 scale can be composed as shown below:

	Least important										Most important
Scale	-5	-4	-3	-2	-1	0	$+1$	$+2$	$+3$	$+4$	$+5$
Category value	1	2	3	4	5	6	7	8	9	10	11

And a ± 4 scale can be composed as follows:

	Least important									Most important
Scale	-4	-3	-2	-1	0	$+1$	$+2$	$+3$	$+4$
Category value	1	2	3	4	5	6	7	8	9

To understand the mechanics of a Q-Sort that produces both a rank and a weight, assume that ten criteria were identified by survey. (The example limits the number of criteria to ten to ease presentation of the concepts. There would be no need to sort these few criteria in practice.) The criteria are to be sorted into the following categories:

	Least important				Most important
Number to be selected	1	2	4	2	1
Category value	0	1	2	3	4

The numbers above the line indicate the number of criteria to be selected in each sort. The respondent begins with most important category and selects one criterion. This is followed by the selection of the least important criterion. In the next step, the two most important criteria and the two least important criteria are selected from the criteria that remain. The four criteria that remain are placed in the final category. As a final step, the category value is assigned to each criterion.

Q-Sort permits a decision maker to carefully construct his or her attitude toward a large set of criteria. The technique is ideally suited to ranking more than thirty criteria and can be quickly administered and scored. Divisions of opinion in rankings among key stakeholders can yield important insights. Coalitions can be isolated by comparison of sorts to identify disagreements among stakeholders. The criteria supported by each coalition suggest potential disagreements that can be explored before consensus is sought.

Comparison of Weighting Techniques. Each weighting technique has strengths and weaknesses. Below is a comparison of the techniques in terms of their speed, precision, and adherence to assumptions about additivity requirements.

Technique	Speed	Precision	Assumptions
1. ARS scales	High	Moderate	Moderate
2. Paired comparison	Low (for more than 10 items)	High	Moderate/high
3. Rank-weight	Moderate/high	High	Moderate
4. Direct assignment	High	Low/moderate	Low/moderate
5. Q-Sort	Moderate	High	Moderate

To satisfy the additivity requirement, a rater must establish weights according to scale values and descriptors that are
perceived in the same way by other raters. If the scales and
descriptors are not clear, they will suggest different things to different people and cause weights to vary capriciously. None of the
techniques can provide assurance that this requirement is met,
but most are workable. Paired comparisons provide the clearest
and least ambiguous way to specify criterion importance.

Paired comparison also has the best precision in the
assignment of values, but it is not practical for large numbers of
criteria. When paired comparisons are used to weight ten or
more criteria, the number of pairs becomes unwieldy and dealing with them time-consuming. Using paired comparisons in
conjunction with a survey, such as Delphi (Chapter Fifteen), may
also create problems. Respondents may not see how the values
will be computed and become suspicious that they are being
manipulated.

Rank-weight methods can be used in meetings, but the
technique is cumbersome in a survey. In a meeting, the rank-
weight technique is superior to ARS scales and direct assignment because of its precision and relative speed. ARS scales are
best in surveys that require ranks with interval scale properties
because the instructions can be brief and easy to understand.
This approach is the easiest for most respondents to grasp
without a face-to-face explanation.

Direct assignment works best in an individual rather than
a group setting. The ranker can sort and then re-sort several
times with relative ease, as compared to the other methods. Q-
Sort is the only practical way to screen large numbers of criteria.

Reconsideration in Groups. Reconsideration and reflection
should be encouraged before final values for weights are set. In a
group, initial views can be influenced by uncertainty in both the
position of the individual and the position of others. To overcome these problems, the following steps have been proposed
(Huber and Delbecq, 1972):

1. Solicit individual judgments.
2. Pool individual judgments into a mean score to specify the initial group consensus.
3. Discuss initial group consensus.
4. Reconsider initial judgment and revote.

Combining these steps into a procedure, a group first weights the criteria without discussion, using any of the techniques previously described. Next, average weights representing the initial consensus are computed and displayed to stimulate group discussion. Discussion is directed toward defending or critiquing the initial weights. The group considers members' views as they emerge during discussion. After this discussion the group re-weights the criteria without discussion. The average weights that result represent an informed group consensus that shows more agreement than the initial weights (Nutt, 1976a).

This procedure is called estimate-discuss-estimate (EDE). EDE was developed to obtain parameter estimates from groups for tasks in which precise estimation is required. EDE was found to be a very accurate way to make these estimates (Gustafson, Shukla, Delbecq, and Wallester, 1973). The procedure works for several reasons. First, it directs criticism at the current group consensus, not at an individual. Second, EDE simulates what a group typically does when faced with a decision (Nutt, 1976a). In most situations, a decision body wants time to reflect. Groups typically treat their initial choices as preliminary, subject to change pending more information on how members feel and the facts they offer. Third, public voting by show of hands or through open discussion subjects a member of a group to social pressure by other members. Members who feel less knowledgeable are reluctant to take a position until they see how others are voting. Any public voting approach will entice some to vote in ways that differ from how they would vote prior to the showing of public sentiments. The independent weighting step gets each member to think through his or her preferences, thereby avoiding the pressures to conform. After the initial weighting, changes stem more from the persuasiveness of the other members' arguments than from their status or personality.

Estimating the Likelihood of Future Conditions

Many of the same techniques used to weight criteria can be used to estimate the likelihood of future conditions. Discussion in this section shows how these techniques can be applied to estimate likelihoods.

Anchored Rating Scales. The ARS technique can be used to help an expert assign probabilities to future conditions. For example, the experts could be sales representatives, or others acquainted with a market, who are asked to estimate the sales prospects for a particular product. As described in the previous section, the ARS scale is continuous to encourage fine discriminations in ratings that can range from 0, never occur, to 100, is certain to occur. The descriptors help the expert select a likelihood value that is congruent with a mutually understood concept. The scale lists states adjacent to it (Table 17.2). In the table, 150 percent of past demand, 100 percent of past demand, 75 percent of past demand, and 50 percent of past demand (defining past demand as last year's sales) are used. The expert draws a line from each condition to a point on the scale to indicate the condition's likelihood. The probabilities are drawn directly from the scale. An average can be used to capture the views of a sales or marketing department or other types of groups.

Paired Comparisons. Paired comparisons can sort out the likelihood of future conditions by asking experts knowledgeable about demand prospects which of two conditions is more likely. Considering the conditions in pairs permits the experts to concentrate on the differences between any two conditions, thereby simplifying the judgment to be made. The expert is presented with all combinations, considers each pair, and indicates which is more important. For example, consider conditions where demand is 200 percent, 150 percent, and 50 percent of last year's demand. (Finer discriminations are desirable but unnecessary for purposes of illustration.) Assume that the following choices were made:

Table 17.2. The ARS Technique for Estimating Future Conditions.

State		Descriptor
150 percent of last year's demand	1.0	Certain
125 percent of last year's demand	.75	Likely
Last year's demand	.50	May or may not occur
75 percent of last year's demand	.25	Unlikely
50 percent of last year's demand	0	Never occurs

Pairs	More Likely Outcome
200 vs. 150	150
200 vs. 100	100
200 vs. 50	200
150 vs. 100	150
150 vs. 50	150
100 vs. 50	100

The probabilities for each condition are sorted out in Figure 17.4. Averages can be used to capture a group's views.

Rank-Weight Technique. The rank-weight technique has the expert first rank the future conditions and then specify each condition's importance (Kneppreth, Gustafson, Rose, and Leifer, 1973). Each condition is placed on an index card. The expert ranks the conditions by ordering the cards and then records the "times more important" on each card. An odds

Figure 17.4. Paired Comparisons for Making
Subjective Estimates of Likelihood.

	200%	150%	100%	50%
200%		1	1	0
150%	0		0	0
100%	0	1		0
50%	1	1	1	

	200%	150%	100%	50%
Raw Score	1	3	2	0
Probability	17%	50%	33%	0

procedure can be used. The most important condition is given a
value of 100. Each of the remaining conditions is compared to
the most important and a "times more important" value is
recorded. If the second condition is seen as twice as important
as the first, a value of one-half or 50 percent is recorded for the
second condition. Alternatives to the odds procedure include
weighting the importance of conditions according to index
numbers (for example, 1 = unimportant and 5 = critically
important), a linear scale like that used in the ARS technique, or
a log scale.

   Direct Assignment. To estimate probability for each future
condition, values and labels can be created as follows:

Label	Value
Certain	10
High certainty	8
Considerable certainty	6
Some certainty	4
Little certainty	2
No certainty	0

When large numbers of conditions are to be compared, each is placed on an index card. The experts sort them into piles with labels as shown above. Considerable sorting and re-sorting are required.

The likelihood of each future condition is estimated by converting the values assigned to the condition in this way to percents (for example, 10 = 100 percent, 8 = 80 percent, and so on). Finer discriminators can be made for up to about ten categories. When the number of categories exceeds ten, people's ability to make the required designations declines rapidly. The errors produced offset any increase in precision.

Reconsideration in Groups. Groups can use the EDE approach to improve the precision of likelihood estimates in the same way this approach is used for criteria weighting (Gustafson, Shukla, Delbecq, and Wallester, 1973). First an initial judgment is made. Next, the group's initial consensus estimate for each condition's likelihood is presented. The initial consensus is used to provoke discussion. Members can argue for a higher or a lower likelihood by citing their past experience and facts. After discussion, the likelihoods are reestimated. These final estimates are averaged to determine the consensus estimate of a group.

Key Points

1. The following techniques can be used to weight criteria and estimate the likelihood of future conditions:
    a. Anchored rating scales
    b. Paired comparisons

    c. Rank-weight

    d. Direct assignment

    e. Q-Sort

2. Decision makers select among these techniques by noting the way in which information must be collected (for example, by using groups in a face-to-face meeting or by mailed survey).

3. Because of the subjectivity of these estimates, the values are often exposed to "what if" questioning to explore how uncertainty in future conditions and values for criteria influence a choice (see Chapters Thirteen, Eighteen, Nineteen, and Twenty).

18

Using Decision Trees
to Deal with Chance Events
and Sequential Choices

The decision tree technique is used to capture complex choice situations that involve many choices and chance outcomes. The technique has several useful features. First, it provides a way to deal with several future conditions in the valuation of alternatives. Second, it offers procedures to treat multiple future conditions as unknowns in order to explore "what if" questions about how changes in key assumptions made for each condition influence a decision. Third, because many tough decisions are sequential, calling for choices that determine what to pay for information that can clarify outcomes, the decision tree technique provides ways to value this clarifying information, drawing on notions of lost opportunity. "What if" questioning is then applied to explore the risk in the decision to purchase clarifying information. Figure 18.1 shows how these topics support the decision process.

Uses of Decision Trees

Most tough decisions must deal with several future conditions. For example, hospitals contemplating an expansion must consider the prospect of endowments and the likelihood of a favorable regulatory decision in addition to the level of demand. The decision tree must incorporate utilization, philanthropy,

Figure 18.1. The Decision Process.

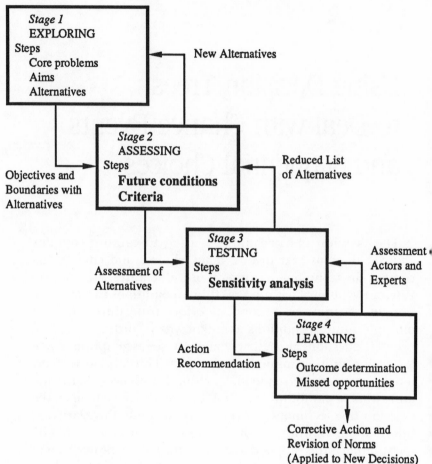

Note: Boldface type indicates topics addressed in this chapter.

and the attitude of regulators, which in this case make up future conditions, into the assessment of alternatives. By incorporating the influence of many types of future conditions, the decision tree technique is useful in supporting the process of making tough decisions.

A new form of sensitivity analysis, using a decision tree, is presented in this chapter. The analysis allows decision makers to conduct "what if" questioning of multiple future conditions to simultaneously relax assumptions about these conditions. A range of values for the future conditions under which various alternatives are preferred is identified. Using this approach, a manager is able to explore various combinations of favorable and unfavorable outcomes for key future conditions. This, in turn, allows the manager to explore the amount of risk inherent in adopting an alternative.

An opportunity to clarify what is known about important future conditions, such as demand, often emerges in a decision process. Such information is both costly and imperfect, but it improves the manager's prospects of selecting the best course of action. Examples include deciding whether to carry out market surveys of customer preferences, conduct lobbying efforts, do seismic studies of prospective oil-drilling sites, use various laboratory tests to confirm a diagnosis or select a treatment, and compile sales histories of comparable homes to decide how to price your home for sale.

Decision makers are frequently uncertain about the value of this additional information. A separate decision is necessary to determine whether the cost and delay of an information search can be justified. A sequence of choices results. First, decision makers determine what additional information they need, its costs, and its ability to clarify the payoffs associated with plausible alternatives. The minimal commitment rules suggested by Lindblom (1965) are often followed. For instance, a manager may pick an option that maintains flexibility, such as making a small expansion to a warehouse, believing that additions to the warehouse can be made as needed. This alternative seems desirable because the manager can wait to see whether the need for a larger warehouse materializes before he or she commits to the larger expenditure. However, such a choice may cause the firm to experience inflated building costs and lost sales due to delays in providing needed storage capacity during a period of strong product demand. To deal with this sequence of choices, the manager must find ways to acquire information that can clarify the "building now" or "add on later" alternatives.

Systematically representing such a decision with a decision tree has many benefits. They include the ability to clarify options, specify needed information, manage complex relationships, communicate, manage conflict, uncover and deal with uncertainty, carry out sequential decisions, learn about the value of expert advice, and help decision makers increase their understanding, thereby improving their decisional capacity.

How to Use a Decision Tree

A decision tree provides a flow diagram, much like a road map. There are frequent forks in the road, depicting significant chance events that can occur. At each fork these events are described so that they will be mutually exclusive and exhaustive. As a result, their probabilities always sum to one. The tree depicts the chronological order of a possible set of acts by a decision maker and outcomes flowing from these acts that are governed by chance. The tree's branch points distinguish between chance and choice forks. A choice fork is designated as a square and a chance fork as a circle, as shown in Figure 18.2. The branches of the tree terminate with a payoff. The branches can be traced to specify a series of managerial acts that make up an alternative. A decision tree can incorporate a variety of acts and consequences, including not acting or choosing to continue to use a current system or procedure. The tree provides a graphic representation, listing crucial events that make up a decision.

Five steps are required to construct a decision tree:

1. Identify alternatives, acts that can influence the alternatives, and plausible chance events.
2. Map out the logic flow of the tree by specifying choice and chance nodes and connecting them by specifying hybrid alternatives or outcomes.
3. Determine payoffs or utilities for the ends of the tree's branches.
4. Assign probabilities to all chance nodes.
5. Select a decision rule to value each alternative in the tree.

A basic decision tree is shown in Figure 18.2. A tree has three components: nodes, branches, and valuations. Nodes de-

Figure 18.2. The Decision Tree Framework.

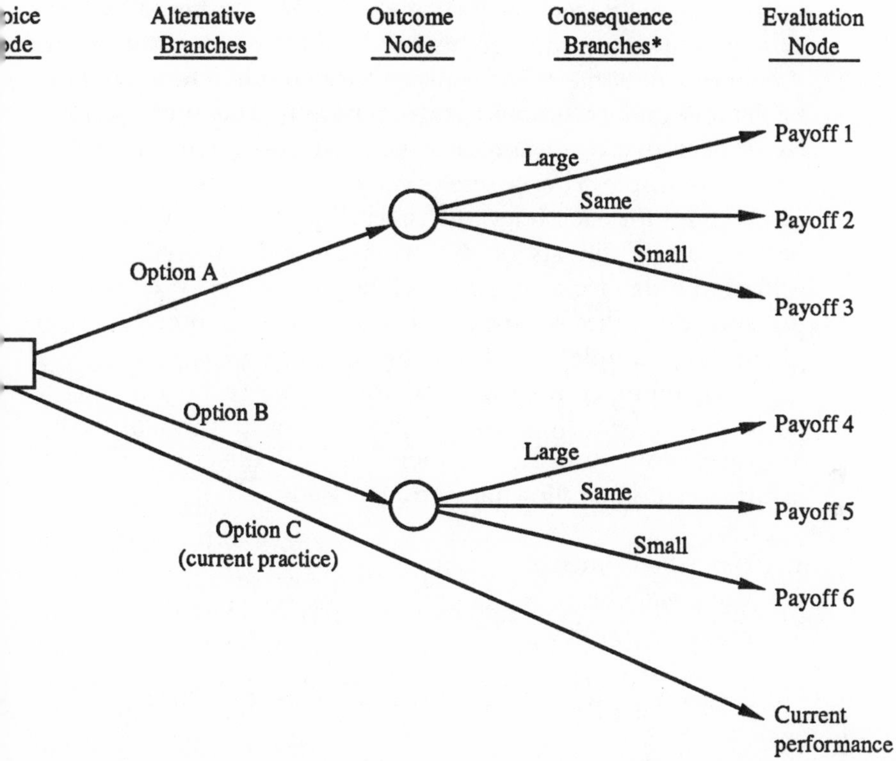

oice de	Alternative Branches	Outcome Node	Consequence Branches*	Evaluation Node

*Consequences are typically measured in terms of demand.

scribe choices and outcomes. Branches depict consequences that flow from an alternative. The branches of the tree terminate with valuations.

The decision maker begins with a choice node and lists the alternative courses of action. Next, outcome nodes are listed, which describe the consequences that stem from the adoption of each alternative. For example, estimates of demand are frequently needed to estimate a payoff, such as profit, for an alternative. Several other types of criteria can be used to value an alternative, including the satisfaction of key power centers (such as the endowers of a foundation), utilization, or product

quality. The current approach (option C in Figure 18.2) describes current system performance, which serves as a baseline.
The current system can also be included to see how it would fare
if demand, or some other consequence factor, were to change.
Each consequence branch creates a payoff valued by a particular set of criteria (for example, cost, satisfaction, benefits, and so
on). For multiple criteria, one of two options can be used. A tree
can be built for each relevant criterion called for to value alternatives, or the effects of the criteria can be merged into a
valuation index for a single tree. The procedure for constructing such an index is illustrated in the next chapter. For simplicity, the examples in this chapter use a single criterion.

In summary, for tough decisions, managers construct a
decision tree by listing options and moving to the right in the
diagram, often drawing on their staff to collect the needed
information. The following steps are used:

1. Describe branches.
2. Value each branch.
3. Estimate payoffs.

Dealing with Several Types of Future Conditions

Several types of future conditions can influence an organization's decisions, such as whether to adopt a new product or
service. Market surveys can be used to estimate product demand
and to determine the prospects of a strike. Future conditions are
given by the strike and no-strike events and various levels of
demand. Decisions to purchase various commodities, such as
land, can be influenced by trends in commodity prices and
forecasts of loan prospects and interest rates.

To illustrate how a decision tree is constructed and analyzed, an example of a hospital deciding whether to expand its
capacity in the face of uncertainty about the future cost of
financing and utilization is provided. Nonprofit hospitals seeking to expand their revenue base under governmental price
controls are being pushed to increase their volume (Nutt, 1984c,
p. 349). A popular approach is to develop ways to direct patients

to a hospital, keeping occupancy at levels that ensure financially viable operations. Satellite operations are often initiated with this intent in mind to produce a "profit" to offset losses in services, such as burn care or coronary care, where reimbursement falls far short of covering costs. To start satellites, a hospital must obtain regulatory approval under state-operated certificate of need (CON) programs. Regulation requires a hospital to submit all expansion plans for approval. However, nearly all of the plans submitted to CON review bodies are approved (Nutt and Hurley, 1981). As a result, administrators often "fast track" plans, making investments to set the plan in place as regulatory review is being conducted. This allows a hospital to stake out turf and discourage competitors from farming the same catchment area for patients.

Two environmental factors are important: the size of demand and the cost of financing. Administrators can use various schemes in an attempt to increase the utilization of a hospital by marketing to physicians. Financing costs act as a constraint. Steps to lobby or exert political pressure do not change interest rates. Assume that the hospital is attempting to choose between two alternatives: the current situation (no clinic) and the construction of a satellite clinic. This example is conceptually identical to a firm's contemplating the expansion of its capacity in the face of uncertainty about the cost of money needed to finance the plant expansion and the level of demand for the products to be manufactured in the larger plant.

Step 1: Describe Branches. To construct the tree, the decision maker lists the options under consideration. Assume, for example, that two options are being considered: constructing a satellite clinic or continuing without a clinic (see Figure 18.3). Next, the marketing effort undertaken to stimulate use is described. For simplicity, the marketing effort will be described as large or small. Assume that the marketing cost can be covered by the hospital's cash reserves but that the clinic construction must be debt-financed. The cost of financing the clinic is dependent upon future interest rates. Assume that the interest market is volatile, suggesting that rates may be favorable or unfavorable when the project has been planned in sufficient detail for the hospital to seek financing. Revenues are estimated according to the demand that marketing with a given type of clinic is predicted to stimulate and with the understanding that interest costs could be favorable or unfavorable. Revenue less cost values each outcome payoff in the tree.

Step 2: Value Each Branch. In this step, the decision maker incorporates information needed to describe each payoff in the tree. First, under each alternative or option, its costs are placed in the tree (Figure 18.3). In this example, the cost needed to operate the clinic is made up of the sum of the cash outlay for the clinic plus the present worth of operating cost increases over the current costs of hospital operation. The cost required to construct and operate the clinic is shown below:

> Option A: Satellite clinic $1,000,000
> Option B: No clinic   0

Next, the costs of marketing the new clinic are incorporated into the tree. Assume that marketing can be major or minor and that the following costs are incurred:

1. Major marketing effort: $100,000
2. Minor marketing effort: $50,000

The clinic option can produce revenues that vary substantially, depending on the level of demand produced by marketing. Assume that the prospect of a large demand for the clinic option has a 60 percent likelihood and leads to revenue of $10 million when a major marketing investment is made or $5 million when a minor marketing effort is made. With a minor marketing effort, the prospect of a large demand falls to 20 percent, with revenue of $1 million, and the prospect of a small demand is 80 percent, with revenue of $500,000. In summary, the following revenues, expressed as the present worth of an income stream, are estimated for the clinic:

Marketing	Demand	Prospects	Revenue
Major	Large	P = .6	$10,000,000
Major	Small	P = .4	$ 1,000,000

Figure 18.3. Decision Tree for the Clinic Decision.

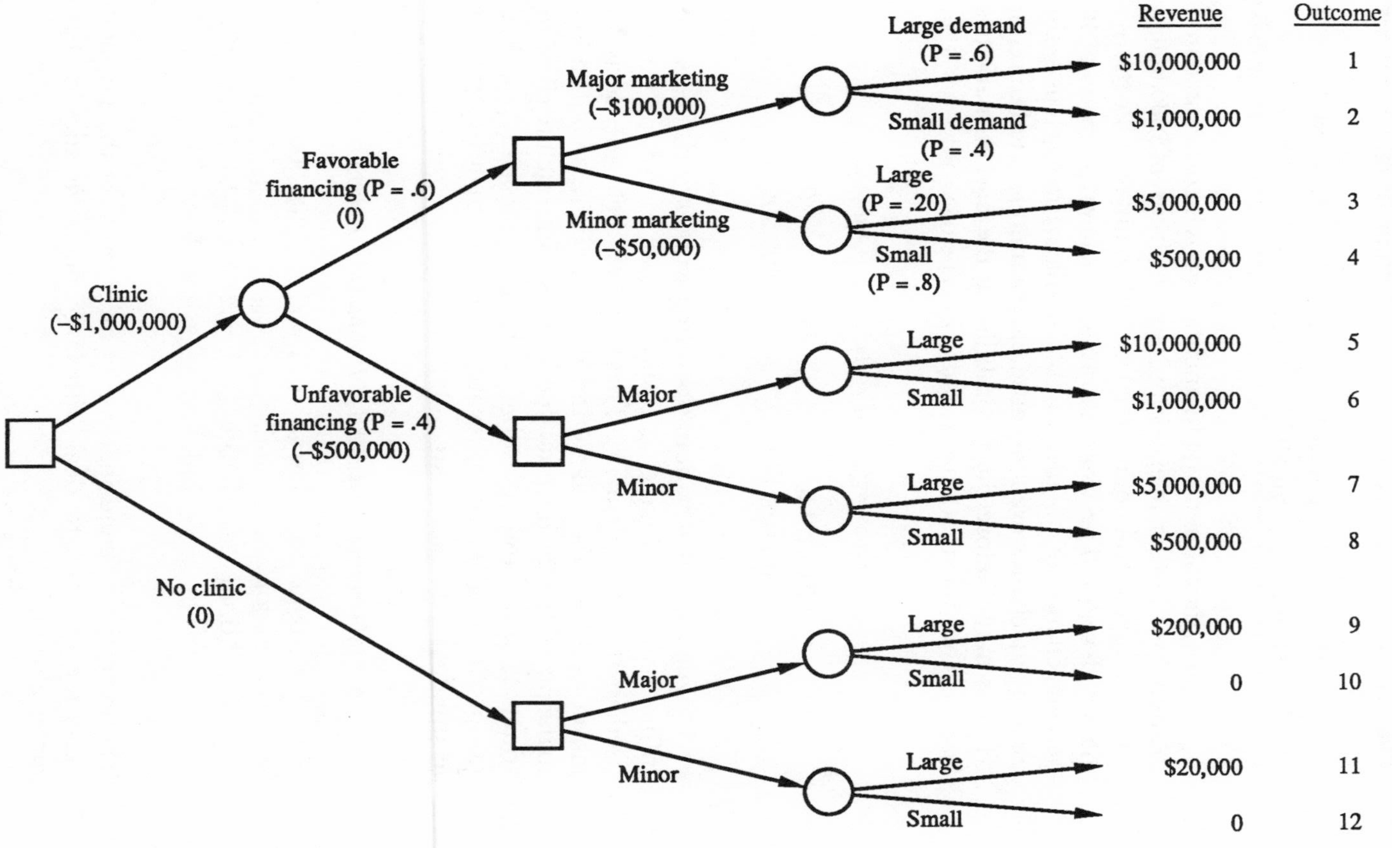

	Revenue	Outcome
Large demand (P = .6)	$10,000,000	1
Small demand (P = .4)	$1,000,000	2
Large (P = .20)	$5,000,000	3
Small (P = .8)	$500,000	4
Large	$10,000,000	5
Small	$1,000,000	6
Large	$5,000,000	7
Small	$500,000	8
Large	$200,000	9
Small	0	10
Large	$20,000	11
Small	0	12

Major marketing (–$100,000)
Minor marketing (–$50,000)
Major
Minor
Major
Minor

Favorable financing (P = .6) (0)
Unfavorable financing (P = .4) (–$500,000)
No clinic (0)

Clinic (–$1,000,000)

| Minor | Large | P = .2 | $ 5,000,000 |
| Minor | Small | P = .8 | $ 500,000 |

Next, the influence of financing costs is incorporated into the tree. Assume that an excess present worth cost of $500,000 in interest expense will be incurred should an unfavorable money market develop. The financial analyst believes there is a 40 percent chance of an unfavorable market. Interest costs are treated as a chance event because the commitment to build the clinic is made before the favorability of the money market is known. This information is summarized below:

Outcome	Prospects	Cost
Favorable	.6	0
Unfavorable	.4	500,000

The current situation, operating without a clinic, is not influenced by the financing costs. However, marketing can be used to stimulate demand. These options help the decision maker assess whether marketing alone can increase utilization to the point that the hospital does not need the satellite clinic to stimulate profit (or operating margin, in the jargon of the nonprofit hospital). The following revenue estimates, expressed as present worth values, are obtained:

Marketing	Demand	Prospects	Revenue
Major	Large	P = .6	$200,000
Major	Small	P = .4	$ 0
Minor	Large	P = .2	$ 20,000
Minor	Small	P = .8	$ 0

The expected revenue increase is small because the hospital lacks the capacity to deal with large demands should they materialize.

Figure 18.4. The First Collapse of the Decision Tree.

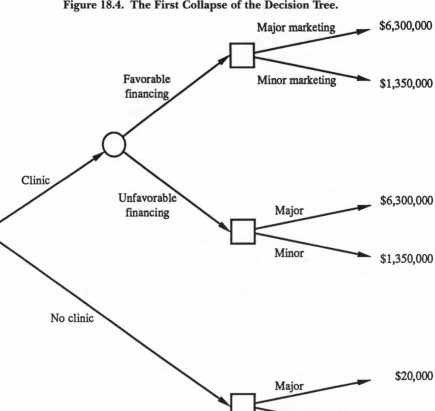

Step 3: Estimate Payoffs. To estimate the payoff (profit) for each option, the decision maker merges the paths in the tree to get a net expected value. First, the outcome node is replaced with the net expected value, as shown in Figure 18.4. The following format is used for the computations:

$$\text{Marketing with or without a clinic} = \text{Cost of marketing} + (\text{Large demand prospects}) \times \text{Revenue} + (\text{Small demand prospects}) \times \text{Revenue}$$

The payoffs are computed below:

Clinic with
major marketing = − $100,000 + .6($10,000,000) + .4($1,000,000)
= $6,300,000

Clinic with
minor marketing = − $50,000 + .2($5,000,000) + .8($500,000)
= $1,350,000

No clinic with
major marketing = − $100,000 + .6($200,000) + .4(0) = $20,000

No clinic with
minor marketing = − $50,000 + .2($20,000) + .8(0) = − $46,000

These values become the payoffs for the first collapse of the decision tree, as shown in Figure 18.4.

The decision tree is reduced a second time to take into account the prospects of financing. The calculation format follows:

$$\frac{\text{Expected value}}{\text{of option}} = \frac{\text{Cost of}}{\text{option}} + \left(\frac{\text{Unfavorable interest}}{\text{prospects}}\right)\text{Excess cost} + \text{Revenue}$$

The expected values of the options are as follows:

Option A:
clinic with
major marketing = − $1,000,000 + .4(− $500,000) + $6,300,000
= $5,100,000

Option B:
clinic with
minor marketing = − $1,000,000 + .4(− $500,000) + $1,350,000
= $150,000

Option C:
no clinic with = 0 + $20,000 = $20,000
major marketing

Option D:
no clinic with = 0 − $46,000 = − $46,000
minor marketing

Figure 18.5. The Second Collapse of the Decision Tree.

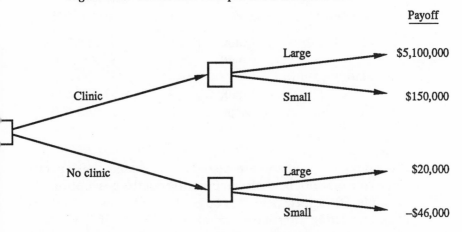

These values represent the payoffs expected for each option. As shown in Figure 18.5, the choice among options is now clear. According to the expected-value decision rule, major marketing makes the clinic the best alternative because it has the best payoff.

Sensitivity Analysis

Conclusions drawn from a decision tree depend on the precision of likelihood estimates for future conditions. These estimates, like those in Chapter Thirteen, can be treated as assumptions to be progressively relaxed. "What if" questions are posed to find out what must be assumed about the estimates to change a decision. Expanding on the previous example, assume that a modest clinic alternative is also being considered. This alternative calls for a smaller investment (Nutt, 1984c, p. 355). Now there are three options to choose from: an elaborate clinic (at a cost of $1 million), a modest clinic (at a loss of $100,000), and no clinic. The information below depicts the present worth of operating profits produced by the level of demand for each option. (The present worth of operating profit is computed as expected revenue less the cost of operations for each option, for the expected level of activity, discounting these profit streams with the procedures discussed in Chapter Thirteen.)

Option	Demand	Prospects	Operating Profits (Present Value)
A. Modest clinic	Large	.6	$ 500,000
	Small	.4	$ 200,000
B. Elaborate clinic	Large	.6	$2,300,000
	Small	.4	− $1,000,000
C. No clinic	Large	.6	$ 200,000
	Small	.4	0

If the demand estimates are viewed as unreliable, the expected value rule may not be useful in pointing out the best option. For example, if the prospect of a large demand is overstated, the elaborate clinic alternative would seem viable; if it is understated, the elaborate clinic may not be viable.

Assessing Demand. Sensitivity analysis can be used to examine demand estimates from an optimistic and a pessimistic point of view. Consider the options and payoffs shown in Figure 18.6. The computation to determine payoff can be written as follows:

$$\text{Payoff} = \text{Initial cost} + (\text{P})\text{Optimistic profit} + (1 - \text{P})\text{Pessimistic profit}$$

If prospects for a large demand are P = .6, payoffs for the options are as follows:

Option A = − $100,000 + .6($500,000) + .4($200,000)
   = $280,000
Option B = − $1,000,000 + .6($2,300,000) + .4(− $1,000,000)
   = − $20,000
Option C = 0 + .6($200,000) + .4(0) = $120,000

The modest clinic (option A) is preferred. The elaborate clinic (option B) is expected to run at an operating loss, making it less viable than making no investment to increase capacity.

With a somewhat more optimistic view of demand, differ-

Figure 18.6. Sensitivity Analysis with a Decision Tree.

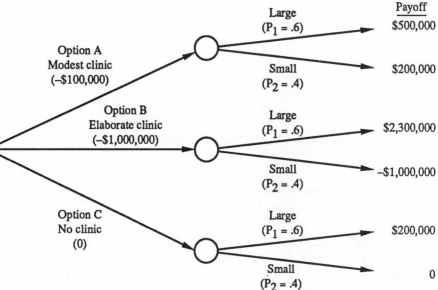

ent payoffs are realized. Merely boosting P to .7 yields the following:

Payoff A = – $100,000 + .7($500,000) + .3($200,000)
    = $310,000
Payoff B = – $1,000,000 + .7($2,300,000) + .3(– $1,000,000)
    = $310,000
Payoff C = 0 + .7($200,000) = $140,000

In this case, the elaborate clinic and modest clinic have the same payoff. The decision maker should now realize the choice between these alternatives changes when the prospect of high demand is above .7. The elaborate clinic is always preferred in this region.

The value of P is considered to be an unknown in sensitivity analysis. For instance, the expected value of payoffs for option A is payoff A = $100,000 + P($300,000)

This linear relationship can be plotted by setting P = 0 and 1.0.

P	Payoff
0	$100,000
1.0	$400,000

A straight line is drawn between these points. The other relationships are as follows:

Payoff B = − $2,000,000 + P($3,300,000)
Payoff C = P($200,000)

Plots of demand likelihood against payoffs are shown in Figure 18.7. Option C (no clinic) can be ruled out at this point because one of the options (option A) is better, no matter what the demand. This assessment applies the dominance decision rule, discussed in Chapter Thirteen. The choice between the elaborate and modest clinic alternatives (options A and B) requires a judgment. The payoff for the elaborate clinic is very sensitive to demand, as shown by the steep line in Figure 18.7. Huge losses can be incurred if prospects for a large demand fall below 50/50. If the decision maker believes that a large demand is likely, specifically, more than 70 percent, the elaborate clinic would be built. If not, the modest clinic would be preferred.

Assessing Financing. A similar analysis can be carried out for financing costs. "What if" questions address the likelihood of favorable financing costs that result from low interest rates. Using data drawn from the previous example, incorporating the best estimate for the prospects of a large demand produces six options. Note that the six "hybrid" alternatives are created by merging the three clinic and two marketing alternatives. The linear relationships between P (the likelihood of favorable financing) and payoffs are shown below:

$$\frac{\text{Option 1}}{\text{(modest clinic and major marketing)}} = -\$100,000 + P(700,000)$$

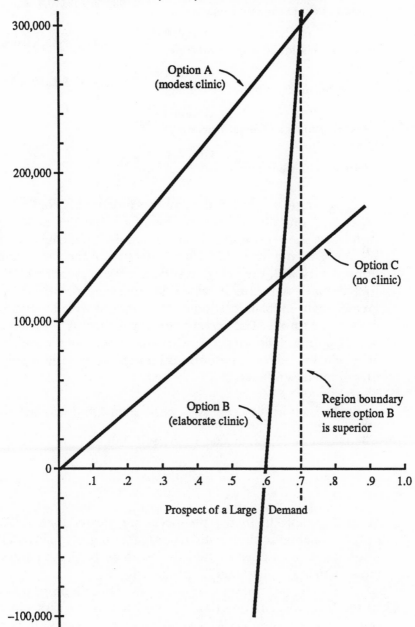

Figure 18.7. Sensitivity of Payoff to Demand Likelihood.

$$\frac{\text{Option 2}}{\text{(modest clinic and minor marketing)}} = -\$100,000 + P(\$10,000)$$

$$\frac{\text{Option 3}}{\text{(elaborate clinic and major marketing)}} = -\$1,000,000 + P(\$5,500,000)$$

$$\frac{\text{Option 4}}{\text{(elaborate clinic and minor marketing)}} = -\$1,000,000 + P(\$550,000)$$

$$\frac{\text{Option 5}}{\text{(existing clinic and major marketing)}} = \$20,000$$

$$\frac{\text{Option 6}}{\text{(existing clinic and minor marketing)}} = -\$46,000$$

For options 5 and 6, the payoff is independent of financing costs. Promoting the use of current facilities was paid for by cash reserves, so this option does not require financing at market rates. Figure 18.8 shows how payoffs for the other four options vary with financing. Two domains are identified. The first domain is profit. If favorable financing prospects are greater than .1425, at least one of the options will always produce a net profit. The second domain concerns the choice among options. The lines cross where the payoffs for the options are equal. For example, for options 1 and 3, the breakeven point is computed as follows:

$$-\$100,000 + P(\$700,000) = -\$1,000,000 + P(\$5,500,000)$$

$$\$900,000 = P(\$4,800,000)$$

$$P = \frac{9}{48} = .1875$$

When favorable financing prospects are greater than .1875, option 3 (elaborate clinic with major marketing) is preferred. If favorable financing seems unlikely, less than .1875, the modest clinic with major marketing is preferred.

The decision maker uses two types of questioning tactics. In the first "what if" question, the decision maker asks which option is best, assuming various likelihoods for favorable financ-

Figure 18.8. Sensitivity Analysis for Financing Prospects.

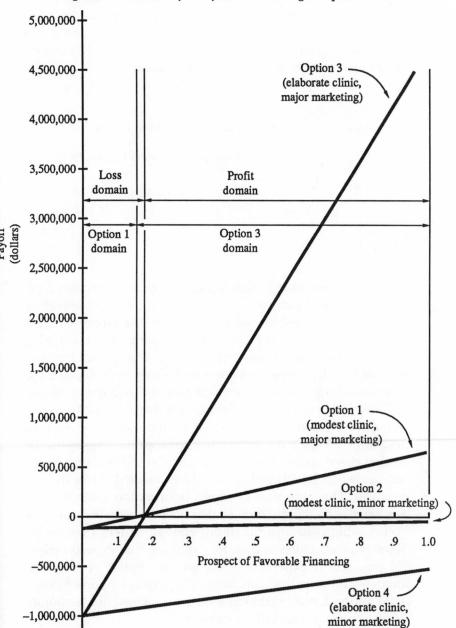

ing. In the second, the decision maker identifies the "domain" for various options, defined in this example by financing prospects. The range of conditions under which each option is best is elicited by the decision maker. Using Figure 18.8, the decision maker can identify the following conditions:

Option	*Conditions Where Option Is Best*
1	Favorable financing prospects below .1875
2	None
3	Favorable financing prospects above .1875
4	None
5	None
6	None

Using Sensitivity Analysis to Make a Decision. Sensitivity analysis offers two kinds of insight. First, the minor marketing option is dominated by major marketing. The larger expenditure for marketing can be justified, no matter what financing terms result. At this point, the decision maker can eliminate options 2 and 4, using a dominance decision rule. Second, the decision is largely insensitive to the cost of financing. A conservative estimate of favorable financing terms, above 20 percent, creates a condition in which option 3 is superior to option 1. To determine whether the elaborate clinic option dominates the modest clinic option, the decision maker could consult a financial banker to get his or her best guess about shifts in interest expenses. The consensus of expert information, collected this way, can clarify the situation so that the choice is clear-cut. This occurs when one option dominates all others (has better payoffs) for all values of a future condition that experts believe are possible. If experts believe that the chance of favorable financing is better than one in five (20 percent), option 3 dominates option 1, making the decision to adopt option 3 (elaborate clinic and major marketing) clear-cut.

Sensitivity Analysis with Two Future Conditions

Many decisions require assumptions about several future conditions. A different type of analysis is required if none of these future conditions can be treated in expected-value terms to be explored one at a time, as in the previous example. Treating the likelihoods of all future conditions as unknowns allows the decision makers to penetrate a tough decision characterized by uncertain or unreliable information about several important future conditions.

To demonstrate the analysis, assume that a large women's department store, called Disfederated, is considering opening a new branch. The cost of leasing a building, buying fixtures, and other fixed costs is $1 million. Experience shows that such funds, once committed, are not recoverable. Leases cannot be broken and fixtures have little salvage value. The standard practice of Disfederated is to offer a large selection of goods and engage in advertising to stimulate sales when the store first opens. In the past, Disfederated has used two advertising firms that offer different advertising plans. Experience suggests that advertising improves the prospect of a strong demand. Payoffs in this illustration are expressed as the present worth of "operating profits," determined by discounting an income stream of revenues expected under each alternative less the costs needed to operate a store at the volume produced by advertising. Data that summarize the present worth of operating profits that have been produced by the two advertising plans for the store option are shown below:

Level of Advertising	Advertising Cost	Demand	Prospects	Profits (Present Worth)
Major	$100,000 (firm 1)	Large Small	P = .6 P = .4	$10,000,000 − $1,000,000
Minor	$ 50,000 (firm 2)	Large Small	P = .2 P = .8	$ 5,000,000 − $500,000

Disfederated has a specialty competitor called Unlimited. Unlimited has an uncanny ability to identify a selection of clothing that sells better than anything Disfederated has to offer. The competitor does not compete with all of Disfederated's items, but in areas where it does compete, Unlimited always manages to capture what it wants of the market. The president of Disfederated has become paranoid about competition from Unlimited. For one in every four previous store openings, Unlimited opened at the same time as Disfederated and took volume valued at $3 million in present worth terms from Disfederated, no matter what steps Disfederated took to counter Unlimited's market entry. To reflect the impact of competition when it occurs, $3 million must be subtracted from the profits that result from the two advertising programs.

Disfederated does not want to enter any market that Unlimited has selected. However, the time needed to set up a store makes it impossible to back out of a market after Disfederated finds out that Unlimited has decided to enter. Disfederated has no way to determine whether Unlimited has decided to enter a market before Disfederated must make its own commitments. To make matters worse, Unlimited seems to have inside information on Disfederated's plans. The president of Disfederated hopes that the company's strategy leaks have been plugged. As a result, there are not good data on the prospect of competition.

Disfederated is competing with several stores at all of its current locations. It can choose to concentrate advertising on present stores, which creates a "no store" alternative. However, in this case, advertising would have a smaller impact because of competition from Unlimited and others. The payoffs for the no-store alternative are also expressed as the present worth of increases in operating profit that may occur when increased advertising is used for a store that has been in operation for several years. The payoffs are as follows:

Level of Advertising	Advertising Cost	Demand	Prospects	Payoff
Major	$100,000	Large	P = .6	$750,000
	(firm 1)	Small	P = .4	$300,000

| Minor | $ 50,000 | Large | P = .2 | $500,000 |
| (firm 2) | | Small | P = .8 | $ 0 |

The decision is summarized by the decision tree shown in Figure 18.9.

Estimation of Payoffs. The decision tree in Figure 18.9 is collapsed according to the following format:

Payoff = − Store Cost − Advertising cost

$$+ \frac{\text{Large demand}}{\text{prospects}} \left(\frac{\text{No competition}}{\text{prospects}} (\text{Profit}) + \frac{\text{Competition}}{\text{prospects}} (\text{Profit}) \right)$$

$$+ \frac{\text{Small demand}}{\text{prospects}} \left(\frac{\text{No competition}}{\text{prospects}} (\text{Profit}) + \frac{\text{Competition}}{\text{prospects}} (\text{Profit}) \right)$$

Using the expected-value decision rule with the best estimates of demand prospects (large demand = .6, small demand = .4, competition = .25, no competition = .75) and profits (present worth of operating profit), the decision maker finds the following payoffs for the options:

Store and = − $1,000,000 − $100,000 + .6[.75($10,000,000) + .25($7,000,000)]
major advertising   + .4[.75(− $1,000,000) + .25(− $4,000,000)]
= $3,750,000

$$\frac{\text{Store and}}{\text{minor advertising}} = -\$1,200,000$$

No store and = 0 − $100,000 + .6($750,000) + .4($300,000)
major advertising = $470,000

$$\frac{\text{No store and}}{\text{minor advertising}} = \$50,000$$

The expected values suggest that opening a store with a major advertising package is the best alternative. However, Disfederated's president worries that if the strategy leaks have not been plugged, the chance of competition from Unlimited may increase. The president also believes that the historical impact of advertising may have been eroded because local markets have

Figure 18.9. Decision Tree for Store Purchase Decision.

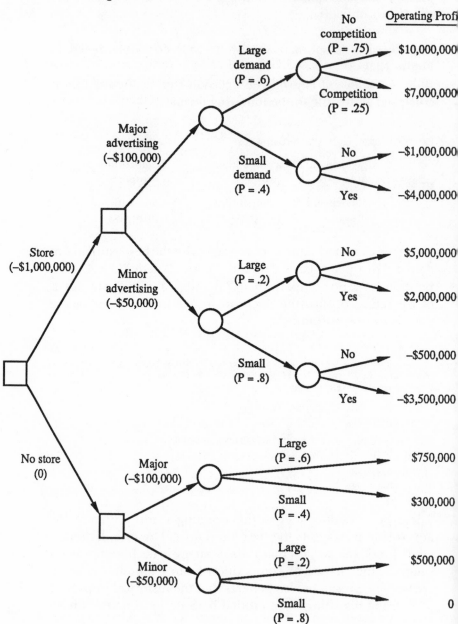

been flooded with advertising recently, which seems to have diluted its impact.

Treating the Prospects of Competition and Advertising as Unknowns. Each of the four options can be subjected to a sensitivity analysis that treats the likelihood of both future conditions as unknowns. The option calling for a store and major advertising, with the likelihoods expressed as unknown, is shown below:

Target profit = $-$ \$1,100,000 + P[p(\$10,000,000) + (1 $-$ p)(\$7,000,000)]
$\qquad$ + (1 $-$ P)[p($-$ \$1,000,000) + (1 $-$ p)($-$ \$4,000,000)]

Simplifying the equation in terms of the unknowns yields:

Target profit = $-$ 5,100,000 + 11,000,000P + 3,000,000p

P represents the prospects of a large demand and p the likelihood that Disfederated can avoid competition from Unlimited. Solving for P yields:

P = [(5,100,000 + target profit) $-$ 3,000,000p]/11,000,000

To carry out sensitivity analysis with three unknowns and one equation, the value of P is determined by selecting feasible values for target profit and all possible values for p, the chance of avoiding competition from Unlimited. The maximum profit (in present worth terms) that the store can produce is \$8.9 million, the \$10 million maximum operating profit less the \$1 million in store costs and \$100,000 in advertising. For the purpose of exploration, the decision maker sets profit at zero, beginning with the smallest target value of any interest. Setting the target profit at zero reduces the equation as shown:

P = (5,100,000 $-$ 3,000,000p)/11,000,000

Now let p, the prospect of avoiding competition, take the extreme values of zero and one. Letting p = 0, or making competition a certainty, yields:

$$P = (5,100,000 - 0)/11,000,000 = .4636$$

Letting p = 1, making *no* competition a certainty, yields:

$$P = (5,100,000 - 3,000,000)/11,000,000 = .191$$

Considering target profit in $1 million increments and solving for extreme values of p produces the following values for P, the prospect of a large demand:

	Values of P When	
Target Profit	*p = 0*	*p = 1*
0	.4636	.191
$1,000,000	.545	.282
$2,000,000	.645	.372
$3,000,000	.736	.464
$4,000,000	.82	.554
$5,000,000	.92	.645
$6,000,000		.736
$7,000,000		.827
$8,000,000		.918

A family of straight lines results, which can be plotted on a grid for the unknowns P (prospects of a large demand) and p (prospects of avoiding competition), as shown in Figure 18.10.

Figure 18.10 is subjected to "what if" questioning by the decision maker. To conduct a sensitivity analysis, Disfederated's president notes that the previous estimates of p and P were .75 and .6, respectively. Entering these values in Figure 18.10 produces the expected value for profit of between $3 and $4 million.

A more conservative estimate would be to assume a 50/50 chance of avoiding competition and having a large demand. Using the graph and entering p = .5 and P = .5, the decision maker discovers that profit for this contingency would be about $2 million (see Figure 18.11). Using this kind of logic, the decision maker can carry out various kinds of interrogations. For

**Figure 18.10. Sensitivity Analysis for Two Future Conditions
According to Expected Values.**

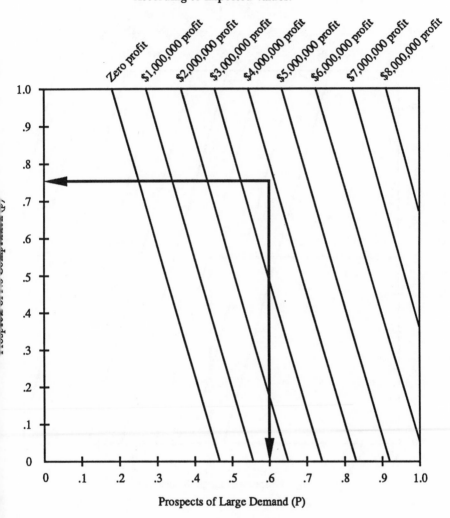

Prospects of Large Demand (P)

instance, the prospect of a large demand can be clarified by
experts who may contend that it falls between .4 and .6. Drawing
vertical lines at these points on Figure 18.10 allows the decision
maker to explore the implications of making a range of support-
able assumptions about a competitor. To make these assump-

Figure 18.11. Sensitivity Analysis with Equal Likelihoods.

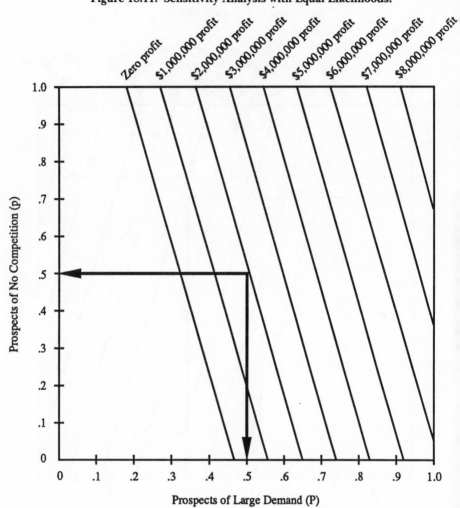

Prospects of Large Demand (P)

tions clear, the payoff lines outside the expected demand region are shown as dashed lines (see Figure 18.12). Payoff possibilities outside the .4 to .6 region are ruled out.

To conduct sensitivity analysis, various assumptions about competition are entertained. Competition must be quite likely (80 percent) to push profit to zero, shown as the lowest horizon-

Figure 18.12. Sensitivity Analysis for Ranges of Expectation.

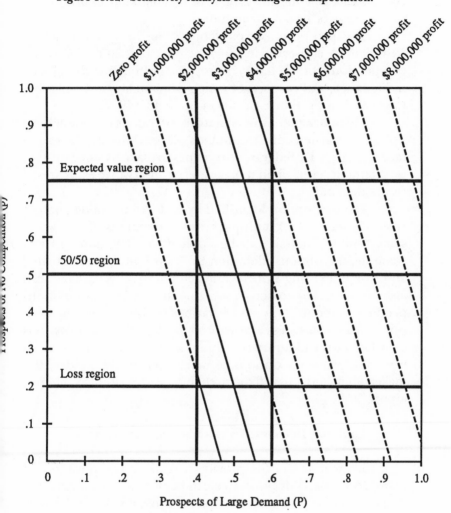

Prospects of Large Demand (P)

tal line in Figure 18.12. A 50/50 competition assessment results in a minimum profit of $1 million and a maximum profit of $4 million. If the competitor's past history is used as a guide (75 percent chance of no competition), a zero profit results only when the prospect of a large demand falls below 30 percent, well below the demand thought by experts to be attainable. A *very* conservative one-in-five estimate of no competition produces a profit range of zero to $2 million.

The prospects of competition can be given a similar treatment. A conservative range of values of .20 to .75 for no competition is bracketed by the top and bottom horizontal lines in Figure 18.12. Prospects of a high demand above .4 will avoid losses and can produce profits of up to $8 million.

This assessment shows that Disfederated's president need not be concerned with Unlimited's plans. Unlimited does not take enough of Disfederated's revenues to make its store strategy unprofitable, even when it makes very conservative estimates of future demand.

The best option identified by an expected-value analysis is usually selected for multiple sensitivity analysis. However, the same type of analysis can be applied to all options. In this example, the options identified by "store – minor advertising" and "use of existing stores with each advertising package" can also be subjected to sensitivity analysis. If the computations produce different choices with various decision rules, the decision maker can assess the choices by treating the prospects associated with all future conditions as unknowns. The analysis is used to prune the options, as well as to reassure the decision maker about how payoffs can change as the result of chance events.

Applying Decision Trees to Sequential Decisions

Sequential choices provide a realistic complication in many decisions. A decision tree can be used to break down the decision into several smaller decisions confronted by a decision maker analyzing each as it occurs, using the best available information.

In sequential decisions, decision makers are confronted with a choice of whether or not to seek additional information describing possible outcomes. This choice must be made before the choice among alternatives can be made. Decision makers must first consider whether to pay for information that may clarify their options. The information-seeking process itself can be sequential, with one set of information suggesting possible benefits in acquiring other types of information. For example, consider a new restaurant's decision of whether or not to advertise. A general purpose market survey may reveal a market segment with a large potential. This segment can be explored in a second market survey to determine whether directing advertising toward the high-potential segment is likely to increase customers.

There are several types of decisions for which an information decision step is essential. For example, a department store could purchase a market survey prior to making a decision about the size of its promotion to stimulate sales. The market analysis would be used to clarify the prospects of the promotion. Promotion in a saturated market would have only a small impact on sales, but in an open market the store could expect a large impact on sales. The decision maker would have to decide what to pay for the market survey.

The purchase of stocks and many other kinds of investments also calls for an information purchase decision. A two-step process results. The decision maker decides whether to acquire expert advice and then decides on the merits of the investment with and without the advice. The investor needs to know what can be justified as a payment to the expert.

Many other decisions present opportunities to purchase clarifying information. Wildcatters must decide whether they should purchase information on rock formations that influence the cost of drilling before deciding whether to drill for oil at a particular site. State governments are influenced by economic conditions that increase or decrease the amount of taxes businesses and individuals pay. How much should the state pay for more accurate forecasts of economic conditions? Nursing home chains must decide whether or not to purchase a study of past regulatory decisions prior to deciding whether they should attempt to expand their bed capacity. A part-time consultant specializing in lawsuits involving three-wheel vehicles determines the cost of information that predicts the number of future lawsuits and the prospect of governmental regulation before deciding whether to go into consulting full-time. In decisions regarding defense contracts or public work projects, a decision to seek information about other bidders precedes a firm's choice of whether to bid or what to bid. Finally, hospitals confronted with price controls that severely limit future revenue increases consider the cost of learning about various types of acquisitions, such as insurance companies or the *National Lampoon*, to use their cash reserves to underwrite their forecasted losses. In all of these cases, the decision makers need to know how much they can justify paying to learn more about their options before they make irrevocable commitments.

To conduct this type of analysis, the decision maker applies an expected-value formulation that is based on what is initially known about the decision to determine the value of additional information. In the analysis, the decision maker considers the loss of opportunity, using regrets, as described in Chapter Thirteen, to determine the value of additional information.

An Example. To demonstrate the analysis steps in a sequential decision, consider an organization that is contemplating the purchase of mineral rights as part of its diversification strategy. Assume that the firm has committed to investments in minerals and assesses each new site as it materializes. This assessment is complicated by several factors. Not all sites have high yields. Decision makers can improve their information by paying to have each site evaluated for its mineral prospects. This information can be costly and accurate only within certain ranges. Decision makers must decide how much to pay for the additional information.

To add specifics to the illustration, assume that an oil-producing site is being assessed (Raiffa, 1970). The site is known to have oil, but the amount of oil can vary from "wet" to "soaking." The wet outcome is much less desirable than the soaking one, often failing to produce revenues sufficient to cover costs. A soaking site can be a bonanza. Assume that the cost of site purchase and development is $700,000 and would be incurred no matter what the site's ultimate production level. Assume that a wet site produces $500,000 in revenue and a soaking site produces $20 million. The payoffs are expressed as profit. A wet site results in a $200,000 loss, $500,000 revenue less $700,000 in costs, and a soaking site results in a $19.3 million profit, $20 million revenue less $700,000 in costs, as shown below:

Alternatives	C_1 *(Wet)* $P_1 = .99$	C_2 *(Soaking)* $P_2 = .01$
A_1 (purchase)	– $200,000	$19,300,000
A_2 (do not purchase)	0	0

The alternatives are A_1 (purchase) and A_2 (do not purchase). There are two future conditions: wet and soaking. The company mineralogist, drawing on past experience, indicates that only one site in 100 is soaking but that this type of information may not apply to the site under consideration. The expected-value rule applied to this information produces these assessments:

$$A_1 \text{ (purchase)} = -\$200,000(.99) + 19,300,000(.01) = -\$5,000$$
$$A_2 \text{ (do not purchase)} = 0$$

The strategic manager should realize that a very small increase in the prospects of a soaking site would tip the decision to the purchase alternative.

Information that can assess the oil-producing prospects of a site can be derived from seismic soundings that determine the nature of the site's rock formations. Assume that these soundings taken over the entire site would cost $1 million. The soundings reduce uncertainty by providing a site-specific assessment on which to base the decision of whether to purchase. If seismic soundings find a closed rock structure, the prospects of a soaking site are enhanced. If the site lacks this structure, the prospects that the site is merely wet increase. The decision maker must decide whether to purchase the soundings to help make the decision.

Determining the Value of Information. The strategic manager must decide whether to purchase seismic soundings to help make the mineral site purchase decision. Initially, all the manager has to go on is the information presented on page 457, with

Table 18.1. Results of Seismic Soundings of Mineral Site.

		Future Conditions		Sounding Likelihoods
		Wet	Soaking	
Seismic Sounding Results	Open structure	.60	.05	.65
	Closed structure	.10	.25	.35
	New state likelihoods	.70	.30	
	Old state likelihoods	.99	.01	

site prospect estimates from the company mineralogist based on experience with other sites. Because of the uncertainty, these estimates appear to be overly conservative. The manager must decide how much he or she can justify paying for a study that provides information on the prospects of the site under consideration. The information shown in Table 18.1 is unknown at this point but would be available in the format shown, at a cost of $1 million.

The manager examines this information and determines regret in terms of lost opportunity. First, the manager assumes that a wet site will occur and determines lost opportunity of this outcome by subtracting the payoffs in the first column from the largest payoff in the column. If condition 1 (a wet site) occurs, purchase of the site produces a lost opportunity to save $200,000 (the loss incurred). The lost opportunity is zero if the site is not purchased. Now assume that condition 2 (a soaking site) occurs. Lost opportunity for A_1 (purchase) is zero because the $19.3 million profit is realized. For A_2 (no purchase), the lost opportunity is equal to the profit that would have been obtained had the purchase been made. These data are summarized in Table 18.2.

The expected value for the opportunity loss is computed

Table 18.2. Lost Opportunity in the Mineral Site Purchase Decision.

	Wet (P = .99)	Soaking (P = .01)
A₁ (Purchase)	$200,000	0
A₂ (No Purchase)	0	$19,300,000

according to what is known about the prospects of a wet or a soaking site. The expected values of opportunity loss are

$$A_1 \text{ (purchase)} = \$200,000(.99) + 0(.01) = \$198,000$$
$$A_2 \text{ (no purchase)} = 0(.99) + \$19,300,000(.01) = \$193,000$$

Note that the expected values of opportunity loss and expected values of the payoffs must be constant across alternatives (see Table 18.3).

Without additional information, the decision maker adopts A_2 (no purchase) because its expected value of zero is larger than the $-\$5,000$ expected loss for A_1 (purchase). The decision maker now asks what the return would be after learning whether the site is wet or soaking. The best return with a wet site is zero; with a soaking site it is $19.3 million. The expected value is

$$.99(0) + .01(19,300,000) = \$193,000$$

Table 18.3. Expected Gains and Losses.

	Expected Values for Gains	Expected Values for Losses
A₁ (Purchase)	− 5,000	198,000
A₂ (No Purchase)	0	193,000

The incremental value of the difference between the expected values when one knows and does not know what will occur identifies the maximum that can be justified to seek more information. In this example, the expected value when the decision maker knows is $193,000 and the expected value when the decision maker does not know is zero. In this case, the decision maker can justify spending up to $193,000 for the seismic soundings and would not acquire the information.

Another way to determine the value of the information is to consult the expected values for losses computed thus far. The minimal expected loss for the alternatives ($193,000) specifies the maximum value of additional information. A third approach to computing this value is to determine what to do if a wet or a soaking site occurs. The best alternative for a wet site, A_1 (no purchase), produces a zero return, and the best alternative for a soaking site, A_2 (purchase), produces a $19.3 million return. The wet site has a probability of .99 and a soaking site a probability of .01, so their expected value specifies the largest amount one would spend to learn more about the chance that a wet or dry site will occur. This is computed as follows:

$$\begin{bmatrix} \text{Maximum justifiable} \\ \text{payment for information} \end{bmatrix} = .99(0) + .01(19,300,000) = \$193,000$$

This analysis produces the same values as in the first approach applied to the example, but it may not in other applications that have different payoffs.

Sensitivity Analysis. The conservative nature of the estimates of a soaking site severely limits the amount that can be paid for additional information. The curious strategist may wish to treat these probability estimates as assumptions and relax them to find out what must be assumed about the site to justify investing $1 million for site exploration.

To compute this value, the state probabilities are treated as unknowns and substituted into the relationship used to compute the value of the information. This computation is shown as follows:

$$\begin{matrix} \text{Site exploration} \\ \text{cost} \end{matrix} = \begin{pmatrix} \text{Probability of} \\ \text{wet site} \end{pmatrix} \begin{matrix} \text{Best payoff} \\ \text{from wet site} \end{matrix} + \begin{pmatrix} \text{Probability of} \\ \text{soaking site} \end{pmatrix} \begin{matrix} \text{Best payoff} \\ \text{from soaking site} \end{matrix}$$

Treating the probability of a soaking site as an unknown, designated P, the probability of a wet site becomes $1 - P$. Substituting what we know into the relationship yields

$$\$1,000,000 = (1 - P)(0) + P(\$19,300,000)$$

Solving for P (the chance of a soaking site) yields

$$P = 1,000,000/19,300,000 = .052$$

A 5 percent chance of a soaking site would justify the site exploration expenditure of $1 million.

Representing the Decision with a Decision Tree. Assume the strategic manager applies sensitivity analysis and decides to take the implied risks and purchase the site survey. At this point, the decision can be represented as foreclosed opportunities and opportunities that remain. Figure 18.13 summarizes these choices in a tree format. The dashed lines in Figure 18.13 identify foreclosed choices, and the solid lines represent choices that remain.

The tree is filled in according to the seismic-sounding information purchased by the strategic manager. The results of the soundings are expressed as the likelihood of a wet or a soaking site. The likelihoods in the top set of branches are contingent on whether the site is found to be open or closed, which alters the likelihood that the site is wet or soaking. The seismic soundings have clarified the decision, but the true condition of the site is still known only in terms of likelihoods. The four likelihoods must sum to one, just as the likelihoods in the now pruned part of the tree also sum to one.

The payoff for each remaining branch in the tree can be computed by determining its expected value. This value is computed as follows:

Figure 18.13. Decision Tree for the Mineral Site Purchase.

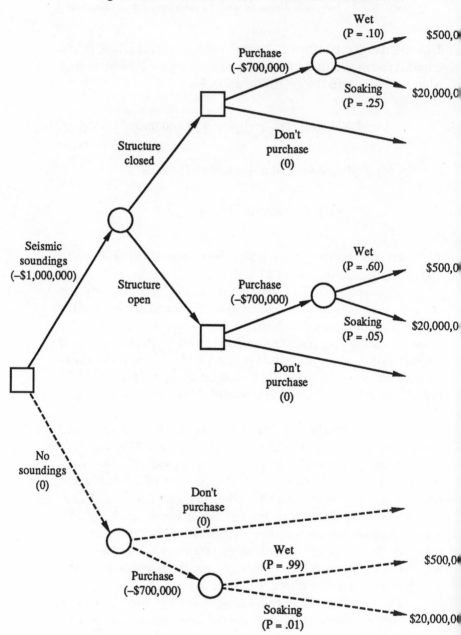

$$\underset{\text{payoff}}{\text{Net}} = -\underset{\text{site assessment}}{\text{Cost of}} - \underset{\substack{\text{purchase} \\ \text{and exploration}}}{\text{Cost of}} + \underset{\text{payoff}}{\text{Realized}}$$

Valuing each of the remaining four alternatives yields:

Purchase = $-\$1,000,000 - \$700,000 + [.1(-\$500,000) + .25(\$20,000,000)]$
(closed structure) = $\$3,250,000$

Purchase = $-\$1,000,000 - \$700,000 + [.6(\$500,000) + .05(\$20,000,000)]$
(open structure) = $-\$400,000$

$\underset{\text{(closed structure)}}{\text{No purchase}} = -\$1,000,000$

$\underset{\text{(open structure)}}{\text{No purchase}} = -\$1,000,000$

The decision can be approached in one of two ways. Unfavorable information can be used as a decision rule. In this example, the strategist may decide ahead of time to forgo the purchase if an open structure is found on the site. Seismic sounding information clarifies the prospects of a wet or soaking site but rules out neither. A decision under uncertainty remains. The expected values show that the site would be purchased because, no matter which structure actually results, profits are realized. A profit of $3,250,000 is expected if the information purchase is made, and a closed structure results. A loss of $1 million is incurred if the purchase is not made. Should a closed structure result, the expected payoff is − $400,000. Treating the $1 million site exploration expenditure as a sunk cost, this loss can be offset somewhat by the expected profit that stems from purchasing and developing the site under the conditions of a closed structure. There is a net revenue of $600,000 to be realized by exploiting the site: $-\$700,000 + .6(\$500,000) + .05(\$20,000,000)$. An unambiguous decision to purchase and develop the site can now be made.

Bushy Trees for Complex Decisions

In practice, a mineral site selection decision is far more complex than the illustration. The simplified version has the strategist deciding whether or not to conduct site exploration and using this information to decide whether to purchase and develop the site. Other information decisions and consequence factors can be incorporated into the decision, expanding the tree to include many layers of complexity. For example, there can be several types of site surveys, each with different costs and prospects of clarifying the decision. The cost of drilling can be uncertain, with costs escalating should certain types of obstructions be encountered at the spots selected for drilling. A decision to move the rig or continue may be required and should be anticipated. The future price of oil can be considered, as well as contingencies about the specific production level of the site, whether to bid on land adjacent to the site, leasing choices that parcel the site in various ways (for example, half or third shares). A chance fork or node can capture factors such as oil prices and obstructions and decision mode options such as leasing and buying adjacent land. However, the same basic principles are used to manage the information and make a choice.

A bushy tree is often needed to incorporate all the factors meriting consideration in making a decision. Complex or bushy trees can be approached in two ways. First, sensitivity analysis can be applied to trim the tree. For example, the clinic decision was shown to be fairly insensitive to the cost of financing. Had the loss domain in Figure 18.8 been only a little smaller, the decision maker could have concluded that the decision was insensitive to this factor and dropped it, thereby pruning the tree. Several chance outcomes often prove to have little or no impact following this type of analysis, which allows the decision maker to simplify (trim) the tree.

Second, no matter how bushy or complex the tree becomes, the analysis procedures described in this chapter can be used to move systematically through the decision. The decision maker arrays choices and chance events and values information, making purchasing decisions that seem justified. Decision makers apply sensitivity analysis along the way to reflect on the uncertainty and to decide whether the cost of acquiring additional information to clarify the prospect of various outcomes

can be justified. The tree helps the decision maker organize the
decision and identify essential information.

Key Points

1. The decision tree clarifies a decision to be made. Without
    such a structure, stakeholders may clutter a choice with
    alternatives drawn from several problem situations (Hayes,
    1969), as discussed in Chapters Eleven and Twelve. The tree
    makes incongruous alternatives obvious, eliminating this
    type of confusion.
2. The tree identifies needed information and eliminates the
    cost and time wasted in searching for information that is
    superfluous. Experts can give testimony that can be incor-
    porated into the tree at appropriate points in the valuation
    of alternatives.
3. The tree shows how various factors are interrelated, allow-
    ing the decision maker to view all aspects of a tough deci-
    sion without being overwhelmed by its complexity. Even
    when future conditions, such as demand prospects, cannot
    be quantified, a qualitative understanding of these rela-
    tionships reduces the decision's ambiguity by focusing on
    key unknowns. Decision makers can explore their attitude
    toward these unknowns by using sensitivity analysis.
4. The tree eases the difficulty of communicating complex
    decisions. It distinguishes preferences from consequences
    and chance outcomes from the deliberate acts of a decision
    maker. The rationale behind a choice can be laid out to rally
    support and keep opposing views in perspective.
5. The tree can act as a mediating device for situations in
    which major disagreements often arise. Decomposition of
    the decision through use of the tree makes key assumptions
    explicit. Debates can be focused on what must be assumed
    to make each position valid; this enhances the likelihood of
    a constructive dialogue.
6. The tree makes all those involved think through the deci-

sion to uncover new factors and contingencies and select those that offer the most fruitful way to arrive at a decision.

7. Decision trees create a framework for continuous evaluation. New information can be incorporated as it is uncovered. A record of results is provided to permit decision makers to reflect on which experts provided the most accurate and useful information.

19

Applying Multiple Criteria to Assess Alternatives

Several criteria, such as cost, various effectiveness measures, and user satisfaction, are often needed to value alternatives in tough decisions. For instance, decisions that locate an office building, select a new hospital service, or choose among peak period staffing options call for cost, the satisfaction of key people, marketability, need, and still other criteria to compare the merits of alternatives. In addition, an alternative may have several unique features that have intrinsic value. A comparison of these features, called *attributes*, also helps to identify the best alternative. For example, computer systems may have attributes such as color graphics, touch update, and memory. A "multi-criteria" assessment incorporates criteria and important attributes to value alternatives.

This chapter offers two ways to deal with multicriteria decisions. Decision makers faced with the need to explore alternatives using many criteria under time pressure can use a tactic called *elimination by aspects*. This tactic allows decision makers to become efficient and reliable information processors, but it ignores uncertainty. A second tactic formally deals with uncertainty but takes more time to collect data and conduct analysis. This approach uses the expected-value decision rule described in Chapters Thirteen and Eighteen to create a valuation index that incorporates what is known about uncertainty. The valuation index captures the extent to which the criteria are satisfied, how the criteria are influenced by future conditions, and the criteria's importance. Techniques to establish criteria weights that determine the relative importance of criteria were presented in Chapter Seventeen.

Finally, the logic of a valuation index is extended to introduce the concept of utility. Utility deals with the value that is produced by increases in the level of a criterion. Sometimes more is not better. For instance, the U.S. Department of Agriculture's women-infants-children (WIC) program offers food supplements to expectant mothers that increase the average birth weight of newborns by 25 percent (Nutt and Wheeler, 1980). However, a 25 percent increase in birth weight has little practical value if the average weight of newborns is five pounds as compared to three pounds. This chapter describes how to elicit the information needed to scale the utility of a criterion, such as birth weight, and shows how this information can be merged into a valuation index.

Figure 19.1 shows how the material treated in this chapter supports the decision process.

Dealing with Multicriteria Decisions

Multicriteria decisions seriously test a decision maker's powers of intuition, often making systematic information handling impossible. To overcome these problems, tactics that permit a decision maker to search for and use information systematically and consistently are required. Elimination by aspects ignores uncertainty by applying criteria one at a time to rule out alternatives that do not satisfy minimal expectations. This tactic is useful for short-fuse decisions in which there are many criteria that the decision maker wants to consider. Elimination by aspects, however, cannot be used to consider tradeoffs among critera because it ignores potentially critical assumptions about criterion importance that can be tested with sensitivity analysis.

The second tactic applies the expected-value decision rules to capture what is known about the uncertainty associated with future conditions and value differences in the importance of criteria to make a decision. In multicriteria decisions, decision makers can subject these value differences to "what if"

Figure 19.1. The Decision Process.

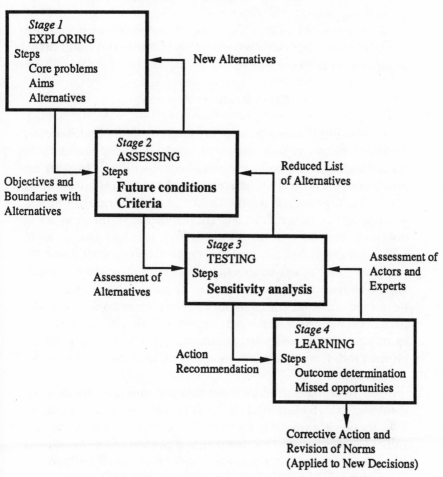

Note: Boldface type indicates topics addressed in this chapter.

questioning to determine how values, expressed as criterion weights, must shift to change a choice from one alternative to another.

Both elimination by aspects and the expected-value approach help decision makers identify needed information and use their intuition systematically, provide an external memory capability, and allow the implications of hunches to be extracted. Without the use of these tactics, human information-processing limitations, discussed in Chapters Four and Five, would create serious problems for decision makers who are attempting to cope with several value-laden criteria and many uncertain future conditions.

Elimination by Aspects

The elimination by aspects tactic calls for the decision maker to scan the alternatives in each state for undesirable outcomes, using a given criterion (Tversky, 1972). Consider an apartment decision. The apartment seeker can prepare a spread sheet that lists criteria as row headings and alternatives as column headings. Several criteria are important in the apartment decision, such as rent, location (safety), contract length, pool and other amenities, amount of security deposit, work commuting time, and access to downtown. Each apartment option is valued with each of these criteria in the spread sheet. The would-be renter scans all the apartment alternatives to rule out the unacceptable, using the most important criterion first. In our example, alternatives with unacceptably high rent could be eliminated first, followed by those with unsafe locations, and so on.

Site selection tactics used by oil companies for gas stations and used by fast-food chains for their restaurants illustrate how to use elimination by aspects. In these cases, no single indicator can be used to determine a preferred site because it must meet several criteria. For example, Rax restaurants, adopting a scheme used by Wendy's, applies seventeen criteria in categories that describe the area, site features, and competition. The criteria used by Rax are as follows:

Area Characteristics
1. Retail activity
2. Employment
3. Traffic
4. Population density
5. Population growth

6. Income
7. Overall activity

Site Features
8. Lot size
9. Visibility
10. Ingress/egress
11. Convenience
12. Cost

Competition
13. Number of units
14. Location of units
15. Volume of units
16. Lunch business
17. Dinner business

Car counts and proximity to intersections give an indication of traffic. The volume of retail activity in competitive fast-food outlets, such as McDonald's or Wendy's, being at least 20 percent above their national average provides a norm for projected volume. Cost is measured in dollars per square foot and is limited to no more than $2 per square foot above the average prices in the area. Convenience is measured by proxies such as time to turn through traffic to get to site and time to get back into the flow of traffic from the site. Demographic data from census tracts identify population growth, income, and local business activity. Market research firms provide the remaining information. Market research for Rax estimated that 70 percent of its volume is determined by retail activity and employment in the area, making these factors the dominant criteria. No other criterion accounts for more than 10 percent of the volume.

If Rax is faced with choosing among a large number of sites, elimination by aspects would be a useful way to systematically eliminate sites until the best site alternative emerges. The criteria are ranked with the most important used first. This is done with a large chart on which the proposed sites (alternatives) are numbered and listed across the top and the seven-

Table 19.1. Using Elimination by Aspects to Select Restaurant Sites.

	Site #1	Site #2	Site #3	Site #4	Site #5	Site #6	... #n
Area Characteristics							
Retail activity							
Employment							
Traffic							
Population density							
Population growth							
Income							
Overall activity							
Site Features							
Lot size							
Visibility							
Ingress/egress							
Convenience							
Cost							
Competition							
Number of units							
Location of units							
Volume of units							
Lunch business							
Dinner business							

teen criteria down the left side, as shown in Table 19.1. The decision maker deals with the criteria one at a time, applies a norm, and draws a line through all sites (more generally options) that fail to meet the norm. In the Rax cases, sites with unacceptably low business volume projections would be ruled out first. Next, sites with competitors doing below 20 percent more than their national average volume would be ruled out. The process continues until one site remains.

The approach can be used without the criteria-ranking step. The process can be repeated several times with different stakeholders to reveal their views regarding the importance of criteria and norms that should be applied. For instance, some people in the organization may rule out sites that have to compete with Wendy's, thinking that Rax is more apt to lose business to Wendy's than to other fast-food outlets. This procedure unobtrusively reveals the extent to which this view is shared by others.

When several criteria are applied in this way, the list of alternatives can be quickly narrowed in a cognitively simple and efficient manner. The tactic is good for minimizing both decision costs and time. The disadvantage stems from its inability to consider trade-offs. A desirable outcome in one future condition may be offset by an undesirable outcome in another. The elimination by aspects tactic is called *noncompensatory* because compensating criteria values are not considered in the decision.

Valuing Alternatives with Multiple Criteria Under Several Possible Future Conditions

To value alternatives with multiple criteria, the decision maker must consider the weight, or relative importance, of the criteria. Criteria weights provide a new type of subjective information that is uncertain because it is value-based, depending on the values of decision makers. This chapter and the next present a discussion of values expressed as criteria weights and their role in decision making. Techniques that can be used to estimate criteria weights were discussed in Chapter Seventeen.

To draw together these ideas, alternatives are valued according to both future conditions and criteria. The valuation index is made up of objective information, such as the level of cost and quality for each alternative in a given state, and subjective information, such as the relative value of the cost and quality criteria. Computations for the valuation index are as follows:

$$V_{ij} = \Sigma_k b_k X_{ijk}$$

where V_{ij} = the value determined for alternative i in state j
  b_k = the weight of importance of criteria k, set by the decision maker
  X_{ijk} = the value of criteria k for alternative i in state j

The index amalgamates the objective and subjective information. The decision maker (or group), aided by staff, identifies future conditions that could occur, estimates the likelihood that each condition will occur, and provides a set of criteria derived from the decision's objective that can be used to assess each alternative. The criteria are used to measure various kinds of benefits of an alternative, incorporating the influence of environmental factors, such as level of demand. For example, several levels of usage for a counseling service are conceivable. The valuation of alternatives must consider how different use rates may influence cost, client satisfaction, and other criteria.

An Example

A numerical example illustrates these computations. Assume that the administrator of an outpatient clinic operated by a hospital found that waiting time for appointments was so long that many patients left before their appointment was kept, causing lost revenue. A search was conducted to reduce this performance gap and produced one seemingly viable alternative: extended hours of service. Assume that the outpatient clinic has salaried physicians and that current demand is not being met through normal working hours.

To begin the valuation of this alternative, the decision maker conducts a survey of comparable clinics that have extended hours of service. A forecast is made of the demand that appears to have been stimulated by evening hours of operation. Assume the forecast suggests that a future demand of 200 percent of the current demand has a likelihood of 0.3; a demand of 150 percent has a likelihood of 0.65; and a demand of 105 percent has a likelihood of 0.05. Two valuation criteria will be used: profit and physician satisfaction. Profits will be weighted twice as high as physician satisfaction.

The decision framework helps the decision maker identify and combine objective and subjective information. First, each alternative is assessed. Questionnaires can be distributed to physicians, asking how they feel about expanded hours, which might require them to work late one night a week on rotation for extra compensation. The questionnaire would compare their satisfaction with extended hours and with current hours, if there

Table 19.2. Satisfaction Scores from Physician Questionnaire.

	C_1 Considerable Latent Demand	C_2 Some Latent Demand	C_3 Little Latent Demand
A_1 Current hours	0.60	0.80	1.00
A_2 Expanded hours	0.65	0.40	0.10

turned out to be a considerable latent demand (200 percent of current demand), some latent demand (150 percent), and little new demand (105 percent). Physician answers could be scored on a scale of zero percent (totally unacceptable) to 100 percent (no objections). Assume that the satisfaction data shown in Table 19.2 were obtained.

Next, profits would be projected on a monthly basis. To project revenue under each demand assumption, the various levels of demand are multiplied by the average charge for a visit, subtracting a figure that captures bad debt expectations. Costs are estimated according to current costs and the costs incurred with expanded hours, such as after-hours costs for physicians and costs for heat and lights. Profit is computed for each of the six combinations of alternatives and conditions by subtracting costs from revenues. Table 19.3 summarizes these values in terms of *increases* over current profit levels.

Values for the profit criterion must be rescaled to make them comparable to the satisfaction scores. The values for profit are made to fall on a zero-to-one scale. (See Table 19.3). The lowest value for profit (– $20,000) becomes a zero; the highest ranked value ($110,000) becomes one. The intermediate values are made proportional (20/130 = 0.15, and 30/130 = 0.23), according to this scale.

The valuation index is given by the following equation:

$$V_{ij} = 2/3(\text{profit}) + 1/3(\text{satisfaction})$$

For the current hours alternative with considerable latent demand, the index yields:

Table 19.3. Monthly Profit Estimates.

Actual Values	C_1 Considerable Latent Demand	C_2 Some Latent Demand	C_3 Little Latent Demand
A_1 Current hours	0	0	0
A_2 Expanded hours	+ $110,000	+ $10,000	– $20,000

Rescaled Values	C_1	C_2	C_3
A_1 Current hours	0.15	0.15	0.15
A_2 Expanded hours	1.00	0.23	0

$$V_{11} = 2/3(0.15) + 1/3(0.60) = 0.30$$

This calculation is repeated for each matrix cell to create the values shown in Table 19.4.

To compute a value for an alternative by applying the expected-value decision rule, each future condition's probability is multiplied by each value (V_{ij}) that captures the profit and satisfaction in each alternative:

Expected value of $A_1 = 0.30(.30) + 0.65(.37) + 0.05(0.43) = 0.35$
Expected value of $A_2 = 0.30(.89) + 0.65(.29) + 0.05(0.03) = 0.45$

Table 19.4. Expanding Hours of Service in a Third-Sector Organization.

	Considerable Latent Demand C_1 $P_1 = 0.30$	Some Latent Demand C_2 $P_2 = 0.65$	Little Latent Demand C_3 $P_3 = 0.05$
A_1 Current hours	0.30	0.37	0.43
A_2 Expanded hours	0.89	0.29	0.03

The expanded hours option (A_2) yields the highest composite value according to the expected-value rule, making that option preferable.

Other Decision Rules

The choice above applies the expected-value decision rule. As pointed out in Chapter Thirteen, many other decision rules can be used, including dominance, pessimism, optimism, LaPlace or ignorance, and regret.

The dominance principle produces no clear-cut choice between the alternatives. The expanded hours alternative is no better than the current hours alternative for all of the future conditions (Table 19.4).

The pessimism or maximin decision rule can be used if the decision maker feels considerable threat from the physicians, fearing that they will rebel against evening hours, and from the trustees, who are demanding actions that can generate profit. The decision maker scans the values in Table 19.4, finds the poorest payoff (lowest value) for each alternative, and selects the alternative with the highest minimum payoff. This assessment leads the decision maker to continue with the current hours alternative because expanded hours produce lower net benefits (payoff) under the "little latent demand" state in Table 19.4.

An optimism or maximax rule can be used if the decision maker sees few threats. The decision maker finds the maximum payoff associated with each alternative and compares them, selecting the alternative with the best payoff. The expanded hours option has a maximum value of .89 and the current hours option .43 (on a zero-to-one scale), leading to the selection of the expanded hours. The minimax rule calls for the smallest regret, which favors the expanded hours alternative.

To use the LaPlace decision rule, both the probabilities for future conditions and criteria weights would be ignored, creating a new decision matrix. For V_{11}, the valuation index yields:

Table 19.5. Other Decision Rules Applied to Expanded Hours of Service.

LaPlace Rule	Considerable Latent Demand	Some Latent Demand	Little Latent Demand
Current hours	.375	.475	.575
Expanded hours	.825	.315	.050

Regret Rule	Considerable	Some	Little
Current hours	−.450	0	0
Expanded hours	0	−.165	−.525

$$V_{11} = 1/2(\text{profit}) + 1/2(\text{satisfaction})$$
$$= 1/2(.15) + 1/2(.60)$$
$$= .375$$

The results of these computations are shown in Table 19.5.

The payoffs for the alternatives are computed under the assumption that each future condition is equally likely:

Value for A_1 = 1/3(.375) + 1/3(.475) + 1/3(.575) = .475
Value for A_2 = 1/3(.825) + 1/3(.315) + 1/3(.050) = .397

This analysis suggests that the current hours alternative (A_1) should be adopted.

To apply the regret decision rule, a matrix of regrets is formed by subtracting the largest value from the others in each condition (see Table 19.5). Applying the minimax regret rule, the decision maker would adopt the alternative with the smallest maximum regret. The current hours alternative would be adopted because the maximum regret for the current hours is −.450 and the maximum regret for expanded hours −.525.

A comparison of the choices preferred by the decision rules is shown below. The expanded hours option is preferred under all but the most pessimistic conditions.

Decision Rule	Favored Alternative
Uncertainty (LaPlace)	Current hours
Sure Thing (dominance)	No decision

Pessimism (maximin)	Current hours
Optimism (maximax)	Expanded hours
Regret (minimax)	Current hours
Expected Value	Expanded hours

Sensitivity Analysis

It is often useful to explore how preferences among alternatives can change as the weights assigned to the decision criteria shift. This analysis is similar to that applied to the likelihood of future conditions. To conduct a sensitivity analysis for criteria weights, the likelihood estimates are treated as constraints and the criteria weights are treated as unknowns.

For instance, consider the expanded hours example discussed in the previous section. The expected value is the sum of the payoffs for each criterion for a particular future condition times the criterion weight, with this amount multiplied by the likelihood of the future condition. According to the expected-value decision rule for each alternative, the payoff can be expressed by means of a scale ranging from 0 to 100:

$$\text{Payoff} = \Sigma_i[(1 - b)(\text{satisfaction value})_i + b(\text{profit value})_i]P_i$$

In this relationship, b represents the weight assigned to the profit criterion and P_i the probability of each future condition according to the values previously described for the hours of service example (see Tables 19.2 and 19.3). Substituting values drawn from these tables yields:

$$A_1 \text{ (current hours)} = [(1 - b)60 + b15].30$$
$$+ [(1 - b)80 + b15].65$$
$$+ [(1 - b)100 + b15].05$$
$$A_2 \text{ (expanded hours)} = [(1 - b)65 + b100].30$$
$$+ [(1 - b)40 + b23].65$$
$$+ [(1 - b)10 + b(0)].05$$

Solving for the unknown criteria weight, b, these equations reduce to:

$$A_1 = 75 - 60b$$
$$A_2 = 46 - 1.05b$$

The payoffs can be plotted by letting the weight of the profit criterion, b, take on values of one and zero.

	$b = 0$	$b = 1$
A_1	75	15
A_2	46	45

The payoff relationships for the two alternatives are plotted in Figure 19.2. The breakeven point is determined by setting the payoffs for current hours and expanded hours equal to each other and solving for b.

$$75 - 60b = 46 - 1.05b$$

$$b = 29/58.95 = .492$$

Figure 19.2 shows that when profit is about the same as satisfaction (weighted at b = .492), the expanded hours alternative is preferable. The decision maker must search for a situation in which satisfaction is more important than profit to prefer the current hours alternative.

This type of analysis removes considerable uncertainty and ambiguity, making clear which alternative is best for the organization. As shown in Figure 19.2, the expanded hours alternative is insensitive to the importance accorded profit. The current hours alternative produces large payoffs but only when profit is rendered less important than physician satisfaction.

This analysis removes much of the ambiguity about how physician satisfaction trades off with profit prospects. It gives the decision maker a justification to act and provides a basis for the decision maker to defend his or her actions. The decision maker can defend the decision by pointing out that the views of physicians were carefully taken into account. The organization must subordinate profit to physician satisfaction before the current hours option provides a better payoff for the organiza-

Figure 19.2. Sensitivity Analysis Applied to Criteria Weights.

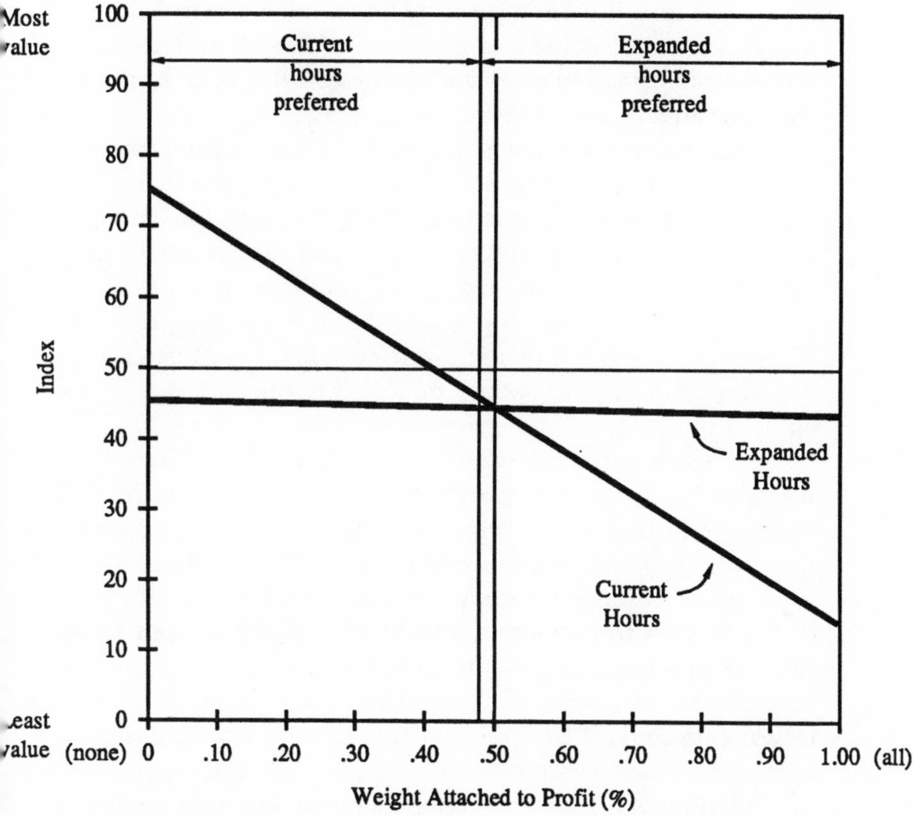

tion. In most cases, this argument would put proponents of the current hours alternative on the defensive. For example, the benefits to the organization make it hard for physicians to argue against the policy without appearing to be grossly self-serving.

The Concept of Utility

Utility is an essential concept in valuing alternatives because linear changes in profit, cost, revenue, and the like, measured in dollars, often fail to capture the preference of a decision maker. As pointed out in Chapter Five, some decision makers are risk-averse, being more concerned about losses than gains. The disutility for a possible loss is much greater than the actual magnitude of the loss, as expressed in dollars (Kahneman and Tversky, 1982). In cases such as these, utility must be used to capture value.

In the department store peak period staffing example cited in Chapter Thirteen, several criteria in addition to cost can be important. The alternative of restricting vacations and calling for overtime during a holiday season may result in good people resigning. Other responses could be absenteeism or bogus sick claims, causing unanticipated staffing shortfalls. These shortfalls could drive morale even lower because employees who come to work would be asked to put in longer hours without notice, to compensate.

This example raises several questions about how to deal with changes in a criterion such as morale. Above certain levels, surrogate indicators of morale may have no important consequences. However, when morale falls below a certain point, turnover or absenteeism may begin to increase. The notion of utility is used to capture this relationship. Utility can be expressed with objective or subjective measures.

Objective Measures of Utility

Utility is not an "objective" concept. However, a kind of objectivity is possible when utility is measured by a criterion that can be related to a factor that measures consequences. Payoff is expressed in units of the consequence factor. An example is job satisfaction, measured by a survey, and its link to absenteeism or turnover. Job satisfaction is the criterion, and turnover or absenteeism is the consequence factor expressing utility. A survey made up of several questions designed to measure job satisfaction can be administered to all employees. The responses to the questions can be measured by a 0-to-100 ARS scale, where 0 reflects no job satisfaction and 100 reflects complete job satisfaction. One way to link the consequence factor to the job satisfaction scale is by means of empirical knowledge based on research findings. Specific points on the scale measuring job satisfaction can be associated with actual absenteeism rates according to the results of studies conducted in comparable work settings.

Two results can be imagined. The first calls for a linear relationship. Figure 19.3 illustrates this relationship with the top curve, assuming that a 50 percent or greater absenteeism rate has 0 utility because this level of absence would severely limit productivity in the organization. However, a linear relationship may be unrealistic because moderate levels of job satisfaction may have no consequences expressed as absenteeism. Job satisfaction must fall below a threshold before consequences (absenteeism) occur.

The lower curve in Figure 19.3 captures another way to view the job satisfaction–absenteeism relationship. In this relationship, chronic absenteeism will result until job satisfaction rises above a threshold. This threshold is likely to be organization- or industry-specific. To illustrate, General Motors and other U.S. automakers report severe absenteeism problems, which have been attributed to working conditions. Working conditions, however, are often far worse in steel mills and foundries and much better in shopping centers and hospitals. In the peak period staffing example, discussed in Chapter Thirteen, job satisfaction must rise above a threshold level (neutral on the scale) before absenteeism will dramatically decline. A fairly steep reduction can be imagined until a moderate level of job satisfaction is approached. At this point, absenteeism may represent legitimate sick days that cannot be lowered further, no matter what steps are taken.

Very different decisions would be made if these curves were used to capture job satisfaction as an outcome of a peak period staffing alternative. In the upper curve in Figure 19.3, the consequences of positive levels of job satisfaction are overstated and at low levels are understated. Complete job satisfaction will not yield zero absenteeism, and an unworkable level of absenteeism (50 percent) will be reached when job satisfaction falls just below neutral. The most important aspect of job satisfaction would be missed: When satisfaction falls below a certain point, absenteeism increases dramatically.

An objective index of utility has been used to describe a

Figure 19.3. Utility Expressed as Turnover.

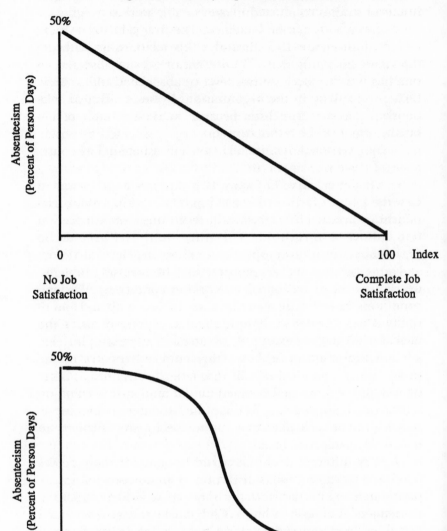

variety of relationships useful in decision making. For example, financial indicators (criteria) have been related to a utility expressed as a bond rating. Utility captures how a rating changes as some indicator, such as peak debt service coverage, changes (Cleverley and Nutt, 1984). This information points out, among other things, the level of debt coverage associated with a bond rating that falls below an investment grade (below a BBB rating). Similar analyses can be carried out for each criterion thought to be important in the rating decision.

Staffing ratios for nursing wards in a hospital also illustrate an objective utility index, in this case expressed as nursing hours per patient day. Hours per patient day provide a measure of severity (or negative utility). As hours go up, the severity of a patient's condition should also go up. In keeping with this notion of severity, nursing hours per patient day have been linked to clinical indicators (criteria) for nurse staffing decisions (Nutt, 1984a). Objective indices can be used in a variety of other decisions, such as budgeting and funding decisions of federal programs, in which allocated dollars can be used to capture utility. Measures of objective utility are expressed as budget allocations and the amount of funding in these examples.

A limitation in the use of objective utilities stems from practicality. To sum the effects of several types of criteria that have different scales, such as satisfaction and cost, a common referent or indicator of value must be used. The consequence factor for the objective index—for example, cost—is converted to a utility-like scale. In a linear transformation, the extreme (highest and lowest) cost values become the end points of a 0-to-100 scale. Such a scale is similar to scales used to capture satisfaction and other criteria for which value must be measured in terms of subjective utility. As a result, objective indices are usually converted to subjective scales to aggregate the effects of the criteria. This step makes the consequence values associated with cost comparable to those of satisfaction, so they can be summed to form a valuative index. The transformation of cost to a satisfaction scale can be made because cost can be viewed in terms of satisfaction, such as low costs have high satisfaction. If some criteria must be expressed with a subjective index, such as

Figure 19.4. Utility Curve for Experience in Managerial Selection.

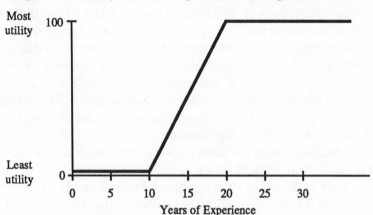

the utility associated with satisfaction, it is often convenient to express all of the consequence factors subjectively. For example, in the clinic expanded hours decision described in the previous section, outcomes are related to the utility of each alternative for each future condition.

Subjective Measurers of Utility

Value can also be captured with a subjective measure of utility. The subjective utility measure attempts to capture worth, satisfaction, value, or payoff. A link is made between a criterion and the subjective utility or value attached to various levels of that criterion. For example, a decision that selects among candidates for a management position can be made on the basis of a criterion, such as experience. The decision maker may attach no value to experience of less than ten years and little value to experience beyond twenty years, treating this amount of experience as superfluous and unnecessary. "More is better" within the range of ten to twenty years, but nowhere else. This relationship between a subjective measure of utility and years of experience is shown in Figure 19.4.

Subjective utilities are often used to express value. *Consumer Reports*, for example, rates the performance of products, such as the video reception of VCRs and the audio fidelity of stereo speakers, on a scale that runs from 0 to 100. The scale is used to order products according to their performance so that consumers can evaluate trade-offs between performance and cost when making a purchase decision.

The National Football League uses the "National" and "Blesto" scales to rate college players prior to its annual draft. The Blesto scale gets its name from an acronym of the Bears, Lions, Eagles, and Steelers Talent Organization, its four founders. The Blesto scale runs from 0 (best) to 5 (worst). The National scale, used by the other nineteen NFL teams, runs from 1 (worst) to 10 (best). A player's potential is linked to the scale. For example, projected first-year starters (except quarterbacks) are rated 0 to .99 on the Blesto and 9.0 to 9.99 on the National scale. Such scales allow NFL teams to aggregate the views of their scouts and to evaluate the performance of particular scouts. The performance of a player, say, a first year starter, can be tied to the ratings of specific scouts to see which one has the best track record of projecting starters drafted by any NFL team. The scale can also identify scouts whose ratings are too optimistic or too pessimistic and whether a scout is best at rating players for certain positions, such as linemen or quarterbacks. This type of system has been credited with making the Dallas Cowboys the most consistently competitive team in the NFL.

Constructing Utility Curves

The construction of a valuation index that incorporates utilities is best illustrated by way of examples. In the first, assume that an investment banker wants to capture the way in which the bond rating agencies Moody's and Standard & Poor's are likely to rate taxable issues used by firms to raise investment capital. Investors use these credit ratings to assess the risk and set interest rates accordingly. Securities must be rated above a threshold level (BBB for Standard & Poor's and BAA for Moody's) to be termed "investment" grade. This designation is critical because the policies of many large potential buyers, such as retirement plans, prohibit investment in bonds that fall below investment grade.

Assume that three criteria are thought to be crucial in the rating agencies' decision: size, debt service, and leverage. Size is determined by a firm's revenues. Firms ranging from $200 million to $10 billion in annual revenues are likely to float bonds. Debt service indicates the coverage ratio, indicating cash flow to be used to pay back the debt service. Leverage is the ratio of long-term debt to equity.

To create a valuation index for the investment banker, two additional steps are added to the procedure. First, utilities must be drawn to capture how a rating changes with changes in each criterion. The curves shown in Figure 19.5 were drawn by an expert in capital financing and illustrate the use of objective utilities. Second, the three criteria must be weighted to indicate their relative importance. An index which corresponds to a value that is assigned in the form of a bond's rating is made up of the value drawn from each curve, multiplied by its weight.

For the second example, assume that an agency such as the American Heart Association or the National Heart Institute of the National Institutes of Health is evaluating potential program areas to target for funding priorities. To develop priorities, criteria such as target group size, disability relieved, quality of life achieved, years of life gained, and cost are to be used (Nutt, 1984c). (These criteria are defined later in the discussion.) A list of possible program areas and information that describes how each program meets each criterion is obtained to describe the outcomes expected for state-of-the-art treatment in each potential program. To identify the high-priority programs, the same two steps are required. First, utility curves must be drawn for each criterion. Utility in this case is subjectively measured, providing a contrast to the bond rating case. Second, these criteria must be weighted to reflect their relative importance.

The Valuation Index

For both the bond rating and the heart disease priority examples, the valuation index is written as follows:

Figure 19.5. Utility Curves in Bond Rating Decisions.

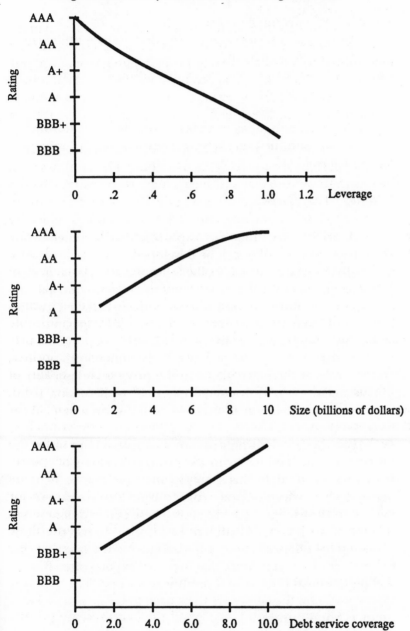

$$V_j = \Sigma_i W_i U(X_{ij})$$

where W_i = weight of criterion i

           $U(X_{ij})$ = a value for alternative j drawn from utility curve for criterion i

           V_j = the valuation index indicating the merit of alternative j

The valuation index merges information drawn from the utility curves and the criteria weights into a priority, valuation score, or payoff.

Sketching Utility Curves

A utility curve that can capture either a subjective or objective index of utility can be developed with a scaling technique. To create a utility curve, the following steps are required: orientation, criterion definition and refinement, and participant graphing. Either an individual or a group can sketch utility curves. Although the procedure was developed for groups, it can be readily adapted for use by an individual.

Setting the Stage. The purpose of sketching a utility curve and the role of the participants in the process is described to initiate activity in the orientation step. This discussion is followed by a presentation illustrating utility curves that others have sketched.

For the bond-rating case, an example of the utility inferred for gains and losses in the project decisions of middle managers was used. In this example, shown in Figure 19.6, the managers had a decided preference to avoid losses and were not enticed by the likelihood of big gains. These curves demonstrate that the "more is better" dictum does not apply to real decisions involving the financial choices of managers. The example helps to break down the resistance that financial experts often have to scaling financial criteria in a nonlinear fashion. The expert is then shown how the curves are to be used to create a model that predicts bond ratings.

For the heart disease program priorities case, the curves

Figure 19.6. Utility Curves Showing Asymmetrical Preferences for Gains and Losses in Executive Decisions.

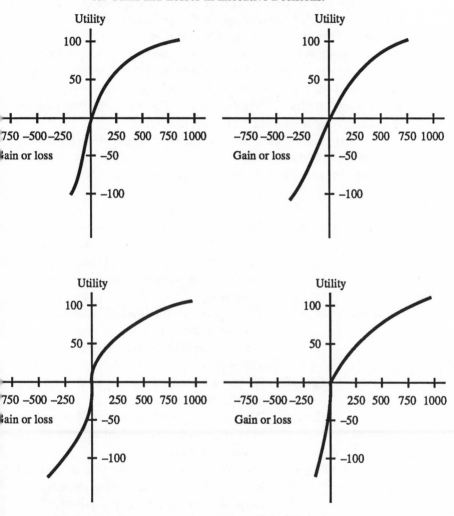

Source: Adapted from Swalm, 1966, pp. 123–136.

shown in Figure 19.7 can be used to suggest how a subjective utility, medical underservice in this illustration, changes with changes in the various criteria (Fryback, Gustafson, and Detmer, 1978). The curves in Figure 19.7 illustrate how utility or value was found to change with changes in physicians per one thousand population, percentage of people in a region below the poverty level, and percentage of the population over sixty-five. The implications of these curves are then explained. The demonstration shows how values for the criteria (physician numbers and population age and income) can be related to the concept of medical scarcity. The nonlinear relationships between the criteria and utility are highlighted to illustrate why one cannot always assume a simpler linear relationship.

Next, the criteria are presented and defined. A display such as the one shown below is created to identify and define the criteria for selecting heart disease programs (Nutt, 1984c, p. 319):

Net target group:	The total number of people affected defines the population of risk. The net target group is the target group times the expected survival rate following treatment.
Disability relieved:	The change in the level of disability, after treatment, is defined by a disability level. The levels are defined as follows:
Class I:	People with no symptoms and no limitations.
Class II:	People with problems who suffer no limitations where physical activity would cause fatigue.
Class III:	People with problems that cause a slight limitation, experienced when engaging in mild forms of ordinary activity.
Class IV:	People with problems that cause a marked limitation, experienced when engaging in mild forms of ordinary activity.
Class V:	People with problems that cause severe limitations that occur with any physical activity and at rest.

Figure 19.7. Utility Curves for Possible Medical Program.

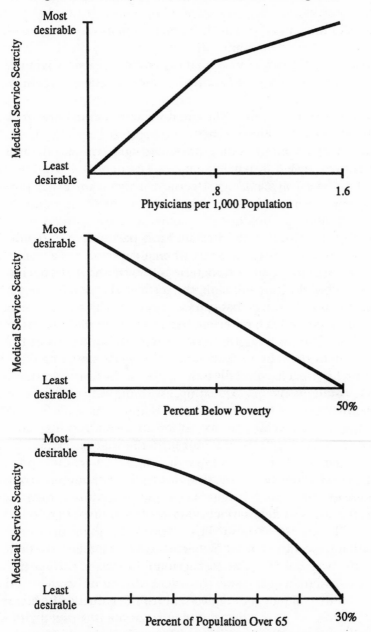

Source: Reprinted from Health Services Research Group, "The Development of an Index of Medical Underservice," *Health Services Research*, Summer 1975 (168–180).

Quality of life:	Defined as the residual disability after treatment.
Years of life gained:	The difference in years of survival with and without treatment.
Cost:	The total expenditures per individual to apply the best available treatment.

(Criteria for the bond rating example were defined previously.) On occasion, additional criteria are suggested at this point. It is wise to be prepared to incorporate new criteria into the materials to be scaled by participants.

Participant Graphing. Decision makers are given graph paper with the vertical axis labeled by utility (or its equivalent according to a consequence factor) and the horizontal axis labeled by values for a criterion. Each participant in the decision is asked to assign a utility when a criterion has a minimal value, assuming that nothing else is known about the decision. For the bond rating decision, the vertical axis (see Figure 19.5) lists the bond ratings that can be assigned. The horizontal axis has a range for each criterion, beginning with the smallest and ending with the largest criterion value, which describes firms that might use a bond for financing. Experts would be participants. First, each expert finds the value for the leverage criterion that would justify an AAA rating, assuming that nothing else is known about the firm. Next, a value is found that calls for a BBB rating. Finally, values are found for all possible ratings in between, switching from the lowest to the highest rating, until none remain. A smooth curve is drawn to connect these points. The curve is reviewed to ensure that its implications are consistent with the expert's beliefs. The same procedure is then used for the size and debt service coverage criteria (see Figure 19.5).

To scale criteria for heart disease program priorities, a similar procedure is used. To begin, assume that the lowest value for the "years of life gained" criterion is two years. Each decision maker assigns a utility level consistent with his or her view of the importance of a benefit of two years of life gained, which is apt to be close to zero. The value that is assigned is noted and its implications discussed with the participant(s). If a comparatively high utility value is assigned, it would be interpreted, for example, as "This means two years of life gained may be as important as ten years of life gained." If the participants agree, the value is not changed. Typically, some revision follows each explanation. The process is then repeated with the highest number of years gained, forty-four years, and then for five to ten points between these extremes. After each point, the implications are explained until the participants become comfortable with the scale and the implications of their designations. The number of intermediate points is determined by the nature of the criterion scale. For instance, if outcomes all along the scale can be imagined, more points are required. This procedure would be repeated for the other continuously scaled criteria, cost and target group size, to produce curves like those shown in Figure 19.8.

The participant connects all the points by drawing a smooth curve. If a group is participating, the curves are then superimposed. A composite curve is drawn to represent the group's consensus. This technique can be used with individuals or groups of up to nine or so. Beyond nine, the discussion needed can become unwieldy, and a two-step process called for in order to merge views of separate groups.

In a discussion period, the implications of each curve are explored. For example, using Figure 19.7, the decision maker or group is asked if the difference between 0.8 and 1.6 physicians per thousand population really has comparatively little effect on medical service scarcity. During the ensuing discussion, group members attempt to reconcile their views with those of others as they emerge. After discussion, the participants are asked to resketch the curve they believe best describes the relationship between utility and each criterion.

When points along a criterion scale are discrete categories, such as the disability relieved and quality of life criteria, some minor changes in approach are required. In such cases, a criterion's categories may not have a clear ordering. A ranking step must precede scaling to sort out these criterion levels.

Consider, for example, the diagnosis criterion that was used in nurse staffing decisions (Nutt, 1984a). Using the pro-

Figure 19.8. Utility Curves for Program Priorities.

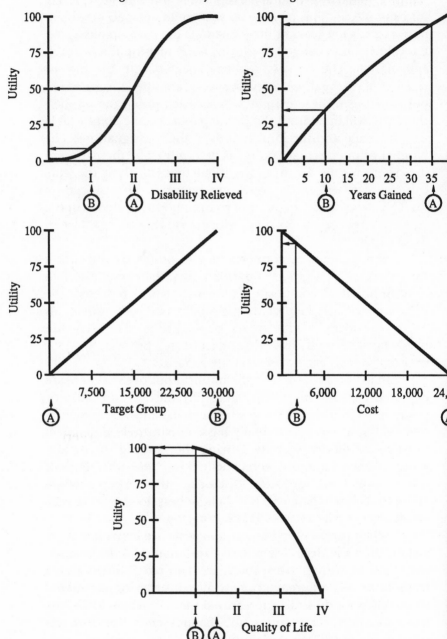

cedure summarized in Table 19.6, the decision maker first ranks each diagnosis in terms of the demand that a patient places on staff time. After levels of a criterion have clear-cut ordering, the decision maker systematically compares all of the categories. First, the decision maker finds the extreme levels of the criterion and assigns anchor values, 0 and 100, as shown in Table 19.6. Next, the remaining levels are reviewed to find the least and most important levels, and utility values between 0 and 100 are assigned to each. Each participant proceeds in this way, assigning utility values in pairs of least and most. This procedure reduces the information-processing demands of the task. If a group is used, the values are averaged and discussion proceeds as before, following the EDE format discussed in Chapter Seventeen. Final values for the utilities are determined by averaging the group's final selection of utility values.

Table 19.7 provides a format that can be used to order criterion levels. For instance, a treatment that eliminates one level of disability may be more important when the initial disability level was high than when it was low. In this case, the ranking and weighting procedure would systematically compare changes in each level by using a paired comparison approach (Chapter Seventeen) to get a ranking. The weighting proceeds as described above. Assuming that one level of disability relieved is the same as another, the disability criterion can also be treated as shown in Table 19.8. In this example, the ordering is clear, so the ranking step can be skipped.

Valuing Alternatives. Curves are drawn for both the categorical and continuously scaled criteria, as shown in Figures 19.5 and 19.8. These curves allow each alternative to be scored according to each criterion. (The utility curves in Figure 19.8 for the program priorities were constructed by consumer panels in a study of consumer preferences, according to the techniques described in this chapter.) Consider two possible programs from Table 19.9, Tetralogy of Fallot (A.3) and Hypertension (B.2). Values for these programs are drawn from Table 19.4 and located on each of the criterion's axis. The utility is read off the vertical axis in Figure 19.8.

Table 19.6. Procedure to Establish Utility Values for Criteria
with Unclear Ordering and Discrete Levels.

Procedure (Consider each diagnosis as an independent factor)

1. Rank diagnoses from least to most important.
2. Assign the most important a value of 100 and the least important a value of 0.
3. Find the second least important diagnosis and assign it a value larger than 0.
4. Find the second most important diagnosis and assign it a value smaller than 100 to depict its relative importance.
5. Repeat, comparing each diagnosis to the previous rankings.
6. Check for consistency (all ratios should be meaningful, no matter how large).

Diagnosis	Rank	Weight
Hyperbilirubinemia	1	0
Congenital anomaly		
R/O sepsis		
Prematurity		
PDA and hyperbilirubinemia		
Hyperbili and R/O sepsis		
RDS and hyperbili		
PDA		
RDS		
RDS and R/O sepsis		
PDA and R/O sepsis		
RDS and PDA		
RDS, PDA, and hyperbili		
PDA, hyperbili, and R/O sepsis		
RDS, PDA, and R/O sepsis		
BPD		
RDS, R/O sepsis, and hyperbili		
Meconium aspiration		
RDS, PDA, hyperbili, and R/O sepsis	19	100

Table 19.7. Utility Values for Criteria with Unclear Ordering
and Discrete Levels.

	Rank	Utility
4 levels relieved (Class V to Class I)	1	100
3 levels relieved (Class IV to Class I)		
(Class V to Class II)		
2 levels relieved (Class III to Class I)		
(Class IV to Class II)		
(Class V to Class III)		
1 level relieved (Class II to Class I)		
(Class III to Class II)		
(Class IV to Class III)		
(Class V to Class IV)		
0 levels relieved	11	0

Table 19.8. Utility Values for Criteria with Clear Ordering
and Discrete Levels.

Quality of Life	Utility
Class IV	0
Class III ½	
Class III	
Class II ½	
Class II	
Class I ½	
Class I	100

Table 19.9. Criteria Values for the Potential Programs.

	Years of Life Before Treatment	Years of Life After Treatment	Limitations Before Treatment	Limitations After Treatment	Incidence	Prevalence	Percent of Survival	Cost ($)
A. *Congenital Heart Disease*								
1. Ventricular septal defect	35	65	II	I	52	328	90	6,000
2. Ductus arteriosus	35	70	III	I	35	239	99	2,000
3. Tetralogy of Fallot	15	50	III	I or II	21	154	85	8,000
4. Transposition	1	45	IV	II	16	119	60	24,000
5. Atrial septal defect	65	72	II	I	14	97	99	6,000
6. Pulmonary stenosis and coarctation	34	70	III	II	27	87	97	4,000
7. Miscellaneous	—	—	—	—	41	7		
B. *Acquired Heart Disease*								
1. Rheumatic (valvular)								
a. Mytrial stenosis	45	65	III	I	—	5744	90	12,000
b. Aortic stenosis	50	68	III	II	—	2872	85	14,000
c. Combined	40	65	IV	II	—	2872	50	20,000
2. Hypertensive	55	65	I or II	I	—	30025	98	2,000
3. Metabolic (collagen, nutritional, thyrotic, bacterial)	30	70	III	I	—	14360	90	2,000
C. *Degenerate Heart Disease*								
1. Coronary artery disease (surgical treatment)	60	68	IV	II	—	28196	97	20,000
2. Vascular								
a. Peripheral	65	67	III	II	—	11488	95	4,000
b. Cerebral	65	68(?)	IV	III	—	5744	95	6,000

	Disability Relieved	Quality of Life	Years Gained	Target Group	Cost
Program A Tetralogy of Fallot	50	90	90	0	0
Program B Hypertension	5	100	30	100	85

Priorities are created by merging the utility values that describe the two program areas. These values are drawn from Figure 19.8. The priority scores for programs A and B are as follows:

Program A = (50 + 90 + 90 + 0 + 0)/5 = 230/5 = 46
Program B = 320/5 = 64

Adding these values to give an overall program priority score applies a LaPlace decision rule, which assumes that the criteria have equal weight. In most instances, this assumption cannot be made, and techniques to weight the criteria are needed to merge the utility values.

The same procedure is used for the bond rating example. Values for the criteria that describe a firm are entered into the curves in Figure 19.5. The utility values drawn from the curves can be averaged (with a LaPlace rule) to predict the bond rating for that firm. Alternatively, criteria weights can be determined with the techniques presented in Chapter Seventeen to differentiate among the criteria in terms of importance. Incorporating criteria weights produces a weighted average rating. To simplify this averaging, integers from 9 to 1 can be used in place of the bond rating categories (for example, AAA = 9, and so on). This procedure assumes that the ratings all have equal value increments between each category. This assumption is discussed in Chapter Twenty.

A Summary of Steps

The key steps in the procedure to deal with multiple criteria in tough decisions are selecting criteria, linking attributes to criteria, developing utility-criteria relationships, weighting attributes, weighting criteria, and computing a utility score for each alternative.

Step 1: Selecting Criteria. Some criteria, such as costs, are obvious, but others can be overlooked. To avoid the use of habitual decision criteria and to ensure that pertinent concerns are addressed, care must be taken in selecting criteria. Decision makers working alone or with the aid of staff can use partitioned thinking in generating criteria, as described in Chapter Sixteen. The decision maker ponders the objective and lists primary and secondary concerns. The group process techniques discussed in Chapter Fifteen can also be used to help uncover new criteria. This procedure often provides extensive lists of criteria that can be pruned by the Q-Sort technique, described in Chapter Seventeen.

Step 2: Linking Attributes to Criteria. Attributes can be derived from the features of an alternative. For instance, the attributes of a computer system, such as memory capacity and speed, provide useful features that help in selecting among competing systems. This type of attribute is often treated as a criterion. In other cases, attributes can provide somewhat redundant measures of a criterion. For instance, the criterion "management capability" can be measured by years of experience, supervisor's fitness reports, peer relations, and the like. Questions in a morale survey provide another example in which attributes must be merged into a criterion with the same tactics that are applied to merge criteria into an index of value. In complex valuations, several sets of attributes must be merged to form criteria that are used to capture the value of an alternative.

Step 3: Developing Criteria-Utility Relationships. Some criteria have a single measure (for example, cost). Other criteria can each have several attributes, and a utility curve must be prepared for each attribute (Edwards and Newman, 1982). In still other instances, several attributes that make up a criterion can be merged without resort to a utility curve, such as a survey of satisfaction that merges the response to various questions into an overall satisfaction score. Utility is equated with the average satisfaction score. Levels of this average satisfaction score are linked to a consequence factor to create a utility curve. A sketching approach for the construction of a utility curve was described for continuously scaled criteria (for example, years of life gained). For discrete criteria (for example, disability level) a rank-weight procedure is used.

Step 4: Weighting Attributes. Where a criterion has several attributes, a weight is developed for each attribute. The techniques described in Chapter Seventeen for criterion weighting are also used to weight attributes.

Step 5: Weighting Criteria. The importance (weights) of the criteria are determined with the techniques described in Chapter Seventeen.

Step 6: Computing Multiattribute Utility Scores. In the final step, scores for each criterion that depict the value of an alternative are drawn from utility curves. The criteria weights are multiplied by these scores to produce a utility score for each alternative. The alternative with the highest utility would be selected if the expected-value decision rule were used.

Key Points

1. Elimination by aspects and expected value provide two ways to deal with multiple criteria and incorporate them into the valuation of alternatives. Elimination by aspects is quick and efficient and is used for multicriteria short-fuse decisions. The expected-value approach provides a more precise way to assign values to alternatives and can deal with the uncertainty in tough decisions. The expected-value approach creates a valuative index that links the payoff of an alternative, measured by several criteria, to plausible future conditions.

2. In valuing alternatives with several criteria, a decision maker's key concern is the stability of preferences, expressed as criteria weights. Sensitivity analysis can be applied to criteria weights to treat the weights as assumptions that can be relaxed. This type of analysis determines alternatives that are sensitive and those that are insensitive to preferences expressed as weights. This assessment reveals condi-

tions under which each alternative is preferred as preferences about criteria weights shift.

3. The concept of utility allows a decision maker or expert to
    specify how preference or value changes with changes in the
    level of a criterion, such as satisfaction. This step is essential
    for situations in which increases in the level of a criterion
    may have no practical value, such as birth weight in the
    women-infants-children program. Techniques are available
    to draw utility curves that link value with changes in the
    level of a criterion to capture this relationship.

20

Using Decision Analysis to Foster Learning

This chapter shows how decisions can be analyzed to aid in learning. Decision analysis is used to infer norms and values, create training exercises, and uncover sources of conflict among decision makers. Both actual and simulated decisions are amenable to this kind of analysis. Actual decisions can be assessed by correlating choices that have been made with decision criteria that should have been used. For instance, rate hike decisions by an organization empowered to regulate utilities are made with criteria such as the utility's recent earnings, size of hike, and current rate of return. The regulatory body's decision to grant or not to grant the rate increase can be correlated with these criteria to determine their relative importance in rate hike decisions. For some decisions, archival information of this type is not available. To deal with this type of situation, simulated decisions with hypothetical choices can be used. Feasible options are defined according to the criteria, and decision makers are asked to make judgments. For both constructed and actual data bases, decisions are correlated with levels of the criteria in the decision by means of statistical techniques to identify the importance decision makers attached to each of the criteria. This type of analysis has been directed toward a variety of topics pertinent to decision making, including the thinking processes people use in judgmental tasks (Slovic, Fischhoff, and Lichtenstein, 1977), making predictions (Libby, 1976), simulating decision processes for training (Goldberg, 1968), evaluating policy questions (Gustafson and others, 1975), and exploring bias,

505

accuracy, and conflicts found in a decision process (Huber, 1974).

The inferred criteria weights have several uses. First, norms and the values that they imply can be identified. Making these values explicit helps one clarify assumptions and facilitate communication. Second, the protocol that decision makers contend should be applied often slips away without periodic review. Reflecting on a model that captures how decisions are actually made provides such a review. Finally, comparing differences in weights assigned to decision criteria by decision bodies or factions provides a vehicle for dealing with real or potential conflict among the groups or factions. In some instances, differences will prove to be overstated. In this case, a sensitivity analysis will reveal that these differences do not produce different decisions, suggesting that value differences have no practical significance. When value differences do influence choices, the debate can be focused on the magnitude of compromises that must be made by each faction to support each of the viable alternatives. Reflecting on the changes in values that are implied can be instructive and lead to a compromise. Figure 20.1 shows how these topics support the decision process.

Studying Decisions to Promote Learning

Decision makers must address three issues as they analyze decisions to promote learning. To address these issues, decision makers draw on their staff or other resources to carry out the required analyses. First, the decision maker must clarify how a decision was made in order to uncover hidden assumptions and how values influence or fail to influence choices. Second, a policy focus can be used to identify information needs, which is a critical step in understanding when decision aids, such as information systems, are necessary. The policy focus also provides a way to assess a decision process. Finally, the dilemmas of cognitive overload can be highlighted, posing problems that decision makers must contend with when making tough choices.

Figure 20.1. The Decision Process.

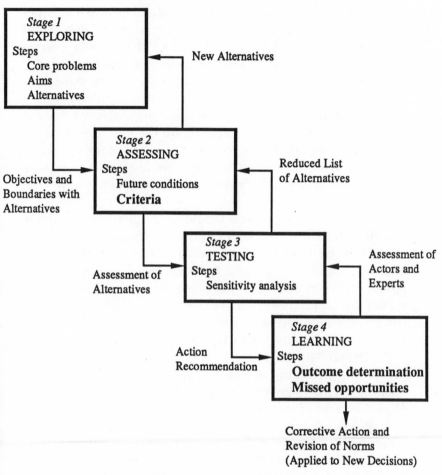

Note: Boldface type indicates topics addressed in this chapter.

Hidden Assumptions

Policymakers often debate the importance that should be attached to various criteria. For example, Fryback, Gustafson, and Detmer (1978) illustrate how a decision by federal policymakers to designate geographical areas as medically underserved was delayed by disputes about the importance of criteria such as infant mortality rates and numbers of physicians per one thousand population. The "need versus supply" debate was resolved when decision analysis showed that supply criteria advocates included need criteria in their decisions and vice versa. Both need and supply were implicitly used to make decisions by the need and supply factions. When members of each faction designated the level of need in hypothetical areas, the need-supply debate had no bearing on the decision of which areas were designated as high in need. Analysis of the simulated decision uncovered hidden assumptions, in this case, showing that the policymakers made similar choices, which resolved the conflict.

In other cases, criteria weighting by factions may differ and the differences may lead to different choices. The level of conflict can be lowered by focusing on differences in the weights and the justifications offered for each position. For instance, debates between various parties to regulatory decisions, such as a land use commission and a city council that disagree on zoning decisions, can be explored by comparison of differences in the criteria weights that each party applies to make a decision (Nutt, 1980a). The analysis of decisions sharpens arguments and provides a mediating device for working out disagreements. Spelling out the values of parties to a decision can create a focus on real instead of imagined differences.

A decision process can be assessed to identify hidden values or what is valued. For example, Nutt and Hurley (1981) measured the values that review agencies have attached to criteria stipulated by legislation to decide whether to allow an expansion in capacity or new services in the health care industry. Criteria that were deemed important and unimportant were identified. The importance that various groups attached to criteria in making decisions was compared to indicate the values of these groups, opening them up for discussion and analysis. Determining the extent to which extraneous factors, such as an applicant's bed size, influence a decision provides another type of assessment.

The analysis of decisions clarifies how a decision maker

deals with essential trade-offs. By segregating fact from value, such as the cost of an alternative and the importance of cost compared to other criteria, the analyst can explore how values dictate trade-offs in which valued criteria, such as cost and stakeholder satisfaction, must be balanced. Decision makers are often surprised to see how they carry out this balancing act.

Learning and training are promoted by reflecting on how decisions have been made. For example, Goldberg (1968) shows how radiologists improved their ability to select between a diagnosis of stomach ulcers and one of stomach cancer by systematically processing information gleaned from stomach X rays in a decision model. This approach provides the equivalent of a decision support system that can be used for applications as diverse as common stock assessment, bond rating, medical diagnosis, graduate school admission, and job selection (Dawes, 1975).

Policy Focus

The analysis of decisions makes ground rules clear to key participants. Two major benefits are realized. First, information needs are clarified. This clarification is an essential step in the design of management information systems and other mechanisms that support decision processes (Keen and Scott-Morton, 1978). Second, process consistency can be used to assess a decision process. This step is essential for situations in which limitations are imposed on the evaluation of decisions because the merits of nonselected alternatives are unknown. Examples include staffing, capital budgeting, and regulatory decisions. There is no way to know whether other staffing plans, capital budgets, and regulation options could have provided superior decisions.

Expert decision makers typically claim that a particular protocol should be used for decision making (Slovic, Fischhoff, and Lichtenstein, 1977). Despite this agreement, the protocol is seldom followed in practice (for example, Anderson, Dean, and Hammond, 1981). Physicians, for instance, claim to use a process called *differential diagnosis*. They claim they examine levels of several criteria to ensure that each exceeds a critical value before they take action. Studies of physician decisions show that information is processed one criterion at a time, not simultaneously, as the differential diagnosis protocol requires. Decision makers who seem to know how to make a decision cannot reliably process information in the way that their protocol demands.

Bootstrapping is offered for decision support in these instances. A model is built to capture the decision maker's protocol and used to support the decision-making process (Nutt, 1984a). The virtue of the model is its strict adherence to the protocol and ability to reliably process information. Variations of this approach are called *expert systems* and *artificial intelligence*. In each case, a decision support system is created (Keen and Scott-Morton, 1978). Its purpose is not to supplant the decision maker but to provide external memory and allow for sensitivity and other forms of analysis that can explore the ramifications of a decision before it is made. All decision support systems should have these capabilities.

Decision analysis also provides a way to assess a decision process (Nutt, 1980a). Decisions are correlated with criteria and extraneous factors. A reliable process will consistently approve of an action when important criteria are satisfied. If decisions differ when the same set of criteria are present, the process can be labeled capricious. Capricious decisions are hard to justify and defend, and they create a basis for legal action.

Dealing with Cognitive Overload

The procedures outlined in Chapters Thirteen and Nineteen lay out key steps used to select one alternative from several. To value the alternatives, both the likelihood of future conditions and the importance attached to criteria must be estimated. Establishing these likelihoods and criteria weights constitutes the subjective and inherently uncertain aspects of decision making. Procedures that help decision makers apply formal rules of choice were offered in Chapter Thirteen to overcome systematic errors inherent in estimating these factors. The analytical process merges fact and value so that information overloads and other cognitive limitations do not result in unreliable information processing.

Profiling Actual Decisions

To capture the way that decisions have been made, the decision outcome, such as approval or disapproval, is associated with facts that surround the decision. For example, the land use decisions of a city council, expressed as zoning changes, can be correlated with a developer's claims about providing jobs, the environmental impact, the character of the contiguous neighborhoods, and the developer's connections. The analysis reconstructs how the criteria were weighted to make the decision and the consistency with which the criteria were used in making the decision. Criteria weights reveal values, such as sacrificing environmental impact to jobs in zoning decisions. Consistency is one way to evaluate a decision process.

Decision analysis can be time-consuming. It is applied by staff members or consultants to significant decisions that occur repeatedly. As noted in Chapter Fourteen, the importance of these decisions calls for an understanding of both expected and actual decision maker performance. When this situation arises, an organization can gain considerable knowledge about how well its decision makers measure up by underwriting the costs of analysis. Managers should have a basic understanding of assessments that can be made and how to interpret them. The purpose of the following discussion is to describe the steps and results of decision analysis.

A variety of decisions have been successfully analyzed in this manner. For example, Goldberg (1970) derived the norms used by radiologists in diagnosing stomach cancer by having them read X rays from patients after surgery revealed their true condition. The radiologists examined each X ray and, using cues (criteria) that they contend are contained in an X ray, selected between a diagnosis of stomach cancer and a diagnosis of ulcers. Psychologists who use Minnesota Multiphasic Personality Index profiles to judge whether patients in a mental hospital are neurotic or paranoid, in order to provide a basis to grant weekend furloughs, can be assessed in the same manner (Gold-berg, 1968). In each case, a behavioral model of the decision maker(s) can be developed. The regression parameters in the model specify the importance decision makers have attached to criteria when making decisions. This type of model is helpful because it defines criteria, identifies criteria weights, specifies how criteria and weights were combined, and provides a way to evaluate a decision process by comparing predictions to outcomes.

The decision maker should be able to match the perfor-mance of the model by using it as a decision support device. This model provides a performance norm that decision makers should be able to meet. To evaluate a decision maker, or any group of decision makers, actual performance is compared to this norm. For example, the proportion of correct cancer diag-noses for radiologists or radiology departments could be com-puted with a comparison of simulated diagnostic decisions to actual outcomes and to the bootstrapped model. The com-parison to actual outcomes measures departures from perfor-mance ideals, and the comparison to the model measures depar-tures from attainable performance.

Profiling actual decisions requires three steps: specifying the form of the decision, identifying criteria and contextual factors that can express the values of the decision makers, and conducting statistical analyses that correlate criteria and con-textual factors with the decisions.

Form

A decision can be rendered in several ways. The most common rendering is yes-no or approve-disapprove. For in-stance, a regulatory body deciding on rate hikes proposed by a utility, or a city council making zoning decisions, typically has an approve-disapprove outcome. Some decisions are expressed in several ways. For example, a rate hike decision can be de-scribed as the amount of the hike that was granted in approved requests. Decisions in lawsuits such as malpractice claims (Nutt and Emswiler, 1979) can be expressed in terms of the amount of the award. A zero award or rate hike implies a loss or disapproval. Finally, some decisions are rendered as one of an ordered set of values. Examples include bond rating and staffing. In bond rating, the rating agencies, Moody's and Standard & Poor's, rate an applicant's bond by putting it in one of several categories that imply risk and thus interest called for by the market. Staffing decisions are expressed in units of time, such as hours.

Criteria and Contextual Factors

Criteria are identified by studying decision makers' protocols and asking decision makers to describe how they make decisions or by using external referents, such as legislation that stipulates criteria. Contextual factors are inferred from the situation and should *not* influence a decision. For example, the capital improvement plans of a firm are often made annually, in part by considering requests from work units (for example, divisions) in the form of proposed projects. The time since a division's last approved request for capital improvements should not influence whether the division's current request is approved, but it often does. Contextual factors also stem from an interest in exploring situational influences. For example, the year in which a decision was made may have special significance because of the entry or exit of regulatory controls. Airline route decisions provide an illustration.

Analysis

Statistical techniques are used to correlate criteria and contextual factors with decisions. Regression techniques are used to carry out this analysis. (Discussion of these techniques is beyond the scope of this text.) In the analysis, the decision is the dependent variable, and the criteria and contextual factors are the independent variables. Decisions expressed as approvals or disapprovals create a dichotomous dependent variable. (Variance can be explained by regression techniques as long as the proportion of yes-no decisions has less than an 80/20 split; see

Nerlove and Press, 1973. Discriminant analyses can also be used to build models of the approvals and disapprovals; see Nutt and Caswell, 1988.) Two key results of this analysis identify the importance attached to each criterion and contextual factor in decision making and the extent to which these factors can explain how a decision was made. Subsidiary questions are posed in the same way for various parties to the decision, such as factions in an organization or decision group.

Two cases are presented to illustrate how this type of analysis can be used. The first deals with an assessment of regulatory decision making. The case profiles decisions that were made by regulatory bodies charged by federal legislation to control the expansion of capacity in the health care system. The second identifies criteria and procedures used by Moody's and Standard & Poor's in their rating of revenue bonds for money markets. These cases were selected because they illustrate the kind of information that is required in actually conducting a decision analysis and the precision of assessments that such an analysis can provide. Both cases describe tough decisions because there is ambiguity and uncertainty in how the criteria were used to render a judgment.

A Regulation Case

Regulation in the health care industry was initiated in 1972 by federal legislation with the goal of preventing unwarranted capital expenditures and is still being used in most states. Under the legislation, providers, including nursing homes, hospitals, and community health centers, must receive approval before initiating a project that exceeds a cost threshold, requires more capacity, or involves a new service. The cost threshold was initially set at $100,000 and has been gradually increased to account for inflation and to reduce review activity and thereby review costs. The law made reimbursement for Medicare and Medicaid services contingent upon this approval. Most providers receive a significant proportion of their revenues from Medicare and Medicaid, so approval has been a practical necessity.

Proposals are submitted by the applicant to the appropriate health system agency (HSA) and to the state health planning and development agency (SHPDA). Review is carried out separately by each agency. The staffs of both agencies review the application to determine its completeness. Consultation with the applicant is carried out locally by the HSA. This initial review may lead the applicant to withdraw the application or to modify it.

When the application is complete, the clock begins running on the review process, which must be finished within a stipulated period, usually 120 days. Typically, review in an HSA moves through a subarea committee and a project review committee before going to the HSA board of directors. In each review, the findings and recommendations from previous reviews are considered. This process varies among HSAs. For instance, staff members make formal recommendations in some HSAs, while in others they merely provide information. The findings of an HSA are submitted to the SHPDA as a recommendation. State review groups typically receive documentation from the HSAs and analysis from their own staff from which to make a decision. After the SHPDA decision, both judicial and administrative appeal processes are available to the applicant, and both are often used.

Data for the study were drawn from files of a state agency that conducted capital expenditure review (Nutt and Hurley, 1981). Two project categories, CT scanners and bed expansions, were selected for analysis because each was relatively homogeneous, with relatively large numbers of projects, and had some history of disapproval. Scanners and bed expansions presented widely different types of review decisions. Scanners represented new technology at the time of the study, and bed expansions represented generic capacity expansion in the health care industry.

Decision analysis was used to evaluate the review process, correlating decisions with factors that surrounded them (Nutt and Hurley, 1981). Several questions were posed in the study, including the reliability or consistency of the process, the criteria used, and the amount of agreement among review groups.

A reliable decision process will consistently approve and disapprove comparable applications that have similar criteria values. If decisions differ when the same set of facts is presented, the process can be labeled capricious. Capriciousness seems an excellent basis for appeal by an applicant. In an appeal, the applicant can contend that the project meets criteria to the same extent as other approved projects. Decisions can be defended by a demonstration of consistency. Reliability can be measured by the percent variance explained in a regression that treats decisions for comparable projects as the dependent variable and values for criteria and contextual factors as the independent variables. Agencies with a role in decisions can be compared in terms of their reliability, and the absolute level of reliability of the decision process can be compared to standards found in the decision analysis literature.

Review agencies' values can be measured by the weights they attach to legislatively stipulated criteria when making decisions. A criterion such as utilization is deemed important when the level of utilization in approved and disapproved projects is significantly different. Criteria can be ranked according to their statistical significance, to depict importance. The rankings of criteria used by each review group indicate the values held by these groups. By considering the criteria viewed as important by one agency and not by another, applicants can draw inferences. The average values of significant criteria in approved, as compared to disapproved, projects suggest which standards are being used, which opens them up to review and discussion.

Finally, the review process can be tested to determine the extent to which legislative criteria or contextual factors influence a decision. Ideally, contextual factors, such as an applicant's size, should have much less importance than the criteria. Collectively, this information provides an assessment of the review process and offers guidance for its improvement.

Two strategies were used to determine measures for each of the legislatively stipulated criteria (need, staffing, cost containment, economic feasibility, and quality of care) as they apply to CT scanners and bed expansion reviews. Agency staff were interviewed to isolate information they considered in the review process. At the same time, the applications were carefully reviewed to identify the level of quantification and clarity of this same information. These steps were taken to verify that the decision makers attempted to use pertinent information and that this information was available. The measures identified for the review criteria are summarized in Table 20.1.

Two dependent variables were defined: SHPDA decisions and HSA board recommendations. The independent variables were made up of legislatively stipulated criteria and contextual factors. To obtain approval, applicants' projects had to demonstrate need, show adequate staffing and feasible financing, avoid inflationary effects in the pricing of services, and demonstrate that quality could be maintained or enhanced. Applicants had to decide how best to defend their projects by discussing each of these criteria in their applications.

In the study, contextual factors were collected to determine how variables external to the process influenced the decision. These factors included applicant characteristics, review factors, and characteristics of the region. The applicant was described by bed size, a service intensity index, and percent occupancy. Review factors included the year that a decision was made, the duration of the review process, and the reviewer who developed documentation used in the review process. Characteristics that described the region included measures of urbanness and population density. The decisions and values for the criteria were taken from each application.

Profiling the Decisions

The approval rates from the review groups were compared and found to be comparable but not identical (see Tables 20.2, 20.3). The SHPDA approved a higher proportion of CT scanner projects than the HSA did. The approval rates for bed projects were comparable, but the SHPDA and HSAs did not always agree on which projects should be approved.

The number of decisions by the SHPDA that overturned recommendations by HSAs elaborates these differences. Eleven percent of the decisions represented overturns. To explore these

Table 20.1. Measures for Project Review Criteria.

| Criteria | Criteria Measures | |
	CT Scanners	Bed Expansions
	Common Measures	
Need	Scanners per 1,000 HSA population	Beds per 1,000 HSA population
	Number of scans in second year	Occupancy by third year
	Other Measures	
	Presence of written standards to guide review	Number of new beds proposed
	Consistency of HSA decision with standards	Type of beds (acute; special)
	Special purpose (none; teaching and/or research)	Faculty (expansion; satellite; new)
Staffing	Professional staffing (needed; not needed)	No information
	Number of nonprofessional staff to be recruited	
	Common Measures	
Economic Feasibility	Project cost	Project cost
	Source of funds (cash reserve; lease; loan)	Source of funds
	Other Measures	
	Margin or markup	
	Common Measures	
Cost Containment	Shared service attempts (none; use attempts by others; joint)	Shared service
	Competing applications (one; two or more)	Competing applications
	Other Measures	
	Charges per scan	
	Cost containment documentation (missing; asserted; attempts to measure)	
Quality Improvement	No information	No information

Table 20.2. Mean Values of Review Criteria for CT Scanners.

		SHPDA		HSA	
	N	Approved	Disapproved	Approved	Disapproved
	41	34	7	32	8
Total					
Need Criteria					
Special purpose					
None	30	77%	23%ᵃ	72%	28%ᵃ
Teaching/research	11	100%	0%	100%	0%
Conformity to HSA standards					
No	8	63%	37%ᵃ	50%	50%ᵃ
Yes	33	88%	12%	88%	12%
Written standards					
No	15	73%	27%	64%	36%
Yes	26	88%	12%	88%	12%
Number of scans in second year		2,997	2,335ᵃ	3,000	2,649ᵃ
Scanner density		2.0	3.3	1.9	3.75ᵃ
Staffing Criteria					
Professional staff					
None	30	87%	13%	86%	14%
Some	11	73%	27%	81%	19%ᵃ
Nonprofessional added		1.3	1.9ᵃ	1.4	1.7
Economic Feasibility					
Project cost		$574,000	$629,000	$581,000	$616,000
Source of funds					
Reserves	22	77%	23%	64%	36%
Lease	15	87%	13%	81%	19%
Loan	4	100%	0%	73%	27%
Margin		21%	2%ᵃ	22%	4%ᵃ
Cost Containment					
Shared service					
None	10	50%	50%ᵃ	40%	60%ᵃ
Letters	28	96%	4%	96%	4%
Joint application	3	67%	33%	67%	33%
Competing application					
None	37	84%	16%ᵃ	80%	20%ᵃ
Two or more	4	50%	50%	50%	50%
Charges per scan		$133	$137	$129	$141
Cost containment documentation					
None	1	0%	100%	0%	100%
Asserted	34	85%	15%	85%	15%
Quantified	6	83%	17%	67%	33%

ᵃ Statistically significant difference, p<.05.

Table 20.3. Mean Value for Review Criteria for Bed Expansions.

Criteria/Measures	N	SHPDA		HSA	
		Approved	Disapproved	Approved	Disapproved
Number of Projects	17	9	8	8	8
Need Criteria					
Beds per 1,000 population		4.4	4.6	4.3	4.6[a]
Projected occupancy in 3 years		86%	87%	87%	87%
New beds		42 beds	136 beds[a]	67 beds	115 beds
Service					
Special	12	58%	42%	45%	55%
Acute	5	40%	60%	60%	40%
Facility					
Expansion	11	82%	18%[a]	70%	30%[a]
Satellite	3	0%	100%	33%	67%
New	3	0%	100%	0%	100%
Staffing (none available)					
Economic Feasibility					
Project cost		$4,000,000	$15,000,000[a]	$4,000,000	$16,000,000[a]
Source of funds					
Reserves	2	0%	100%	0%	100%
Lease	1	100%	0%	100%	0%
Loan	14	50%	50%	50%	50%
Cost Containment					
Shared services					
None	3	0%	100%	0%	100%[a]
Letters	12	69%	31%	58%	42%
Joint	1	0%	100%	100%	0%
Competing applications					
No	13	64%	36%[a]	54%	46%
Yes	3	0%	100%	33%	67%

[a] Statistically significant differences, p<.05.

differences, overturns were categorized as positive or negative. A positive overturn would change a disapproval to an approval, whereas a negative overturn would do the opposite. Overall, overturns were evenly split: 50 percent positive and 50 percent negative. Seventy-five percent of the CT scanner overturns were positive. In contrast, only 25 percent of the bed expansion projects had a positive reversal. The SHPDA was found to encourage more CT scanners and discourage more bed projects than HSAs. This suggests that the SHPDA sought to make new technology available and attempted to constrain generic capacity. Some contend that this posture by the SHPDA led to a proliferation of scanners. The HSAs' attitude was to constrain the growth of all resources, although some — specifically HSAs in rural areas — found it difficult to deny bed expansions.

Values Expressed as Decision Criteria

Criteria and contextual factors were screened to determine the importance of each. The screening sorted projects into approval and disapproval categories and then compared the distribution of values for each criterion and contextual factor that fell into these two categories. Statistical significance for each sort was determined. This analysis produced a ranking of factors based on their statistical significance.

The rankings can be interpreted in two ways. First, the objectivity of the review process is suggested by the proportion of criteria to contextual factors found to be important. Ideally, the legislatively stipulated criteria should dominate. A second interpretation stems from differences in how criteria were weighted by the review groups. When the SHPDA and HSAs use the same criteria, their decision processes should be comparable.

The ranking of factors important in CT scanner decisions is shown below:

SHPDA Decision Criteria
1. Shared services (cost containment)
2. Margin (economic feasibility)

3. Competing applications (cost containment)
4. Population density (contextual)
5. Special purpose (need)
6. Conformance to standards (need)
7. Nonprofessional staff (staffing)
8. Projected scans (need)

HSA Decision Criteria
1. Duration (contextual)
2. Shared services (cost containment)
3. Conformity to standards (need)
4. Scanner density (need)
5. Applicant bed size (contextual)
6. Special purpose (need)
7. Margin (economic feasibility)
8. Year (contextual)
9. Professional staff (staffing)
10. Competing applications (cost containment)

The factors influencing CT scanner decisions were largely dictated by the decision criteria. Seven of the eight factors that influence SHPDA decisions and seven of the ten factors used by the HSAs were based on legislatively stipulated criteria. The dominant consideration in both review processes was cost containment, followed by need. Cost containment was measured by the applicant's commitment to share services, and competition among hospitals was measured by more than one attempt by applicants to provide the same service. The SHPDA and HSA review processes stressed need measures. Both viewed "conformity to HSA standards" and "special-purpose use" as important. Differences cropped up in terms of utilization, defined for CT scanners as "projected scans," and capacity, expressed as "scanner density." Finally, there was substantial agreement between the SHPDA and HSAs in terms of the criteria used. Seven of the eight criteria measures that influenced the decisions reached were used by both the SHPDA and HSAs.

Factors that influenced a bed expansion decision were ranked as follows:

SHPDA Decision Criteria
1. Facility (need)
2. Number of beds (need)
3. Project cost (economic feasibility)
4. Competing applications (cost containment)

HSA Decision Criteria
1. Facility (need)
2. Project cost (economic feasibility)
3. Shared services (cost containment)
4. Beds-to-population ratio (need)

The same general conclusions can be drawn from this analysis. Only legislatively stipulated criteria influenced bed project decisions. On the basis of their decisions, HSAs and the SHPDA both ranked "type of facility" requested by the applicant very high, and both used cost as a measure of economic feasibility. Differences cropped up in terms of the way need and cost containment were measured. Number of new beds was the key factor in the SHPDA decisions, whereas the beds-to-population ratio was used by HSAs as a measure of need. Cost containment was measured by the state agency in terms of competing applications, and shared services served as a cost containment measure in the HSA reviews.

Decision Norms

Decision norms or standards can be inferred from the average values of the criteria measures for approved and disapproved projects. A listing of these values is shown in Tables 20.2 and 20.3.

Assessing the Decision Process

Regulatory decisions cannot be validated because there is no way to tell whether a disapproved project would have had good or bad effects. When faced with this situation, decision analysts use tests of reliability (Fisher, 1979). Reliability measures the extent to which a decision process produces a consistent result when comparable information is considered. In decision analysis, reliability is measured by percent variance explained in a multiple regression that correlates the values for the review criteria with the decisions reached. The percent variance explained can be interpreted by the use of both relative and absolute tests. Relative tests compare the level of reliability among the various review groups. Absolute tests compare the percent variance explained (R^2) to norms found in the decision analysis literature. The R^2 values for the multiple regression equations are shown below:

Decision Group	CT Scanners	Bed Expansions
SHPDA	60 percent	68 percent
HSA	64 percent	65 percent

These data suggest that the differences in reliability between the state and the local review agencies were minor. The variance explained compares favorably with norms found in the decision analysis literature. Generally, decision processes have 60 to 70 percent of the variance explained, so values in this range provide a norm (Slovic, Fischhoff, and Lichtenstein, 1977). This norm, however, is based on an assessment of individual decisions, not a decision group or an entire organization, as attempted by this study. Considering this qualification, the decision process appeared to be reliable.

The Bond Rating Case

Hospital construction has been debt-financed since 1960 (Cleverley and Nutt, 1984). The dominant source of financing has been tax-exempt revenue bonds. By 1980, tax-exempt financing made up 50 percent of all hospital construction requirements.

The interest rate that hospitals pay for borrowed funds is based on an investor's perception of risk. Risk can be categorized into the following four factors: default risk, interest rate risk, purchasing power risk, and marketability risk. Of these four factors, only default risk is related directly to the borrower's operating conditions, both current and projected, and to the specific provisions of the bond issue. The assessment of default risk has considerable impact on the borrower's cost.

Investors rely upon credit ratings issued by the national rating agencies Moody's and Standard & Poor's to assess default risk. The effect that credit ratings have on the interest rates of tax-exempt bonds is summarized below:

Moody's	Standard & Poor's	Interest Rate
Aaa	AAA	5.59%
Aa	AA	7.15
A	A	8.13
Baa	BBB	8.97

On a bond issue of $25 million, the difference between an Aa and an A rating could have cost a hospital $250,000 per year. Any security receiving a rating lower than Baa or BBB is assumed to be below investment grade. The market for securities with ratings below investment grade is reduced significantly. The regulatory policies controlling investment funds, such as retirement plans and commercial banks, often prohibit such investments, viewing them as too risky. Moody's uses six rating categories for investment-grade bonds: Aaa, Aa, A', A, Baa', and Baa. Standard & Poor's also uses six categories but labels them differently: AAA, AA, A + , A, BBB + , and BBB. These ratings are treated as equivalent by financial analysts. Ratings for hospital revenue bonds typically fall between Aa-AAA and Baa-BBB.

Data were taken from Moody's municipal credit reports for hospital bonds and rated from 1974 through 1977. Abstracts of 165 reports were drawn up to identify the rating assigned by Moody's as well as other indicators that appeared to influence the rating process. The Standard & Poor's rating was taken from the *Standard & Poor's Municipal Report.*

Analysis determined the degree of association between the bond rating, treated as a dependent variable, and criteria

used by the rating agencies in rendering a rating, the independent variables. The bond ratings were correlated with the criteria to determine the extent to which the ratings could be
explained by the criteria. The data were analyzed with an all-
possible-subsets stepwise regression to identify the best predictors (criteria) for each decision model. A multiple regression was
used to determine the importance of each predictor in the regression equation. The importance of criteria in the model was
measured with F-tests of statistical significance. The percent variance explained by the Moody's and Standard & Poor's decision
models provides a measure of the extent to which the criteria can
explain the bond ratings by Moody's and Standard & Poor's.

The scale for the dependent variable was defined by the
categories in which a rating agency places a bond. To permit
analysis, these rating categories were converted to a scale with
values ranging from 1 to 9, with the higher values associated
with a higher bond rating. To test the properties of this scale, a
comparison between the letter rating and its interest rate was
made for each rating category. The differences between ratings
were found to be proportional, with the exception of the AAA
category. In this case, there was a disproportionate change in
interest rate from the AA to the AAA category. However, there
were no AAA ratings in the data, so this nonlinearity could be
ignored. As a result, integers could be used to construct an
interval scale to represent the bond ratings categories in the
analysis, which permitted the use of parametric statistical
techniques.

Decision Criteria

Criteria used by rating agencies fell into three categories:
hospital financial, hospital nonfinancial, and bond indenture.
These categories were identified from a review of existing bond
rating literature and from discussions with personnel at
Moody's, Standard & Poor's, and investment banking firms.

Financial Criteria

Financial variables included liquidity, debt, profitability,
and coverage. Profitability and coverage were identified by bond

rating personnel as the most important. The following seven financial variables were used:

1. *Peak debt historical coverage* is a coverage ratio that indicates the ability of a hospital to meet the maximum debt service on the new issue from present or existing cash flow. It is defined as the ratio of the present year historical cash flow, before interest expense, to the estimated maximum annual principal and interest on all outstanding bonds and the bonds to be issued. A value greater than 1 implies less risk because no increase in cash flow is required to meet the maximum debt service on the new bond issue.

2. *Peak debt first-year coverage* is a prospective coverage ratio. It is defined as the ratio of estimated cash flow, before interest expense during the first full year following completion of the construction program, to the estimated maximum annual principal and interest on all outstanding bonds and on the bonds to be issued. The measure indicates the ability of the organization to cover its maximum debt service on the new bond issue in its first year of operation after the construction program is complete.

3. *Net take down* is a profitability measure, defined as the ratio of present period cash flow plus interest to revenue. Larger values of this ratio imply greater profitability and thus better debt repayment potential.

4. *Sales to net fixed assets* is a profitability measure defined as the ratio of present period sales or revenue to net fixed assets. Higher values imply better use of capital in generating revenue and may be regarded as a measure of efficiency.

5. *Cash flow change* is a profitability measure that attempts to measure historical variability in cash flow. For this study, three years of historical data were available. The measure of cash flow change was defined as the ratio of present year cash flow to average cash flow in the preceding two years. A value greater than 1 implies cash flow growth. However, very large values for this ratio may imply some manipulation by the organization to dress up its financial statements in anticipation of new financing.

6. *Net working capital to sales* is a liquidity measure that indicates the proportion of current year revenue held in net working capital. It is defined as the ratio of present period net working capital (current assets less current liabilities) to present period sales or revenue. Values that are "very low" indicate little liquidity and thus suggest some short-term risk. Conversely, values that are too high may imply an overinvestment in lower-earning liquid assets.

7. *Debt per bed* is a debt ratio defined as the amount of debt per bed currently outstanding. Higher values for this ratio indicate that the organization may have more risk because of its greater indebtedness. However, interpretation of this measure must be made in conjunction with debt service coverage. Organizations with heavy debt may still carry less risk because of better debt service coverage ability.

Nonfinancial Criteria

Both rating agency personnel and the bond rating literature contend that nonfinancial variables are important in rating decisions. The classes of variables most often cited were utilization, medical staff characteristics, major third-party sources of operating funds, rate control agencies, socioeconomic characteristics of the market area, competitive position of the hospital, management ability, and accreditations. All agree that hospital bed size has considerable importance. The following eight measures were used to capture these criteria:

1. *Beginning beds.* The organization's beginning bed size was selected because it is unaffected by inflationary adjustments. For example, the total asset value of a hospital will be affected by the average age of its physical plant. Newer facilities will have higher values even though no absolute differences in size may exist. Larger hospitals should have better ratings because risk and size are believed to be inversely related.

2. *Bed occupancy.* Utilization of existing facilities is a measure of

current need. Hospitals with low bed occupancy may not have an adequate demand for their services and perhaps less need for expansion or replacement.

3. *Relative occupancy.* A measure of a hospital's competitive position within its market area, called *relative occupancy*, is defined as the ratio of the hospital's current occupancy to the average occupancy of all other hospitals in its market area. A value greater than 1 indicates better relative utilization and thus a better competitive position.

4. *Percentage of Medicaid revenue.* A measure of the hospital's relative reliance on Medicaid as a source of operating revenue, the percentage of Medicaid revenue is defined as the ratio of Medicaid revenue to total revenue. As the percentage of Medicaid revenue increases, the perceived risk of the hospital also increases. In the past, Medicaid payments have been subject to delays and underpayment because of financial difficulties in some of the states processing the payments. Medicaid pays only allowed costs, which eliminates any margin of profit that could improve debt service coverage. A large percentage of Medicaid patients suggests that the hospital operates in an economically depressed area. Such hospitals often have large write-offs stemming from the provision of charity care.

5. *Location.* The increasing importance and incidence of state rate control organizations was thought to have a negative influence on risk assessment. A state rate control system reduces the profitability of hospitals. Bond rating agency personnel singled out the state of New York as a case of adverse rate control effects. To test the importance of rate control, a binary-valued factor was defined, with two levels that determined whether the hospital was or was not in New York State.

6. *Status.* Religious affiliations may also affect the perceived riskiness of a hospital. Religious affiliation may reduce the inherent risk of default because such an affiliation can provide supplemental funding in a financially distressed period. A religious affiliation may also imply linkage with a larger system of hospitals and thus some spreading of risk

among its members. To recognize this possible impact, a variable called *status* was defined, with two levels: church- and nonchurch-affiliated.

7. *Market share.* Another variable used to measure competitive position, called *market share*, was defined as the ratio of hospital patient days to total patient days provided in all hospitals in the market area. Larger values of this variable would imply a more dominant position, or a monopolistic position, and thus less risk.

8. *Expense per patient day.* One intangible factor mentioned frequently by bond rating personnel was management capability. They mentioned days in accounts receivable, budgetary systems, management engineering activities, presence of internal auditor, full-time employee equivalents per patient day, and expense per patient day as measures they used to determine management capability. Of these measures, only expense per patient day could be drawn from the data set.

Bond Indenture

Subordination status, the presence of other creditors, did not occur for bonds in the study. This factor may be important for hospitals with numerous creditors. Two bond indenture provisions were included.

1. *Depreciation reserve.* A depreciation reserve requirement is an additional burden placed upon the borrower. The borrower is required to set aside in a trust fund specified sums of money over and above the normal debt service requirements. This fund provides a stable source of funds for future capital replacement, which tends to reduce the risk of default. A depreciation reserve requirement should reduce risk. But only the weaker hospitals would be required to maintain a depreciation reserve. Thus, there may be a negative relationship between the existence of a depreciation reserve and financial strength. This criterion determined

whether or not hospitals were required to establish a depreciation reserve.

2. *Percentage term financing.* Typically, the longer the payment period of a loan, the greater the risk of default. Most hospital tax-exempt revenue bonds are characterized by two patterns of repayment, a serial and a term portion. The serial portion provides for an annual (or semiannual) amortization of the principal, whereas the term portion provides for a lump sum payment at maturity. A higher risk, and thus a lower rating, was expected for the term payment mode. This criterion was measured as the ratio of term principal to the total amount borrowed.

Contextual Factors

Two of the more important contextual factors were thought to be the bond underwriter and the feasibility consultant. Certain feasibility consultants (usually Big Eight CPA firms) may provide better estimates of future financial performance than others. Also, there was some feeling that certain underwriters may have a political advantage with the rating agencies in securing favorable ratings for their issues. Unfortunately, no information was available to test the influence of these factors.

Values Expressed in the Criteria

Some of the criteria identify ways for the hospital anticipating a rating to enhance its position. Others represent constraints because they can be altered only in the long term, if at all. For instance, the hospital can alter the terms surrounding the indenture, such as depreciation reserve and percent term financing, more easily than bed size. In other instances, the hospital may conclude that its financial position makes it virtually impossible to obtain acceptable financing via revenue bonds. Location illustrates a constraint: Hospitals in certain areas of the country find it easier to finance with tax-exempt revenue bonds.

The analysis identified criteria used by each rating agency

in its rating decisions. Seven criteria were found to explain 62 percent of the variance in the bond ratings of both rating agencies.

The ranking of criteria for Moody's was:

1. Expenses per patient day
2. Net take down
3. Beginning beds
4. Cash flow change
5. Peak debt first year
6. Sales to net fixed assets
7. Bed occupancy

For Standard & Poor's, the ranking was:

1. Beginning beds
2. Expenses per patient day
3. Percent Medicaid revenue
4. Depreciation reserve
5. Net take down
6. Peak debt first year
7. Debt per bed

Four of the seven criteria used by the rating agencies were identical, suggesting that the agencies used very similar, but not identical, rationales in rating hospital revenue bonds. Regression results for different time periods had striking similarities. The key variables remain the same, suggesting that dominant criteria were identified.

The rating agencies appear to provide an incentive for bigness in the hospital industry. Two criteria, beginning beds and expense per patient day, were found to be significant in both the Moody's and Standard & Poor's rating decisions. Since higher expense per patient day values are usually associated with higher intensity of service, it would appear that the rating agencies have provided an incentive for growth in full-service hospitals. This incentive seems consistent with public policy, and it may be a more effective way to encourage efficiency in the hospital industry than that provided for in capacity regulation (see previous case). However, there is no evidence that significant operating efficiencies stem from the scale of hospital operations. Most excess beds exist in urban areas, where the typical full-service hospital is also located.

Second, the rating agencies appear to place an emphasis on both current and future profitability. Net take down and peak debt first-year coverage were key criteria in both rating models. This emphasis on profitability is understandable, since profits ultimately determine the ability of a hospital to meet its debt service obligations. However, one of the rating agencies, Standard & Poor's, does not consider prior profitability. Earnings variability is a significant factor in rating corporate issues. Its absence in the Standard & Poor's model was curious.

Note that Tables 20.4 and 20.5 indicate a positive average change in cash flow for all rating categories of both rating agencies. This would imply that in the year preceding debt issuance, hospitals apparently increased, by rather sizable amounts, their cash flow from operations. It is likely this was accomplished by increasing the prices charged for most hospital services. Furthermore, there is a significant positive correlation between cash change and net take down. This implies that hospitals with high current levels of net take down apparently reached that position in the most recent year. Greater increases in current cash flow from prior years are associated with higher ratings in the Standard & Poor's model (Table 20.5).

Standard & Poor's emphasis on current profitability may be justifiable. Perhaps the most recent year of actual operating performance is the best indicator of future debt service ability. Prior profit experiences may not be relevant to future performance if the hospital can sustain its current-year profits into the future. However, if there is some association between prior years' profits and future profit levels, Standard & Poor's may be over-emphasizing current performance in its rating of hospital issues. From the hospital's perspective, hospital administrators were enticed to emphasize current financial performance.

Factors such as the ratio of long-term debt to total capitalization and the average age of the medical staff—which

Table 20.4. Decision Rules Implied by Moody's Ratings.

Criteria	Baa	Baa'	A	A'	Aa
Peak debt historical coverage	0.53 (6)[a]	0.48 (13)	0.94 (74)	1.36 (55)	2.29 (13)
Peak debt first-year coverage	1.61 (5)	1.76 (11)	1.96 (69)	2.34 (47)	3.30 (11)
Debt per bed	$56,088 (6)	$63,079 (13)	$52,045 (75)	$42,405 (55)	$32,653 (14)
Net take down	0.11 (6)	0.08 (13)	0.10 (75)	0.11 (55)	0.12 (14)
Cash flow change	1.39 (5)	1.13 (12)	1.54 (70)	1.43 (49)	1.40 (13)
Net working capital to sales	0.14 (3)	0.19 (9)	0.29 (70)	0.31 (50)	0.20 (14)
Sales to net fixed assets	2.42 (3)	2.85 (9)	1.61 (70)	1.34 (50)	1.28 (14)
Beginning beds	98 (6)	237 (13)	282 (76)	465 (54)	789 (14)
Bed occupancy	0.72 (6)	0.76 (13)	0.81 (75)	0.81 (55)	0.85 (14)
Relative occupancy	0.94 (6)	0.99 (13)	1.04 (73)	1.04 (53)	1.05 (14)
Percentage of Medicaid revenue	0.13 (5)	0.09 (11)	0.07 (65)	0.08 (46)	0.06 (14)
Location	1.00 (6)	1.00 (13)	1.01 (76)	1.04 (55)	1.00 (14)
Status	1.00 (6)	1.00 (13)	1.17 (76)	1.25 (55)	1.29 (14)
Expense per patient day	$141 (5)	$138 (13)	$140 (75)	$148 (52)	$177 (14)
Market share	0.22 (6)	0.41 (13)	0.40 (74)	0.37 (53)	0.57 (14)
Depreciation reserve	0.83 (6)	0.62 (13)	0.52 (75)	0.44 (55)	0.29 (14)
Percentage term financing	0.64 (5)	0.68 (12)	0.60 (66)	0.53 (53)	0.59 (12)

[a] Value in parentheses represents the number of observations used to compute the mean.

Table 20.5. Decision Rules Implied by Standard & Poor's Ratings.

Criteria	BBB	BBB+	A	A+	AA
Peak debt historical coverage	0.80 (2)[a]	0.62 (18)	.88 (62)	1.38 (57)	1.65 (11)
Peak debt first-year coverage	1.38 (1)	1.85 (16)	1.96 (58)	2.33 (51)	2.86 (9)
Debt per bed	$52,266 (2)	$58,916 (19)	$52,675 (62)	$45,226 (57)	$33,429 (12)
Net take down	0.16 (2)	0.10 (18)	0.10 (62)	0.11 (57)	0.11 (12)
Cash flow change	1.13 (2)	1.35 (18)	1.35 (57)	1.39 (54)	1.42 (11)
Net working capital to sales	0.10 (1)	0.33 (12)	0.29 (59)	0.30 (53)	0.20 (12)
Sales to net fixed assets	1.39 (1)	1.73 (12)	1.80 (59)	1.42 (53)	1.21 (12)
Beginning beds	0.85 (2)	188 (19)	262 (62)	463 (56)	748 (12)
Bed occupancy	0.57 (2)	0.76 (18)	0.81 (62)	0.82 (57)	0.87 (12)
Relative occupancy	0.77 (2)	1.01 (18)	1.05 (61)	1.04 (54)	1.07 (12)
Percentage of Medicaid revenue	0.19 (1)	0.10 (18)	0.07 (51)	0.07 (49)	0.06 (12)
Location	1.00 (2)	1.00 (19)	1.00 (62)	1.01 (57)	1.00 (12)
Status	1.00 (2)	1.16 (19)	1.16 (62)	1.21 (57)	1.33 (12)
Expense per patient day	$147 (2)	$141 (17)	$142 (62)	$149 (54)	$175 (12)
Market share	0.06 (2)	0.40 (18)	0.40 (62)	0.35 (54)	0.32 (12)
Depreciation reserve	0.50 (2)	0.58 (19)	0.55 (62)	0.51 (57)	0.17 (12)
Percentage term financing	0.22 (2)	0.70 (17)	0.63 (55)	0.54 (38)	0.56 (10)

[a] Value in parentheses represents the number of observations used to compute the mean.

investment bankers as well as rating agency personnel contend should be important — did not appear in either decision model. Rating agents, who are inundated with information before and during the rating session, are seemingly unable to use all of the information they would like to use. Whether this is caused by information overload or other factors, bond ratings were not influenced by these criteria.

Public financing programs seem to affect the Standard & Poor's bond ratings. The percentage of Medicaid financing was found to be a significant criterion in the Standard & Poor's rating. This evaluation was probably justifiable in light of the nature of Medicaid reimbursement formulas and their deleterious influence on hospital profitability. Negative associations between the percentage of Medicaid revenue and peak debt historical, peak debt first year, and net take down were observed. This might imply a causal relationship between profitability and Medicaid revenue in the hospital, and it could explain why the percent of Medicaid criterion was not found in the Moody's model.

To the extent that bond ratings direct the flow of capital and determine the cost of that capital, the decision analysis findings suggest the need to reevaluate Medicaid reimbursement policies. Hospitals that service large Medicaid populations increasingly find themselves closed out of the private capital markets. Direct subsidies by the government became a reality in the late 1980s.

Decision Norms

Tables 20.4 and 20.5 indicate the average value of criterion measures that were found in bonds that had investment-grade ratings. These norms or standards can be interpreted in two ways. First, the norms seem consistent. Most values decrease or increase in the manner predicted in the discussion of criteria. Second, the criterion values provide a way for a hospital to gauge how rating agencies will react to a proposed bond.

Profiling and Assessing the Decisions

Both Moody's and Standard & Poor's had 62 percent of the variance in their decisions explained by decision criteria. These values fall within an acceptable range, identified in the previous case as between 60 and 70 percent.

To determine the consistency with which information was used, values for each of the seven criteria were substituted into the regression equation to compare the actual and predicted ratings. The Moody's model correctly classified 66.7 percent of the bonds. All predicted ratings were no more than one rating category from the actual ratings (Table 20.6). The decision model suggests that twenty (or 18.5 percent) were rated too high and sixteen (or 14.8 percent) were rated too low. The Standard & Poor's model correctly classified 65.4 percent of the actual ratings, with 20.2 percent rated too high and 14.4 percent rated too low (Table 20.6). Again, all predicted ratings were no more than one rating category from the actual ratings. The accuracy of the models is good enough to predict future ratings by applying the bootstrapped rating model.

Table 20.7 summarizes interagency rating consistency. Of the 152 issues jointly rated, 111 received identical ratings from Moody's and Standard & Poor's, and 40 of the remaining 41 issues differed by only one rating category. While these differences are minimal, a change of a single rating category can create significant differences in interest rates. A change from an A+ to an A rating for an issue could, over the life of a bond issue, result in an interest cost increase of $50,000 per year on a $25 million bond issue.

Differences both in criteria used and in weightings attached to criteria explained much of the rating difference. This suggests that Standard & Poor's was more likely than Moody's to grant a higher rating. In the forty-one cases of split ratings, Standard & Poor's gave a higher rating twenty-five times. Differences in rating outcome were due to differences in criteria used by the agencies. Note that bonds with an adjusted rating could be used to validate the rating models. This opportunity was not

Table 20.6. Comparing Predicted and Actual Bond Ratings.

		Baa	Baa'	A	A'	Aa
		Moody's Predicted Rating				
	Baa	0	2	0	0	0
Actual	Baa'	0	2	3	0	0
Moody's	A	0	3	44	9	0
Rating	A'	0	0	10	22	2
	Aa	0	0	0	7	4

Correctly classified: 72 of 108, or 66.7%
Rated too high: 20 of 108, or 18.5%
Rated too low: 16 of 108, or 14.8%

		BBB+	A	A+	AA
		Standard & Poor's Predicted Rating			
Actual	BBB+	0	9	0	0
Standard	A	0	40	5	0
&	A+	0	14	25	1
Poor's	AA	0	0	6	3
Rating	AA+	0	0	0	1

Correctly classified: 68 of 104, or 65.4%
Rated too high: 21 of 104, or 20.2%
Rated too low: 15 of 104, or 14.4%

Table 20.7. Comparing Bond Ratings.

		Aa	A'	A	Baa'	Baa
		Moody's Rating				
Standard	AA	9	3	0	0	0
&	A+	3	42	12	0	0
Poor's	A	0	5	52	5	0
Rating	BBB+	0	1	6	7	5
	BBB	0	0	0	1	1

possible in the regulatory case because decisions are not reconsidered.

Simulated Decisions

A different approach must be used if data files do not exist or if archives lack needed information. Decision processes are simulated to elicit choices or judgments from decision makers. Decision makers are confronted with hypothetical but feasible courses of action described by values for several criteria and are asked to make a judgment or a prediction. For example, hypothetical health projects have been described by their "costs" and the "target group's size," "residual disability," and "years of life gained" so that members of a decision panel could rate the funding prospects for each project (Nutt, 1980c). A score of 100 implied virtually certain support, a score of 0, no prospects of support, and ratings in between suggested the likelihood of funding. The ratings made of each hypothetical project were correlated with criteria levels in the proposals, using regression techniques to form a simulated decision model. The model indicates how a panel believes that funding decisions should be made. The hypothetical cases represent all conceivable decisions and are defined by all combinations of the decision criteria.

Regression techniques are used to identify the important (statistically significant) criteria and criteria interactions that make up the decision model. Tests are required to ensure that the criteria are independent and that the dependent (decision) variable is intervally scaled. Independence is tested by examining correlations between criteria. Scale properties are tested to ensure that scale zero points and intervals for the rating scale are clearly defined.

Some Applications

Simulated decisions have been used to elicit choices or judgments from decision makers to build decision models for a variety of decisions. For example, simulations of patient conditions have been used to develop nursing staff models. A model was built with consideration given to clinical indicators such as white blood count, platelets, temperature, stage of disease, and diagnosis (Nutt, 1984a). A factorial of clinical indicators, each with two levels, was used to identify hypothetical patients. Nurses estimated the number of nursing hours needed for each hypothetical patient. Decisions, expressed as nursing hours, were correlated with the criteria levels to identify the importance of each criterion.

To permit a comparison of outcomes (for example, mortality, morbidity, length of stay) in hospital emergency rooms, patient condition must be considered. Gustafson and others (1983) constructed a severity index that measures patient condition. One portion of the index assessed the condition of patients with ischemic heart disease (Nutt, 1982a). Profiles were created that represented two levels for primary arrhythmias, three levels for types of myocardial infarction, two levels for patient age, two levels for the time since the onset of symptoms, and four types of complications. All combinations of levels for these criteria created 96 profiles ($2 \times 3 \times 2 \times 2 \times 4$). Physicians skilled in the treatment of ischemic heart disease rated the severity of each of the 96 patient profiles on a continuous scale of 0 (no possible threat to life) to 100 (certain death). The ratings were correlated with criteria to specify how each criterion was weighted by the panel.

The Procedure

The "case approach" is used to simulate decisions (Nutt, 1980c, 1984a). Six steps are required: determine criteria and identify realistic ranges of criteria values, construct cases, pose hypothetical decisions, select a rating scale, rate each case, and derive weights. To illustrate the procedure and to allow a comparison of methods, examples from the previous chapter will be used. In the first example, recall that a predictive model of taxable revenue bond rating used by firms in their debt financing was constructed. The second example ranked potential heart disease programs for agencies such as the National Heart Institute or the American Heart Association.

The Bond Rating Example

Moody's and Standard & Poor's rate a variety of bonds, including taxable issues used by firms to raise capital. Three criteria were identified in Chapter Nineteen as important: size, debt service, and leverage. Size was measured by the firms' revenue, debt service by a coverage ratio, and leverage by the ratio of long-term debt to equity. (Recall that this example was greatly simplified to illustrate the mechanics.)

Step 1: Identify Criteria Ranges. Permissible ranges for each criterion were identified. Investment bankers and other experts were consulted to identify these ranges. Firms with revenues ranging from $100 million to $10 billion often attempt to finance their projects with bonds. A relevant range for debt service was set at 1.5 to 10.0 and leverage at .10 to .80. The ranges within which most issues fall are shown below:

Criterion	Range
Size	$1 to $4 billion
Debt service	3.0 to 7.0
Leverage	.25 to .65

More elaborate steps are typically required to isolate relevant criterion ranges and will be illustrated in the priority-setting example that follows.

Step 2: Construct Cases. To define cases, all combinations of criteria levels that span the relevant ranges noted above were identified. There were three criteria, each with two levels, producing eight combinations (2 × 2 × 2). These eight combinations were used to define eight hypothetical bonds for experts to rate, as shown below:

Bond	Debt Service Coverage	Revenue	Leverage
1	3.0	$1 billion	.25
2	7.0	$1 billion	.25
3	3.0	$4 billion	.25
4	7.0	$4 billion	.25

5	3.0	$1 billion	.65
6	7.0	$1 billion	.65
7	3.0	$4 billion	.65
8	7.0	$4 billion	.65

Step 3: Pose Hypothetical Decisions. Cases are described in a narrative form to create each hypothetical bond. An expert or panel would consider each of the eight hypothetical revenue bonds, specified by the criteria. For example, bond 1 could be described to panel members as follows:

> Consider a taxable revenue bond with these characteristics:
> 1. The firm's debt service coverage is 3.0.
> 2. The firm has $1 billion in revenue.
> 3. The firm's leverage (long-term debt/equity) is .25.
> Please indicate the rating you would expect from:
>   Moody's __
>   Standard & Poor's __

The decision could also be captured as the expected interest rate.

The panel is often made up of experts in the area to be considered, making expertise the key factor in the selection of panel members. In the example, either rating agency representatives or investment bankers represent reasonable choices for panel members.

Step 4: Select a Rating Scale. Rating scales take several forms. As discussed in Chapter Nineteen, either an objective or subjective utility can be used to capture the value a decision maker assigns to each bond. In this example, an objective utility (a rating) is preferred because it is expressed in terms understandable to the participants. Either a rating (for example, AAA, AA) or the expected interest rate can be obtained.

Step 5: Rate the Cases. Participants are given a brief orientation to describe their role, set expected time requirements, and define the criteria. The criteria definition step can be quite important if experts are used. Comments are solicited to ensure that the selected ranges make sense.

Step 6: Determine Criteria Weights. The decisions are recorded. Bond ratings are converted to integers. (The rationale for the procedure was described in a previous section of this chapter.) If the decision was captured as an interest rate, this value can be used without transformation. The ratings assigned to each hypothetical bond are correlated with the decision criteria by using regression techniques. The statistical analysis determines the implicit weight assigned to the criteria by decision makers as they make decisions.

The Program Priority Case

Establishing rankings for program areas in heart disease differ in several respects from rating bonds. First, the values sought are not those of experts but those of the public on the desirability of various outcomes that result from medical interventions. Second, an actual case is used. This project demonstrated how a panel of consumers rated cases that represented feasible outcomes that can be produced by heart disease treatment. Third, the case is more complex than the previous example and shows how to deal with larger numbers of criteria and manage the information-processing problems.

Step 1: Identify Criteria Ranges. Permissible ranges for each criterion are identified by constructing a frequency distribution for each criterion. Table 19.9 lists outcomes that are possible for heart disease treatment. Using these data, a frequency distribution for the quality of life criterion is created, as shown below:

Quality of Life Categories	*Frequency*
I	6
I ½	2
II	5
II ½	0
III	1
III ½	0
IV	0

The most frequently used categories are I and II. These values capture the relevant range for the quality of life criterion. The outcomes for the remaining criteria are listed below:

Criterion	Outcome	Number of Categories
Quality of life	Class I or II	2
Disability relieved	1 or 2 levels	2
Years gained	5, 10, 20, 25, 40	5
Cost	$1,000, $2,000, $3,000, $10,000	4
Target group	500, 3,000, 6,000, 30,000	4

Step 2: Construct Cases. Criteria can be treated as having discrete or continuous levels. In this example, the outcomes fell into specific categories, which make a strictly discrete classification possible. To define cases, all combinations of the categories can be used. This approach would require 320 cases ($2 \times 2 \times 5 \times 4 \times 4$), which covers nearly all of the outcomes that can arise for the heart disease programs shown in Table 19.9.

To reduce the number of cases or to capture criteria with a continuous scale, a two-level factorial can be used to define cases (Nutt, 1982a). The factorial requires the use of end points to describe the most common outcomes. The two most common outcomes for the criteria in the example above are as follows:

Criterion	End Point
Quality of life	Class I or II
Disability relieved	1 or 2 levels
Years gained	5 or 40
Cost	$1,000 or $10,000
Target group	500 or 30,000

The factorial design is shown in Table 20.8. This approach cuts the cases that define programs from 320 to 32 (2^5, or $2 \times 2 \times 2 \times 2 \times 2$).

Cases must be checked for feasibility. For instance, had disability levels I and III been used, not I and II, programs 3, 7,

Table 20.8. Defining Hypothetical Programs.

Program	Quality of Life (Class)	Disability Relieved (No. of Levels)	Years Gained	Number in Target Group	Cost ($)
1	II	1	5	500	10,000
2	I	1	5	500	10,000
3	II	2	5	500	10,000
4	I	2	5	500	10,000
5	II	1	40	500	10,000
6	I	1	40	500	10,000
7	II	2	40	500	10,000
8	I	2	40	500	10,000
9	II	1	5	30,000	10,000
10	I	1	5	30,000	10,000
11	II	2	5	30,000	10,000
12	I	2	5	30,000	10,000
13	II	1	40	30,000	10,000
14	I	1	40	30,000	10,000
15	II	2	40	30,000	10,000
16	I	2	40	30,000	10,000
17	II	1	5	500	1,000
18	I	1	5	500	1,000
19	II	2	5	500	1,000
20	I	2	5	500	1,000
21	II	1	40	500	1,000
22	I	1	40	500	1,000
23	II	2	40	500	1,000
24	I	2	40	500	1,000
25	II	1	5	30,000	1,000
26	I	1	5	30,000	1,000
27	II	2	5	30,000	1,000
28	I	2	5	30,000	1,000
29	II	1	40	30,000	1,000
30	I	1	40	30,000	1,000
31	II	2	40	30,000	1,000
32	I	2	40	30,000	1,000
33	II	1	5	500	1,000
34	I	1	5	500	1,000
35	II	2	5	500	1,000
36	I	2	5	500	1,000

11, 15, 19, 23, 27, 31, and 35 would have been infeasible. In each of these cases, three levels of disability would be relieved. But adding three levels to a residual disability of two requires that the patient begin with a level V classification, which was not defined. All hypothetical decisions must be carefully checked in this manner to be sure they can occur.

Step 3: Pose Hypothetical Decisions. The cases defined in Table 20.8 are described in a narrative form. In the heart disease program priority example, a decision maker would be asked to consider thirty-two possible programs. Program 1 can be described as follows:

Consider a possible program that can produce these outcomes.

Quality of life:	Class II
Disability relieved:	2 levels
Years gained:	5
Number affected:	500 people
Cost:	$10,000/person

Please indicate your view of the value of this program. ____

Because such judgments may exhibit sequential changes, such as exhibit learning, the cases should be randomized so that a different order is considered by each person in the group.

Step 4: Select a Rating Scale. Rating scales that permit the decision maker to indicate his or her views of each hypothetical program can be constructed in several ways. Common scales are categorical or linear, and the odds procedure can be used. (See Chapter Seventeen for a complete discussion of the scale options.) A categorical scale has the decision maker assign a value to each course of action. For example, the programs defined in Table 20.8 could be rated as excellent (80–100), good (60–80), average (40–60), fair (20–40), or poor (0–20). This approach is summarized by scale 1 in Figure 20.2.

A linear scale can also be used. This type of scale has the

Figure 20.2. Rating-Scale Options.

Instructions. Please consider the program that has the following features:

Quality of life: Class I
Disability relieved: 2 levels
Years gained: 40
Number affected: 30,000
Cost: $1,000/patient

Scale 1:

Using the following definitions, please assign a value
that depicts your view of the program's importance. _____

80 – 100   Excellent
60 – 80   Good
40 – 60   Average
20 – 40   Fair
0 – 20   Poor

Scale 2:

Check the scale below to predict your view of the
program's adoptability.

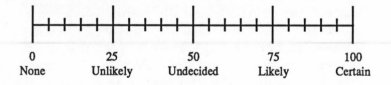

0	25	50	75	100
None	Unlikely	Undecided	Likely	Certain

Scale 3:

Steps: 1. Sort the profile for each alternative.
        2. Compare the profiles and assign a "times
           more important" value to each alternative.

decision maker check along a continuous scale to indicate his or her prospects of adopting each hypothetical alternative. For example, the decision maker could be asked to indicate the prospects of adopting each program in Table 20.8 by scale 2 in Figure 20.2.

The odds procedure places the criteria values, which describe hypothetical courses of action, on index cards. The decision maker first ranks the alternatives and then compares the alternatives one at a time by sorting the cards. The most important alternative is given a value of 1. Each of the remaining alternatives is compared to the most important, and a "times more important" value is recorded. If the first alternative was seen as three times as important, a value of one-third would be assigned to it. This creates the "odds ratio" for each alternative. The odds values are normalized prior to the regression analysis. Scale 3 in Figure 20.2 summarizes this procedure.

Step 5: Rate the Cases. To initiate the rating process, participants are given a brief orientation to describe their role and the time required and to define the criteria. One of the three rating scales shown in Figure 20.2 is selected and added to each program description. Participants are asked to examine each program and assign a value that best describes their view of the program's importance.

Figure 20.3 provides a scale that can be used to rate a large number of hypothetical alternatives (Gustafson and others, 1983). The best and worst programs are located at the end points to anchor the scale. An index card that describes an alternative is moved along the scale to find an appropriate distance from these best and worst case extremes. The procedure that a group can use to rate large numbers of profiles is summarized below:

1. Anchor points on severity scale (see Figure 20.3).
2. Locate first profile on the scale and discuss.
3. Select next four profiles and rate 0 to 100.
4. Record scores for first five profiles.
5. Discuss agreement (differences of fewer than fifteen points are ignored).

Figure 20.3. Rating Scale for Large Numbers of Projects.

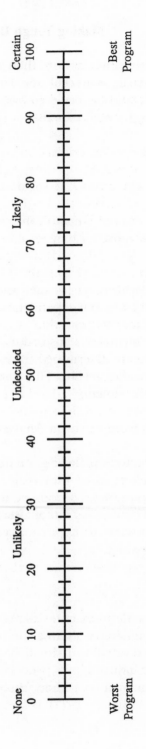

Adoption Prospects

None	Unlikely	Undecided	Likely	Certain
0	10 20 30 40 50 60 70 80 90			100

Worst
Program

Best
Program

Quality: Class II
Disability: 2 levels
Years: 5
Number: 500
Cost: $10,000

Quality: Class I
Disability: 2 levels
Years: 40
Number: 30,000
Cost: $1,000

(Locate each patient profile on the scale to judge the approximate severity)

6. Discuss reasons behind ratings when more than a fifteen-point spread occurs. (Consensus is *not* required. Discussion ensures that the same factors are considered and that the task is seen in the same way by each panelist.)
7. Collect profiles and code.
8. Repeat, five profiles at a time.
9. Impossible alternatives:
   a. Any way alternatives can occur? If so, describe on profile.
   b. If not, make *minimal* changes in indicator levels, so alternatives are plausible, even if they would rarely occur in practice.

Step 6: Determine Criteria Weights. The values assigned to each hypothetical alternative become the dependent variables. The dependent variables are correlated with the criteria values (the independent variables) by means of statistical techniques. The weights assigned to criteria are determined from the beta weights provided in most regression results. These values are normalized to convert them to a percent.

What We Have Learned from Decision Analysis

Decision analysis studies have revealed a good deal about the capabilities of decision makers faced with tough choices. These studies find that few criteria are used, that decisions have low reliability, that information processing is often incomplete, and that decision aids can be useful in supporting a decision process.

Few Criteria

Decision makers insist that far more criteria are necessary than they actually use when making decisions. Information-processing limitations may play a role in this behavior (see Chapters Four and Five). People have difficulty processing more than a few discrete items of information without external aids because of cognitive limitations (Simon, 1977). Differences are

Table 20.9. Comparison of Criteria Weights.

	Indirect (Regression)	Direct
Bond Rating (Three Criteria)		
Debt service	.12	.29
Size	.35	.42
Leverage	.53	.29
	1.00	1.00
Staffing (Four Criteria)		
Birth weight	.18	.18
Days from birth	.19	.25
Gestational age	.10	.25
Condition (diagnosis)	.53	.32
	1.00	1.00
Program Priorities[a] (Five Criteria)		
Cost of treatment (per case)	.20	.37
Disability relieved	.21	.24
Quality of life[b]	.21	.01
Target group size	.20	.32
Years of life gained	.18	.06
	1.00	1.00

[a] Typical panel.
[b] Disability after treatment.

always found in the weights assigned by direct methods, described in Chapter Seventeen, as compared to indirect inference of the weights from a regression. A comparison of weights for three-, four-, and five-criterion decisions is shown in Table 20.9. The indirect or case method produces considerable spread in the weights. Weighting criteria with direct methods bunches the weights. Criteria are typically seen as having about equal importance when direct methods are used. Decision makers appear to mull over several criteria but at the moment of decision actively consider only a few of these criteria. Information overload may play a role in this behavior.

Decision makers may try to convey an image of being comprehensive, which provides another explanation. A comprehensive posture may be used to avoid the appearance of superficiality. Exploring how decisions are made can be threatening and may cause decision makers to contend that they were exhaustive in their search for diagnostic information. Decision makers may also claim that they use lots of information as a smokescreen to cover up the blatant adoption of their pet ideas. Whatever the reasons, decisions are based on relatively few criteria.

Decisions Lack Reliability

Studies of decision making can explain between 60 and 70 percent of the variance in the decisions made in field settings. Put differently, between 30 and 40 percent of the variance remains unexplained. Nearly 40 percent of the variance in the ratings assigned to hospital revenue bonds could not be attributed to criteria that Moody's and Standard & Poor's claim they used in assigning the ratings. And about 40 percent of the variance in certificate-of-need decisions was not related to measures of need, cost containment, and the other legislatively dictated criteria. This unexplained variance may represent attempts to make a decision work out in a way that is helpful to the decision maker or his or her inability to assimilate all the information.

Information Is Processed in a Highly Simplified Manner

Decision makers use information describing the value of alternatives in a simple, additive manner. For instance, physicians contend they use "differential diagnosis," in which values from two or more criteria, such as blood pressure and heart rate, are considered jointly, when they make a diagnosis. That is, blood pressure and heart rate must both exceed some critical value before a positive diagnosis is made. Studies of clinical decision making find that physicians consider criteria such as blood pressure and heart rate separately. This finding may not generalize to all decision tasks, but there is considerable evidence supporting simplistic information processing and little that supports a more complex process. Decision makers embrace valid principles to guide them in their decisions but tend to abandon them when faced with tough choices (Dawes, 1975).

Models Outperform the Decision Maker

When a model based on the decision maker's historical decisions is tested against the decision maker, the model outperforms the person from whom it was derived (Hammond, McClelland, and Mumpower, 1980). The model provides an abstraction of the decision process. However, the model makes better decisions than the decision maker because decision makers use information in an unreliable manner. Decision makers often make different decisions when faced with similar facts. Bootstrapping, replacing the decision maker with a model, is desirable and provides a way to support the decision process. Decision aiding for tough decisions should be given considerable impetus as a result of these findings. Examples include computer-aided diagnosis and computer interpretation of EKGs in health care, and decision support systems for most tough decisions, such as those that involve capital plans, stock selection, and the like.

Key Points

1. The analysis of actual and simulated decisions can be used to clarify the way in which values, expressed as differences in the weights assigned to criteria, influence a decision. Conflict can be managed by showing that differences in value do not influence a choice. When value differences are important, isolating differences that matter (for example, those that influence the choice among alternatives) avoids distraction by focusing discussion on areas in which differences are important.
2. Through demonstrations of how decision makers use information, the need for decision aids, such as analysis and information systems, becomes obvious. Decision makers cannot reliably carry out the necessary computations to value alternatives without conducting some analysis.

3. Learning about decision making is dependent on appreciating how well decision makers can perform under various conditions. By using analytical techniques to support the decision process, decision makers can reduce the error rates for medical diagnoses, graduate admissions, and other tough decisions.

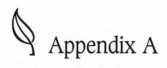

Appendix A

Measuring Tolerance for Uncertainty

Uncertainty Survey Form

Instructions. On the following pages, you will find a series of situations that are likely to occur in everyday life. The central person in each situation is faced with a choice between two alternative courses of action, which we might call X and Y. Alternative X is more desirable and attractive than alternative Y, but the probability of attaining or achieving X is less than that of attaining or achieving Y.

For each situation on the following pages, you will be asked to indicate the minimum odds of success you would demand before recommending that the more attractive or desirable alternative, X, be chosen.

Read each situation carefully before giving your judgment. Try to place yourself in the position of the central person in each of the situations. There are twelve situations in all. Please do not omit any of them.

1. Mr. A, an electrical engineer who is married and has one child, has been working for a large electronics corporation since graduating from college five years ago. He is assured of a

Adapted with permission from Kogan, N., and Wallach, M. A. *Risk Taking: A Study in Cognition and Personality.* New York: Holt, Rinehart & Winston, 1964, Appendix. The male-oriented nature of the questions reflects the era in which the form was developed. Changing the questions to make them less sexist is desirable but would create problems of reliability.

lifetime job with a modest, though adequate, salary and liberal pension benefits upon retirement. On the other hand, it is very unlikely that his salary will increase much before he retires. While attending a convention, Mr. A is offered a job with a small, newly founded company that has a highly uncertain future. The new job would pay more to start and would offer the possibility of a share in the ownership if the company survives the competition of larger firms.

Imagine that you are advising Mr. A. Listed below are several probabilities or odds of the new company's proving financially sound.

Please check the lowest probability that you would consider acceptable to make it worthwhile for Mr. A to take the new job.

____ The chances are one in ten that the company will prove financially sound.

____ The chances are three in ten that the company will prove financially sound.

____ The chances are five in ten that the company will prove financially sound.

____ The chances are seven in ten that the company will prove financially sound.

____ The chances are nine in ten that the company will prove financially sound.

____ Place a check here if you think Mr. A should not take the new job, no matter what the probabilities.

2. Mr. B, a forty-five-year-old accountant, has recently been informed by his physician that he has developed a severe heart ailment. The disease is sufficiently serious to force Mr. B to change many of his strongest life habits—reducing his work load, drastically changing his diet, giving up favorite leisure-time pursuits. The physician suggests that a delicate medical operation could be attempted; if successful, it would completely relieve the heart condition. But its success cannot be assured, and in fact the operation could prove fatal.

Imagine that you are advising Mr. B. Listed below are

several probabilities or odds that the operation would prove successful.

Please check the lowest probability that you would consider acceptable for the operation to be performed.

____ Place a check here if you think Mr. B should not have the operation, no matter what the probabilities.

____ The chances are nine in ten that the operation would be a success.

____ The chances are seven in ten that the operation would be a success.

____ The chances are five in ten that the operation would be a success.

____ The chances are three in ten that the operation would be a success.

____ The chances are one in ten that the operation would be a success.

3. Mr. C, a married man with two children, has a steady job that pays him about $30,000 per year. He can easily afford the necessities of life but few of the luxuries. Mr. C's father, who died recently, carried a $4,000 life insurance policy. Mr. C would like to invest this money in stock. He is well aware of the secure blue-chip stocks and bonds that would pay approximately 6 percent on his investment. On the other hand, Mr. C has heard that the stock of the relatively unknown Company X may double its present value if a new product currently in production is favorably received by the buying public. However, if the product is unfavorably received, the stock will decline in value.

Imagine that you are advising Mr. C. Listed below are several probabilities or odds that Company X stock will double in value.

Please check the lowest probability that you would consider acceptable for Mr. C to invest in Company X stock.

____ The chances are one in ten that the stock will double in value.

____ The chances are three in ten that the stock will double in value.

____ The chances are five in ten that the stock will double in value.

____ The chances are seven in ten that the stock will double in value.

____ The chances are nine in ten that the stock will double in value.

____ Place a check here if you think Mr. C should not invest in Company X stock, no matter what the probabilities.

4. Mr. D is the captain of College X's football team. College X is playing its traditional rival, College Y, in the final game of the season. The game is in its final seconds, and Mr. D's team, College X, is behind in the score. College X has time to run one more play. Mr. D, the captain, must decide whether it would be best to settle for a tie score with a play that would be almost certain to work or try a more complicated and risky play, which could bring victory if it succeeded but defeat if it failed.

Imagine that you are advising Mr. D. Listed below are several probabilities or odds that the risky play would work.

Please check the lowest probability that you would consider acceptable for the risky play to be attempted.

____ Place a check here if you think Mr. D should not attempt the risky play, no matter what the probabilities.

____ The chances are nine in ten that the risky play would work.

____ The chances are seven in ten that the risky play would work.

____ The chances are five in ten that the risky play would work.

____ The chances are three in ten that the risky play would work.

____ The chances are one in ten that the risky play would work.

5. Mr. E is president of a light metals corporation in the United States. The corporation is quite prosperous and has strongly considered the possibility of business expansion by building an additional plant in a new location. The choice is between building another plant in the United States, where there would be a moderate return on the initial investment, or

building a plant in a foreign country. Lower labor costs and easy access to raw materials in the foreign country would mean a much higher return on the initial investment. On the other hand, there is a history of political instability and revolution in the foreign country under consideration. In fact, the leader of a small minority party is committed to nationalizing, that is, taking over all foreign investments.

Imagine that you are advising Mr. E. Listed below are several probabilities or odds of continued political stability in the foreign country under consideration.

Please check the lowest probability that you would consider acceptable for Mr. E's corporation to build a plant in the foreign country.

____ The chances are one in ten that the foreign country will remain politically stable.

____ The chances are three in ten that the foreign country will remain politically stable.

____ The chances are five in ten that the foreign country will remain politically stable.

____ The chances are seven in ten that the foreign country will remain politically stable.

____ The chances are nine in ten that the foreign country will remain politically stable.

____ Place a check here if you think Mr. E's corporation should not build a plant in the foreign country, no matter what the probabilities.

6. Mr. F is currently a college senior who is very eager to pursue graduate study in chemistry leading to a Ph.D. He has been accepted by both University X and University Y. University X has a worldwide reputation for excellence in chemistry. While a degree from University X would signify outstanding training in this field, the standards are so rigorous that only a fraction of the degree candidates actually receive a degree. University Y, on the other hand, has much less of a reputation in chemistry, but almost everyone admitted is awarded a Ph.D., though the degree

has much less prestige than the corresponding degree from University X.

Imagine that you are advising Mr. F. Listed below are several probabilities or odds that Mr. F would be awarded a degree at University X, the one with the greater prestige.

Please check the lowest probability that you would consider acceptable to make it worthwhile for Mr. F to enroll in University X rather than University Y.

_____ Place a check here if you think Mr. F should not enroll in University X, no matter what the probabilities.

_____ The chances are nine in ten that Mr. F would receive a degree from University X.

_____ The chances are seven in ten that Mr. F would receive a degree from University X.

_____ The chances are five in ten that Mr. F would receive a degree from University X.

_____ The chances are three in ten that Mr. F would receive a degree from University X.

_____ The chances are one in ten that Mr. F would receive a degree from University X.

7. Mr. G, a competent chess player, is participating in a national chess tournament. In an early match he draws the top-favored player in the tournament as his opponent. Mr. G has been given a relatively low ranking in view of his performance in previous tournaments. During the course of his play with the top-favored man, Mr. G notes the possibility of a deceptive though risky maneuver that might bring him a quick victory. At the same time, if the attempted maneuver should fail, Mr. G would be left in an exposed position and defeat would almost certainly follow.

Imagine that you are advising Mr. G. Listed below are several probabilities or odds that Mr. G's deceptive play would succeed.

Please check the lowest probability that you would consider acceptable for the risky play in question to be attempted.

___ The chances are one in ten that the play would succeed.
___ The chances are three in ten that the play would succeed.
___ The chances are five in ten that the play would succeed.
___ The chances are seven in ten that the play would succeed.
___ The chances are nine in ten that the play would succeed.
___ Place a check here if you think Mr. G should not attempt the risky play, no matter what the probabilities.

8. Mr. H, a college senior, has studied the piano since childhood. He has won amateur prizes and given small recitals, suggesting that Mr. H has considerable musical talent. As graduation approaches, Mr. H has the choice of going to medical school to become a physician, which would bring certain prestige and financial rewards, or entering a conservatory of music for advanced training with a well-known pianist. Mr. H realizes that even upon completion of his piano studies, which would take many more years and a lot of money, success as a concert pianist would not be assured.

Imagine that you are advising Mr. H. Listed below are several probabilities or odds that Mr. H would succeed as a concert pianist.

Please check the lowest probability that you would consider acceptable for Mr. H to continue with his musical training.

___ Place a check here if you think Mr. H should not pursue his musical training, no matter what the probabilities.
___ The chances are nine in ten that Mr. H would succeed as a concert pianist.
___ The chances are seven in ten that Mr. H would succeed as a concert pianist.
___ The chances are five in ten that Mr. H would succeed as a concert pianist.
___ The chances are three in ten that Mr. H would succeed as a concert pianist.
___ The chances are one in ten that Mr. H would succeed as a concert pianist.

9. Mr. J is an American who has been captured by the enemy and placed in a prisoner-of-war camp. Conditions in the

camp are quite bad, with long hours of hard physical labor and a barely sufficient diet. After spending several months in this camp, Mr. J notes the possibility of escape by concealing himself in a supply truck that shuttles in and out of the camp. Of course, there is no guarantee that the escape would prove successful. Even if it did, recapture by the enemy could well mean execution.

Imagine that you are advising Mr. J. Listed below are several probabilities or odds of a successful escape from the prisoner-of-war camp.

Please check the lowest probability that you would consider acceptable for an escape to be attempted.

____ The chances are one in ten that the escape would succeed.
____ The chances are three in ten that the escape would succeed.
____ The chances are five in ten that the escape would succeed.
____ The chances are seven in ten that the escape would succeed.
____ The chances are nine in ten that the escape would succeed.
____ Place a check here if you think Mr. J should not try to escape, no matter what the probabilities.

10. Mr. K is a successful businessman who has participated in a number of civic activities of considerable value to the community. Mr. K has been approached by the leaders of his political party as a possible congressional candidate in the next election. Mr. K's party is a minority party in the district, though the party has won occasional elections in the past. Mr. K would like to hold political office, but to do so, he would have to make a serious financial sacrifice because the party has insufficient campaign funds. He would also have to endure the attacks of his political opponents in a hot campaign.

Imagine that you are advising Mr. K. Listed below are several probabilities or odds of Mr. K's winning the election in his district.

Please check the lowest probability that you would consider acceptable to make it worthwhile for Mr. K to run for political office.

_____ Place a check here if you think Mr. K should not run for political office, no matter what the probabilities.

_____ The chances are nine in ten that Mr. K would win the election.

_____ The chances are seven in ten that Mr. K would win the election.

_____ The chances are five in ten that Mr. K would win the election.

_____ The chances are three in ten that Mr. K would win the election.

_____ The chances are one in ten that Mr. K would win the election.

11. Mr. L, a married thirty-year-old research physicist, has been given a five-year appointment by a major university laboratory. As he contemplates the next five years, he realizes that he might work on a difficult, long-term problem that, if he could find a solution, would resolve basic scientific issues in the field and bring him high scientific honors. If he could not find a solution, however, Mr. L would have little to show for his five years in the laboratory, and this would make it hard for him to get a good job afterward. On the other hand, he could, as most of his professional associates are doing, work on a series of short-term problems that are of lesser scientific importance but whose solutions would be easier to find.

Imagine that you are advising Mr. L. Listed below are several probabilities or odds that he would find a solution to the difficult, long-term problem that he has in mind.

Please check the lowest probability that you would consider acceptable to make it worthwhile for Mr. L to work on the more difficult long-term problem.

_____ The chances are one in ten that Mr. L would solve the long-term problem.

_____ The chances are three in ten that Mr. L would solve the long-term problem.

_____ The chances are five in ten that Mr. L would solve the long-term problem.

____ The chances are seven in ten that Mr. L would solve the long-term problem.

____ The chances are nine in ten that Mr. L would solve the long-term problem.

____ Place a check here if you think Mr. L should not choose the long-term, difficult problem, no matter what the probabilities.

12. Mr. M is contemplating marriage to Miss T, a woman whom he has known for a little more than a year. Recently, however, a number of arguments have occurred between them, suggesting some sharp differences of opinion in the way each views certain matters. Indeed, they decide to seek professional advice from a marriage counselor as to whether it would be wise for them to marry. On the basis of their meetings with the marriage counselor, they realize that a happy marriage, while possible, would not be assured.

Imagine that you are advising Mr. M and Miss T. Listed below are several probabilities or odds that their marriage would prove to be a happy and successful one.

Please check the lowest probability that you would consider acceptable for Mr. M and Miss T to get married.

____ Place a check here if you think Mr. M and Miss T should not marry, no matter what the probabilities.

____ The chances are nine in ten that the marriage would be happy and successful.

____ The chances are seven in ten that the marriage would be happy and successful.

____ The chances are five in ten that the marriage would be happy and successful.

____ The chances are three in ten that the marriage would be happy and successful.

____ The chances are one in ten that the marriage would be happy and successful.

Norms Using the Uncertainty Preference Scale

Source: The Tolerance for Uncertainty Scale

Basis   The survey asks twelve questions about personal and
and self- work-oriented situations with uncertainty. You were
scoring: asked to choose between two options (two jobs, and so
           on) indicating the likelihood that you would adopt a
           low uncertainty–low payoff or a high uncertainty–
           high payoff option. To determine your score, average
           your responses to the twelve questions. The scale runs
           from 1, high uncertainty tolerance, to 9, low uncer-
           tainty tolerance.

The Scale:

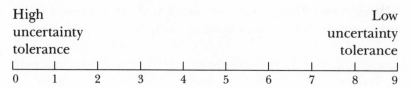

High   Low
uncertainty   uncertainty
tolerance   tolerance

Norms:

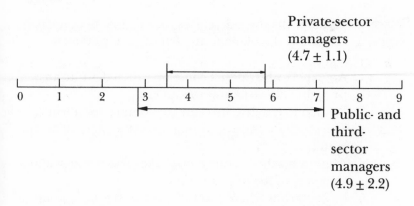

Private-sector
managers
(4.7 ± 1.1)

Public- and
third-
sector
managers
(4.9 ± 2.2)

Source: Nutt, 1980d.

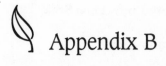 Appendix B

Measuring Tolerance for Ambiguity

Tolerance for Ambiguity Survey Form

Please read each of the following statements carefully. Then use the following scale to rate each of them in terms of the extent to which you either agree or disagree with the statement.

Completely disagree		Neither agree nor disagree				Completely agree
1	2	3	4	5	6	7

Place the number that best describes your degree of agreement or disagreement in the blank to the left of each statement.

____ 1. An expert who doesn't come up with a definite answer probably doesn't know too much.

____ 2. I would like to live in a foreign country for a while.

____ 3. The sooner we all acquire similar values and ideals, the better.

____ 4. A good teacher is one who makes you wonder about your way of looking at things.

____ 5. I like parties where I know most of the people more than ones where all or most of the people are complete strangers.

Adapted with permission from Budner, S. "Intolerance of Ambiguity as a Personality Variable." *Journal of Personality*, 1962, *30*, 29–50.

____ 6. Teachers or supervisors who hand out vague assignments give a chance for one to show initiative and originality.

____ 7. A person who leads an even, regular life in which few surprises or unexpected happenings arise really has a lot to be grateful for.

____ 8. Many of our most important decisions are based on insufficient information.

____ 9. There is really no such thing as a problem that can't be solved.

____ 10. People who fit their lives to a schedule probably miss most of the joy of living.

____ 11. A good job is one in which what is to be done and how it is to be done are always clear.

____ 12. It is more fun to tackle a complicated problem than to solve a simple one.

____ 13. In the long run, it is possible to get more done by tackling small, simple problems than large and complicated ones.

____ 14. Often the most interesting and stimulating people are those who don't mind being different and original.

____ 15. What we are used to is always preferable to what is unfamiliar.

____ 16. People who insist upon a yes or no answer just don't know how complicated things really are.

Norms Using the Tolerance for Ambiguity Scale

Source: The Tolerance for Ambiguity Scale.

Basis   The survey asks sixteen questions about personal and
and self- work-oriented situations with ambiguity. You were
scoring: asked to rate each situation on a scale from 1 (toler-
           ant) to 7 (intolerant). (Alternating questions have the
           response scale reversed.) A perfectly tolerant person
           would score 16 and a perfectly intolerant person, 112.
           Scores between 20 and 80 are reported with means of
           45. To determine your score, add your responses to the
           even-numbered questions to 7 minus the score of your
           responses to the odd-numbered questions.

The Scale:

Perfectly   Perfectly
tolerant   intolerant

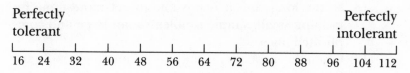

16   24   32   40   48   56   64   72   80   88   96 104 112

Norms:

Private-sector managers
(44.6 ± 8.5)

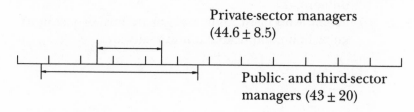

Public- and third-sector
managers (43 ± 20)

Source: Nutt, 1988.

 Appendix C

Measuring Decision Style

Decision Style Survey Form

Instructions. For each numbered item, circle either a or b. If you feel both a and b are true, decide which one is more like you, even if it is only slightly more true.

1. I would rather
   a. Solve a new and complicated problem
   b. Work on something I have done before
2. I like to
   a. Work alone in a quiet place
   b. Be where "the action" is
3. I want a boss who
   a. Establishes and applies criteria in decisions
   b. Considers individual needs and makes exceptions
4. When I work on a project, I
   a. Like to finish it and get some closure
   b. Often leave it open for possible changes
5. When making a decision, the most important considerations are
   a. Rational thoughts, ideas, and data
   b. People's feelings and values
6. On a project, I tend to
   a. Think it over and over before deciding how to proceed
   b. Start working on it right away, thinking about it as I go along

7. When working on a project, I prefer to
   a. Maintain as much control as possible
   b. Explore various options
8. In my work, I prefer to
   a. Work on several projects at a time, and learn as much as possible about each one
   b. Have one project which is challenging and keeps me busy
9. I often
   a. Make lists and plans whenever I start something and may hate to seriously alter my plans
   b. Avoid plans and just let things progress as I work on them
10. When discussing a problem with colleagues, it is easy for me
    a. To see "the big picture"
    b. To grasp the specifics of the situation
11. When the phone rings in my office or at home, I usually
    a. Consider it an interruption
    b. Don't mind answering it
12. Which word describes you better?
    a. Analytical
    b. Empathetic
13. When I am working on an assignment, I tend to
    a. Work steadily and consistently
    b. Work in bursts of energy with "down time" in between
14. When I listen to someone talk on a subject, I usually try to
    a. Relate it to my own experience and see if it fits
    b. Assess and analyze the message
15. When I come up with new ideas, I generally
    a. "Go for it"
    b. Like to contemplate the ideas some more
16. When working on a project, I prefer to
    a. Narrow the scope so it is clearly defined
    b. Broaden the scope to include related aspects
17. When I read something, I usually
    a. Confine my thoughts to what is written there
    b. Read between the lines and relate the words to other ideas
18. When I have to make a decision in a hurry, I often
    a. Feel uncomfortable and wish I had more information
    b. Am able to do so with available data

19. In a meeting, I tend to
    a. Continue formulating my ideas as I talk about them
    b. Only speak out after I have carefully thought the issue through
20. In work, I prefer spending a great deal of time on issues of
    a. Ideas
    b. People
21. In meetings, I am most often annoyed with people who
    a. Come up with many sketchy ideas
    b. Lengthen meetings with many practical details
22. Are you a
    a. Morning person?
    b. Night owl?
23. What is your style in preparing for a meeting?
    a. I am willing to go in and be responsive
    b. I like to be fully prepared and usually sketch an outline of the meeting
24. In a meeting, would you prefer for people to
    a. Display a fuller range of emotions
    b. Be more task oriented
25. I would rather work for an organization where
    a. My job was intellectually stimulating
    b. I was committed to its goals and mission
26. On weekends, I tend to
    a. Plan what I will do
    b. Just see what happens and decide as I go along
27. I am more
    a. Outgoing
    b. Contemplative
28. I would rather work for a boss who is
    a. Full of new ideas
    b. Practical

In the following, choose the word in each pair which appeals to you more.

29. a. Social
    b. Theoretical

30. a. Ingenuity
    b. Practicality
31. a. Organized
    b. Adaptable
32. a. Active
    b. Concentration

Scoring Key for Decision Style Form

Count one point for each item listed below that you circled in the inventory.

Score for I	*Score for E*	*Score for S*	*Score for N*
2a	2b	1b	1a
6a	6b	10b	10a
11a	11b	13a	13b
15b	15a	16a	16b
19b	19a	17a	17b
22a	22b	21a	21b
27b	27a	28b	28a
32b	32a	30b	30a

Total

Circle the one with more
points: I   E

Circle the one with more
points: S   N

Score for T	*Score for F*	*Score for J*	*Score for P*
3a	3b	4a	4b
5a	5b	7a	7b
12a	12b	8b	8a
14b	14a	9a	9b
20a	20b	18b	18a
24b	24a	23b	23a
25a	25b	26a	26b
29b	29a	31a	31b

Total

Circle the one with more
points: T   F

Circle the one with more
points: J   P

After totaling:

Score I if I > E
Score E if E ≥ I   ___

Score N if N ≥ S
Score S if S > N   ___

Score P if P ≥ J
Score J if J > P   ___

Score F if F > T   If T = F and you are male, score F.
Score T if T > F   ___   If T = F and you are female, score T.

List the scores you tallied and circle the letter in each pair with
the highest value. This is your style.

I ___   N ___   T ___   J ___
E ___   S ___   F ___   P ___

Glossary

Action learning. Learning focused on outcomes and the future conditions that should have been foreseeable and that produced these outcomes.

Actor learning. Determining the accuracy of information offered by experts in a decision process, such as the likelihood of a future condition (interest rates), and norming by what has been obtained by the typical expert.

Alternatives. Optional courses of action from which a decision maker is expected to choose that are obtained from memory, vendor search, research and development, and the like and provide ways to achieve objectives.

Ambiguity. The inability to characterize or describe important aspects of a decision, such as core problems, future conditions, alternatives, or criteria.

Analysis. Separating or breaking up the component parts needed to value alternatives so that estimates for each component can be made and their effects combined.

Analytical decision process. The process by which a dominant stakeholder can act as the decision maker by applying steps to explore possibilities, access alternatives, ask "what if" questions, and reflect in order to learn.

Anchor effect. The failure to make adjustments after the initial estimate has been proved incorrect. This resistance is greater when the initial estimate was very high or very low.

Arena. The context in which a decision is made that captures background and motivating information that characterize a decision. Arenas identify contexts that are *assumed* by decision makers, which may or may not frame a decision in the most opportune manner.

Assumptions. Suppositions about values for key factors in a decision process, such as future conditions, that are taken for granted unless subjected to sensitivity analysis.

Availability heuristic. A rule of thumb that is used to acquire information in which easily accessible information is treated as diagnostic.

Bad decisions. Failures to deal with foreseeable events and cope with behavioral factors that inhibit and mislead decision makers, whether the outcome is favorable or unfavorable.

Behavioral. A description of how decision makers act when making decisions without the aid of normative tactics (also called *descriptive*).

Bias. Partiality or prejudice in interpreting information and applying it to a decision situation.

Causal attribution. The assignment of causes to outcomes or events that are observed.

Coalition. A temporary union or alliance of stakeholders as a decision group to make a particular decision.

Conflict. Disagreement among people with different interests, views, or agendas, causing emotional disturbance and stress.

Conspicuous alternatives. Traditional or habitual ways of responding to core problems that arise early in a decision process.

Context. The situation that captures background information and insights relevant to a decision and from which meaning and understanding are extracted (also called *environment*).

Core problem. The most important and most central problem provoking action, which can be difficult to identify.

Criteria. The means used to make a comparison among alternatives such as cost and quality.

Criteria weight. A quantitative value that specifies the relative importance of criteria.

Criterion domain. The proxy measure selected to capture a criterion, such as a morale survey that is used to measure satisfaction.

Decision analysis. A technique used to explore various facets of a decision, such as consistency or accuracy, the importance of criteria, the influence of extraneous factors, and norms within and among factions to promote insight that leads to learning.

Decision levels. A level corresponds to increases in the complexity of decisions, as assumptions about future conditions become more ambiguous.

Decision rules. Guides that specify how to use objective and subjective information to compare the merits of alternatives.

Decision tree. An analytical technique that merges chance occurrences about several future conditions with information that describes hybrid alternatives to value courses of action open to a decision maker.

Diagnosis. The action taken by decision makers to determine the underlying factors prompting a decision, using powers of observation and intuition.

Dominance decision rule. Find an alternative that is better or worse than all other alternatives, no matter what future conditions arise.

Elimination by aspects. A technique used with multicriteria to speed decision making in short-fuse situations. Many alternatives are ruled out, one at a time, on the basis of criteria norms (for example, budget constraints or user views), thus eliminating all of the alternatives that fail to satisfy these norms.

Emotional inoculation. A technique used to reduce stakeholders' fears about decision outcomes over which they have no control.

Empirical decisions. Information-poor decisions that have an accepted way to generate and analyze information for decision-making purposes.

Ethical consideration. Identification of actions that seem acceptable according to organizational standards and modes of conduct but that would be unacceptable or questionable according to personal standards and personal modes of conduct.

Expected-value decision rule. Value alternatives by weighting payoffs according to the relative importance of criteria and the likelihood of all future conditions. This is the only decision rule that incorporates what can be determined about uncertainty and applies compensatory logic.

Feedback. Information gleaned about a decision after its outcome has been observed.

Form. Shape or outline as a criterion in decisions, such as the style of a building that gives it a distinctive appearance.

Formal simulation. A tactic used to promote learning by creating hypothetical decision situations. Decision makers consider the hypothetical decisions and make choices that are correlated to the cues (criteria) buried in them to extract values and determine consistency in the use of information.

Frame. A window that focuses attention on what a decision is about, thereby providing direction to subsequent steps in a decision-making process.

Function. Use as a criterion in decisions, such as the use of a building that gives rise to space allocations and other user requirements that stipulate its design.

Future conditions. Factors beyond the decision maker's control that influence the payoffs associated with alternatives, such as the demand for a product (also called states of nature or states).

Gambler's fallacy. Treating random events such as a dice roll as if the outcome of one roll implies something about the outcome of the next roll.

Group decision process. The process used when there are many known stakeholders. In this process, a decision group made up of these stakeholders takes steps to explore possibilities, assess options, ask "what if" questions, and reflect in order to learn.

Group process. A set of procedures used to manage the activities of a group engaged in decision-making activities, such as identifying problems and uncovering alternatives.

Heuristic. A trial-and-error tactic used by a decision maker to speed the process of learning or finding out.

Hindsight bias. The tendency to treat observed outcomes as if they were more likely than facts would warrant or even as if they were preordained.

Illusion of control. An act of prediction that makes the predicted outcome seem more certain — for example, attributing good outcomes to skill and bad ones to chance, which leads to treating out-of-control situations as if they were under control and to minimal learning about missed opportunities.

Illusory associations. Misleading connections between signs and conditions they are thought to predict.

Individual learning. Decision makers' gaining of insight as they reflect on decision outcomes and missed opportunities.

Inference. A conclusion that is drawn by applying reasoning to available information to arrive at a decision.

Informal simulation. A technique applied in important and recurring decisions to promote learning by recreating actual decision situations. The parties involved are disguised, and the decision is described with the facts available when the actual decision was rendered. A comparison of the simulated decisions and the original choices in terms of outcomes indicates how well one can do.

Informational decisions. Unique or problematic interpretations drawn from information-rich situations in which the means used to assess information are controversial.

Information-processing capability. The ability of decision makers to observe, catalogue, and make judgments on the basis of information they observe.

Innovate. To use a new, not necessarily better, way of responding to aims or objectives.

Intuition. Knowing without the conscious use of reasoning or logic.

Janusian thinking. The ability to hold multiple views while making a decision. The term comes from the Roman god Janus, who was the patron of beginnings and endings and is usually shown with two faces to symbolize these multiple views. These two faces symbolize the need for multiple views as a decision is made.

Judgment. The act of deciding by an individual or group vested with authority.

Knowledge structure. A set of beliefs formed by experience and assembled as theories or scripts that suggest relationships among people, events, and objects.

LaPlace decision rule. Assume nothing about the likelihood of future conditions, making the valuation of alternatives an average of the payoffs under each future condition (also called the uncertainty rule).

Learning. Discovering pitfalls to avoid in future decisions and ways to avoid these pitfalls.

Learning to learn. A form of learning in which reflection on both process and outcome occurs, leading to a reappraisal of norms and values applied in making decisions and the steps to follow (also called double-loop learning and learning two).

Missed opportunities. Ways of responding to core problems that were overlooked or rejected during a decision process.

Mixed-mode decision process. The process recommended when unknown or competing factions can be identified as stakeholders. A coalition of stakeholders with aims that correspond to those of the organization is formed to explore possibilities, assess options, ask "what if" questions, and reflect in order to learn.

Multicriteria decisions. Decisions in which several outcomes can occur and in which each outcome has a value that must be considered in order to compare the merits of alternatives.

Multiple perspectives. Technical, personal, and organization views of a decision that are used to incorporate a balanced view of factors that merit consideration.

Norm. A standard identifying a level of performance that is expected or required.

Normative. A type of statement that suggests how a decision should be carried out (also called *prescriptive*).

Objective estimates. Estimates of quantitative information obtained by traditional means, such as accounting systems for costs.

Objectives. The intentions of the decision process that set out what is to be strived for or sought (also called *aims*).

Optimism decision rule. Use a maximax rule to find the best payoff for the most likely future conditions or the best payoff regardless of future conditions.

Order effect. Information received early in a decision process is given more weight than information received later in the process.

Organizational learning. Improving the capacity of the organization to make good decisions, neutralizing coverups by removing the incentives for decision makers in the organization to offer only good news.

Outcomes. The results of a decision process that value the alternative that was selected by measuring the results in terms of the decision criteria (for example, cost, satisfaction, quality, use).

Pallid. A characteristic of information that makes it hard to recall because of a lack of personal identity, distance, or abstractness.

Participation. The involvement of stakeholders in key steps of the decision process.

Pessimism decision rule. When high stakes call for conservative choices, a minimax rule is used to identify future conditions that lead to the worst outcomes and to make choices that avoid these future conditions by selection of the alternative with the best payoff that is left.

Prediction. The act of estimating something before it occurs.

Problem situations. Concerns that specify what a decision is about, including background information that depicts its origins and the motivations of stakeholders.

Puzzlement. A condition that arises when cues that describe what a decision is about are obscure or vague.

Qualitative information. Descriptions of the basic nature of a decision according to features that characterize sentiments of key stakeholders, winners and losers for particular options, problem definitions, and so on, expressed as criteria weights and likelihood of future conditions.

Quantitative information. Measurements of factors pertinent to decisions, such as costs or questionnaire results that capture sentiments.

Rationality. A way of thinking about a decision that stresses political, logical, and ethical means of drawing an inference to make a judgment.

Regret decision rule. Use a minimax rule to find alternatives with the greatest "lost gain" if not adopted and select the alternative that best manages the postdecisional regret of missed opportunity.

Representational decisions. Choices for which there is a rich informational base and an accepted way to manipulate the data.

Representation heuristic. Use of a past decision as an example from which premises about important relationships are drawn and used to make future decisions.

Risk. The chance that a bad outcome will occur, no matter what precautions are taken.

Root cause. The source or origin of a decision that indicates the necessity to act.

Rule of thumb. An approach that is based on experience, not scientific knowledge, and is thought to be useful in carrying out some aspect of decision making.

Satisficing. A decision rule calling for the first alternative that meets preset norms to be adopted.

Schema. A systematic program of action to attain an objective that is often unspoken and applied intuitively.

Search decisions. Decisions made in situations that are information-poor and in which there is no obvious or agreed-upon way to formulate the decision to collect and analyze information.

Selective perspective. Recognition of information only when it is consistent with the decision maker's inclinations or prejudices, a tendency that often leads the decision maker to ignore all other information.

Sensitivity analysis. A technique used to examine the risk in assumptions about key factors, such as interest rates and the relative weight of cost and quality criteria, in the choice among alternatives.

Sequential decisions. Decisions in which opportunities to purchase clarifying information arise throughout the decision process.

Stakeholders. People who have legitimate interests or stakes in the decision.

Structured opportunities. Opportunities that are clear because the set of favorable circumstances that can be exploited is known.

Structured problems. Problems that are understood because most of their component parts can be identified.

Subjective estimates. Best guesses about factors influenced by chance events, such as the prospects of high demand for a product or high usage for a service, and the relative importance of criteria used to compare alternatives.

Symptomatic problems. Signs and signals that suggest superficial concerns and not the underlying issues that are prompting the need to act.

Tactics. Procedures that specify one or more steps to be taken to deal with a particular stage of the decision process.

Theories. Propositions that describe what one believes to be true about people, object, and event relationships.

Tough decisions. A class of decisions plagued by ambiguity, conflict, and uncertainty.

Uncertainty. Doubt about the magnitude of key future conditions, such as the level of demand, interest rates, or inflation.

Unstructured opportunities. Opportunities that are vague because key events needed to produce favorable outcomes are uncertain.

Unstructured problems. Problems that are poorly understood because most of their component parts are unknown or contentious.

Utility. The relationship between value and changes in the level of a criterion, such as increases in satisfaction.

Valuation information. Criteria, such as cost or profit, used to determine the merit of alternatives so that those with the greatest merit can be selected.

Values. In decision making, values are expressed in terms of weights given to the criteria, either explicitly or implicitly. Implicit values are derived by examining several similar decisions and noting which criteria must have been emphasized for a series of choices to have been made.

Vividness. A characteristic of information that makes it memorable because of its emotional appeal, proximity, or seeming reality.

Warrant. A basis for drawing a conclusion, such as statistical significance, mathematical proof, or agreement among experts.

"What if" questioning. The logical inquiry applied to examine assumptions about key factors, such as product demand or level of endowments, to isolate the level of risk inherent in seemingly viable alternatives.

References

Allison, G. *Essence of Decision: Explaining the Cuban Missile Crisis.* Boston: Little, Brown, 1971.

Anderson, B. F., Dean, D. H., and Hammond, K. R. *Concepts in Judgment and Decision Research.* New York: Praeger, 1981.

Argyris, C., Putnam, R., and Smith, D. *Action Science: Concepts, Methods, and Skills for Research and Intervention.* San Francisco: Jossey-Bass, 1985.

Argyris, C., and Schön, D. A. *Organizational Learning: A Theory of Action Perspective.* Reading, Mass.: Addison-Wesley, 1978.

Asch, S. "Forming Impressions of Personality." *Journal of Applied and Social Psychology,* 1946, *41,* 258–290.

Bales, S. F. *Interaction Process Analysis.* Reading, Mass.: Addison-Wesley, 1951.

Bardach, E. *The Implementation Game.* Cambridge, Mass.: MIT Press, 1977.

Bartlett, F. C. *Remembering.* Cambridge, England: Cambridge University Press, 1932.

Bass, B. M. "When Planning for Others." *Journal of Applied Behavioral Science,* 1970, *6,* 151–171.

Bennis, W., and Nanus, B. *Leaders.* New York: Harper & Row, 1985.

Blake, R. R., and Mouton, J. S. *The Managerial Grid.* Houston, Tex.: Gulf, 1964.

Blaylock, B. K., and Rees, L. P. "Cognitive Style and the Usefulness of Information." *Management Science,* 1984, *15,* 74–91.

Bouchard, T. J., Jr., and Hare, M. "Size, Performance, and Potential in Brainstorming Groups." *Journal of Applied Psychology,* 1970, *54* (1), pt. 1, 51–55.

Bowman, E. H. "Consistency and Optimality in Decision Making." *Management Science*, 1963, *9* (2), 310–321.

Bristol, L. H., Jr. "The Application of Group Thinking to the Problems of Pharmaceutical Education." *American Journal of Pharmaceutical Education*, 1958, *22*, 146–156.

Brown, S. R. *Q-Sort Analysis*. New Haven, Conn.: Yale University Press, 1980.

Brown, S. R., and Coke, J. G. "Public Opinion on Land Use Regulation." *Urban and Regional Development Series*, no. 1. Columbus, Ohio: Academy of Contemporary Problems, 1977.

Budner, S. "Intolerance of Ambiguity as a Personality Variable." *Journal of Personality*, 1962, *30*, 29–50.

Burnberg, J. G., Pondy, L. P., and Davis, C. L. "Effects of Three Voting Rules on Resource Allocation Decisions." *Management Science*, Feb. 1970, pp. B356–B371.

Burns, T. "The Direction of Activity and Communication in a Departmental Executive Group." *Human Relations*, 1984, *7* (1), 73–87.

Carr, A. Z. "Is Business Bluffing Ethical?" *Harvard Business Review*, Jan.-Feb. 1978, p. 144.

Catron, B. L. "Ethical Postures and Ethical Posturing." *American Review of Public Management*, 1983, *17* (2/3), 155–159.

Christensen, P. R., Guilford, J. P., and Wilson, R. C. "Relations of Creative Responses to Work Time Instructions." *Journal of Experimental Psychology*, 1957, *53*, 82–88.

Churchman, C. W. *On the Design of Inquiring System: Basic Concepts in Systems and Organization*. New York: Basic Books, 1971.

Churchman, C. W. *The Systems Approach and Its Enemies*. New York: Basic Books, 1979.

Cleverley, W. O., and Nutt, P. C. "The Decision Process Used for Rating Hospital Revenue Bonds and Its Implications." *Health Services Research*, 1984, *19* (5), 615–637.

Cohen, M. D., March, J. P., and Olsen, J. P. "A Garbage Can Model of Organizational Choice." *Administrative Science Quarterly*, 1976, *17*, 1–25.

Collaros, P. W., and Anderson, L. R. "Effect of Member Participation and Commitment on Influence Satisfaction, and Decision Riskiness." *Journal of Applied Psychology*, 1974, *59*, 127–134.

Collins, B., and Guetzkow, H. A. *A Social Psychology of Group Process for Decision Making.* New York: Wiley, 1964.

Cummings, L. L., Huber, G. R., and Arndt, S. "Effects of Size and Spatial Arrangements on Group Decision Making." *Academy of Management Journal,* 1974, *17*, 460–475.

Cyert, R. M., Dill, W. R., and March, J. G. "The Role of Expectations in Business Decision Making." *Administrative Science Quarterly,* 1958, *3*, 307–340.

Cyert, R. M., and March, J. G. *A Behavioral Theory of the Firm.* Englewood Cliffs, N.J.: Prentice-Hall, 1963.

Dalky, N. *Delphi.* Santa Monica, Calif.: Rand Corporation, 1967.

Dawes, R. M. "The Mind, the Model, and the Task." In F. Restle and others (eds.), *Cognitive Theory.* Vol. 1. Hillsdale, N.J.: Erlbaum, 1975.

Dawes, R. M., and Corrigan, B. "Linear Models in Decision Making." *Psychological Bulletin,* 1974, *81*, 95–106.

Dean, J. *Blind Ambition: The White House Years.* New York: Simon & Schuster, 1976.

Dearborn, D. C., and Simon, H. A. "Selective Perception: A Note on the Departmental Identification of Executives." *Sociometry,* 1958, *21*, 140–144.

Delbecq, A. L. "The Management of Decision Making in the Firm: Three Strategies for Three Types of Decision Making." *Academy of Management Journal,* 1967, *10* (4), 329–339.

Delbecq, A. L. "The World Within the Span of Control." *Business Horizons,* 1968, *11*, 47–56.

Delbecq, A. L., and Van de Ven, A. "A Group Process Model for Problem Identification and Program Planning." *Journal of Applied Behavioral Science,* 1971, 7 (4), 466–492.

Delbecq, A. L., Van de Ven, A., and Gustafson, D. H. *Group Techniques for Program Planning.* Middleton, Wis.: Greenbrier Publications, 1986.

Deutsch, A. "The Effects of Cooperation and Competition upon Group Process." In D. Cartwright and others (eds.), *Group Dynamics.* New York: Harper & Row, 1962.

Dewey, J. *How We Think.* Boston: D. C. Heath, 1910.

Dickson, G. W., Senn, J. A., and Chervany, N. L. "Research in

Management Information Systems: The Minnesota Experiments." *Management Science*, 1977, *23*, 913–923.

Dill, W. R. "Business Organizations." In J. March, *Handbook of Organizations*, pp. 1071–1114. Skokie, Ill.: Rand McNally, 1965.

Doktor, R. H., and Hamilton, W. F. "Cognitive Style and the Acceptance of Management Science Recommendations." *Management Science*, 1973, *19* (8), 889–894.

Downey, H. K., Hellriegel, D., and Slocum, J. W. "Environmental Uncertainty: The Construct and Its Applications." *Administrative Science Quarterly*, 1975, *20* (4), 613–629.

Downs, A. *Inside Bureaucracy*. Boston: Little, Brown, 1967, p. 63.

Drucker, P. *The Practice of Management*. New York: Harper & Row, 1964.

Ebert, R. J., and Mitchell, R. R. *Organizational Decision Processes*. New York: Crane, Russak, 1975.

Eckenrode, R. T. "Weighting Multiple Criteria." *Management Science*, 1965, *12* (3), 180–192.

Edwards, W. "Conservatism in Human Information Processing." In B. Kleinmuntz (ed.), *Formal Representation of Human Judgment*. New York: Wiley, 1968.

Edwards, W., and Newman, J. R. *Multiattribute Evaluation*. Beverly Hills, Calif.: Sage, 1982.

Epstein, S., and Fenz, N. P. "Steepness of Approach and Avoidance Gradients in Humans as a Function of Experience: Theory and Experiment." *Journal of Experimental Psychology*, 1965, *70*, 1–12.

Erwing, D. W. "Discovering Your Problem-Solving Style." *Psychology Today*, Dec. 1977.

Estes, W. K. "The Cognitive Side of Probability Learning." *Psychological Review*, 1976, *83*, 37–64.

Etzioni, A. *Modern Organizations*. Englewood Cliffs, N.J.: Prentice-Hall, 1964.

Faust, W. L. "Group Versus Individual Problem Solving." *Journal of Abnormal Psychology*, 1959, *59*, 68–72.

Fiedler, F. "Engineering the Job to Fit the Manager." *Harvard Business Review*, 1965, *43*, 115–122.

Filley, A., and Grimes, A. J. "The Basis for Power in Decision

Processes." Paper presented at the Academy of Management proceedings, Chicago, Dec. 1967.

Filley, A., House, R., and Kerr, S. *Managerial Process and Organizational Behavior.* (2nd ed.) Glenview, Ill.: Scott, Foresman, 1976.

Fischhoff, B. "Hindsight-Foresight: The Effect of Outcome Knowledge on Judgment Under Uncertainty." *Journal of Experimental Psychology, Human Perception, and Performance,* 1975, *1,* 288–299.

Fisher, G. W. "Utility Models for Multiple Objective Decisions: Do They Accurately Reflect Human Preferences?" *Decision Sciences,* 1979, *10* (3), 451–479.

Fleishman, A. "Leader Behavior Descriptions for Industry." In R. M. Stogdill and others (eds.), *Leader Behavior: A Description and Measurement.* Monograph no. 88. Columbus: Bureau of Business Research, Ohio State University, 1975.

Ford, J. "The Effects of Causal Attributions on Decision Makers' Responses to Performance Downturns." *Academy of Management Review,* 1985, *10,* 770–786.

Foster, R. *Innovation: The Attacker's Advantage.* New York: Summit Books, 1986.

Freeman, R. E. *Strategic Management: A Stakeholder Approach.* New York: Pitman, 1983.

French, J., Jr., and Raven, B. H. "The Bases of Social Power." In D. Cartwright (ed.), *Studies in Social Power.* Ann Arbor, Mich.: Institute of Social Research, 1959.

Fryback, D. G., Gustafson, D. H., and Detmer, D. E. "Local Priorities for Allocation of Resources: Comparison with the IMU." *Inquiry,* 1978, *15,* 265–274.

Galbraith, J. R. "Matrix Organization Designs." *Business Horizons,* Feb. 1971, pp. 20–40.

Ghiselli, E. E. *Exploration in Managerial Talent.* Pacific Palisades, Calif.: Goodyear, 1971.

Ginsberg, A. S., and Offensend, F. L. "An Application of Decision Theory to a Medical Diagnosis-Treatment Problem." *IEEE Transactions on Systems and Cybernetics,* 1968, *SSC-4* (3), 335–362.

Goldberg, L. R. "Simple Models or Simple Processes—Some

Research on Clinical Judgments." *American Psychologist*, 1968, *23* (7), 483–496.

Goldberg, L. R. "Man Versus Model of Man: A Rationale Plus Some Evidence for a Method to Improve Clinical Inference." *Psychological Bulletin*, 1970, *73*, 422–432.

Golding, S., and Roper, L. "Illusory Correlation and Subjective Judgment." *Journal of Abnormal Psychology*, 1972, *80*, 249–260.

Gordon, W.J.J. *The Metaphorical Way*. Cambridge, Mass.: Propoise, 1971.

Grossman, R. M. "Voting Behavior of HSA Interest Groups: A Case Study." *American Journal of Public Health*, 1978, *68* (12), 1191–1193.

Gueschka, H., Shaude, G. R., and Schlicksupp, H. "Modern Techniques for Solving Problems." In M. M. Baldwin (ed.), *Portraits of Complexity*. Columbus, Ohio: Battelle Monograph Series, 1975.

Guetzkow, H. "Differentiation of Roles in Task-Oriented Groups." In D. Cartwright and others (eds.), *Group Dynamics: Research and Theory*. New York: Harper & Row, 1960.

Guetzkow, H., and Dill, W. R. "Factors in the Development of Task-Oriented Groups." *Sociometry*, 1957, *20*, 175–204.

Guetzkow, H., and Simon, H. "The Impact of Certain Communication Nets upon Organization and Performance in Task-Oriented Groups." *Management Science*, 1950, *21*, 233–250.

Gustafson, D. H., Pai, G. K., and Kramer, G. G. "A 'Weighted Aggregate' Approach to R&D Project Selection." *AIIE Transactions*, 1971, *3* (2), 22–31.

Gustafson, D. H., Shukla, R., Delbecq, A., and Wallester, G. "A Comparative Study in Subjective Likelihood Estimates Made by Individuals, Interacting Groups, Delphi Groups, and Nominal Groups." *Organizational Behavior and Human Performance*, 1973, *9*, 280–291.

Gustafson, D. H., and others. "The Development of an Index of Medical Underservice." *Health Service Research*, Summer 1975, pp. 168–180.

Gustafson, D. H., and others. "An Evaluation of Multiple Trauma Severity Indices Created by Different Index Development Strategies." *Medical Care*, 1983, *21* (7), 674–691.

Hall, D. T., Bowen, D. D., Lewicki, R. H., and Hall, F. S. *Experiences in Management and Organizational Behavior*. New York: Wiley, 1982.

Hall, P. *Great Planning Disasters*. Berkeley: University of California Press, 1980.

Hall, R. H. *Organizations: Structure and Process*. Engelwood Cliffs, N.J.: Prentice-Hall, 1972.

Halpin, A. W. "The Leadership Behavior and Combat Performance of Airplane Commanders." *Journal of Abnormal and Social Psychology*, 1954, *49*, 19–22.

Hammond, K. R., McClelland, G. H., and Mumpower, J. *Human Judgment and Decision Making*. New York: Praeger, 1980.

Hampden-Turner, C. *Maps of the Mind: Charts and Concepts of the Mind and Its Labyrinths*. New York: Macmillan, 1981.

Hare, A. P. *Handbook of Small-Group Research*. New York: Free Press, 1962.

Hare, A. P., Bogatala, E. F., and Bales, R. F. (eds.). *Small Groups: Studies in Social Interaction*. New York: Knopf, 1955.

Hayes, R. H. "Qualitative Insights from Quantitative Methods." *Harvard Business Review*, July-Aug. 1969, pp. 108–117.

Hearn, G. "Leadership and the Spatial Factor in Groups." *Journal of Abnormal Psychology*, 1957, *54*, 259–272.

Heider, F. *Psychology of Interpersonal Relations*. New York: Wiley, 1958.

Henderson, J. C., and Nutt, P. C. "The Influence of Decision Style on Decision Behavior." *Management Science*, 1980, *26* (4), 317–386.

Herbert, T. T., and Yost, E. B. "A Comparison of Decision Quality Under Nominal and Interacting Consensus-Group Formats: The Case of the Structured Problem." *Decision Sciences*, 1979, *10* (3), 358–370.

Hinton, B. L., and Reitz, H. J. *Groups and Organizations: Analysis of Social Behavior*. Belmont, Calif.: Wadsworth, 1971.

Hogarth, R. *Judgment and Choice: The Psychology of Decision*. New York: Wiley, 1980.

Holloman, C. R., and Hendrich, H. W. "Adequacy of Group Decisions as a Function of the Decision-Making Process." *Academy of Management Journal*, 1972, *15*, 175–184.

House, R. "Leader Initiating Structure and Performance, Satisfaction, and Motivation: A Review and Theoretical Interpretation." Toronto, Canada: University of Toronto, 1974. (Mimeographed.)

Howell, I. T., and Becker, S. W. "Seating Arrangements and Leadership Emergence." *Journal of Abnormal and Social Psychology*, 1962, *64*, 148–150.

Hoy, F., and Hellriegel, D. "The Kilmann Herden Model of Organizational Effectiveness Criteria for Small Business Managers." *Academy of Management Journal*, 1982, *25* (2), 308–322.

Huber, G. P. "Multiattribute Utility Models: A Review of Field and Fieldlike Studies." *Management Science*, 1974, *20* (10), 1393–1402.

Huber, G. P. *Managerial Decision Making*. Glenview, Ill.: Scott, Foresman, 1980.

Huber, G. P., and Delbecq, A. L. "Guidelines for Combining the Judgments of Individual Members in Decision Conferences." *Academy of Management Journal*, 1972, *15*, 159–174.

Janis, I. L. *Victims of Groupthink: A Psychological Study of Foreign Policy Decisions and Finances*. Boston: Houghton Mifflin, 1972.

Janis, I. L. "Preventing Group Think." In D. R. Hampton, C. E. Summer, and R. A. Webber (eds.), *Organizational Behavior and the Practice of Management*. Glenview, Ill.: Scott, Foresman, 1980, 269–278.

Janis, I. L., and Mann, L. *Decision Making: A Psychological Analysis of Conflict, Choice, and Commitment*. New York: Free Press, 1977.

Jung, C. G. *Psychological Types*. London: Routledge & Kegan Paul, 1923.

Jung, C. G. *Collected Works: Six Psychological Types*. (W. McGuire, ed.) Princeton, N.J.: Princeton University Press, 1970.

Kahneman, D., and Tversky, A. "Subjective Probability: A Judgment of Representatives." *Psychology Review*, 1973, *80*, 237–251.

Kahneman, D., and Tversky, A. "The Psychology of Preferences." *Scientific American*, 1982, *246*, 160–172.

Keen, P., and Scott-Morton, M. *Decision Support Systems: An Organizational Perspective*. Reading, Mass.: Addison-Wesley, 1978.

Keeney, R. L., and Raiffa, H. *Decisions with Multiple Objectives: Preferences and Value Tradeoffs*. New York: Wiley, 1976.

Kepner, C., and Tregoe, B. *The Rational Manager.* New York: McGraw-Hill, 1965.

Kerlinger, F. N. *Foundations of Behavioral Research.* (2nd ed.) New York: Holt, Rinehart & Winston, 1967.

Kerr, S. "On the Folly of Rewarding B While Hoping for A." *Academy of Management Journal,* 1975, *18* (4), 769–783.

Kerr, S., Schriesheim, C., Murphy, C. J., and Stogdill, R. M. "Toward a Contingency Theory of Leadership Based on Consideration and Interaction Structure Literature." *Organizational Behavior and Human Performance,* 1974, *12,* 62–82.

Kneppreth, N. P., Gustafson, D. H., Rose, J., and Leifer, R. P. "Techniques for the Assessment of Worth." In R. Berg (ed.), *Health Status Indicators.* Chicago: Hospital Research and Educational Trust, 1973.

Kogan, N., and Wallach, M. A. *Risk Taking: A Study in Cognition and Personality.* New York: Holt, Rinehart & Winston, 1964.

Kogan, N., and Wallach, M. A. "Risk Taking as a Function of the Situation, the Person, and the Group." In N. Kogan and M. Wallach (eds.), *New Directions in Psychology III.* New York: Holt, Rinehart & Winston, 1967.

Kolb, D. A. "Problem Management: Learning from Experience." In S. Srivastva and Associates, *The Executive Mind: New Insights on Managerial Thought and Action.* San Francisco: Jossey-Bass, 1983.

Landro, L. "RCA Reaches Crossroads on Its Troubled Video Disk Player." *Wall Street Journal,* Sept. 13, 1983, p. 37.

Langer, E. J. "The Illusion of Control." *Journal of Personality and Social Psychology,* 1975, *32,* 311–328.

Laswell, H. *The Decision Process: Seven Categories of Functional Analysis.* College Park: University of Maryland, Bureau of Governmental Research, College of Business, 1956.

Laswell, H. "The Technique of Decision Seminars." *Journal of Political Science,* 1960, *4,* 213–236.

Laswell, H. "The Policy Sciences of Development." *World Politics,* 1965, *17* (2), 286–309.

Laswell, H. *A Preview of Policy Sciences.* New York: American Elsevier, 1974.

Lewin, K. "Group Decisions and Social Change." In J. E. Maccoby, T. W. Newcomb, and E. Hartley (eds.), *Reading in Social Psychology*. New York: Holt, Rinehart & Winston, 1958.

Libby, R. "Man Versus Model of Man: Some Conflicting Evidence." *Organizational Behavior and Human Performance*, 1976, *16* (1), 1–12.

Lindblom, C. E. *The Intelligence of Democracy: Decision Process Through Adjustment*. New York: Free Press, 1965.

Linstone, H. *Multiple Perspectives for Decision Making: Bridging the Gap Between Analysis and Action*. New York: North Holland, 1984.

Linstone, H., and others. "The Multiple Perspective Concept: With Applications to Technology Assessment and Other Decision Areas." *Technological Forecasting and Social Change*, 1981, *20*, 275–325.

Locke, E. A. "Knowledge of Results: A Goal-Setting Phenomenon." *Psychological Bulletin*, 1968, *70*, 474–485.

Loomis, C. J. "How ITT Got Lost in a Big Bad Forest." *Fortune*, Dec. 17, 1979, pp. 42–55.

Machiavelli, N. *The Prince*. Oxford, England: Oxford University Press, 1952. (Orig. tr. L. Ricci, 1903.)

McKenney, J. L., and Keen, P. "How Managers' Minds Work." *Harvard Business Review*, May-June 1974, pp. 79–90.

Maier, N.R.F. "Reasoning in Humans: The Solution of a Problem and Its Appearances in Consciousness." *Journal of Comparative Psychology*, 1931, *12*, 181–194.

Maier, N.R.F. *Problem Solving and Creativity: In Individuals and Groups*. Monterey, Calif.: Brooks/Cole, 1970.

March, J., and Simon, H. *Organizations*. New York: McGraw-Hill, 1958.

Mason, R. O. "A Dialectical Approach to Strategic Planning." *Management Science*, 1969, *15* (8), B403–B444.

Mason, R. O., and Mitroff, I. I. "A Program for Research on Management Information Systems." *Management Science*, 1973, *19* (5), 475–487.

Mason, R. O., and Mitroff, I. I. *Challenging Strategic Assumptions: Theory, Cases, and Techniques*. New York: Wiley-Interscience, 1981.

Matheson, J. E., and Howard, R. E. "An Introduction to Decision

Analysis." In R. Howard (ed.), *Readings in Decision Analysis.* (2nd ed.) Menlo Park, Calif.: Stanford Research Institute, 1972.

May, E. R. *Lessons of the Past.* New York: Oxford University Press, 1973.

Mayo, G. E. *The Human Problems of an Industrial Civilization.* Boston: Division of Research, Harvard Business School, 1933.

Meehl, P. E. *Clinical Versus Statistical Prediction.* Minneapolis: University of Minnesota Press, 1954.

Milliken, F. J. "Three Types of Perceived Uncertainty About the Environment: State, Effect, and Response." *Academy of Management Review,* 1987, *12* (1), 133–143.

Minsky, M. "A Framework for Representing Knowledge." In P. H. Winston (ed.), *The Psychology of Computer Vision.* New York: McGraw-Hill, 1975.

Mintzberg, H. *The Nature of Managerial Work.* New York: Harper & Row, 1973.

Mintzberg, H., Raisinghani, D., and Theoret, A. "The Structure of Unstructured Decision Processes." *Administrative Science Quarterly,* 1976, *21,* 246–275.

Mitroff, I. I., and Kilmann, R. H. "The Stories Managers Tell: A New Tool for Organizational Problem Solving." *Management Review,* 1975, *64,* 18–28.

Mitroff, I. I., and Kilmann, R. H. *Methodological Approaches to Social Science: Integrating Divergent Concepts and Theories.* San Francisco: Jossey-Bass, 1978.

Mitroff, I. I., Mason, R. O., and Nelson, J. "On the Management of Myth Information Systems." *Management Science,* 1974, *21* (4), 371–382.

Mitroff, I. I., Mohrman, S., and Little, G. *The Global Solution: The New Rules for Doing Business in a World Economy.* San Francisco: Jossey-Bass, 1987.

Mohrman, S. "A New Look at Participation in Decision Making: The Concept of Political Access." Paper presented at the Academy of Management proceedings, Atlanta, Ga., Aug. 1979.

Myers, I. B. *Introduction to Type.* Gainesville, Fla.: Center for Applications of Psychological Type, 1976.

Myers, I. B., and Myers, P. B. *Gifts Differing.* Palo Alto, Calif.: Consulting Psychologists Press, 1980.

Nadler, G. *Work Design: A Systems Concept.* Glenwood, Ill.: Irwin, 1970.

Nadler, G. *The Planning and Design Approach.* New York: Wiley, 1981.

Nerlove, M., and Press, S. J. "Univariate and Multivariate Log-linear and Logistic Models." Rand Technical Paper R-1306-EDA/NIH. Santa Monica, Calif.: Rand Corporation, 1973.

Nisbett, R., and Ross, L. *Human Inference: Strategies and Shortcomings of Social Judgment.* Englewood Cliffs, N.J.: Prentice-Hall, 1980.

Nussbaum, B. "The Changing Role of the CEO." *Business Week,* Oct. 23, 1987.

Nutt, P. C. "Field Experiments Which Compared the Effectiveness of Design Methods." *Decision Sciences,* 1976a, 7 (3), 739–758.

Nutt, P. C. "The Merits of Using Experts and Consumers as Members of Planning Groups." *The Academy of Management Journal,* 1976b, 19 (3), 378–394.

Nutt, P. C. "Models for Decision Making in Organizations: Some Contextual Variables Which Stipulate Optimum Use." *Academy of Management Review,* 1976c, 1 (2), 84–98.

Nutt, P. C. "An Experimental Comparison of Three Planning Procedures." *Management Science,* 1977, 23 (4), 499–511.

Nutt, P. C. "On the Acceptance and Quality of Plans Drawn by Consortiums." *Journal of Applied Behavioral Science,* 1979a, 15 (1), 7–21.

Nutt, P. C. "The Influence of Decision Styles on the Use of Decision Models." *Technological Forecasting and Social Change,* 1979b, 14 (1), 77–93.

Nutt, P. C. "Some Considerations in Selecting Interactive and Analytical Decision Approaches." *Medical Care,* 1979c, 17 (2), 152–167.

Nutt, P. C. "Calling Out and Calling Off the Dogs: Managerial Diagnosis in Public Service Organizations." *Academy of Management Review,* 1979d, 4, 203–214.

Nutt, P. C. "Comparing Methods for Weighting Decision Criteria." *Omega,* 1980a, 8 (2), 163–172.

Nutt, P. C. "Evaluating Regulatory Decisions Using Decision Analysis." Working Paper Series 80-86. Columbus: College of Administrative Science, Ohio State University, 1980b.

Nutt, P. C. "On Managed Evaluation Process." *Technological Forecasting and Social Change*, 1980c, *17*, 313–328.

Nutt, P. C. "Linking Decision Style and Risk." Paper presented at the Midwest Academy of Management proceedings, Cincinnati, Ohio, Apr. 1980d.

Nutt, P. C. "Some Guides for the Selection of a Decision Process." *Technological Forecasting and Social Change*, 1981a, *19*, 133–145.

Nutt, P. C. "The Acceptance and Accuracy of Decision Analysis Methods." *Omega*, 1981b, *9* (6), 619–622.

Nutt, P. C. "Decision Theory." In W. O. Cleverley (ed.), *Handbook of Health Finance*. Washington, D.C.: Aspen, 1982a.

Nutt, P. C. *Evaluation Concepts and Methods*. (Rev. ed.) New York: Spectrum, 1982b.

Nutt, P. C. "Hybrid Planning Methods." *Academy of Management Review*, 1982c, *7* (3), 442–454.

Nutt, P. C. "Implementation Techniques for Planning." *Academy of Management Review*, 1983, *8* (4), 600–611.

Nutt, P. C. "Decision Modeling Methods Used to Design Decision Support Systems for Staffing." *Medical Care*, 1984a, *22* (11), 1002–1013.

Nutt, P. C. *Planning Methods*. New York: Wiley, 1984b.

Nutt, P. C. "Types of Organizational Decision Processes." *Administrative Science Quarterly*, 1984c, *29* (3), 414–450.

Nutt, P. C. "Decision Style and Its Influence on Managers and Management." *Technological Forecasting and Social Change*, 1986a, *29*, 341–366.

Nutt, P. C. "Decision Style and Its Influence on the Strategic Decisions of Top Executives." *Technological Forecasting and Social Change*, 1986b, *30*, 39–62.

Nutt, P. C. "Evaluating MIS Design Principles." *MIS Quarterly*, June 1986c, pp. 139–155.

Nutt, P. C. "The Tactics of Implementation." *Academy of Management Journal*, 1986d, *24* (2), 230–260.

Nutt, P. C. "Identifying and Appraising How Managers Install Strategy." *Strategic Management Journal*, 1987a, *8*, 1–14.

Nutt, P. C. "Processes of Formulation Used to Set Intentions in Decision Making." Working Paper Series 87-129. Columbus: College of Business, Ohio State University, 1987b.

Nutt, P. C. "The Tolerance for Ambiguity and Decision Making." Working Paper Series 88-291. Columbus: College of Business, Ohio State University, 1988.

Nutt, P. C. "How Bank Executives Deal with Risk in Their Loan Decisions." *Omega*, 1989, *17* (3).

Nutt, P. C., and Backoff, R. W. "Mutual Understanding and Its Impact on Formulation During Planning." *Technological Forecasting and Social Change*, 1986, *29*, 13–31.

Nutt, P. C., and Backoff, R. W. "A Strategic Management Process for Public and Third-Sector Organizations." *American Journal of Planning*, 1987, *53*, 44–57.

Nutt, P. C., and Backoff, R. W. *Regenerating the Non-Profits: Change Through Strategic Management.* San Francisco: Jossey-Bass, forthcoming.

Nutt, P. C., and Backoff, R. W. "Strategic Issues as Tensions." *Strategic Management Journal*, forthcoming.

Nutt, P. C., and Caswell, R. J. "The Influence of Biased Forecasts in Regulatory Decision Making." *Medical Care*, forthcoming.

Nutt, P. C., and Emswiler, S. M. "Factors Influencing the Size of Malpractice Awards in Hospitals." Paper presented at the Midwest Academy of Management proceedings, Cleveland, Ohio, Mar. 1979.

Nutt, P. C., and Hurley, R. "Factors Affecting Capital Expenditure Review Decisions." *Inquiry*, Summer 1981, pp. 151–164.

Nutt, P. C., and Wheeler, M. "Social Program Evaluation Revisited: The WIC Program." *American Institute of Decision Science Proceedings*, 1980, *12*.

Osborn, A. F. *Applied Imagination.* (3rd ed.) New York: Scribner's, 1963.

Parker, A. W. "The Consumer as a Policy Maker: Issues of Training." *American Journal of Public Health*, 1970, *60*, 2139–2153.

Parnes, S. J. "Effects of Extended Effort in Creative Problem Solving." *Journal of Educational Psychology*, 1961, *52*, 117–122.

Parnes, S. J., and Meadow, A. "The Effects of Brainstorming Instructions on Creative Problem Solving by Trained and

Untrained Subjects." *Journal of Educational Psychology*, 1959, *50*, 171–176.

Parsons, T. "On the Concept of Influence." *Public Opinion Quarterly*, 1963, *27*, 37–62.

Perrow, C. "A Framework for the Comparative Analysis of Organizations." *American Sociology Review*, 1967, *32*, 194–208.

Perrow, C. *Complex Organizations*. Glenview, Ill.: Scott, Foresman, 1979.

"Playing Nuclear Poker." *Time*, Jan. 31, 1983, p. 23.

Pribaum, K. H. "The Brain, Cognitive Commodities, and the Enfolded Order." In K. E. Boulding and L. Senesh (eds.), *The Optimum Utilization of Knowledge: Making Knowledge Serve Human Betterment*, pp. 29–40. Boulder, Colo.: Westview Press, 1983.

Quinn, R. E. "Applying Leadership: Toward an Integrating Framework." In J. J. Hunt, R. Stewart, C. Schriessheim, and D. Hosking (eds.), *Managerial Work and Leadership: An International Perspective*. New York: Pergamon, 1983.

Quinn, R. E. *Beyond Rational Management: Mastering the Paradoxes and Competing Demands of High Performance*. San Francisco: Jossey-Bass, 1988.

Quinn, R. E., and McGrath, M. R. "Moving Beyond the Single-Solution Perspective: The Competing-Values Approach as a Diagnostic Tool." *Journal of Applied Behavioral Science*, 1983, *18* (4), 463–472.

Raiffa, H. *Decision Analysis: Introductory Lectures on Choices Under Uncertainty*. Reading, Mass.: Addison-Wesley, 1970.

Ramaprasad, A., and Mitroff, I. I. "On Formulating Strategic Problems." *Academy of Management Review*, 1984, *9* (4), 597–605.

Rappaport, A. "Mathematical Aspects of General Systems Analysis." *General Systems*, 1969, *11*, 3–11.

Ritti, R. R., and Funkhouser, G. R. *The Ropes to Skip and the Ropes to Know: Studies in Organizational Behavior*. (3rd ed.) Columbus, Ohio: Grid Publishing, 1986.

Schein, E. H. "The Mechanisms of Change." In W. Bennis, E. Schein, A. Stelle, and A. Berlow (eds.), *Interpersonal Dynamics*. Homewood, Ill.: Dorsey Press, 1964.

Schlisinger, L., Jackson, S. M., and Butman, J. "Leader-Member Interaction in Management Committees." *Journal of Abnormal and Social Psychology*, 1960, *61*, 350–354.

Schriesheim, C. J., Tolliver, J. M., and Behling, O. C. "Leadership, Some Organizational and Managerial Implications." In P. Hersey and J. Stinson (eds.), *Perspectives in Leader Effectiveness*. Athens, Ohio: Center for Leadership Studies, 1980.

Scott, W. E., and Cummings, L. L. *Reading in Organizational Behavior.* (Rev. ed.) Homewood, Ill.: Irwin, 1973.

Simon, H. A. *Administration Behavior.* New York: Macmillan, 1947.

Simon, H. A. *The New Science of Management Decision.* (Rev. ed.) Englewood Cliffs, N.J.: Prentice-Hall, 1977.

Simon, H. A., and Newell, A. "Human Program Solving: The State of the Art in 1970." *American Psychologist*, 1971, *26*, 145–159.

Simon, M. A. *Understanding Human Action.* Albany: State University of New York Press, 1982.

Skinner, B. F. *Contingencies of Reinforcement.* East Norwalk, Conn.: Appleton-Century-Crofts, 1969.

Slovic, P. "Analyzing the Expert Judge: A Descriptive Study of a Stockbroker's Decision Process." *Journal of Applied Psychology*, 1969, *53*, 255–263.

Slovic, P. "Choice Between Equally Valued Alternatives." *Journal of Experimental Psychology: Human Perception and Performance*, 1975, *1*, 280–287.

Slovic, P., Fischhoff, B., and Lichtenstein, S. "Behavioral Decision Theory." *Annual Review of Psychology*, 1977, *28*, 1–39.

Snyder, R. C., and Paige, G. D. "The U.S. Decision to Resist Aggression in Korea: The Application of an Analytical Scheme." *Administrative Science Quarterly*, 1958, *3* (3), 341–378.

Sommers, R. "Further Studies on Small-Group Ecology." *Sociometry*, 1965, *28*, 337–340.

Sorensen, T. C. *Kennedy.* New York: Harper & Row, 1966.

Souder, W. E. *Management Decision Methods for Managers of Engineering and Research.* New York: Van Nostrand Reinhold, 1980.

Stein, M. I. *Stimulating Creativity.* New York: Academic Press, 1975.

Stephenson, W. *The Study of Behavior.* Chicago: University of Chicago Press, 1953.

Stogdill, R. M. *Individual Behavior and Group Achievement.* New York: Oxford University Press, 1969.

Stogdill, R. M., and Coons, A. E. (eds.). *Leader Behavior: Its Description and Measurement.* Monograph no. 88. Columbus: Bureau of Business Research, Ohio State University, 1975.

Strumpf, S. A., Zand, D. E., and Freeman, R. D. "Designing Groups for Judgmental Decisions." *Academy of Management Review,* 1979, *4* (4), 589–600.

Suchman, E. A. *Evaluation Research: Principles and Practice in Public Service Organizations.* Thousand Oaks, Calif.: Sage, 1967.

Sudman, S., and Bradburn, N. M. *Asking Questions: A Practical Guide to Questionnaire Design.* San Francisco: Jossey-Bass, 1982.

Susman, G. I. "Action Research: A Sociotechnical System Perspective." In G. Moran (ed.), *Beyond Method: Strategies for Social Research.* Thousand Oaks, Calif.: Sage, 1983.

Swalm, R. O. "Utility Theory—Insights into Risk Taking." *Harvard Business Review,* 1966, *44,* 123–136.

Taggart, W., and Robey, D. "Minds and Managers: On the Dual Nature of Human Information Processing and Management." *Academy of Management Review,* 1981, *6* (2), 187–195.

Thibaut, J. W., and Kelley, H. H. *The Social Psychology of Groups.* New York: Wiley, 1959.

Thompson, J. D. *Organizations in Action.* New York: McGraw-Hill, 1967.

Torbert, W. R. "Executive Mind, Timely Action." *Revision,* 1983, *6* (1), 3–21.

Toulmin, S. *Knowing and Acting: An Invitation to Philosophy.* New York: Macmillan, 1979.

Tversky, A. "Elimination by Aspects: A Theory of Choice." *Psychological Review,* 1972, *79,* 281–299.

Tversky, A., and Kahneman, D. "The Belief in Small Numbers." *Psychological Bulletin,* 1971, *76,* 105–110.

Tversky, A., and Kahneman, D. "Availability: A Heuristic for

Judging Frequency and Probability." *Cognitive Psychology*, 1973, *5*, 207–232.

Tversky, A., and Kahneman, D. "Judgment Under Uncertainty: Heuristics and Biases." *Science*, 1974, *185*, 1124–1131.

Utterback, J. M. "The Process of Technological Innovation in Firms." *Academy of Management Journal*, 1971, *14* (1), 75–87.

Van de Ven, A., and Delbecq, A. "Nominal Versus Interacting Group-Process Effectiveness for Committee Decision Making." *Academy of Management Journal*, 1974, *14* (2), 203–217.

Volkema, R. "Problem Formulation as a Purposive Activity." *Strategic Management Journal*, 1983, *7* (3), 267–279.

Von Neuman, J., and Morgenstern, O. *Theory of Games and Economic Behavior*. Princeton, N.J.: Princeton University Press, 1947.

Vroom, V. H. "A New Look at Managerial Decision Making." *Organizational Dynamics*, Spring 1973, pp. 66–80.

Vroom, V. H., Grant, L. P., and Cotton, T. S. "The Consequences of Social Interaction in Group Problem Solving." *Organizational Behavior and Human Performance*, 1969, *4* (1), 77–95.

Vroom, V. H., and Yetton, P. W. *Leadership and Decision Making*. Pittsburgh, Pa.: University of Pittsburgh Press, 1973.

Walster, E. "Assignment of Responsibility for an Accident." *Journal of Personality and Social Psychology*, 1966, *3*, 73–79.

Warfield, J. N. *Societal Systems: Planning Policy and Complexity*. New York: Wiley, 1976.

Warner, D. M., and Holloway, D. C. *Decision Making and Control for Health Administration*. Ann Arbor, Mich.: Health Administration Press, 1978.

Wilber, K. *The Holographic Paradigm and Other Paradoxes*. Boulder, Colo.: Shambhala, 1982.

Wildavsky, A. "Rescuing Policy Analysis for PPBS." *Public Administration Review*, Mar./Apr. 1969, pp. 189–202.

Wildavsky, A. *Speaking Truth to Power*. Boston: Little, Brown, 1979.

Ziller, R. C. "Group Size: A Determinant of the Quality and Stability of Group Decisions." *Sociometry*, 1956, *20*, 165–173.

Index

603